EVERY-DAY
Light

Light for the Path

Light for the Path

DAILY INSPIRATIONS FROM

Selwyn Hughes

FEATURING THE PAINTINGS
OF LARRY DYKE

BROADMAN
&HOLMAN
PUBLISHERS

NASHVILLE, TENNESSEE

Published by Broadman & Holman Publishers, Nashville, TN
Editorial Team: Leonard G. Goss, John Landers, Sandra Bryer
Cover and Interior Design: Paul T. Gant Art & Design
Typesetting: TF Designs, Mt. Juliet, Tennessee
0-8054-2143-2

Dewey Decimal Classification: 242.2
Subject Heading: DEVOTIONAL EXERCISES

Unless otherwise noted, Scripture quotations are from the Holy Bible, New International Version, copyright © 1973, 1978, 1984 by International Bible Society. Other translations are identified as follows:

Amplified. The Amplified Bible, Old Testament copyright © 1962, 1964 by Zondervan Publishg House, used by permission, and the New Testament © The Lockman Foundation 1954, 1958, 1987, used by permission.

KJV. King James Version.

NASB. The New American Standard Bible, © The Lockman Foundation, 1960, 1962, 1963, 1968, 1971, 1972, 1973, 1975, 1977; used by permission.

Moffatt. The Bible. A New Translation. © 1922, 1924, 1925, 1926, 1935, by Harper & Row, Publishers, Inc. © 1950, 1952, 1953, 1954 by James A. R. Moffatt.

NLT. *Holy Bible,* New Living Translation, copyright © 1996. Used by Permission of Tyndale House Publishers, Inc., Wheaton, Illinois 60189. All rights reserved.

Phillips. Reprinted with permission of Macmillan Publishing Co., Inc. fromm J. B. Phillips: The New Testament in Modern English, revised edition, J. B. Phillips 1958, 1960.

RSV. Revised Standard Version of the Bible, copyrighted 1946, 1952, © 1971, 1973.

TLB. The Living Bible, copyright © Tyndale House Publishers, Wheaton, Ill., 1971, used by permission.

Contents

Publisher's Foreword

*P*ainting is a continual process of discovery for Larry Dyke: experimenting with new techniques, finding new subjects, standing in awe of yet another miracle of God's creation and wondering how he will ever capture it on canvas. The search is never ending, because there are more new experiences waiting for him than he can possibly get to in a lifetime.

Faith is a lifelong journey too. There's always something new to discover about our relationship with God, a passage of Scripture or an insightful thought that encourages and refreshes us as we make our way in the world. In *Light for the Path*, Selwyn Hughes guides us from one incredible discovery to another with a full year's worth of commentaries, Bible readings, and prayers. His wisdom and understanding, built on more than thirty years as a pastor, counselor, and teacher, make these daily readings exceptionally helpful and meaningful.

In Dyke's search for inspiration as an artist, he has hiked through Yosemite, gotten lost in the Appalachians, and ridden a helicopter into the middle of a South American rain forest. A lot of times the journey is just as exciting as the final result. Selwyn Hughes' journey is exciting in a different way. Though it is a spiritual journey instead of a physical one, it's still filled with the exhilaration that comes from experiencing some long-anticipated moment for the first time. And while the sight of Angel Falls cascading more than two thousand feet down a mountainside in Venezuela is awesome, it's nothing compared with the discovery Hughes makes: new assurance that God is always watching over us, Jesus is our Savior, and that no matter how much we see and learn of the Creator's love for us, there is more grace and blessing ahead of us than we can even imagine.

The world longs for the light of Christ. These pages will light your way to Him.

Leonard G. Goss

Introduction

*M*any things make it hard to believe that God wants to illuminate our daily path. The vastness of the universe makes it hard. You may wonder whether the Creator and Sustainer of such a vast universe notices the needs of individuals on this microscopic earth. Wonder no longer. He does.

Many Biblical texts make this clear. Here are just a few: "He guides the humble in what is right and teaches them his way" (Ps. 25:9). "You guide me with your counsel, and afterward you will take me into glory" (Ps. 73:24). "You will seek me and find me when you seek me with all your heart" (Jer. 29:13).

God has many ways of shedding light on a Christian's pathway (through prayerful reasoning, counsel from others, circumstances, etc.) but the most powerful way is the illumination that He brings to us from His Word, the Bible. The Psalmist put it like this: "Your word is a lamp to my feet and a light for my path" (Ps. 119:105). Exposing ourselves daily to the Scriptures is the best way I know for finding light and direction in life.

In this third one-year edition you will find six themes that I think will help illuminate your Christian walk. The themes are taken from the long-running Every Day with Jesus series (now in its thirty-fifth year) which has proved to be helpful to thousands of people. The Twenty-Third Psalm was one of the most popular themes I ever presented. So was The Search for Meaning—a verse-by-verse exposition of the book of Ecclesiastes. The other themes were also very popular. My prayer and wish once again is that your perusal of these themes will deepen your relationship with the Lord and cause God's light to flood your path.

Selwyn Hughes

Topical Index

Topical Index (continued)

PSALM 91:1

Section One

The Uniqueness of Our Faith

The Uniqueness of Our Faith

Though light comes from an almost endless variety of sources, there is only one sun. It is the brightest, strongest, steadiest, most reliable source of all, and every other kind of light depends on it one way or another. Moonlight is a soft, shimmering reflection of sunlight. Even electric light comes mostly from fossilized material once nurtured by the sun's rays.

As a painter, Larry Dyke is interested in every kind of light. But he knows that behind each highlight and shadow, every reflection and candle glow, the massive unfathomable power of the sun is at work. In a similar way, Selwyn Hughes describes Christianity as a uniquely powerful faith. There are other religions that on the surface seem somewhat like Christianity—it may seem at first like the light is there. It's not until we dig deeper that we realize the apparent brilliance of their center is weak and fleeting.

Only Christianity has a sun because only Christianity has Christ. It is the Incarnation of God in human form that makes us as Christians different from all the rest. As Selwyn Hughes says, no other faith claims its teacher is God. Jesus isn't first in his class, he's a class no other historical or religious figure can claim: God as flesh and blood.

Christianity is absolute and final: It is light, and all else is darkness. Highlight and shadow are the essence of painting. With every brush stroke Dyke tries to convince the eye that the light flashes here, reflects there, and contrasts with the dim, indistinct images adjacent to it. But the light of Christ falls equally on all of creation with life-giving power, even in the darkest places of our lives. Jesus, after all, rose from the pitch-black tomb to bring the light of salvation to the world.

There are many apparent sources of spiritual light in our world. All of them exist only in the reflected glory of God in Christ.

L.G.G.

One Faith, One Lord

"... contend for the faith that was once for all entrusted to the saints." (v. 3)

For reading & meditation—Jude vv. 1–16

*W*hat makes the Christian faith different from every other faith? Prince Charles, who is next in line to the British throne, has let it be known that if and when he becomes king he would like to be regarded as Defender of all faiths rather than Defender of the faith—the Christian faith. Living now as we do in a multi-faith rather than a Christian society, he said, it is important that this shift be reflected in the duties of the monarch.

No Christian would want to deny any individual or group the right to follow or practice the faith of their choice, but we must be careful that tolerance of other religions does not cause us to fall into the trap of thinking that Christianity is just one religion among many. Decidedly, it is not. Christianity is in a category all by itself. If that belief opens us up to the charge of arrogance, then so be it.

Recently, I heard a religious commentator say on television that one religion is as good as another. One religion as good as another? How utterly absurd. It sounds broadminded but actually it is the judgment of ignorance. No one would ever make that statement if they understood the purpose of Christ's coming to this world, His atoning death on the cross, and His glorious resurrection. We are not unmindful of the spiritual glow which comes from other lamps, but our claim for Jesus is the claim He made for Himself—He alone is the Light of the world, and thus utterly indispensable to salvation.

FURTHER STUDY

Phil. 1:1–27;
Gal. 2:1–8;
1 Cor. 9:17

1. What did Paul admonish the Philippians for?
2. What was Paul entrusted with?

Prayer

O Father, help me comprehend even more fully and clearly the truths of the faith into which, by Your grace, You have brought me. I cannot live by opinions, I must live by convictions. May Your truths become my convictions. In Christ's Name I pray. Amen.

No Other Name

"Salvation is found in no one else . . ." (v. 12)

For reading & meditation—Acts 4:1–12

*W*e looked yesterday at the statement to the effect that all religions are the same. We must watch out for such statements, for when they are repeated over and over again, and by seemingly sincere people, we can be brainwashed into accepting them.

In 1966, when the first multi-faith service was held in an Anglican church in London, in which Hindus, Buddhists, Muslims, and Christians took part on equal terms, some Christian newspapers described it as a "betrayal of the faith." Nowadays there is hardly a mention of such services although they take place regularly in different parts of our nation, and also in other countries. People seem to have given up the idea of syncretism—the idea that all religions can be fused into one—and are focusing more on pluralism—the recognition of each faith as being of equal value. I take my stand with Dr. Visser't Hooft who said: "It is high time that Christians should rediscover that Jesus Christ did not come to make a contribution to the religious storehouse of mankind, but that in Him God reconciled the world unto Himself."

The words of our text for today were displayed outside a church in London until the minister was told by the local authority to take the poster down as it offended some local inhabitants who were adherents of other faiths. "It is not the best way to love one's neighbor as oneself" was how one critic put it. But how can we love our neighbor as ourselves if we make no attempt to share with them the knowledge of salvation in Jesus Christ?

FURTHER STUDY

John 3:1–17; 6:35; 14:6

1. *What Old Testament example shows there is only one way to salvation?*
2. *What did Jesus declare about Himself?*

Prayer

O Father, in an age when the faith once delivered to the saints is being watered down, deepen my understanding of it so that I may contend for it without being contentious. In Christ's Name I pray. Amen.

Pluralism's Persuasiveness

Day 3

"The life I live in the body, I live by faith in the Son of God . . ." (v. 20)

For reading & meditation—Galatians 2:11–21

The argument presented by pluralists that Christians must view their religion as one among many, and Jesus as only one Savior among others, must be firmly resisted. It may sound arrogant to say so but it is nevertheless a fact that Christianity is unique, absolute, definitive, ultimate, and final.

Critics of the uniqueness of Christianity can be very persuasive. "The world is under great threat," they tell us, "because of environmental pollution, economic injustice, and many other problems. Nothing that divides us, including our religions, should be considered as important as the need to live together in harmony." Another emphasis is on the need to study comparative faiths. There is a sense in which understanding what other people believe is useful, but not until the claims of Christianity are seen to be definitive and final. Christianity is not a comparative religion; it reveals God's one and only way of entering into a personal relationship with Him.

The text before us today in the Amplified Bible reads: "The life I now live . . . I live by faith—by adherence to and reliance on and [complete] trust—in the Son of God, Who loved me and gave Himself up for me." Bishop Leslie Newbigin put it well: "If it is really true, as it is, that 'the Son of God loved me and gave himself up for me,' how can I agree that this amazing act of matchless grace should merely become part of a syllabus for the 'comparative study of religions'?" Christ is not first in a class; He occupies the category all by Himself.

FURTHER STUDY

Acts 4:1–12;
1 Tim. 2:1–6;
1 Cor. 3:11

1. What did Peter declare to the Sanhedrin?
2. What did Paul declare to Timothy?

Prayer

My Father and my God, may the Person of Your Son become as real and as precious to me as He is to You. And teach me more about Him so that I can make clear to others why He is a Savior beyond compare. For His own dear Name's sake. Amen.

The Last Is the Best

". . . he has spoken to us by his Son, whom he appointed heir of all things . . ." (v. 2)

For reading & meditation—Hebrews 1:1–14

*T*he words of our text today point out that though God spoke in times past through prophets and sages (referring to the religion of Judaism), His final Word to this world is in His Son. That is our claim as Christians. Not that the Jewish religion contains nothing of value. God forbid! But it is not God's last Word to the men and women of His creation.

No other world faith claims that its great teacher was God incarnate. Yet we claim for Christ just that—and also that as God He meets every human need. He comes to us where we are and *He* does the work. He can relieve any plight of the human soul, and He has the power to meet every human need. Every spiritually sensitive person is aware of the presence of guilt which arises from indwelling sin, and is aware too that he or she alone can do nothing to dissolve it. Christ atoned for sin and is able to forgive it. Every normal person also stands in awe of death, knowing it is impossible to escape it. But Christ has conquered death and has opened the way to eternal life.

Christ's call is to all humanity. He does not differentiate between groups of people or races. He abides no barriers of class or creed. "Whosoever will may come" is His constant message. Devotees of other faiths regard Christians as intolerant when they cannot concede even by implication that there are any "gods" or prophets equal to Him. He is unique in His Person, His mission and in His finished work.

FURTHER STUDY

Phil. 2:1–11;
Eph. 1:22;
1 Cor. 8:6

1. Why has God exalted Christ?
2. What does Paul acknowledge? What is his conclusion?

Prayer

O God, how can I express my gratitude that I have found the best, or rather that the Best has found me? May I lay hold of all that is in Jesus and reflect Him to the world, not in arrogance but in humility. Amen.

"Nothing!"

"... He appeared in a body, was vindicated by the Spirit ..." (v. 16)

For reading & meditation—1 Timothy 3:1–16

Max Muller, a writer on religious issues, once made this arresting statement: "You do not know the worth of your Christian faith until you have compared it to others." The first article of belief we look at is the fact that God has appeared in this world in the Person of His eternal Son. Our faith is not the word of a prophet but, as we saw yesterday, the Word of the Son Himself. No other world faith even attempts to represent its great teacher as God incarnate. Yet we claim for Christ just that. As God, He comes to us from the highest, and He comes all the way.

I remember hearing a missionary to India say that he was forced to rethink his faith in the light of other faiths and other ways of life. "All the old shibboleths and modes of expression and accepted outlooks on life are challenged," he said, "and one begins to see where the relevant lies." He started discussions with Hindu, Buddhist, and Muslim leaders, as well as representatives of India's many other religions. The gatherings were called "Round Table" discussions to suggest that everyone could present what they considered to be the distinctives of their faith. One could see scintillations of truth, the missionary recalled, as people spoke from experience or from their sacred books. But whenever a Christian spoke and unfolded the truth of the Incarnation, the meeting would lapse into silence. Sometimes the silence would last for many minutes, only to be broken with the remark: "We have nothing in our faith that compares to that. Nothing!"

FURTHER STUDY

Acts 1:1–5;
1 Cor. 15:1–8;
Acts 9:1–6

1. What was Paul's testimony?
2. How did he substantiate it?

Prayer

Dear God and Father, if You hadn't come down to us, how could we have ever come up to You? What humiliation this must have meant for You. Yet what love. Our hearts sing with gratitude. Blessed be Your Name forever. Amen.

The Great Divide

"The Word became flesh and made his dwelling among us." (v. 14)

For reading & meditation—John 1:1–18

We continue meditating on the fact that the Christian faith is unique in that it is the Word not of a prophet but of the Son of God Himself. And when I refer to the Son of God I mean also God the Son. The Son is as much God as God Himself. One commentator says of the verse before us today: "If I were to put my finger on the most important verse in Scripture I would unhesitatingly put my finger on this one: 'And the Word became flesh.'"

This verse has been described as "The Great Divide," because no other religion can claim that the word they received from God became flesh. In all other religions the essential element is a word become word—a philosophy, a moralistic system, and so on. Only in Christianity does God appear in human form; the Word become flesh.

Early in my career as a minister I found that whenever I tried to present the Christian gospel to people of other faiths, everything I said brought the bland reply: "Yes, what you say is good, but we have the same teaching in our sacred books also." The Sermon on the Mount? Muslims have something similar in the *Qur'an*. Turning the other cheek? Hindus would reply: "Our sacred books tell us the same." Caring and sensitivity to the needs of others? Buddhists would respond: "We believe in that too, perhaps even more than you." Every issue I raised had its parallel. I was puzzled. Where was Christianity's uniqueness? Then it dawned upon me—the Incarnation. No other religion has anything like the Incarnation.

FURTHER STUDY

*Isa. 9:1–6; 7:14;
Gal. 4:4;
Luke 1:30–33*

1. How did Isaiah depict the Incarnation?
2. What was the message of the angel?

Prayer

O God our Father, just to reflect on the Incarnation is to be filled with amazement and joy. We are not knocking at the door of heaven. You are knocking at the lowly doors of our hearts. How can such a thing be true? Yet it is. I am so thankful. Amen.

The Thrilling Truth

"... but made himself nothing ... being made in human likeness ..." (v. 7)

For reading & meditation—Philippians 2:1–11

W e are reflecting on the fact that the Christian faith is not just a little better than other faiths but radically different. Religion is mankind's search for God; Christianity, however, is God's search for man. Therefore there are many religions, but only one gospel. Religion is the word become word; the gospel is the Word become flesh.

The commentator William Barclay, when writing on the verse "And the Word became flesh" which we looked at yesterday, said that this phrase explains why John wrote his Gospel. John apparently could not get over the fact that God had become man in the Person of His Son, and he sustained that thought throughout the whole of his writings. Augustine, the great saint of the fourth and fifth centuries, remarked that in his pre-Christian days he had never read anything comparable to that phrase: "And the Word became flesh."

One thing the ancient Greeks could never contemplate was that God could reveal Himself in bodily form. To the Greeks the body was a prison in which the soul was shackled, a tomb in which the spirit was confined. Plutarch, the wise old Greek, believed it was nothing short of blasphemy to expect God to involve Himself in the affairs of the world. Yet in the face of this, the highest thought of the New Testament world, the gospel unfolded the thrilling truth that the Son of God became the Son of Man in order that the sons of men might become sons of God. Could anything in heaven or earth be more wonderful than that? If so, I have yet to hear it.

FURTHER STUDY

1 John 4:1–2;
Rom. 1:1–4; 8:1–4

1. What does a true believer always acknowledge?
2. How did Paul put it?

Prayer

Blessed Lord Jesus, how can we thank You enough for taking on Yourself a human form and showing us what God is really like? For we could never have known unless we had seen. Having seen, it is sufficient. We want no other. Amen.

9

God Came Himself

"... God ... sent his one and only Son into the world that we might live through him." (v. 9)

For reading & meditation—1 John 4:7–21

There have been two great attempts to find God throughout the ages," said Dr. E. Stanley Jones, "one, philosophy, the other, moralism." The attempts of philosophy to find God are represented by the three great philosophical nations—Greece, India, and China. These three nations have taken men and women about as far as it is possible to go by philosophical reasoning. Philosophy has strained itself to the utmost and yet it has not been successful in finding God. Lao-tzu, the Chinese philosopher, said the final word about God is Silence, and Shankaracharya, the Indian philosopher, said the final word about God is not that. They both concluded at zero.

Moralism, likewise, cannot lead to God. The attempt to find God through the law was the noble effort made by the Jews. Never was such a moral system devised as theirs, nor an end result so disappointing. It produced, for instance, the Pharisee who stood in his pride and said: "God, I thank you that I am not like other men" (Luke 18:11). Jesus pronounced doom on the Pharisee's attempt to find God through moralism when He said: "Unless your righteousness surpasses that of the Pharisees and the teachers of the law, you will certainly not enter the kingdom of heaven" (Matt. 5:20). They could not reach the kingdom by even their greatest self-effort alone. Both philosophy and moralism fall short.

When our best was not good enough, when our highest attempts could not lead to the kingdom, God came down Himself to lift us. Now no one need say in his or her quest for God: "Not that."

FURTHER STUDY

Rom. 5:1–8;
Eph. 2:4–5;
John 3:16;
2 Tim. 3:5

1. What is the result of moralism?
2. What is the heart of Christianity?

↤═══ Prayer ═══↦

O God, Your down-reach is my only hope. My up-reach is feeble and goes little higher than my head.
Your down-reach, however, goes to the lowest of the low—it reaches me. I take hold of
Your grace and I am lifted—to You. Blessed be Your Name forever. Amen.

"I Have Jesus Christ"

"But when the time had fully come, God sent his Son . . ." (v. 4)
For reading & meditation—Galatians 4:1–8

The Incarnation, we are saying, is one of the chief distinctives of the Christian faith. But there are some within the Church today who cast doubt on this and many other aspects of Christianity. The Christian faith is being attacked not only from the outside but also from within.

The source of these attacks can be traced to those theological seminaries and training establishments which adopt a liberal approach to Christianity. Christ was not born of a virgin, they say, the miracles can be accounted for psychologically, and though Christ died on a cross His resurrection was not a physical one but a spiritual one. A theological student, who is taking a course in comparative religions, said: "If I were to accept what I am being taught, then I would leave college with the idea that the Christian faith has slightly higher moral teaching than other religions, is a little more consistent in its view of God and man, and is a little better in general, but not unique." Is it any wonder that so many students graduate from such institutions with few or no convictions and with nothing to preach—no gospel, no good news—nothing except philosophical arguments or a moral code? How sad that from so many pulpits one hears nothing more than a word become word—moralism, philosophy, and so on.

In a radio interview the interviewer asked me: "You go around the world preaching. What do you have that other religions do not have?" It was a good question and valid. The answer was simple and simply given: "I have Jesus Christ, the Word become flesh."

FURTHER STUDY

Luke 2:1–11;
Mark 1:15;
Rom. 10:15

1. How does the Bible describe the Incarnation?
2. Share the good news with someone today.

Prayer

O Father, though we see You faintly through the lattice of nature, that would never have been sufficient to satisfy the longing of our hearts. You have come to us in the Person of Your Son. Now we are satisfied. All praise and glory be unto Your worthy Name. Amen.

Shadow Boxing

"The law is only a shadow of the good things that are coming—not the realities themselves." (v. 1)

For reading & meditation—Hebrews 10:1-18

*W*e talked two days ago of humanity's efforts to try to reach God through philosophy and moralism or the law. The inadequacy, even bankruptcy, of trying to find God through the law is brought out most clearly in the passage before us today. The law, we are told, contains no true image, merely a shadow. It was the Word become word, hence a shadow and not an image. It follows that all discussion about the law being the route to finding God is nothing more than shadow boxing. It ends in futility.

One day, after centuries of sacrificing animals—during which time God instilled in human minds the important idea of substitution—the unexpected happened. The writer to the Hebrews put it in these words: "Sacrifice and offering you did not desire, but a body you prepared for me" (v. 5). Christ said to the Father: "Here I am . . . I have come to do your will." When the Son of God compressed Himself into a human body, the greatest miracle of the ages took place. *This* was the substance; all else was shadow.

The substance—the Incarnation—superseded all previous manifestations of God and now holds the field as the greatest and indeed the only real revelation. No one would ever have thought that the God of the universe would take a body and become man in order to redeem humankind. A love like that does not exist in the categories of philosophy. But seeing is believing. Every time we write the date we affirm it: God has been here on our planet in the form of a man.

FURTHER STUDY

Eph. 2:14–18;
Col. 2:13–15;
Heb. 7:18; 8:13

1. What has Christ abolished?
2. How is the law described?

Prayer

O God, what can I say? I am speechless at the wonder of it. I am in the dust. But that is where I find You—in the dust ready to receive me and lift me to the highest heaven. O gracious condescension.
I am Yours forever. Amen.

Attainment or Obtainment?

Day 11

"... he is the beginning and the firstborn from among the dead ..." (v. 18)

For reading & meditation—Colossians 1:1–20

*D*oes salvation come up from mankind through striving, helped by the Divine, or does it come down to us from above, through the act of God and our receptivity of that act? Is it an attainment or an obtainment? The answers separate Christianity from all other religions. Non-Christian religions teach that salvation is the work of mankind; the Christian faith teaches that salvation is the gift of God—Christianity alone falls into the category of obtainment.

Some people try to blunt the sharpness of the question "Does mankind strive to reach up to God or does God come down to redeem mankind through the incarnate Jesus?" by saying the answer is both. But by the very nature of things it cannot be both. The starting points are different. One begins with mankind; the other begins with God. Since the beginnings are different, the endings will be different. The whole of the New Testament revolves around the Person and work of Jesus. In some form or another He is on every page.

A letter I received protested against a statement I made which went something like this: "There is only one Person around whom the universe can unite, and that Person is Jesus." "There have been good persons in history," said my correspondent, "why not unite around all of them rather than just one?" Because Christ is the meeting point of the human and the divine. No one else can hold that position. An Indian Hindu said recently: "There is no one else bidding for the heart of humanity except Jesus. There is no one else on the field." There isn't!

FURTHER STUDY

*Eph. 1:1–23;
John 3:31;
1 Cor. 8:6*

1. List some of the things
that we have obtained
in Christ.
2. What did John declare
about Jesus?

Prayer

O Father, we want to thank You that when we couldn't come to You, You came down the ladder to us through the Incarnation. We are eternally grateful. Amen.

13

The Genius of Christianity

"... The virgin will be with child and will give birth to a son,
and will call him Immanuel." (v. 14)

For reading & meditation—Isaiah 7:13-17

*S*ome religions, such as Hinduism, claim that their gods incarnate themselves, but those so-called incarnations are rooted in fantasy, not in fact. The Incarnation of Jesus Christ is not just a great idea—it really happened. There were eyewitnesses and a written record.

The genius of Christianity is that it is not just a religion of influences, values and principles. It is a religion of happenings, of events, of plain but wonderful historical occurrences. The Incarnation belongs to the very marrow of the gospel; therefore, we can assert that God in the Person of His Son came to earth at a certain hour in history, lived and died among us, and afterwards rose from the dead. Those who say, "I admire the ethics of the Sermon on the Mount, I applaud the work and teachings of Christ and follow His principles in my daily life, but I cannot believe the historical part of it, that God took a body and became man," cannot really claim to be Christians. If they do not believe Christ's statements concerning Himself and the reason why He came into this world, then though they may be many splendid things they are not disciples of Christ.

To be a Christian means first and foremost accepting the great fact of the Incarnation—that Christ, the second Person of the Trinity, was born at Bethlehem in the way the Scriptures describe. Of this be certain—the Christian faith carries certain facts at its heart, and the greatest of them is this: "The Word became flesh and made his dwelling among us."

FURTHER STUDY

*1 Tim. 1:1-17;
Isa. 59:16;
John 15:13*

*1. What is a trustworthy
saying?
2. What was Paul's
testimony?*

Prayer

O Father, I pray that nothing will ever diminish the wondrous truth of Your Incarnation in my soul.
For without that You would be a distant deity, vague and unapproachable. In Jesus
You have come close to me. And how! I shall be eternally grateful. Amen.

Without a Rival

"From this time many of his disciples turned back and no longer followed him." (v. 66)

For reading & meditation—John 6:60-71

The next aspect of Christian uniqueness we consider is the Person of our Lord Himself. "Christianity is Christ," said one great preacher. "He is not just the Founder of Christianity but its very foundation. On Him rests the weight of bringing all men and women to God."

It is important to reflect at this point, as John Stott reminds us, that Christians must claim uniqueness and finality only for Christ, not for Christianity. We have to admit that over the centuries things have been done in the name of Christianity of which our Lord would not approve. The historical figure of Jesus and His teaching is the criterion by which everything must be measured. "Jesus Christ," said Bishop Stephen Neill, "is not in the least like anyone else who has ever lived." No one else in history can be compared to Him. You do not select Jesus Christ from rivals; He stands alone. He is not the first of a class; He occupies the category all by Himself.

Simon Peter realized this, as we see from the passage before us today. When Christ's followers started to drift away because He began to disappoint the hopes they had of Him, it seems the disciples started reconsidering their position too. Jesus knew what was going on in their minds and broke in on their thoughts with the question: "You do not want to leave too, do you?" (v. 67). Somehow that question seemed to clarify their minds. They saw in a flash His inevitability. Peter answered for them all: "To whom shall we go? You have the words of eternal life" (v. 68).

FURTHER STUDY

Phil. 1:21;
Col. 1:27;
Rev. 3:20

1. *What is the hope of glory?*
2. *What has Christ promised to those who respond to His voice?*

Prayer

O God, drive this thought more deeply than ever into my soul that there is just no substitute for Jesus.
He has no rivals. How glad I am that I belong to Him and He belongs to me.
May the wonder of this fact grow and glow within me day by day. Amen.

Exposed Realism

"... he taught as one who had authority, and not as their teachers of the law." (v. 29)

For reading & meditation—Matthew 7:13–29

*I*f the men and women of this world took an unbiased look at Jesus as presented to us in the four Gospels, they would see, as Bishop Stephen Neill put it, that "Jesus Christ is not in the least like anyone else who has ever lived." The way He taught, for example, is not the same as that of any other religious teacher. When He concluded the Sermon on the Mount, which some believe to be idealism, the people "were astonished and overwhelmed with bewildered wonder at His teaching, for He was teaching as [One] Who had [and was] authority ..." (Amp. Bible).

What was this "authority"? An authority imposed from without? No, it was the authority of the facts. Jesus was divulging the meaning of life. He was uncovering reality. It was the authority of God; when *He* spoke, God spoke. It was the authority of truth, deed, and love.

A good many people make the mistake of thinking that Jesus came to impose upon humanity a moral code. But Jesus was not a moralist in that sense at all. He was a revealer of the nature of reality. He revealed first the nature of God, and that the nature of God is the ground of God's conduct and ours. He then lifted up the laws written into the universe, written in the warp and woof of our being, and showed us that the only way to live is God's way. Instead of being an imposed idealism, it was exposed realism—Reality itself was speaking. No wonder it was authoritative. Here was the indicative become the imperative.

FURTHER STUDY

Mark 1:1–27;
Matt. 28:18;
John 5:27;
Matt. 8:27

1. What amazed the people?
2. What amazed the disciples?

Prayer

Lord Jesus Christ, revealer of all that is hidden, thank You above everything that You have revealed God to me. You are the Way, the Truth, and the Life. All of Your ways become the way—for everybody, everywhere. Now I am on the way. Hallelujah!

Good Man or God-Man?

"Can any of you prove me guilty of sin?" (v. 46)
For reading & meditation—John 8:31–47

*J*esus publicly made the challenge: "Can any of you prove me guilty of sin?" Here we are face to face with a kind of person who had not been seen since Adam in his pre-fallen condition—a man without sin.

The disciples had shared every kind of experience with Him that mortals can share, had seen Him at all hours of day and night, had seen Him tired, hungry and disappointed, scorned, abused and hunted to death, had ridden with Him on a wave of popularity and hidden with Him from inquisitive miracle-mongers, yet they certainly could find no fault in Him. It is quite possible to know too much about some people. A gardener who was employed by a minister was asked why he did not come to hear him preach. Half in jest but half in earnest he replied: "I know too much about him." But none of the disciples ever said that concerning Jesus. They saw no flaw in Him.

Moreover, not only were His intimates unable to discover sin in Him; He had no awareness of it in Himself. He lived intimately with God His Father, but the holiness of God did not rebuke Him. It didn't because it couldn't. He was sinless, spotless, perfect. If it be granted that Jesus was a good man, and if it be granted that a good man is ready always to tell the truth, are we not constrained by His own words to believe that He was something more than a good man? He is much much more than a good man; He is the God-Man.

FURTHER STUDY

Luke 23:47;
2 Cor. 5:1–21;
Isa. 53:9;
Heb. 4:15;
1 Pet. 1:18–20

1. What did the centurion declare?
2. How did Peter describe Christ's sinlessness?

Prayer

O Jesus, my Savior and my God, when I think of how You, the sinless One, took on Yourself my sins and bore them all away, I feel it must be too good to be true. But yet I know it is too good not to be true. Thank You, my Father. In Jesus' Name. Amen.

"Not on Trial"

"I tell you that one greater than the temple is here." (v. 6)
For reading & meditation—Matthew 12:1–14

We continue reflecting on the thought that Jesus Christ is not like anyone else who has ever lived. Take the claim which He made in our text today: "One greater than the temple is here." Jesus in effect compared Himself with the temple's grandeur and significance as the center of Jewish life and said: "I am greater than all this." It seemed preposterous. And yet the ages have vindicated Him. The temple is gone; all that is left is the Wailing Wall. Yet Christ lives on—and is the most potent power in human affairs.

A man looking at some pictures in a famous art gallery commented to a friend: "I don't think much of these pictures." "Excuse me, Sir," said an attendant who overheard him, "the *pictures* are not on trial." He meant, of course, that the pictures had been approved by the highest authorities. It was not the pictures that were on trial but the people who viewed them.

Some people think Jesus is on trial now, but in truth He is not. We judge ourselves by our judgment of Him. One greater than the temple was there in that first century and is still here today. Jesus is bigger than every system whether it be religious, political, or economic. They are related to Him, not He to them. They must all stand before the judgment bar of His Person. If they accord with Him, reflect His mind and Spirit, then they are valid. If not, they are invalid. Jesus is not just the greatest the world has ever seen; He is the greatest it will ever see.

FURTHER STUDY

Luke 11:14–32;
Isa. 53:12; 63:1;
Phil. 2:9–10

1. What does an evil generation look for?
2. What comparison did Jesus make?

Prayer

Lord Jesus, You are my center and my circumference. I begin with You and end with You. If I don't begin with You, then I end in disillusionment. Help me to begin every thought, every project with You. For Your own dear Name's sake. Amen.

Lord and God

"Thomas said to him, 'My Lord and my God!'" (v. 28)

For reading & meditation—John 20:24–31

*J*esus Christ accepted worship as God. What other person in his right mind has ever made such a claim?

Earlier Simon Peter had made the confession "You are the Christ, the Son of the living God" (Matt. 16:16), which was a profound and powerful statement. Some Bible scholars believe Peter did not perceive the complete significance of the words when he uttered them, but came to see their full meaning later. The twelve disciples, we must remember, were Jews to a man. They had been steeped in their high and ancient faith, and the belief in one God was firmly embedded in their minds. "Hear O Israel," they had said a thousand times, "the Lord our God is one Lord." They were sure the Messiah, the Promised One, would come, but they hardly expected God to come Himself, in Person, and in the garb of a working man. It was difficult for the disciples to grasp the doctrine of Christ as we know it today, or even the truth of the Trinity. They glimpsed it but did not fully understand it.

It was Thomas the doubter, as we call him, who stepped nearer to the truth in the Upper Room after Christ had come back from the grave. If Jesus was a good man but not God then when Thomas said, "My Lord and my God," He should have turned to Thomas and told him: "You can admire Me but you must not worship Me. I am not God." He didn't because He is God, and thus the right recipient of worship.

FURTHER STUDY

Matt. 16:1-16;
Mark 5:1-7; 15:39;
John 1:49; 4:42;
11:24–27

1. *List some of the people who acknowledged Jesus as God.*
2. *Who else acknowledged Him in this way?*

Prayer

Lord Jesus, I stand in awe and almost dumbfounded wonder at the fact that You being God came to this world as a working man. My heart echoes Thomas's cry: "My Lord and my God." And in worshipping You, Lord Jesus, I know I am worshipping God. Amen.

Greater than the Bible

"You diligently study the Scriptures. . . .
These are the Scriptures that testify about me . . ." (v. 39)
For reading & meditation—John 5:31–47

Jesus claimed to be greater than the Scriptures. Everyone else has to put themselves under the authority of the Scriptures. In one sense, of course, Christ subjected Himself to the Scriptures, but in another sense He was superior to them. He did not emerge from the Bible; the Bible emerged from Him. The Amplified Bible puts our text for today: "You search and investigate and pore over the Scriptures diligently, because you suppose and trust that you have eternal life through them . . . And still you are not willing . . . to come to Me, so that you might have life." We saw the other day how Christ declared: "One greater than the temple is here." He could also have said: "One greater than the Scriptures is here."

A prominent theologian stated: "The Bible is the supreme method of communication between God and man." Is it? I thought Christ is the supreme method of communication between God and man. "There is one God and one mediator between God and men, the man Christ Jesus . . ." (1 Tim. 2:5). It is true that we would know little of Christ were it not for the New Testament. But Christ existed before the New Testament. I do not say this to denigrate the Scriptures in any way. They are divinely inspired and thus they inspire me. But the Person is greater than the product. We honor the product but only as it leads us to Christ's feet and to an allegiance to Him. Indeed, one greater than the Bible is here.

FURTHER STUDY

*John 10:1–10; 1:4; 11:25;
Rom. 5:21;
1 John 5:12*

*1. What is Jesus the
source of?
2. What does this mean
for us?*

──══ Prayer ══──

Lord Jesus, I am thankful for the Scriptures for many reasons, but most of all because they lead me to You.
You are the Word that is bigger than men's words. Not a page but a Person.
All honor and glory be to Your Name. Amen.

Our Code Is a Character

"A new command I give you: Love one another. As I have loved you . . ." (v. 34)

For reading & meditation—John 13:1–38

W hat other teacher has taken the Ten Commandments and had the right to add another commandment to them? But this is precisely what Jesus did, as we see from our text today. "A new command I give you," He said. "Love one another. As I have loved you, so you must love one another."

The Old Testament and other religious writings enjoined loving one another. What was new was this: "As I have loved you." Our Lord's conduct—"as I have loved you"—produced a new code for the human race. Paul, writing to the Philippians, catches the spirit of it when he says: "Treat one another with the same spirit as you experience in Christ Jesus" (Phil. 2:5, Moffatt). Here morality reaches its high-water mark. From the moment Jesus uttered the words that are occupying our attention, there came into human life something more than a code—there came a Character. Now, therefore, our code is a Character—the Character of Jesus.

When someone asks me if I believe in the Ten Commandments I say: "Yes, and very much more besides. I believe in Jesus." The Ten Commandments are an injunction—and a God-given one. But Jesus is an injunction plus an inspiration. To follow an injunction is to obey an imposed morality, but to follow a Person and do the things He does is an inspired morality. One is legalism, the other love. One binds you, the other frees you. One makes you feel trammelled, the other relaxed and spontaneous. Our code is not a commandment but a Character. One greater than the commandments is here.

FURTHER STUDY

John 15:1–17;
James 2:8;
Matt. 7:12

1. *What was the basis of Christ's love?*
2. *What is the basis of our being able to fulfill the Royal Law?*

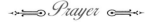

Prayer

O Christ, Your law lays upon me an injunction, but Your life entering into my life inspires me to live up to that injunction. It is this that makes Your yoke so easy. I am deeply, deeply grateful. Amen.

Who Can Forgive?

". . . the Son of Man has authority on earth to forgive sins . . ." (v. 6)
For reading & meditation—Matthew 9:1–12

*P*erhaps one of the most significant ways in which Jesus is unlike anyone else who has ever lived is that He had the ability to forgive sins. I am sure you will know the words of the famous hymn which refers to the forgiveness offered by Christ:

> He breaks the power of cancelled sin,
> He sets the prisoner free.

I know of no one else who can do that. Some psychoanalysts try to rid the soul of guilt, but though they may be successful with pseudo-guilt (guilt that is imagined rather than real), they are powerless to deal with the stain of sin that is deeply ingrained in every human soul. The secular therapist will examine the stuff of your dreams, invite you to answer a series of harmless questions, and then drag out from your forgotten past the source of all your trouble—some past transgression or sin. But even the most highly trained team of psychoanalysts cannot forgive. They may expose an old wound, but they cannot heal it. They may show you that your trouble is an ancient sin, but they cannot cleanse it from the system. And that is what our sick souls need most of all—forgiveness.

A man I talked to the other day said he went to a professional counselor, a non-Christian, who found the root of his trouble—an old and wicked sin. "Now," said the man, "tell me the cure." "Just forgive yourself," said the analyst. Forgive yourself? It's a lot easier to do that when you know that you yourself have been forgiven.

FURTHER STUDY

Matt. 26:17–30;
Acts 2:38;
Heb. 9:22;
Acts 13:38

1. Why is forgiveness available?
2. Seek forgiveness for your sin today.

 *Prayer*

Lord Jesus, You have not only forgiven me but You keep on forgiving me. Help me realize, however, that though Your forgiveness is free, it is not cheap. For You had to die in order to bring me forgiveness. Help me never forget that. Amen.

That One Solitary Life

"The men were amazed and asked, 'What kind of man is this?'" (v. 27)

For reading & meditation—Matthew 8:18–34

Have you ever wondered why Jesus is never referred to as Jesus the Great? We speak of Alexander the Great, Charles the Great, and Peter the Great but never Jesus the Great. And why? Because He dwells in a sphere where no real comparisons are possible. It simply doesn't seem right to use the designation "the Great" of our Lord as we would of others.

Our Lord has no peers, no rivals, and no successors. He is so different from every other leader, so unique, so superior, that He qualifies for a place on His own. The things He said about God are not the same as the sayings of any other religious teacher. The claims He made for Himself are unparalleled. His analysis of human society goes deeper and is more devastating than that pronounced by any other man. The challenges and demands He made on His followers are more searching than those put forward by anyone—past and present. As James Francis said of Him: "He never wrote a book, never held an office, never had a family, never went to college, never did any of the things that usually accompany greatness. But . . . He is the centerpiece of the human race and the leader of its column of progress.

"I am within the mark when I say that all the armies that have ever marched, all the navies that were ever built, all the parliaments that have ever sat, all the kings that have ever reigned, put together, have not affected the life of people upon this earth as powerfully as has that one solitary life."

FURTHER STUDY

Isa. 40:1–31;
Ps. 89:6;
John 1:34

1. What question did Isaiah pose?
2. What was John's testimony?

Prayer

Jesus, my Lord and my God, all the descriptions of You fall short of defining Your real glory and worth. Yet my soul recognizes, even though it cannot put it into words, the glory that belongs to You by sovereign right. I love You Lord Jesus. With all my heart. Amen.

The God Who Seeks

"Rejoice with me; I have found my lost sheep." (v. 6)
For reading & meditation—Luke 15:1–10

We turn now to look at another aspect of Christianity's uniqueness—the issue of personal salvation. The vocabulary of salvation is distasteful to those of other religions and many insist we should give it up. They say, "It smacks of spiritual smugness and arrogance."

But before we answer this criticism we must realize what Christianity is all about. Christianity is essentially a rescue religion; it is the announcement of the good news that God has come in the Person of His Son to save us from the power of sin, the penalty of sin, and one day in the future the presence of sin. In the passage before us today we see that God likens Himself to a shepherd who leaves the rest of the sheep in order to go after one sheep that is lost. The Divine Shepherd, far from abandoning the sheep in the hope that, bleating and stumbling, it may find its own way home, puts His own life on the line to search it out.

Judaism denies that Jesus is the Messiah and that His sin-bearing death is the only ground on which divine forgiveness can be offered. One Jewish scholar, C. G. Montefiore, goes so far as to generously refer to the "greatness and originality" of Jesus in His attitude to sinners that "instead of avoiding them He actively sought them out." However, though Orthodox Jewish teaching recognizes that God receives sinners who return to Him, it fails to see that He also seeks them out. How utterly amazing. The One who *seeks* and saves is God.

FURTHER STUDY

Luke 19:1–10;
Matt. 18:10–14;
John 1:43; 5:14; 9:35

1. What was Jesus' message to Zacchaeus?
2. How did Jesus illustrate the heart of the shepherd?

Prayer

O Father, what a thought: You did not send an angel to seek us out and save us. You came Yourself
in the Person of Your Son. I can never put my gratitude into mere words.
Help me show it by my life. In Jesus' Name. Amen.

The Antechamber of Faith

"... Jesus said, 'It is finished.'" (v. 30)

For reading & meditation—John 19:28-37

The chief difference between other religions and the Christian faith as it relates to the matter of personal salvation is: every other religion teaches a form of self-salvation; Christianity teaches that God came in the Person of His Son to do for us what we could not do for ourselves. One Christian writer, Emil Brunner, refers to "the self-confident optimism of all non-Christian religions, because they teach a gospel of self-salvation, whereas in the Good News the whole emphasis is on the gracious 'self-movement' of God towards sinners and on self-despair as the antechamber of faith."

Buddhism sees the main problem in life as suffering rather than sin, and the "desire" which is at the root of suffering. Deliverance comes, claims Buddhism, through the abolition of desire by self-effort. There is no God and no Savior. The very last words of the Buddha to his disciples were these: "Strive without ceasing." How different from the last words of our Lord from the cross, which included the wondrous cry: "It is finished."

Hinduism teaches the main problem in life is *maya* or *karma*, *maya* being illusion and *karma* retribution through reincarnation. Each person, says Hinduism, must receive the fruit of his or her own wrongdoing in future lives, if not in this one. From this endless cycle of rebirths or reincarnations there is no escape by forgiveness but only the final release of *nirvana*, involving the extinction of being.

If only people of the world would heed the text at the top of this page. What a difference it would make to them. Salvation has been accomplished. It is ours to receive.

FURTHER STUDY

Rom. 10:1–13;
Acts 2:21;
Titus 2:11;
1 Tim. 2:4

1. What is the basis of salvation?
2. What is God's desire?

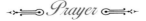 Prayer

O God, I am thankful that I am no longer caught up in precariously trying to save myself. Instead I rest assured in the salvation You have purchased for me on Calvary. Grant that millions more might enter into it by faith this very day. In Christ's Name I pray. Amen.

The Way Begins in a Hole

". . . at just the right time, when we were still powerless, Christ died for the ungodly." (v. 6)

For reading & meditation—Romans 5:1–8

*W*hy should the offer of free salvation in Christ be such a stumbling block to the world? Mainly because it cuts deep into people's pride. Bishop Neill, a writer, says: ". . . that which we ask the Muslim to look for in Jesus is in itself a cause of grave offense to Muslim pride. We suggest—we cannot do otherwise—that he find a Savior. The Muslim affirms that he has no need of such a thing."

Pride adopts the stance: "I can save myself by my fasting, good works, or other meritorious acts." But the message of the gospel is this: there is simply nothing we can do to save ourselves. We must let God save us—or be lost. Helen Woodhouse, another religious writer, says: "We think we must climb to a certain height of goodness before we can reach God, but He doesn't say, 'at the end of the road you may find Me'; rather, 'I am the Way, I am the road under your feet, the road that begins just as low down as you happen to be.'" If we are in a hole, then the way begins in a hole. The moment we give up our pride and turn our face to God, confessing that we can do nothing to save ourselves, that moment we put ourselves in the position where we can be saved. The next step is simply to call out to the Lord and ask Him to save you. If you have never done that before, I urge you—do it today.

FURTHER STUDY

2 Cor. 9:1–15;
Rom. 6:23;
Eph. 2:8;
John 4:10

1. *How is salvation described?*
2. *What two responses can we have?*

 **Prayer**

O God, I see clearly that I can do nothing to save myself, and if I am to be saved then I must look to You to save me. I repent of my sin, and turn to You as Your Word commands. Save me. In Jesus' Name I pray. Amen.

26

No Change—No Conversion

"Greet . . . Epenetus, who was the first convert to Christ in the province of Asia." (v. 5)

For reading & meditation—Romans 16:1–16

A word which the gospel associates with salvation is the word "conversion." Salvation is the offer of divine forgiveness and the gift of eternal life; conversion is the way we enter into that experience and receive the gift. The word "conversion" means to turn about or change one's direction. Though other religions talk about spiritual conversion, the experience they speak of bears no relation whatsoever to the thought in the mind of Jesus when He said: "Except ye be converted . . . ye shall not enter into the kingdom of heaven" (Matt. 18:3 KJV).

We divide people into races, classes, sexes, nationalities, rich and poor, educated and uneducated, but Jesus divided men and women into just two classes—the converted and the unconverted. Apparently, to Him no other distinctions mattered. If you are converted, you are in the kingdom; and if you are not converted, you are not in the kingdom. There are no exceptions.

Listen to the words once again: "*Except* ye be converted . . . ye shall not enter into the kingdom of heaven." I think it sad that the NIV translation of the Bible doesn't use the words "except" or "converted" in Matthew 18:3. It simply says: "unless you change and become like little children." The truth is still there, but in my opinion the words used are not as picturesque or as powerful. Conversion can be explained like this: it is the change, gradual or sudden, by which one passes from the kingdom of self to the kingdom of God. And if there is no change, there is no conversion.

FURTHER STUDY

Isa. 43:25; 55:7;
Micah 7:18;
1 John 1:1–9

1. What does God display toward the unconverted?
2. What is the consequence of conversion?

Prayer

O God, I am thankful that amidst all the awakenings and new experiences I can enter into in this life,
You are eager to give me the supreme awakening—spiritual conversion.
May multitudes enter into it today. In Jesus' Name. Amen.

Two Types of Conversion

". . . they told how the Gentiles had been converted.
This news made all the brothers very glad." (v. 3)
For reading & meditation—Acts 15:1–21

*S*alvation is the word Christians use to describe the experience of sins being forgiven and receiving the gift of eternal life. *Conversion* is the word to describe the way we enter into that experience. Other religions also use the word *conversion*, but usually what they mean by it is the act of changing from one religion to another. Nothing is known of a deep inward spiritual change, which is what happens in the Christian faith when we are saved or converted.

In the book *Mirrors of Downing Street* the author finishes the characterization of Winston Churchill, one of Britain's most famous prime ministers: "General Booth, the founder of the Salvation Army, once told Mr. Churchill that he stood in need of conversion. *That old man was a notable judge of character.*" But Winston Churchill was not alone in his need of conversion. Everyone, says Scripture, has to experience it in order to enter into the kingdom of God.

Sometimes non-Christian religions use the word *conversion* to describe a change of attitude in one of their adherents, but the change is always on the horizontal level rather than a vertical one. By a change "on the horizontal" I mean a change on the human level, a change of thinking or approach, but not a change in relation to God—the vertical level. In Madras once, I read in a local newspaper about a group of Hindus who were ready to fight a court case over the conversion to Islam of a hotel maid. That was a *horizontal* conversion. The Bible knows nothing of horizontal conversions. Conversion in Scripture is always vertical.

FURTHER STUDY

John 15:19–24; 3:17–18;
Rom. 8:1

1. How does Jesus
describe conversion?
2. What does this
remove?

Prayer

O God my Father, is there anything more wonderful in heaven or earth than to be vertically converted—changed by You? I know of nothing. I can do no other than gratefully accept. And am I grateful? I most surely am. Thank You, my Father. Amen.

Vertical vs. Horizontal

"... God, who is rich in mercy, made us alive with Christ even when we were
dead in transgressions . . ." (vv. 4–5)

For reading & meditation—Ephesians 2:1–10

A Hindu once said in my presence: "A man may change his acts but not his character." He was saying that a change is possible, but not a vertical change; there can be improvement, modification, a change of attitude, but no deep radical change.

The Christian church is not without a sprinkling of what yesterday I called "horizontal" conversions. Many historians have called attention to the fact that when Christianity swept through Europe, there were many genuine conversions to Christ but many horizontal ones too—people taking the Name of Christ for political or economic expediency. They were converted horizontally but still in need of a vertical conversion.

When I was about fourteen years of age I was "horizontally" converted. I was a mischievous young man, and one day in church I made up my mind to be "a good boy." I tried hard to give up such things as swearing, stealing, and so on, but it didn't last. Although I felt religious, there was no great inward change. On a horizontal level I was converted, but not in relation to God. About a year later, sitting in the same church and under deep conviction of sin, I made a complete and total surrender to God. I was vertically converted. I walked out of that church feeling as if I had been turned inside out. From that moment my life was changed, old habits began to disappear, and my whole being was flooded with light. I tell you with all the conviction of my being, the vertical was much different than the horizontal.

FURTHER STUDY

Titus 3:1–5;
Ezek. 36:26;
John 3:3–7;
1 Pet. 1:23

1. How is the change in a person described?
2. How is it accomplished?

Prayer

O God, help us not to be converted to the things surrounding Christ—religious rituals for example—but to Christ Himself. For if we don't touch Him we don't touch life, and there will be no deep inward change. In His dear Name we ask it. Amen.

Conversion – a Miracle

". . . in Christ Jesus neither circumcision nor uncircumcision has any value." (v. 6)

For reading & meditation—Galatians 5:1–15

*P*ermit me to pause in our meditations on the chief differences between the Christian faith and non-Christian religions to turn our eyes inward to the state of affairs within the church. We have not been as careful as we might in relation to this matter of vertical conversion. Oftentimes we have been more interested in statistics than in actual true conversions. The church, generally speaking, has a lot to answer for in this respect. The horizontal has outrun the vertical in some sections of institutional Christianity. This is why in a number of countries church leaders will not baptize converts until they have received some clear teaching on what the Christian life is all about.

In Paul's day, as we see from our text, the main question being asked was about circumcision—whether or not that was essential. Paul threw the emphasis on being a new creature. Neither circumcision nor uncircumcision has any value. The only thing that counts, he said, is faith expressing itself through love.

Conversion will involve a miraculous change; when it doesn't then it is not true conversion. What sort of change? There will be the slaying of the beast within, the gathering of the discordant forces of the soul into harmony, the cleansing of a stained conscience, entry into a more abundant life, and a deep inner sense of fellowship with Christ. Conversion doesn't have to be cataclysmic to be real either. The underlying facts are a new life, a new relationship. But it is as much a miracle as the calling forth of Lazarus from the dead.

**FURTHER
STUDY**

*1 Cor. 6:1–11;
Acts 13:39;
Rom. 5:1;
Gal. 3:24*

*1. What word is used to describe the process of conversion?
2. What does it mean?*

Prayer

O God, save us in the church from the peril of horizontal conversions—people changing in relation to one another but not in Your direction. We want the real and only the real. Send us Your Spirit in even greater measure. Amen.

Bankruptcy Confessed

"... you were washed, you were sanctified, you were justified in the name of
the Lord Jesus Christ . . ." (v. 11)

For reading & meditation—1 Corinthians 6:1–11

*I*n his book *Conversion—Christian and Non-Christian*, C. Underwood says that the future of religion lies with the religions of the East, such as Hinduism and Buddhism, where conversions seem to occur. He hears followers discussing such things as self-sacrifice and the practice of good works and labels that as spiritual conversion. When people of any religion begin to become more interested in others than in themselves, then that has to be applauded and recognized as beneficial. But that does not equate with the conversion Jesus talked about.

An acquaintance of mine in India, the principal of a high school, told me of a Christian student who was given to immorality. The student was introduced to a pastor who took him aside, and after a month of deep spiritual counseling he was transformed. Several months later a Hindu student was similarly discovered to be practicing immorality. The principal of the school, hearing of this, said to one of his senior staff, a Hindu: "Tell me of a saintly Hindu that I can talk to, or an institution where there is hope of this young man being reformed." The staff member shook his head and replied: "We don't have such a thing. Hinduism can do nothing for this case. Can't you take him to one of your Christian pastors and get him to pray with him or read the Bible to him?" Here was bankruptcy confessed.

I do not tell this story to put the Hindu religion in a bad light. I tell it simply to establish the fact that when other helpers fail and comforts flee, there is always Jesus.

FURTHER STUDY

Rom. 3:20;
Gal. 2:16;
Eph. 2:8–9

1. Why does observing the law fail?
2. What did Paul underline to the Ephesians?

Prayer

Lord Jesus, I am so thankful that You and You alone are the true Savior. All other Saviors are pseudo-Saviors. Not only do You save me from sin but You save me also from sinning. I am deeply, deeply grateful. Amen.

"I Know I'm Saved"

"... [Jesus] is able to save completely those who come to God through him ..." (v. 25)

For reading & meditation—Hebrews 7:11–28

*I*s it possible to know without any shadow of doubt that one is saved and ready to meet God? This question, says one writer, goes right to the roots of religious experience. Christianity says "Yes." Other religions are not sure. Without exception they will tell you that it savors of presumption to say one is certain that one is saved.

I know some Christians have difficulty here also. They contend that we can hope to be saved, or claim we are being saved, but that no one can state with any degree of assurance that they *are* saved. It is gross self-centeredness, they maintain, and a sign of self-absorption to claim here and now on this earth, "I am saved." Yet John Wesley declared it. On May 24, 1738, he walked into a room in Aldersgate Street, London, where he heard someone read the Preface to Luther's commentary on Romans, and as he listened there was given him "an assurance" that God had taken away his sins and saved him from the law of sin and death.

Millions all over the world can say as Wesley did that they have an assurance they are saved and know that when they die they will go to heaven. It is not presumption to say you are saved providing, of course, you have entered into a personal relationship with Jesus Christ. Indeed, it is offensive for anyone who has given himself or herself to Christ not to say they are saved. As we see from our text today, Christ promises to save and save *completely*. I know I'm saved. How about you?

FURTHER STUDY

2 Tim. 1:1–12;
1 John 3:14;
Job 19:25

1. What was Paul able to write to Timothy?
2. What was Job able to say?

Prayer

O Father, thank You that not only do You save me from my sins and draw me to Yourself but You give me the assurance that I am Yours forever. How can I thank You enough for such wondrous grace? With my stammering tongue, however, I will try. Amen.

M. A. – Mightily Assured

"... let us draw near to God with a sincere heart in full assurance of faith ..." (v. 22)

For reading & meditation—Hebrews 10:19-25

*I*n every religion in the world apart from Christianity there is a note of uncertainty concerning this matter of personal salvation. Many modern religious attitudes are expressed in the limerick:

Forasmuch as without Thee
We are not able to doubt Thee,
O grant us Thy grace
To inform the whole race
That we know nothing whatever about Thee.

Can we be satisfied with this? St. Augustine said he wished to be as certain of things unseen as that seven and three make ten. The human heart longs for certainty—it needs to know without a shadow of doubt that the salvation of the soul is secure. The good news is that in Jesus Christ such security is found. When we turn from other religions to the Word of God, it is like stepping out of thick fog into clear and brilliant sunlight.

Our text today talks not just of assurance but full assurance—the full assurance of faith. What is faith? Faith is simply taking God at His Word, accepting what He asserts and acting accordingly. Listen to just one of the many things God says concerning this matter: "Everyone who calls on the name of the Lord will be saved" (Rom. 10:13). Have you called on Christ and received Him into your heart? Then you have scriptural warrant for believing on that basis alone, quite apart from personal feelings, that you are a child of God, and that you are going to spend eternity with Him. What a salvation! What a Savior!

FURTHER STUDY

1 Thess. 1:1–10;
1 John 2:3–6; 3:16–20;
4:13–16; 5:10

1. What is a recurring theme in 1 John?
2. Why not make the same confession to someone today?

Prayer

My Father and my God, what a joy it is to know that You make available to me not just assurance but full assurance. Fill the cup of my heart until it is overflowing with the sense of divine assurance. And keep it full, dear Father. In Jesus' Name. Amen.

Whose Book Is It?

"All Scripture is God-breathed and is useful for teaching, rebuking,
correcting and training in righteousness . . ." (v. 16)

For reading & meditation—2 Timothy 3:10–17

The next aspect of Christian uniqueness we consider is the Holy Scriptures, which we call the Bible. Nearly every brand of religion is based on a book. Whether ancient or modern, mystical or historical, ceremonial or ethical, it is almost certain to follow the teaching of some allegedly sacred volume. The Hindus have their *Vedas*, the Muslims the *Qur'an*, and the Parsis their *Zend Avesta*. The Sikhs of India treat their sacred book, the *Guru Granth Sahib*, as though it were a person. They fan it in hot weather, offer it food, and put it to sleep under mosquito nets. Western religions have their books too, such as the *Book of Mormon*, *Science and Health*, and so on.

Christianity too is based on a book, a holy book called the Bible. But the Bible is unique. Like the One about whom it speaks, it is in a category all by itself. It is unique because of its Author. Most people would agree that the most important thing about any book is not its title, its topic, its binding, its lettering, or its layout—but how well it is written, in other words its author. In reading and studying Holy Writ, that is the primary and pivotal question: Whose book is it? To that inquiry the Bible itself supplies the answer, as we see from our text today. God is its Author. With other books you have to understand the book in order to know the author. With the Bible you have to know the Author in order to understand the book.

FURTHER STUDY

2 Pet. 1:12–21;
Ezek. 1:3;
Acts 1:16

1. What did Peter think it right to do?
2. Where did God's Word have its origin?

⊷══ Prayer ══⊷

My Father and my God, what new light streams forth from the pages of the Bible since I have come to know You, the Author. The more I love You the more I love Your book, and the more I love Your book the more I love You. Blessed be Your Name forever. Amen.

A Father's Pleasure

"And a voice came from heaven: 'You are my Son, whom I love . . .'" (v.11)
For reading & meditation—Mark 1:1–12

We continue with the thought that what makes the Bible unique is its Author. Some years ago a cartoon appeared in a Christian magazine depicting a woman at the counter of a lending library asking for a copy of the Bible. "Bible?" muses the attendant. "Bible! Never heard of it. Who's the author?"

But don't other religions claim that God is the author of their sacred books also? Mohammed believed that God dictated to him the words of the *Qur'an*, and Joseph Smith maintained that the words written in the *Book of Mormon* came directly from the mouth of God. The crucial question, however, must be this: Do the sacred books of other religions speak of God's Son as the only Savior? And are they inspired by the Father of our Lord Jesus Christ?

What strikes me as strange about the sacred books of other religions that purport to have come from God is that they have no reference to the plan of salvation as brought to us by the Lord Jesus Christ. The main theme of the Bible is Christ. All the Old Testament truths converge on Him and all the New Testament truths emerge from Him. He is the hub of the Bible. In the passage before us today we read how God opened the heavens at Jesus' baptism and called down: "This is my Son whom I love and with whom I am well pleased." If God is so excited about His Son, why is it that in the sacred books of other religions (said to come direct from God) there is no mention of Him?

FURTHER STUDY

Matt. 17:1–13; 3:17;
John 8:18;
1 John 5:9

1. Of what did the voice from heaven instruct the disciples?
2. What is greater than man's testimony?

Prayer

O Father, I can understand the pleasure that You find in Your Son because I find pleasure in Him too.
Your love is so infinitely greater than mine, but such as I have, I give to Him,
and to You, once again this day. Amen.

"A God Who
Has No Son . . ."

"For God so loved the world that he gave his one and only Son . . ." (v. 16)
For reading & meditation—John 3:1-17

*Y*esterday's point about God finding great pleasure in His Son is worth pursuing as so much hangs on it when contrasting the Bible with the sacred books of other faiths. It seems strange to me that God should have so much to say about His Son in the Bible and yet ignore Him when supposedly revealing Himself to the founders of other religions.

Long ago, in India, I sat by a man who, when he discovered I was a Christian, showed me his English translation of the *Qur'an*. I spent several hours perusing it. When eventually I returned it to him I commented: "I notice that though it talks a lot about God (Allah), it never mentions that He has a Son." He looked startled for a moment and replied: "Sir, in our religion such a thing could not be possible." He drew my attention to these words: "Allah forbid that He Himself should beget a Son." I turned to the Bible verse which forms our text for today, and read him the words.

We sat quietly after that, both of us realizing we had touched on the main difference between Islam and Christianity. My heart leaped in gratitude to God that He had an only begotten Son whom He was willing to give up for my sin and the sins of the whole human race. A God who has no Son has to rely on intermediaries to bring people to Himself. And an intermediary who is not God and not man cannot effect complete reconciliation. It would be like a wonderfully constructed bridge that is broken at the farther end.

**FURTHER
STUDY**

*Luke 22:70;
Matt. 16:16;
Heb. 1:3*

*1. What did Jesus confirm
to His questioners?
2. What was Peter's
confession?*

⊸⇒ *Prayer* ⇐⊷

O Father, as I ponder John 3:16 I feel I am putting my heart up against Your heart. I want to feel its beat
and catch its rhythm. For Your heart is here. I am so grateful. Amen.

"Before All Worlds"

"Jesus said . . . 'I am returning to my Father and your Father, to my God and your God.'" (v. 17)

For reading & meditation—John 20:10–18

S ome non-Christian religions claim that God is the Author of their sacred writings as well as of the Bible, but the god they talk about is not the God who has revealed Himself in the Person of His Son. The true God is a *Father*—the Father of our Lord Jesus Christ. Mohammed wrote in the Qur'an (as we saw): "Allah forbid that He Himself should beget a Son." But that is exactly what God did—He begot a Son.

What does "begotten" mean? C. S. Lewis in his book *Mere Christianity* points out that to beget is to become the father of; to create is to make. When you beget, you beget something of the same kind as yourself. A man begets human babies, a beaver begets little beavers, and a bird begets eggs which turn into baby birds. A man can create a statue which looks like a man but is not a real man. This is an important issue to get clear. What God begets is God, just as what man begets is man. That is why human beings are not sons of God in the sense that Christ is. They may be like God in certain ways, but they are not of the same kind.

One of the creeds says that Christ is the Son of God, "begotten not created," and adds: "begotten by His Father before all worlds." "Before all worlds." Christ is begotten, not created. For what purpose? That you and I might have a Divine Father also.

FURTHER STUDY

John 10:22–38; 12:45; 14:1–10

1. What did Jesus declare to the unbelieving Jews?
2. What did Jesus declare to Philip?

Prayer

Gracious and loving God, from the bottom of my heart I want to thank You for begetting a Son in order that through Him I might come to know You as Father. I shall be grateful throughout time and all eternity. Amen

In All the Scriptures!

"Were not our hearts burning . . . while he talked with us . . .
and opened the Scriptures to us?" (v. 32)
For reading & meditation—Luke 24:13–35

The Bible is unique in its varied penmanship. The Scriptures were written over a period of some fifteen hundred years by about forty different penmen, and yet although of such composite character, the book displays an amazing and essential unity.

The most wonderful thing about the written Word is that woven through it from end to end, like a golden thread, the living Word can be observed. Nowhere can this be seen more clearly than in the account of the historic walk to Emmaus, when Luke tells us that "beginning with Moses [he could not go further back in the Bible than that!] and all the Prophets, [Christ] explained to them what was said in all the Scriptures concerning himself" (v. 27). Christ in all the Scriptures! There you have the mystery of the Bible compressed into a single phrase.

Imagine picking up a book written by such contributors as Shakespeare, John Donne, John Bunyan, John Locke, Isaac Newton, Jeremy Taylor, as well as many unknown writers, and then finding it is a complete biography of Sir Winston Churchill. One would turn its pages in utter amazement. Yet we discover something similar when we read the pages of our Bible. Herein lies its uniqueness. Those forty different authors did not know when they were writing that they were putting together a book that tells us as no other the full story of the Lord Jesus Christ. Whatever other faiths claim for their books—that they were inspired or dictated by God—the Bible, so all Christians believe, is God's one and only published work.

FURTHER STUDY

Ps. 119:81–96;
Isa. 40:8;
Matt. 5:18; 24:35

1. How did the psalmist view God's Word?
2. What was Isaiah's conviction?

---⟫═ *Prayer* ═⟪---

O Father, it is no surprise that so much of Jesus comes out of the Bible when so much of Him has gone into it. And the more I see of Him in its pages, the more I see there is to be seen. And the more I want to see. Thank You, my Father. Amen.

The Book of Books

"The grass withers and the flowers fall, but the word of our God stands forever." (v. 8)

For reading & meditation—Isaiah 40:1–11

What do we mean when we say that the Bible is "inspired"? There are various views.

One is *natural inspiration*—that the Bible is inspired in the same way that any work of genius is, like *Pilgrim's Progress* for example. Another view is of *partial inspiration*, which claims that the Bible is not a scientific textbook and therefore cannot be trusted in scientific matters, such as the origin of the species. It is, however, to be trusted in matters that relate to salvation. The third view can be described as *dictational inspiration*—that God dictated the Bible to its writers verbatim, as a businessman would dictate a letter to a secretary. The fourth view is of *verbal inspiration*, which holds that every word in the Bible came from the mouth of God. The fifth and final view is of *supervisal inspiration*—that nothing is included in the Bible which God did not want there and nothing is omitted which was meant to have a place in the sacred book.

I hold to the last view—supervisal inspiration. I rule out natural inspiration and partial inspiration, but not necessarily dictational inspiration, at least in part. Large sections of the Bible were personally dictated to men by God, the Ten Commandments being just one example. The writers of the Bible were, I believe, divinely indemnified against errors of observation, lapses of memory, and unintentional misrepresentation of facts. Their writings were honest, accurate, and supervised by the Holy Spirit before being compiled into this wonderful book we call the Bible. No wonder it is often referred to as the "book of books."

FURTHER STUDY

*Jer. 36:1–7;
Rev. 1:1–20; 2:1; 8, 12, 18; 3:1, 7, 14, 22*

1. What was Jeremiah's experience?
2. What was John's experience?

Prayer

O God, I know Your Word is inspired, for it inspires me. Help me to have Your Word hidden in my heart so deeply that it becomes the hidden spring of action, determining my conduct and my character. In Jesus' Name. Amen.

God's Great Masterpiece

"... and the Scripture cannot be broken ..." (v. 35)

For reading & meditation—John 10:1–18

I said yesterday that I subscribe to the supervisal inspiration of the Bible. I believe God led the minds and hearts of the writers of Scripture to go to the right sources for information, to come up with the required data, and in the process protected them from exposure to error, deceit, or imposture. He supervised them in their research, in their reporting, and when He spoke directly to them He was there also to make sure that they received clearly the message He wanted to convey. Ian Macpherson puts this truth most powerfully in his book *The Faith Once Delivered* when he says: "As in the mystery of the Incarnation, God linked Himself to humanity, so in the mystery of the inspiration of Holy Scripture, God made use of human channels, yet He never surrendered His Divine authorship or permitted the Book to become the word of man rather than the word of God."

Another writer, H. O. Mackey, put it like this: "Who built St. Paul's Cathedral? So many masons, carpenters, iron-workers, carvers, painters—and then there was Wren. He was not a mason, or a carpenter ... and never laid a stone. What did he do? He did it all. He planned it, inspired it with his thought." Mackey does not intend to dishonor the workmen who toiled hard and long, but simply to make the point that in the final analysis St. Paul's Cathedral is Sir Christopher Wren's masterpiece.

Who wrote the Bible? Moses, David, Isaiah, Jeremiah, John, Peter, Paul, and many others. But whose book is it really? It is God's.

FURTHER STUDY

Rev. 22:12–21;
Deut. 4:2; 12:32;
Prov. 30:5–6

1. What was the conclusion of the writer of Proverbs?
2. What was John's warning?

Prayer

O God, it is the entrance of Your Word that brings light and the neglect of Your Word that brings darkness. Help me to expose myself more and more to that light, so that I may walk through life with a sure and steady tread. In Jesus' Name. Amen.

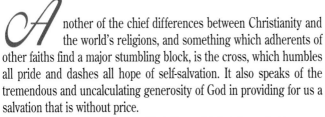

The Unique Cross

"For the message of the cross is foolishness to those who are perishing . . ." (v. 18)

For reading & meditation—1 Corinthians 1:18-31

*A*nother of the chief differences between Christianity and the world's religions, and something which adherents of other faiths find a major stumbling block, is the cross, which humbles all pride and dashes all hope of self-salvation. It also speaks of the tremendous and uncalculating generosity of God in providing for us a salvation that is without price.

Kagawa, the great Japanese Christian, said that it was in the cross that he found Christianity's greatest uniqueness. Listen to his words, spoken some time before his death in 1960: "I am grateful for Shinto, for Buddhism and for Confucianism. I owe much to these faiths. Yet these three faiths utterly failed to minister to my heart's deepest needs. I was a pilgrim journeying upon a long road that had no turning. I was weary, I was footsore. I wandered through a dark and dismal world where tragedies were thick. Buddhism teaches great compassion . . . but since the beginning of time, who has declared 'this is my blood of the covenant which is poured out for many unto the remission of sins'?"

Islam, of course, proclaims the mercy of God. Each chapter of the *Qur'an* is introduced by the words "In the name of Allah, the Compassionate, the Merciful." But they do not tell of a costly and historic display of God's mercy as portrayed by the cross and spoken of in each Gospel. In Islam, Allah is merciful to the meritorious, those who pray, give alms, and fast in Ramadan. In Christianity God is merciful to sinners not because of their good works but because of Christ's sacrifice for them on the cross.

FURTHER STUDY

Gal. 6:1-14;
Eph. 2:14-16;
Col. 1:20

1. How did Paul view the cross?
2. What is at the heart of the message of the cross?

Prayer

Gracious and merciful Lord, through the cross I see right into Your heart. And what I see there sets my heart on fire. I see Love bleeding for me, saving me, delivering me. Now I can never be the same again. Thank You, dear Father. In Christ's Name. Amen.

"The Key to Life"

Whenever I hear a person saying that all religions are the same, my mind runs immediately to the cross. If what is found here is true (and I believe it is), and represents the meaning of life, then clearly all religions are not the same. No authentic note of divine self-sacrifice comes from other faiths. The cross stands out in absolute uniqueness. As Toplady put it in his beautiful hymn:

> In the Cross of Christ I glory,
> Towering o'er the wrecks of time,
> All the light of sacred story
> Gathered round its head sublime.

For weeks and months after I became a Christian I wondered why anyone should preach anything except the cross. The redemptive glowing mystery of it took hold of me in the early days of my conversion, and I think I can honestly say it has never ceased to magnetize my heart.

Among the ancient inscriptions and paintings on the tombs of Egyptian kings, so I am told, one finds everywhere the symbol of the key of life. Strangely enough, it is in the form of a cross. Christ's cross is the only true key to life. This and this alone unlocks the doors to some of life's greatest mysteries. Other religions try, sometimes with great sincerity, to unlock the doors to these profound mysteries, but they are unsuccessful because they do not have the right key. They do not have a cross.

FURTHER STUDY

*Phil. 3:1–18;
Col. 2:14;
Heb. 12:2*

1. *What brought Paul to tears?*
2. *What has the cross abolished?*

 *Prayer*

Father, how can I cease thanking You for the cross? For in it I find the key that unlocks the door of many a mystery, not least the mystery of Your nature—a nature shot through with eternal love.
Help me see it even more clearly. In Christ's Name. Amen.

42

Understanding the Cross

"But God demonstrates his own love for us in this: While we were still sinners, Christ died for us." (v. 8)

For reading & meditation—Romans 5:6–21

*A*n ancient theologian—St. Augustine—suggested that "the answer to the mystery of the universe is God and the answer to the mystery of God is Christ." If this is so then I would like to make a further suggestion: the answer to the mystery of Christ is to be found in His sacrificial spirit, the supreme evidence of which is the cross.

We will never in our mortal state be able to grasp the full meaning of the cross. But what we do grasp gives us a clue to what lies in the heart of the Infinite. Theologians often discuss the various theories of the atonement. Personally, I find myself accepting any theory of the atonement that makes the meaning of the cross more vital and clear. No theory seems to me big enough to fit the facts. As Jesus broke the bars of the tomb and stepped out beyond them, so the fact of Jesus dying seems to transcend our most careful statements or form of words.

To really understand the cross one must have an attitude of mind and heart that responds to its meaning. I came across this: "To understand art one must have art within one; to understand music one must have music within one." I thought to myself, to understand the cross one must have a sacrificial spirit within one. Those who profess to know Christ but live only for self will know something of the cross but will miss its real meaning. The cross is best understood not by an argument but by an attitude.

FURTHER STUDY

John 15:13;
Gal. 1:4;
Eph. 5:2;
1 Pet. 2:24;
Titus 2:1–14

1. How is love demonstrated?
2. What was the greater dimension of Christ's sacrifice?

Prayer

Father, I see that if I am to fully understand the cross I must have a sacrificial spirit within me. May I linger at Your cross until Your nature becomes my nature. Then seeing I shall see. In Jesus' Name. Amen.

One Long Search for God

"For from within, out of men's hearts, come evil thoughts . . ." (v. 21)
For reading & meditation—Mark 7:8–23

We need to be reminded that there is in life a dark and terrible problem—the problem of evil. Herbert Spencer in *Natural Law in the Spiritual World* defines physical life as "inward correspondence with outward environment." When we take in food, air and water, we live. When we don't, we die. There must be a response to our environment. But there is also a spiritual environment to which we must respond, and when we are in correspondence with God we live spiritually. The facts of life fairly faced proclaim with heart-breaking obviousness that human beings are out of touch with their spiritual environment. To be out of touch with God means, inevitably, that we will be out of touch with ourselves and with others.

But the history of humanity is, as one historian put it, "one long search for God." We stand beside our altars, we breathe our prayers, we make our vows, we repeat our ceremonies, we crave with inexpressible yearnings of the inmost heart, we long for fellowship with God. Yet something dark, dreadful, and sinister stands between us and God. We realize God is pure, and because we are conscious of our impurity we hardly dare ask for fellowship with Him. We are separated and guilty.

The object of all religions is to bring those who long for fellowship with God into correspondence with Him. But how is that achieved? Christianity says it can be done only through the cross. Other religions point to other ways, and claim their way is as valid as the Christian way. But God says the cross is the only way.

FURTHER STUDY

*Rom. 1:18–32;
Gen. 6:12;
2 Tim. 3:1–2*

*1. What did men change God for?
2. What was the result?*

Prayer

O God my Father, what way could You have dealt with my sins except through the cross? My sins needed something more than disinfecting; they needed incinerating. In the flames of Calvary that is what happened. Now I am free. And how! Amen.

At-One-Ment

Day 43

"God presented him as a sacrifice of atonement, through faith in his blood." (v. 25)

For reading & meditation—Romans 3:21–31

*H*erbert Spencer, whom we quoted earlier, wrote: "The task of religion is at-one-ment: atonement. If it fails to do this it fails at the vital point." Its ritual may be beautiful, its sanctions may be ancient, its precepts may be good, but if it fails to bring men and women into correspondence with God it fails vitally and irretrievably. All else is useless, for if the problem of evil is ignored or passed over, we are like the person who dreams about and plans next year's happiness while an incurable disease is eating at his vitals.

The wonderful distinctive of Christianity is this—Jesus Christ has done something about the problem of being out of correspondence with God. He puts the hand of a penitent sinner into the hand of a pardoning God. Because of the nature of the problem—the problem of evil—no other solution is possible. Salvation is a task which only God could engineer. As one theologian puts it: "It is a task worthy of God."

The ancient Greek playwrights used to warn their students that when writing a tragedy they should not bring a god onto the stage unless there was an entanglement worthy of a god. The presence of evil in this world, I suggest, presents an entanglement worthy of God. But it is no mere stage affair. It is a tragic fact. To deliver men and women from evil was a problem that challenged God's power and made the deepest claim upon His love. The cross is the answer. If we don't take God's way of salvation, then nothing else will do.

FURTHER STUDY

1 John 2:1–2; 4:10;
2 Cor. 5:11–19

1. What is at the heart of atonement?
2. What did John assure the believers?

Prayer

Father, I rejoice that You have brought me to Your way—the only way. Help the millions who strive to earn their salvation see that the penalty for sin has been fully paid. And all they have to do is humbly receive. In Jesus' Name I pray. Amen.

45

An Unintentional Tribute

"'He saved others,' they said, 'but he can't save himself!'" (v. 42)
For reading & meditation—Matthew 27:32-44

*W*hat humiliation and shame our Lord endured for us on the cross of Calvary. Cicero, a Roman philosopher, said of crucifixion: "Far be the very name of a cross not only from the bodies of Roman citizens, but from their imaginations, eyes and ears." But He, our Lord, though sinless, was crucified on a cross. Although His blood was flowing freely from wounds inflicted by the crown of thorns on His head, from His back that had been lacerated by cruel thongs, from His hands and feet through which He was skewered to the tree, yet He refused the deadening drug offered Him. He underwent the ordeal with brain unclouded and with nerves unsoothed.

The crowd who watched Him cried: "He saved others, but he can't save himself!" But strange as it seems, that mocking phrase became the central truth of the gospel. *He was saving others and therefore He could not save Himself.* That is one of the greatest truths of life—if we are to save others we cannot save ourselves. To quote Spencer again: "It is a great mystery," he says, "yet an everlasting fact, that goodness in all moral natures has the doom of bleeding upon it, allowing it to conquer only as it bleeds. All goodness conquers by a cross."

This law of saving by self-giving runs through life. Those who save themselves cannot save others, and those who save others cannot save themselves—cannot save themselves trouble, sorrow, hurts, disappointments, pain, and sometimes even death. This is a law of the universe, and it applies to God as much as it does to us.

FURTHER STUDY

Gal. 1:1-5; 2:20;
1 Tim. 2:6;
Titus 2:14

1. What does Paul emphasize?
2. What is the implication for us?

 *Prayer*

O God, I have seen this law at work in human nature but I never thought it was part of the divine nature. But where could it have come from other than You? The highest in mankind is the deepest in You. I am staggered by it, but I know it to be true. Thank You, dear Father. Amen.

The Ultimate Discovery

**". . . when the centurion . . . saw how he died, he said,
'Surely this man was the Son of God!'" (v. 39)**

For reading & meditation—Mark 15:16–39

I cannot believe that God would write a law of "saving by sacrifice" within our hearts and evade it Himself. The psalmist asks: "Does he who formed the eye not see?" (Ps. 94:9). And Browning said: "He that created love, shall He not love?" We might add: "He that created sacrificial love, shall He not sacrifice"? The old Chinese scholar was right who, after listening for the first time to a missionary telling the story of the loving sacrifice of God through His Son on the cross, turned to one of his pupils and said: "Didn't I tell you there ought to be a God like that?"

The leaders of the world's religions stumble over this. A leading Muslim said recently during a television debate: "A God who would stoop and suffer is not perfect." And a Hindu commented: "If Brahman would suffer He would be unhappy, and if He were unhappy He would be imperfect, and if He were imperfect He would not be God."

The cross spells out the message that God is prepared to take into Himself the suffering caused by sin and, indeed, to take on Himself the very sins of the ones He created. No other religion can conceive of such a thing. The cross raised on Calvary is but a reflection of an inner cross lying in the heart of God. Through it we see that at the center of the universe is redeeming love. No greater discovery could be made or will be made than that—in earth or in heaven. It is the ultimate in discoveries.

FURTHER STUDY

*John 19:1–15;
1 Cor. 1:1–23; 2:2–8*

1. What was central to Paul's message?
2. How was the message of Christ's crucifixion viewed?

Prayer

O Father, I see that if self-giving love is the meaning behind the cross, and the meaning of the universe, then it must be the meaning behind my life too. May the cross work itself out in all my relationships from this day forward. In Jesus' Name. Amen.

A Sacrificial Head

"For whoever wants to save his life will lose it, but whoever loses his life
for me will save it." (v. 24)

For reading & meditation—Luke 9:18–27

*S*uppose a tiny seed had a will of its own and decided to save itself by refusing to be buried. It would abide alone. It would save itself but would not save others. When it decided to be buried and die, then the result would be a golden harvest. Take a mother: she goes down into the valley of the shadow of death to bring a child into the world. When the child becomes ill, a loving mother forgets herself and spends her strength to give everything she has to the child.

The spirit of self-giving is the most beautiful thing in life. Through it life rises to the highest level. "The extent of the elevation of an animal and of course any free moral agent," said Pascal, the great French Christian and philosopher, "can be infallibly measured by the degree to which sacrificial love for others controls that being." Here is a law by which life may be evaluated and judged. When the sacrificial spirit is absent from life, that life is of the lowest kind; where it is perfectly embodied, that life is highest on the scale of being.

Is this law to be found in God also? I believe it is. If this law holds true on earth but is reversed in relation to God, then laws are meaningless and the universe is without a Head. Then the highest in mankind would be better than God. But such is not the case. God is not a disappointment. The cross shouts out to all who will hear that the universe has a sacrificial Head.

FURTHER STUDY

*John 12:17–26; 10:11;
Rom. 5:6*

*1. What did Jesus liken
Himself to?
2. How did He illustrate
sacrificial love?*

 *Prayer*

O Father, how could I know that there is an unseen cross lying in Your heart unless You had shown me by
the outer cross raised up on Calvary? Such revelation is almost too much for me to comprehend.
Yet it is true. My gratitude will just not go into words. Amen.

The Man of Galilee

"For what I received I passed on to you as of first importance . . . that he was raised on the third day . . ." (vv. 3–4)

For reading & meditation—1 Corinthians 15:1–11

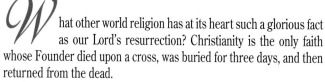

What other world religion has at its heart such a glorious fact as our Lord's resurrection? Christianity is the only faith whose Founder died upon a cross, was buried for three days, and then returned from the dead.

There are voices in today's church trying to persuade us that the resurrection of Christ never took place—that our Lord did not rise from the dead in bodily form. "It is not necessary to believe in the bodily resurrection of Christ in order to be a Christian," says one modern-day religious teacher. He goes on to claim: "We may freely say that the bones of Jesus are still lying somewhere in the land of Israel." "I quite expect," says another religious writer, "that the bones of Jesus will be dug up one day." And a few years ago, David Jenkins, the former Anglican bishop, shocked the Christian world, as you probably know, with the statement: "I have not the slightest interest in a conjuring trick with bones."

In the British Museum in London there used to be a grim exhibit known as "The Galilee Man," so called because the remains were found in the area surrounding Galilee. I remember thinking to myself the first time I visited the British Museum and saw that the exhibit was captioned "The Galilee Man," how wonderful that the disinterred bones of the Galilee man are not the remains of the Man of Galilee.

FURTHER STUDY

*John 20:1–18;
Acts 2:23–24; 3:14–15;
10:39–40*

1. What was Peter adamant about?
2. Share with someone else today the true message of the resurrection.

Prayer

Loving heavenly Father, help me understand even more deeply the truth of Your Son's resurrection, for such an important truth cannot be left to lie in the realm of uncertainty. Take my hand and lead me more deeply into this truth. In Jesus' Name. Amen.

A Basic Precondition

"(They still did not understand from Scripture that Jesus had to rise from the dead.)" (v. 9)

For reading & meditation—John 20:1–18

The late Bishop John Robinson stated: "The resurrection of the body of Christ is no essential belief for Christian people, and it would make no difference to their faith if the Lord's body had been flung into the Valley of Hinnom, like those of the malefactors, to disintegrate among the rotting corpses." Such a statement flies in the very face of Scripture. Paul wrote: "If you confess with your mouth, 'Jesus is Lord,' and believe . . . *that God raised him from the dead, you will be saved*" (Rom. 10:9, italics added). Here Paul makes it crystal clear that acceptance of the fact that Christ rose from the dead is a basic precondition for being a Christian.

But what exactly do we mean by resurrection? "Spiritual survival" is how the liberals in the church define it. But it was not just the spiritual part of Jesus that continued after the tomb—it was the total Christ. True, His body possessed additional powers and properties, but the physical frame which housed His spirit after He left the tomb was the same one that was nailed to the cross. "See my hands," He said to doubting Thomas, "put [your hand] into my side . . . and believe" (John 20:27). Eric Sauer, a writer and Bible teacher, makes the point: "Just as our Lord's body was capable of transfiguration without losing its identity, so it was capable of disfiguration without losing its identity."

Make no mistake about it, our Lord's resurrection was a physical one. If it wasn't, then there is no salvation.

FURTHER STUDY

John 20:19–31; 21:1–13

1. How did Jesus appear to the disciples?
2. What did Jesus participate in?

Prayer

Father, if I am not sure of the resurrection how can I be sure I am saved? However, I am sure, for I live in a resurrected Christ. Since He was resurrected, I know I shall be too. Death has been conquered. Hallelujah!

"The Swoon Theory"

"God has raised this Jesus to life, and we are all witnesses of the fact." (v. 32)
For reading & meditation—Acts 2:29–41

*L*et us pursue the question we asked yesterday: What exactly do we mean by resurrection?

Some try to explain the resurrection as resuscitation—the return to life from *apparent* death. Those holding this view subscribe to what is called "The Swoon Theory." There are two forms of this theory. One maintains that Jesus did not die but fainted on the cross and returned to consciousness when He was laid on the cold rock of the tomb. The other claims that after drinking the wine vinegar that was given to Him when He cried "I am thirsty," He fell into a stupor so deep that it was mistaken for death. But clearly our Lord *actually* died. The Gospels provide us with medical evidence for the fact. One of the soldiers pierced His side and there came forth "blood and water" (John 19:34). A doctor commenting on this says: "The *pericardium* (the sac around the heart) was punctured and the colorless fluid flowing from the wound proves that life would have been extinct."

Was it really a convalescent Christ the disciples encountered on that first Easter Day? Could such a pathetic and powerless figure have convinced them that He had conquered death and was alive forevermore? No, the Master, as it were, had flung from His face the mask of death, and laid down in the hearts and minds of His disciples an impression that stayed with them throughout the whole of their ministry. He who had been dead was now alive—gloriously and resplendently.

FURTHER STUDY

Luke 24:1–53;
Mark 16:12

1. What did the disciples invite Jesus to do?
2. What did Jesus invite the disciples to do?

Prayer

O Father, You whose very nature is truth, would You foist upon us a lie and have us believe Your Son rose from the dead when He did not? I cannot believe it. The life by which I live is resurrection life. I cannot be alive in someone who is dead. Amen.

The True and the False

"... our Savior, Christ Jesus ... has destroyed death and has brought life
and immortality to light ..." (v. 10)
For reading & meditation—2 Timothy 1:1-18

everal of the world's religions, when faced with the perplexing issue of Christ's return from the dead, explain it in terms of reincarnation. A proponent of one of the Eastern religions says: "Christ's resurrection was really a reincarnation—another soul in another body." I once heard a Christian minister declare that Paul's reference to Christ as the firstborn from among the dead (Col. 1:18) was a clear allusion to reincarnation. There is no doubt that our Lord came from a virgin womb and a virgin tomb, but the body that emerged from the sepulchre was not fashioned in the tomb as it had been when He was an infant in Mary's womb. The body was the same one as before.

Others try to explain Christ's resurrection as living on in the recollection of others. "To live in the minds and hearts of those we love," goes a well-known saying often heard at funerals, "is not to die." It has to be acknowledged that some live so vibrantly that it is hard to think of them as dead even after one has attended their funeral. But when we talk about Christ's resurrection, we are not saying He survives in our memories. Recollection is not resurrection.

The body which died upon the cross and was laid in the cool tomb on the evening of the first Good Friday was miraculously infused with life once again early in the morning of the first Easter Day. It is as literal and as factual as that. This—nothing less and nothing else—is what we mean by the resurrection of our Lord from the dead.

FURTHER STUDY

Eph. 1:1-20;
Rom. 4:25;
1 Cor. 15:3-5;
1 Thess. 4:13-15

1. What did Paul say was of first importance?
2. What does this mean for those who have experienced resurrection life?

⊷⊷⊷ *Prayer* ⊷⊷⊷

Father, I am so thankful that in bringing Your Son back to life You brought "life and immortality to light" through the gospel. I know this to be true for in You there cannot be such a thing as death. Life is so sure—as sure as You are. Amen.

52

The Mystery Rolled Back

"Where, O death, is your victory? Where, O death, is your sting?" (v. 55)

For reading & meditation—1 Corinthians 15:50–58

Mark's observation "that the stone, which was very large, had been rolled away" (Mark 16:4) seems a simple statement, but behind it lies a truth that is positively staggering in its implications. One is that no longer can death be an intimidator. "Death," said someone, "is the great enigma of life; humanly speaking, it is the one secret of the universe which is kept, the silence of which is never broken." To the weary and despairing, death may come as a friend; the cynical and disillusioned may meet it with indifference; to the healthy and the happy it may appear as a foe; but it comes to all. Death is like a great stone that blocks the path of human aspiration.

How certain can we be of the continuity of life beyond death? What modest person would find in himself anything worthy to endure for all eternity? Such questions have been asked down the centuries. Death is a mystery—"the undiscovered country from which no traveler returns." Then came the first Easter Day, and the stone was rolled away. One Traveler did return.

Death is an abysmal cavern no longer but a tunnel with light at the farther end. If people have seen it as a blind alley, then they need think no longer in those terms. It is now a thoroughfare, a highway. "'Tis death is dead, not He," said the hymnist. The mystery is a mystery no more. The stone that was rolled away the first Easter morn was not just the rock that sealed the tomb. Our Lord rolled back for us the mystery of death also.

FURTHER STUDY

John 11:1–44;
Matt. 16:21;
Mark 9:9;
John 2:19

1. When did Jesus declare He was the resurrection and the life?
2. What are the implications of this?

Prayer

Lord Jesus Christ, I rejoice and rejoice continually in Your glorious and triumphant victory over death.
For Your victory is my victory. Help me to live by it, in it, and for it.
I am grateful to my depths—grateful forever. Amen.

Not an Exit — an Entrance

"... an angel of the Lord ... going to the tomb, rolled back the stone ..." (v. 2)

For reading & meditation—Matthew 28:1–15

*W*as it really necessary for the stone to be rolled away before our Lord could exit the tomb? Christ's resurrection body was able to pass easily through doors, for He came to His disciples when the doors were shut. The stone was rolled away not that our Lord might come out but that the disciples might go in. It was intended not as a means of exit but as a means of entrance. One preacher put it like this: "God rolled away the stone not that His Son might rise, but that we might know He had risen; that we might steal into the empty tomb and see only the place where they laid Him."

My pastor when I was a young Christian said: "Suppose we live in a home that has no electricity and a young nephew comes to stay with us for a weekend. Suppose also when we put the child to bed there is in the corner of the room a dark curtain which hides such things as traveling cases. And suppose further, when we are about to leave the room taking the light with us, the child falteringly confesses to a fear that on the other side of the dark curtain is someone that might harm him. What do we do? We go to the curtain, fling it aside, flood the gloomy recess with light and say: 'Look, there is nothing to fear.'"

To remove the curtain is to remove the dread. That is why God rolled away the stone. It was not necessary for the resurrection, but it was necessary for its proclamation.

FURTHER STUDY

Heb. 10:1–22;
Rom. 5:1–2;
Eph. 2:18; 3:12;
Ps. 24:3–4

1. Why can we enter the Most Holy Place?
2. What often prevents us from entering in?

Prayer

Lord Jesus, had You stalled at the last ditch, had You been beaten at the barrier of death, then we would be stalled eternally. But now we go through the barrier with You. Nothing can stop us. Amen.

"A Glorious Uprising"

"... 'You will not let your Holy One see decay.'" (v. 35)

For reading & meditation—Acts 13:16–41

We spend one more day considering the implications arising from the rolling away of the stone. What did that rolled-away stone reveal? Well, follow the women into the tomb. It's just a large hole hewn in a rock. What do you see? Just "the place where they laid him" (Mark 16:6). All that was left were the graveclothes. Note that Peter saw "the strips of linen lying there, as well as the burial cloth that had been around Jesus' head" (John 20:6–7). Some scholars say that the Greek words used to describe the head-cloth signify that it still had an annular shape—that it still indicated the outline of His head. Can you see what this suggests? He passed through it without it being unwound. This was no laborious unwinding! This was a glorious up-rising!

There was no possibility that the graveclothes could have looked the way they did without a resurrection. Had the head-cloth been torn apart, the impression gained would have been quite different. It was probably this simple but tremendous fact—the fact that Jesus had clearly passed through the shroud without it being unwound—that convinced the first observers they had witnessed the miracle of resurrection.

Do you think of a tomb as being cold and eerie? That is not our Lord's tomb. No, it is quiet and calm. Our crucified God rested for hours and hours on a cool bed of rock. And to quote the poet Alice Meynell:

All alone ... He rose again behind the stone.

FURTHER STUDY

Ps. 16:1–11;
Matt. 28:9

1. What did the women clasp?
2. What followed?

Prayer

O Jesus, You who are not an evader but a confronter of problems. You have faced everything I face including death. And yet You went through it, not around it. You conquered death by going through it, and now because I am in You I shall conquer it also. Amen.

Anteroom to Glory

"... he raised [Christ] from the dead and seated him at his right hand
in the heavenly realms ..." (v. 20)

For reading & meditation—Ephesians 1:15-23

Young Christians who have just come into the faith often ask: Why is the resurrection so important? How can an event which took place 2,000 years ago have any relevance for us today? Three very simple statements (not original to me) will bring us to the heart of the matter. First, *the resurrection of Christ assures us of God's forgiveness.* Forgiveness is one of humanity's greatest needs. Jack Winslow, in his book *Confession and Absolution,* says that the head of a large English mental hospital remarked that he could dismiss half of his patients immediately if they could be assured of forgiveness. The resurrection is convincing proof that Christ's sacrifice on the cross was accepted, and thus gives us the assurance that all our sins can be forgiven.

Second, *the resurrection of Christ assures us of God's power.* It is one thing to be forgiven; it is another to live above the power of sin. "Men may change their ways," say some writers (as we saw) from non-Christian religions, "but they can't change their character." Well, God can change people's character. He did so with the apostle Paul, with Peter, and with countless others. Paul's prayer in the passage before us today focuses on this—that we might comprehend something of the power released in the world through the resurrection.

Third, *the resurrection assures us of God's ultimate triumph.* Other religions and ideologies have very vague ideas about the future. Some believe in endless cycles of reincarnations; others *nirvana.* Christians, however, have a hope that is different. Death for a believer is nothing more than the anteroom to glory.

FURTHER STUDY

Eph. 2:1-10;
Rom. 8:11;
Col. 3:1

1. To what extent do we experience resurrection life?
2. To what heights does resurrection life raise us?

Prayer

Father, this must be the moment when debate ends and dedication begins. As You have done so much for me, I want to commit myself in a deeper way than ever before to living life in the power of Your resurrection. Help me dear Father. In Jesus' Name. Amen.

Risen . . . and Exalted

". . . he was taken up before their very eyes, and a cloud hid him from their sight." (v. 9)

For reading & meditation—Acts 1:1–11

*B*efore we conclude our meditations on the uniqueness of Christianity, we must mention our Lord's ascension. I much prefer the word *exaltation* to *ascension* to describe Christ's return to the throne of God, for that is what it really was—an exaltation. Paul, in some verses in the passage we looked at yesterday (Eph. 1:20–21), points out that following His resurrection our Lord was elevated above all possible rivals: "far [note the word *far*] above all rule and authority, power and dominion, and every title that can be given, not only in the present age but also in the one to come." Jesus has been exalted to the highest place, and it is this "supremacy" which His Father wants Him to enjoy forever.

This thrilling truth puts into proper perspective the use of the word *superiority* which is a word commonly used by Christians when comparing the faith to others. We must be careful how we use the word. Adopting an air of superiority toward people of other faiths displays nothing more than discourtesy and arrogance. John Stott comments: "It is not 'Christianity' as an empirical institution or system for which Christians should claim superiority. It is Christ, and only Christ. We should not be afraid to affirm without embarrassment that Christ is superior to all other religious leaders, precisely because He alone humbled Himself in love even to the cross and therefore God has raised Him 'above' every other person, rank, or title."

If God has given this supreme position to Jesus and so honored Him, then we should give Him the same honor also.

FURTHER STUDY

Mark 16:9–19;
Ps. 68:18;
Luke 24:50–51;
Phil. 2:9;
1 Pet. 3:22

1. What was Jesus doing when He ascended?
2. What did Jesus do after He ascended?

Prayer

Lord Jesus, I honor You. Oh how I honor You. May Your Church this day and every day give unto You the honor which You so rightly and richly deserve. Blessed be Your wondrous Name forever. Amen.

No Cross without a Crown

"He . . . ascended higher than all the heavens, in order to fill the whole universe." (v. 10)

For reading & meditation—Ephesians 4:1–16

*I*n his autobiography, *A King's Story,* the Duke of Windsor told of a strange thing that happened at the funeral of his father, King George V. He described how, as his father's body was being conveyed on a draped gun carriage through the crowded streets of London, a mishap occurred which only those closest to the scene witnessed.

The imperial crown, removed from the Tower of London, had been placed over the Royal Standard and secured to the lid of the coffin. However, the jolting of the vehicle caused the Maltese Cross, which surmounts the crown, to fall. "Suddenly," said the Duke, "out of the corner of my eye, I caught a flash of light dancing along the pavement. One of the sailors, marching behind the gun carriage, picked it up, took it to his commanding officer, and said, 'This cross fell off, Sir. It must be replaced.' The officer was a little bewildered by the untoward happening and said: 'Must it be replaced now?' 'Yes Sir,' replied the sailor, 'The crown is never complete without the cross.'"

In Christian terms the converse is also true—*the cross is not complete without the crown.* The ascension inevitably followed the atonement; the coronation the crucifixion. One writer says: "One senses a certain embarrassment in some ministers where the subject of the ascension is concerned. They tend to shy clear of the topic or dismiss it lightly as no more than a graphic myth or triumphalist parable." But if there had been no ascension there would be no gospel. The cross would not be complete without the crown.

FURTHER STUDY

Heb. 1:1–9;
Luke 22:69;
Col. 1:18

1. What did God the Father say about the Son?
2. What did God the Father say to the Son?

Prayer

O Father, how can I ever sufficiently thank You that the work of salvation is complete. Nothing more needs to be done than has been done. Your Coronation spells it out in the clearest of terms. I am so deeply, deeply grateful. Amen.

Christ—Our Precursor

"... Jesus, who went before us ..." (v. 20)

For reading & meditation—Hebrews 6:1–20

Out of all the aspects of truth that surround the fact of our Lord's ascension, one of the greatest is surely this—Christ is our Precursor. A precursor is really a forerunner—an advance runner—and that is precisely the term which our text for today applies to the climactic ministry of our ascended Lord.

The NIV translates the word *prodromos* (forerunner) thus: "who went before us." That translation, in my opinion, is not nearly as appealing as that found in other versions, where the word *forerunner* is actually used. "Forerunner" brings to mind a picture of our Lord as a celestial outrider "bringing many sons to glory" (Heb. 2:10), and reminds us of a petition in the great high priestly prayer: "Father, I want those you have given me to be with me where I am, and to see my glory ..." (John 17:24).

Henry Longfellow, in his *Golden Legend,* put it like this:

When Christ ascended
Triumphantly, from star to star,
He left the gates of heaven ajar!

Much as I like Longfellow, I have to disagree. Our Lord left the gates of heaven not just "ajar" but wide open. One of the creeds expresses it more effectively: "When Thou hadst overcome the sharpness of death, Thou didst open the kingdom of heaven to all believers." Whatever the future holds for us, we who are Christ's can be sure of this: our Lord has ascended into heaven. And so, too, shall we.

FURTHER STUDY

*John 17:1–26; 1:12;
Gal. 4:7;
1 Cor. 15:39–44*

1. What does being sons make us?
2. What do we enter into through death?

Prayer

O Father, I see that not only was there an ascension in the life of Your Son, but there is to be one in mine too. According to Your Word, I am to be "caught up in the clouds" and to be with You forever. Lord Jesus, come quickly. Amen.

"Jesus, Yes—Church, No"

"We implore you on Christ's behalf: Be reconciled to God." (v. 20)

For reading & meditation—2 Corinthians 5:11–21

*N*ow that we have looked at the aspects of our faith which make it unique among all world religions, we must face some other important issues before finally drawing to a close.

Being Christians does not mean we therefore have to believe that all other religions are completely wrong. As C. S. Lewis pointed out: "If you are an atheist you have to believe that the main point in all religions is simply one huge mistake. But if you are a Christian you are free to think that all religions, even the queerest of them, contain at least some hint of truth. Being a Christian, however, does mean thinking that where Christianity differs from other religions, Christianity is right and they are wrong. As in arithmetic there is only one right answer to a sum and all other answers are wrong. But some wrong answers are much nearer to being right than others."

While never budging from what we believe, we must show a loving disposition toward those of other faiths. A group of adherents to the Muslim faith gathered outside a church in one of Britain's northern cities shouting: "Jesus, Yes; the Church, No." Their complaint was based on the fact that the minister and people of that particular church had pushed thousands of leaflets through local mailboxes stating: "Islam is a devilish religion; only the Christian religion is of God." We can be passionate in our faith without being discourteous to people. We may disagree with what someone believes, but we must disagree agreeably. As one old preacher quaintly put it: "To win some we must be winsome."

FURTHER STUDY

1 Cor. 9:19–27;
Rom. 10:1;
Matt. 10:16

1. What was Paul's approach to people?
2. What approach were the disciples to take?

Prayer

Father, I see from the text before me today that You want me to implore people to come to You, not intimidate them. Make me a firm but loving witness—one who can disagree without being disagreeable. In Christ's Name I ask it. Amen.

Common Grace

"For in him we live and move and have our being." (v. 28)

For reading & meditation—Acts 17:16–34

God is active not only in the Church but in the world and in those belonging to other religions also. Christians believe that God has revealed Himself in Jesus in a unique way, as declared in the Scriptures, and has nothing more to reveal than He has revealed. But does that mean God is interested only in Christians? Not at all. One of the statements in the passage before us today proclaims: "He is not far from each one of us" (v. 27). By creation all men and women are God's offspring, and they live and move and have their being in Him.

Christians believe that because Jesus is the Light of the world, and is described by John in the Fourth Gospel as "the true light that gives light to every man" (John 1:9). Truth and beauty are derived from Him, even though people may be unaware of their source. Theologians refer to this as "common grace"—the kindness God shows to all human beings even though they know Him not. This is not to be confused with "saving grace," which is the kindness *and* mercy He extends to those who humbly receive the sacrificial offering which His Son made for them on the cross.

Clearly, those who belong to other faiths are of deep concern to God, and that same concern ought to be ours. It should show itself in the way we talk to them, deal with them, and pray for them. There is no better way to end a discussion with an adherent of some other faith than to say and mean: "God loves you, and so do I."

FURTHER STUDY

Matt. 5:38–48;
Job 34:18–19;
Acts 10:34–35

1. How did Jesus describe common grace?
2. What did Peter declare?

Prayer

O God, can it be that sometimes You are hindered in the process of bringing others to Yourself by those of us who are more interested in winning an argument than winning a soul? Infuse us with Your love—Calvary love. In Jesus' Name we ask it. Amen.

Three Important Facts

"Now we are all here . . . to listen to everything the Lord has commanded you to tell us." (v. 33)

For reading & meditation—Acts 10:23–48

*I*f, as the Scripture declares, Jesus is the only way, what about people in other faiths? First, we must be clear that there is no such thing as self-salvation. Nobody can achieve salvation by his or her religion, sincerity, or good works. Second, Jesus Christ is the only way to God and the only Savior. Our Lord Himself said: "No one comes to the Father except through me" (John 14:6). This effectively ends all argument.

Third, we do not know how much knowledge and understanding of the gospel a person needs to have in order to call upon God for mercy and be saved. In the Old Testament, people were justified by faith even though they had little knowledge or expectation of Christ. I believe that when people become aware that they cannot save themselves and need to throw themselves upon God's mercy, in some way God reveals Himself to them and brings them through His Son to a saving knowledge of Himself. I have met many people from other faiths who, realizing that they could not save themselves and yearning to find salvation, were amazingly led by God to a book, a leaflet, or an audiotape, that helped them understand how to come to God through Jesus.

Does this mean we don't need to be concerned about presenting the gospel to people? No, it is much easier for people to believe if they have heard. God worked miraculously to bring the gospel to Cornelius. So too He will work for those who are willing to give up all ideas of saving themselves and look to Him alone for salvation.

FURTHER STUDY

John 6:47–69;
Eph. 2:19–21;
1 Pet. 2:6

1. What was Peter's conclusion?
2. How did Paul describe Christ?

Prayer

O Father, what a glimpse this gives me of Your eagerness to save all that will come to You through Your Son. May this inspire me more than ever to do my part in making Your gospel known. In Christ's Name I pray. Amen.

Christianity Is Unique

"No one comes to the Father except through me." (v. 6)

For reading & meditation—John 14:1–14

We make the claim once again—*Christianity is unique*. It is unique in the sense that it is the divinely appointed way to enter into a relationship with the one true and living God. There is only one way, only one Name, only one God, only one Lord, only one Mediator.

Our claim that Christianity is unique comes not from arrogance but from simple empirical fact. W. A. Visser't Hooft, in his book *No Other Name*, says: "There is no universality if there is no unique event." Uniqueness and universality go together. It is because God has exalted Jesus to the highest place in the universe, "far above all rule and authority," and given Him the unique Name of "Lord," that He towers over every other name. That, too, is the reason why every knee must bow to Him.

And it is precisely because Jesus Christ is the only Savior that we are under an obligation to proclaim Him to as many as we possibly can. In whatever culture we live, we must endeavor to make Jesus known. We must set our face against the faction in today's church that aims to modernize the gospel and says: "Let us recognize all religions as being authentic before God and seek not to convert people from their religion but encourage them to be better adherents of it." Have these people no regard for the honor of Jesus Christ? Do they not care when Christ is seen as just one among many Saviors rather than, as God declares, the *only* Savior. *No true Christian can ever worship Christ without minding that others do not.*

FURTHER STUDY

Matt. 7:15–21;
Acts 20:25–31

1. What did Jesus warn about?
2. What was Paul's charge to the Ephesian elders?

Prayer

Father, help me understand that it is not enough to know about the faith into which You have brought me by Your grace: I must seek also to share it. Help me grasp every opportunity that comes to make the way clear to others. In Jesus' Name. Amen.

Section Two
The Search for Meaning

The Search for Meaning

*I*n Ecclesiastes, King Solomon seems at first to be preaching a message of darkness and doom. He warns that all of life is empty and futile. The classic King James translation renders his admonition as "Vanity, vanity, all is vanity." But a closer look reveals that Solomon's commentary refers specifically to the search for happiness in worldly pleasure and possessions. He isn't out to frighten us; he's out to guide us.

Every painting has a focal point, one feature that stands out in the composition and draws our attention to it. In this series of commentaries, Selwyn Hughes shows us how Solomon makes life with God the focal point of faith. Putting faith in money, appearances, or our own ability guarantees nothing but a life of longing and despair. Recognizing that fact is the first step toward realizing true happiness comes only in knowing and loving God—nowhere else.

The series of rich contrasts in Ecclesiastes chapter 3 is one of the most vivid moments in all of Scripture. "There is a time to be born and a time to die. A time to plant and a time to uproot. A time to kill and a time to heal. A time to mourn and a time to dance." In God's time there is a place and purpose for everything. Solomon paints a dark picture to begin with, but then uses it as a backdrop for the wonderful illumination of a world focused on God. Suddenly, instead of a life of boredom and hopelessness, we experience the light and presence of the Lord. That's where satisfaction is. That's where true pleasure is. That's where fulfilling, lasting peace is.

Selwyn describes the world we make without God as a frightful place. Somehow, though, God gives the courage, energy, and spiritual desire to search beyond the lure of worldly wealth to find meaning only He can give.

Left to our own devices, we choose a life that leads to a dark dead end. Through the wisdom of one of the Bible's greatest leaders, Ecclesiastes takes us from that darkness to the Light of the World.

L.G.G.

Silence!

"'Meaningless! Meaningless!' says the Teacher. 'Utterly meaningless!
Everything is meaningless.'" (v. 2)
For reading & meditation—Ecclesiastes 1:1-2

*W*e begin now a study of what has been described as "the most dangerous book in the Bible"—Ecclesiastes. Why dangerous? Because in it one comes face to face with the utter futility of trying to find happiness and meaning in the things of time. And that discovery, for some people, could lead to opting out of life altogether. An old Jewish tradition says that when the sages met to fix the canon of the Old Testament, they debated fiercely whether to include a book that was so full of cynicism and doubt. But prayer and wisdom prevailed, and it was included. I believe that Solomon is the author of Ecclesiastes, although there is much scholarly discussion about this.

The main message of the book comes through in its opening statement: *"Everything is meaningless."* Seeing the utter futility of life is the first step to an encounter with God. I heard someone say that the first book of the Bible everyone ought to read is the Book of Ecclesiastes— because it silences you. When we see as clearly as Solomon saw that the world does not provide us with the life for which our souls were created, then we are more likely to turn to the true source of happiness—the eternal God Himself.

One of the reasons why some of us do not know God well is because we have never been convinced of the utter futility of trying to find life in *things*. We have not been silenced. Let Ecclesiastes silence you, and in that silence you may experience a deeper awareness of God.

FURTHER STUDY

*Eph. 4:14–19;
1 Chron. 29:15;
Job 7:6*

1. What were the
Ephesians not to do?
2. How did Job describe
his days?

Prayer

O God my Father, if my soul needs silencing, then use Your word once again to accomplish that task.
Do whatever is necessary to bring me to the realization that what my soul longs for
can only be fully found in You. Amen.

Life without God

"Generations come and generations go, but the earth remains forever." (v. 4)
For reading & meditation—Ecclesiastes 1:3–7

Francis Schaeffer wrote that there are times "when a negative message is needed before anything positive can begin." That sums up the Book of Ecclesiastes. It seeks first to silence us with the utter futility of life before turning our gaze to the one and only reality—God. In the passage before us today the author begins the task of dragging us through the undeniable facts manifesting the pointlessness and the emptiness of life in order to show us that we must look elsewhere than the world around us for the water that our souls so deeply crave.

Three things are said about life without God—it is boring, fleeting, and repetitive. "What does man gain from all his labor . . . ?" asks Solomon. Some people enjoy working for a living, but most don't. They watch the clock, fantasize, make up mental games—all designed to fill the time until the workday is over. If we do not see our work as imitating the creativity of God, then it can become exceedingly boring. "Generations come and generations go," says Solomon. Life is so fleeting. How small and insignificant it makes us feel. Then think about this, continues Solomon. Every morning the sun rises, sets, then the next day the same thing happens . . . and the next . . . and the next. Life is so repetitive. The same with the wind. Where does it come from and where does it go?

Life on this planet is not all gloom, of course, but who can escape the conclusion that there is something about earth that just does not satisfy?

FURTHER STUDY

James 4:1–15;
Job 9:25;
Ps. 39:5
1. What question does James ask?
2. How does he answer it?

∼⟹ *Prayer* ⟸∼

Gracious and loving heavenly Father, drive this truth deeply into my spirit that I am made by You, made for You, and my heart will never be content until it is filled with You. Indwell every empty space that is within me. In Jesus' Name. Amen.

"Don't Adjust Your Life"

". . . there is nothing new under the sun." (v. 9)

For reading & meditation—Ecclesiastes 1:8–11

*I*t is surprising how many Christians have never read the Book of Ecclesiastes. One woman told me that Ecclesiastes was the one book in the Bible she could not read. "I am put off by all that pessimism and gloom," she explained. There is, however, a purpose behind this pessimism and gloom. Dr. Cynddylan Jones, a famous Welsh preacher, put it like this: "No Christian will be ready to open himself up to God until he has been gripped, as Ecclesiastes was gripped, by the emptiness and pointlessness of life. It is only when we see, and see clearly, that life is not to be found in the world that we will be ready to move closer toward God."

It is interesting to observe that most philosophers, when they look reality in the face, come to the same conclusion as Solomon. Malcolm Muggeridge, for example, in the days before he found God, saw the world as "an interminable opera." Some graffiti found on the walls of Bath University was even more to the point: "Do not adjust your life, the fault lies in reality."

One of the reasons, I believe, why Solomon uses such vivid illustrations is in order to break through our defensive attempts to avoid reality. Life "under the sun," he has told us, can be boring, fleeting, repetitive, and empty. Life will never be meaningful "under the sun" until we make contact with the One who is above the sun. Those who try to find meaning without linking their lives to the Creator inevitably see life as an "interminable soap opera." Is it any wonder?

FURTHER STUDY

Isa. 55:1–13;
John 4:13–14

1. What question does Isaiah ask?
2. What remedy does he advocate?

Prayer

Gracious and loving Father, wean me off any ideas I may have that life can be found "under the sun." Grant that I might be gripped by the truth that life, real life, is never found in the horizontal but in the Vertical. In You. Amen.

Education without God . . .

"For with much wisdom comes much sorrow; the more knowledge, the more grief." (v. 18)

For reading & meditation—Ecclesiastes 1:12–18

*W*e said yesterday that one of the reasons why Solomon uses so many vivid illustrations is to break through our defensive attempts to avoid reality. It was T. S. Eliot who said that "humankind cannot bear very much reality." Psychologists warn that we should be careful about stripping away people's defenses, as coming face to face with reality too quickly can cause those who are fragile to slide into depression. The author of Ecclesiastes seems unconcerned about this, however, and tells us over and over again, and with deep conviction, that life "under the sun" is futile.

In the passage before us he tells us how his determination to find a purpose for living led him to serious study. But study, and trying to grasp the meaning of the universe by the intellect alone, proved also to be futile. He says that it is like "chasing after the wind" (v. 17). Moffatt translates our text for today: "The more you understand the more you ache."

Life, real life that is, cannot be found through education and intellectual attainment alone. To quote Muggeridge again: "Education—the great mumbo and fraud of the ages," says this highly educated man, "purports to equip us to live and is prescribed as a universal remedy for everything from juvenile delinquency to premature senility. For the most part it serves to enlarge stupidity, inflate conceit, enhance credulity and puts those subjected to it at the mercy of brainwashing with printing presses, radio and television . . ." Lloyd George put it succinctly when he made this caustic comment: "Education without God makes clever devils." Who can deny it?

FURTHER STUDY

Col. 2:1–8;
1 Cor. 3:19–20; 8:1

1. What did Paul warn the Colossians?
2. What does knowledge do?

Prayer

O God, save me from the mistake of believing that life is to be found in deep or profound thinking. Help me see that life is to be found in first knowing You, then thinking Your thoughts after You. Teach me to think as You think, dear Lord. In Jesus' Name. Amen.

"Send in the Clowns"

"'Laughter,' I said, 'is foolish. And what does pleasure accomplish?'" (v. 2)

For reading & meditation—Ecclesiastes 2:1–11

*I*f education, intellectualism and philosophy are not the routes to making life work—then what is? Perhaps life can be found in pleasure. Not so, says Solomon. Pleasure pleases, but it is powerless to quench the ache that exists in the soul. We are provided with a list of the ways in which pleasure can be gained, but all of them are given the "thumbs down" by Solomon.

The first is *laughter*. Send in the clowns. But as almost everyone knows, those who bring laughter to thousands are themselves often desperately unhappy. Billy Graham told the story of a man who went to a doctor for help with his depression. "I'll give you something better than anti-depressants," said the doctor. "Go and see the clown at the local circus. He has just arrived in town and is sending people into hysterics." The man looked at the doctor dolefully and said, "I am the clown."

If laughter cannot satisfy, then perhaps drink will help. "I tried cheering myself with wine," Solomon tells us . . . but clearly that did not satisfy either. He then threw himself into a round of activity—great projects like building a house for himself, planting vineyards, amassing silver and gold, and finally equipping himself with a harem—what he describes as "the delights of the heart of man" (v. 8). But did these things work? Here's his conclusion: "everything was meaningless, a chasing after the wind" (v. 11). He is not saying, of course, that these things didn't bring pleasure. He is making the point that this kind of pleasure is ephemeral; it just does not last.

FURTHER STUDY

Luke 15:11–32;
12:16–21

1. What did the prodigal discover?
2. What did Jesus teach about the "good life"?

Prayer

My Father and my God, I see I am shut up to You. Earth's fountains are unable to quench the deep thirsts of my soul. To whom shall I go? Only You have the words of eternal life. I am so grateful.
Thank You my Father. Amen.

Where Life Ends

"Like the fool, the wise man too must die!" (v. 16)

For reading & meditation—Ecclesiastes 2:12–16

There are some who believe that the writer of Ecclesiastes had lost all objectivity when he wrote this book, and his pessimistic mood affected everything he looked at. As if anticipating that very argument, he says in verse 9: "In all this my wisdom stayed with me." Disillusioned though he was with the fact that things could not fully satisfy, his objectivity never left him.

In the section before us today he re-examines wisdom, this time comparing it with folly. His mind grapples with the idea: "Shall I be a serious thinker, or just go the way of all fools?" His conclusion, initially anyway, is that wisdom has the advantage over folly: "The wise man has eyes in his head, while the fool walks in the darkness" (v. 14). In other words, it is better to be wise than foolish, better to be learned than ignorant. But would wisdom in itself stop him from slipping toward meaninglessness? In the final analysis, both the wise and the foolish have to face the fact of death. That is a card that "trumps" every other card in life. This, then, is his conclusion: "So what if I do have a fine education? What if I enjoy a good standard of living through the application of common sense? What's the point when it all ends in death?"

The answer, of course, is that there is little or no point if life just ends in death. But the reality is—it doesn't. There is life in the hereafter, and the quality of life in the hereafter depends on what you are after here.

FURTHER STUDY

James 3:13–18;
Prov. 4:7;
James 1:5

1. What two kinds of wisdom does James talk about?
2. What are their different qualities?

Prayer

O Father, let me be gripped by the fact, as was the great apostle Paul, that when I know You, life here on earth is too wonderful for words. And to die? There is nothing but gain. All honor and glory be unto Your matchless Name. Amen.

Life in the Real World

Day 68

"I hated all the things I had toiled for . . . because I must leave them to the one who comes after me." (v. 18)

For reading & meditation—Ecclesiastes 2:17-23

When we face the fact that there is nothing in this world—no person, place or thing—that can meet the deepest ache in our soul is probably one of the most solemn moments of our existence. Many can't face that kind of reality so they escape into such things as fantasies, endless rounds of activity, drink, sensual pleasures. It is this quality—the ability to face reality—that endears Solomon to us. We don't have to guess what is going on inside him. He tells us—and in no uncertain terms.

What is the next thing Solomon turned to in his frustration with life? Work; and work, especially creative work, can be very satisfying. Solomon is not knocking work, but he is saying that this is not where life is to be found. Clearly, Solomon had considered throwing himself into activity partly to establish something that could be left to his children. But as he contemplates the idea, he concludes: When you die, you have to leave it all to someone else (v. 18); you cannot be sure if he or she will look after it or ruin it (v. 19); you have no choice but to give it away as a gift to someone who has not worked for it (v. 21); and finally, what benefit does the one who has worked derive from it? (v. 22).

Don't dismiss this as just despairing pessimism. Remember the purpose of Ecclesiastes—to show that true meaning is not found in the temporal but in the eternal. Here is a real person coming to some real conclusions about life in a real world.

FURTHER STUDY

Luke 12:22-34;
Col. 3:1-2

1. *Where does a man's heart focus?*
2. *Where should it focus?*

Prayer

O God my Father, day by day the conviction is quietly being borne in upon me—only in You am I equipped to face the realities of life. I am so grateful that I know the one true reality—whose other Name is Jesus. Amen.

73

It's Tough Out There!

"To the man who pleases him, God gives wisdom, knowledge and happiness . . ." (v. 26)
For reading & meditation—Ecclesiastes 2:24-26

Oswald Chambers said: "No Christian makes much progress in the Christian life until he realizes that life is more chaotic and tragic than orderly." In other words, life in a fallen world can be tough! The sooner we face that fact and allow it to silence us, the fewer expectations we will have of the world, and the more eagerly we will turn to God.

In the section we are looking at now, suddenly we see a small chink of light shining through Solomon's pessimism and gloom. The passage begins with what might appear to be a contradiction: "A man can do nothing better than to eat and drink and find satisfaction in his work. This too, I see, is from the hand of God" (v. 24). The point he is making is this: if life's ultimate meaning can't be found in activities like eating, drinking, and working, it is not to be found in rejecting them either. *Things* in themselves are not bad; what makes them bad is the wrong values we attach to them.

As soon as God is brought into Solomon's musings, notice the change. Enjoyment, he says, is God's personal gift (v. 25). Satisfaction in things is found only when they are seen as being behind God and not in front of Him. When God is not first, then everything around which we wrap our affections is an idol. We can choose either to find life in God and enjoy the provision of His hands; or to find life in things, and turn our back on God. The latter is "meaningless," says Solomon, "a chasing after the wind."

FURTHER STUDY

1 Tim. 5:1-6;
Prov. 21:17;
Luke 8:14

1. What is the plight of those who live for pleasure?
2. What do life's riches and pleasures choke?

Prayer

Father, I see that when You step into my world, then I step out into a new world. Everything looks and appears different. Help me to put nothing in front of You—not even my closest earthly relationship. In Jesus' Name I pray. Amen.

The Time Tunnel

"There is a time for everything, and a season for every activity under heaven." (v. 1)

For reading & meditation—Ecclesiastes 3:1

Solomon turns his attention to the consideration of time. Who can define time? Longfellow asked, "What is time?", and then went on to say that although time could be measured, it could not be clearly defined.

One of the best definitions of discipleship I have ever heard is: "Discipleship is what a person does with his time." Imagine someone who loves you puts into your personal bank account every day the sum of $1,440, with the stipulation that you have to use it all every day, and anything left over will be cancelled by the bank. Sounds too good to be true, doesn't it? However, Someone who loves you puts into your life every day 1,440 minutes—the gift of time. The same condition applies—you have to use it all, and anything left over is forfeited. Ask yourself: How do I manage my time? Do I squander it, or see it as a sacred trust?

Solomon's point is to show how life on this earth breaks down into measurable spans. Take a look at how things happen, he seems to be saying, and you will see a controlling schedule behind all things. Does not this in itself suggest that a loving God presided over the circumstances of life? Kierkegaard said: "Life has to be lived forwards but it can only be understood backwards." Pause now for a moment and reflect on how the things you worried about a year ago look so different with hindsight. Aren't you aware that an eternal God has been marshaling your progress in this tunnel of time?

FURTHER STUDY

Eph. 5:15–20;
Ps. 90:12;
1 Cor. 7:29–31

1. What are we to be careful about?
2. What are we to understand?

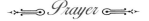

Prayer

O Father, help me to see the issue of time not as a burden, but as a blessing. I want to use my time wisely, but not to become so obsessed by it that I can't stop and smell the roses. Keep me sanely balanced in all this. In Jesus' Name. Amen.

You Will Laugh Again

"... a time to weep and a time to laugh, a time to mourn and a time to
dance. ..." (v. 4)

For reading & meditation—Ecclesiastes 3:2–4a

*P*erhaps no better cross-section of life can be found anywhere than in these beautiful and poetic verses. Solomon unfolds for us the variety of life, all of which takes place under the providential hand of God. There are fourteen contrasts.

(1) *There is a time to be born and a time to die.* No one can negotiate his or her arrival into this world, not the natural time of departure either. Both are beyond our control. (2) *A time to plant and a time to uproot.* Mess around with Mother Nature, and you won't get anywhere. Follow the order and you get results; ignore it and you get consequences. (3) *A time to kill and a time to heal.* This is not to be seen as an approval of killing, but a simple statement of fact—wars and killing are a part of human life. But so, also, is healing. Charles Swindoll puts it like this: "Life seems strangely fixed between a battlefield and a first aid station, between murder and medicine."

(4) *A time to tear down and a time to build.* Demolition is followed by construction, then after a while more demolition and more construction. Isn't this a pattern with which every generation is familiar? (5) *A time to weep and a time to laugh.* Some people have more sorrow than laughter, but no one goes through the world without touching both. Are you shedding a lot of tears over some great difficulty or problem at the moment? I promise you in God's Name, sometime, not too far distant in the future, your heart will laugh again.

**FURTHER
STUDY**

Isa. 58:6–12;
Jer. 31:13;
Isa. 61:3

1. What has God
promised?
2. How will God respond
to those who cry for help?

Prayer

Help me see, dear Father, that though I pass through times of sorrow and difficulty, nothing can shake the
rock of existence on which I stand. In sorrow or in laughter may I never lose sight of You.
In Jesus' Name I ask it. Amen.

The End of Searching

"... a time to scatter stones and a time to gather them ..." (v. 5)

For reading & meditation—Ecclesiastes 3:4b–6a

We continue looking at Solomon's fourteen contrasts of life. (6) *A time to mourn and a time to dance.* We lose a loved one, and then, a year or so later, a family member gets married. Mourning is turned to dancing. Isn't this true of almost every family on earth?

(7) *A time to scatter stones and a time to gather them.* Some commentators believe this refers to the act of scattering stones over a difficult neighbor's field in order to hinder him from plowing; to then go out and retrieve those stones implies an act of sorrow or repentance. The thought here is that life is punctuated with periods when people seem to go out of their way to make it difficult for others, then they have second thoughts, and do everything they can to cancel out their provocative behavior. (8) *A time to embrace and a time to refrain.* There are times when every one of us needs the quiet embrace of a friend who whispers words of comfort. At other times we need not consolation but confrontation. We need to be faced with some hard truths. For life to be balanced, both must be part of our experience.

(9) *A time to search and a time to give up.* How much easier life would be for some if they would learn this lesson and give up searching for something they inwardly sense will never be found. It's good to have hope, but hope must be based on something that is realistic. As someone once put it, "It's better to be a sane pessimist than a silly optimist."

FURTHER STUDY

Acts 17:22–28;
Job 11:7–9;
Jer. 29:13

1. What did Paul point out to the Athenians?
2. What question did Job's friend pose?

Prayer

O Father, how can I sufficiently thank You for helping me to give up searching for satisfaction down paths that were all dead-ends. I need no longer search, for I have found. All honor and glory be to Your peerless and precious Name. Amen.

One Foot in Eternity

"... a time to be silent and a time to speak ..." (v. 7)

For reading & meditation—Ecclesiastes 3:6b–8

We look now at the last of the list of Solomon's fourteen contrasts. (10) *A time to keep and a time to throw (or give) away.* Think at this moment of all the stuff you have that you will never use. Some things you will need to keep, of course, but some things ought to be given away.

(11) *A time to tear and a time to mend.* Some things must never be given up—truth, for example. However, we ought not to be afraid of trying out new ways of doing things. It's not a mark of spirituality to be a "stick in the mud." (12) *A time to be silent and a time to speak.* It's not often someone confesses, "I feel sorry for the things I did not say," but many admit: "I wish I knew how to keep my mouth shut." The sooner we learn when to talk and when to listen the better it will be for us—and for others!

(13) *A time to love and a time to hate.* Love that does not have another person's interests at heart is not love, but mere sentimentality. To love means you must also be willing to hate. Not people, but the thing that may be hindering them from fulfilling their spiritual potential. (14) *A time for war and a time for peace.* Wars start, it is said, "when someone has something somebody else wants." As I write, there are over sixty wars going on somewhere in the world. Solomon's words, therefore, rise to almost cosmic proportions: "there must be a time also for peace."

FURTHER STUDY

James 3:1–11;
Prov. 25:11;
Isa. 50:4

1. What did the Lord give to Isaiah?
2. What is the potential of the tongue?

Prayer

My Father and my God, this focus on the events that take place in time drives home to me my need to have one foot also in eternity. I am grateful that although a creature of time, because I am in You I am bound for eternity. Amen.

78

All Things Beautiful

"He has made everything beautiful in its time." (v. 11)

For reading & meditation—Ecclesiastes 3:9-11

Wouldn't it be wonderful if we knew how to react properly to all of life's events? To do the right thing at the wrong time is almost as bad as not doing right. "What time is it?" we often ask. In regard to life's events, how often we wish we knew!

Solomon follows up his poetic appraisal of time with a question: "What benefit do we get from time?" It might seem a blessing, but actually it is a burden. As he looks at the interesting cycles of time, he concludes that without God all is boring and futile. But here's a sentence that brushes aside futility: *"He has made everything beautiful in its time."* To look at time through mere human eyes alone is to see it as interesting but futile; to look at it through the lens of faith is to see a beautiful picture coming together under the hands of the Divine Artist. He takes our sorrows and turns them into symphonies; He takes our tears and turns them into telescopes; He takes our calamities and turns them into opportunities.

If you could see through your troubles at this moment and catch sight of the beautiful picture God is painting in your life as He mixes the blacks and blues, the reds and crimsons with the whites of His purposes, you would never again shake your fist in His face and tell Him that your life is a mess. The timing of things may not be as you would like them to be but remember, He is making everything beautiful—*in its time.*

FURTHER STUDY

1 Pet. 3:1–5;
1 Chron. 16:29 (KJV);
Pss. 29:2 (KJV);
96:9 (KJV)

1. What is Peter saying about beauty?
2. What is the "beauty of holiness"?

---⇒ *Prayer* ⇒---

O God, save me from the demandingness that wants to change things simply because I see no point or purpose in them. Help me understand that You are working out all things beautifully. But in Your time, not mine. Amen.

What Time Is It?

"He has also set eternity in the hearts of men . . ." (v. 11)

For reading & meditation—Ecclesiastes 3:11

The text before us today reads like a conundrum. God has set eternity in our hearts, yet we cannot understand what He has done.

God has not only established a timetable by which everything is ordered, but He has also placed within our spirits a deep longing for eternity. Because of this, there is something in every one of us that earth cannot satisfy. We live on earth, but we do not belong to it. We belong to eternity. Wordsworth, in his well known "Intimations of Immortality," speaks of this secret reminiscence of the soul when he says:

> But trailing clouds of glory do we come
> From God who is our home.

"From God *who is our home*." This nostalgia we have for heaven is built into every human being, and although with many it is denied, ignored, or overlaid with other things, indisputably it is there. And it is a wonderful moment when a man or woman realizes it is there.

Most people go about their daily tasks largely unaware that there are deep thirsts and deep longings in them which temporal things can never meet. Why is it, they say, that when I have everything I have ever wanted, it still does not satisfy? If only they would stop to consider and ask in relation to spiritual things, "What time is it?", they would then be ready to hear the answer: "It is time to come to terms with eternity."

FURTHER STUDY

*John 6:60–70; 17:3;
Gal. 6:8*

*1. What was Peter's
conclusion?
2. What is eternal life?*

Prayer

O God, it seems too good to be true—that the thing most of humanity is searching for, I have found. You are the Homeland of my soul. In You I am safe, steady, and growing. I shall be eternally grateful. Amen.

God-Given Abilities

Day 76

"That everyone may eat and drink, and find satisfaction in all his toil—this is the gift of God." (v. 13)

For reading & meditation—Ecclesiastes 3:12–13

When God is in our lives, then His presence makes a world of difference. God gives us four things so that we might enjoy our life here on planet earth.

First, *He gives us the ability to be happy* (v. 12). Happiness is a gift. Only God can give us the perspective on life that enables us to remain happy even when things don't go our way. A new Christian put it like this: "I am happier now when I am sad than before when I was happy." Second, *God gives us the ability to do good* (v. 12). It takes God to help us be good to those who are not good to us. We don't have the kind of hearts that want to do good to those who are not good to us; that ability flows from God's heart of love and compassion into ours.

Third, *God gives us the ability to eat and drink* (v. 13). Have you ever considered that your appetite is something that comes from God? It is a gift from our loving Father's hand. Thinking about that will, I promise you, help you enjoy your food much better. Fourth, *God gives us the ability to see good in our labor* (v. 13). The whole workplace could be transformed overnight if men and women saw it from God's perspective. Instead of asking, "What is the least I can do for a day's wages?", our question would be: "What is the most I can do for a day's wages?" Hard to take? That's because it is an "above the sun" perspective.

FURTHER STUDY

Isa. 35:1–10;
Job 19:25;
John 15:11; 17:13

1. What is God's assurance to the redeemed?
2. What was Jesus' promise to the believer?

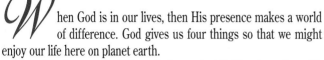

Prayer

O God, when I see how much of my life depends on You, I feel ashamed at how slow I am to appreciate that fact. Forgive me, dear Father, and evoke within me an ever-growing consciousness of Your own continued goodness. In Jesus' Name. Amen.

A Thorough God

"God does it so that men will revere him." (v. 14)
For reading & meditation—Ecclesiastes 3:14–15

*I*n these verses we come face to face with the thoroughness of God. However ragged life may seem in a fallen world, the Creator knows no such imperfections. Everything He does is not only permanent, but complete: "nothing can be added to it and nothing taken from it" (v. 14).

Ever sent for something and found that when it comes a part is missing? God's quality control is 100 percent. Why does God do things with such thoroughness? Solomon tells us: ". . . so that men will revere him." He does it to cultivate in our hearts a climate of reverence. "Religion," it has been said, "begins with a sense of awe, the recognition of God's greatness and our limitations." When do we feel awe? Awe fills us when we stand and look at the works of God—a majestic mountain, a glorious sunset, or a tranquil lake. You don't say as you stand before the Niagara Falls: "Isn't that cute?" You simply stand in silent awe.

But what does Solomon mean when he tells us that whatever is has already been, and that "God will call the past to account" (v. 15)? Moffatt translates this statement: "God is ever bringing back what disappears." It means quite simply that God repeats situations in our lives until we learn the lessons they are meant to teach us. God wants to make a permanent lesson out of something we think is merely passing and temporary. Think of the heartache we would be saved if we could just get hold of this.

FURTHER STUDY

Heb. 13:1–8;
Ps. 102:25–27;
Mal. 3:6;
Heb. 1:12

1. What was the psalmist's conviction?
2. Why is Jesus so trustworthy?

Prayer

O God, when will I learn? I go through the same situations time and time again simply because I have not heeded Your voice. Make me alert to each passing moment, and show me how to draw from it the lessons You want to teach me. In Jesus' Name. Amen.

The Patience of God

"'God will bring to judgment both the righteous and the wicked . . .'" (v. 17)

For reading & meditation—Ecclesiastes 3:16–17

*E*ver found yourself feeling frustrated because of the way in which wickedness seems to win over justice? Then you know something of how Solomon feels in the verses before us today. Every generation, throughout time, has had to face this problem. James Russell Lowell put it this way:

Truth forever on the scaffold,
Wrong forever on the throne.

Solomon struggles, as no doubt you have done (and perhaps still do), with the fact that in the very place where you would expect to see justice, you find wickedness and corruption prevailing. In the days when I was a pastor, I sometimes went to court with people who had a genuine case to be heard, only to see it broken down by tactics that were dishonest and unjust. I have seen enough injustice in my time to share something of Solomon's cynicism.

Are you at this moment a victim of judicial injustice? Then don't allow yourself to become too cynical, for, as Solomon said: "God will bring to judgment both the righteous and the wicked . . ." Wrong will not continue forever. The day is coming when all corruption and injustice will be called to judgment before the throne of God's truth. But of course, being human, we wish the injustices we have received could be put right—now. God seems to be much more patient than we are, and what we must do is to ask for grace to be patient with the patience of God.

FURTHER STUDY

Ps. 58:1–11;
Gen. 18:25;
Ps. 96:13

1. What was the view of the psalmist?
2. How does God judge?

Prayer

O God my Father, give me the divine perspective on things so that present injustices may be swallowed up in the long-term purposes. Help me see that I will have my day in court—Your court.
In Jesus' Name I ask it. Amen.

How Error Occurs

"Man's fate is like that of the animals . . . As one dies, so dies the other." (v. 19)

For reading & meditation—Ecclesiastes 3:18–22

*H*ave you noticed that whenever Solomon looks "above the sun" he gets the right perspective, but when he looks "beneath the sun" his blood pressure rises, along with his cynicism? We saw yesterday that when he looked away from the injustice he observed on earth to the day when all wrongs would be righted, he appeared to be in a better frame of mind, but in the verses before us today he has descended into deep cynicism again.

Listen to what he says: we are like the animals, and will end up like animals—in oblivion. Solomon's cynicism drives him to make a statement that might seem justified under the circumstances, but is quite untrue. We are different from animals and bound for a different destiny. Solomon is not talking truth here; he is talking cynicism. This is what happens when we take our eyes off God, and the truths He unfolds in His Word—we can descend into making the same kind of rash and heretical statements as Solomon. His words are the musings of a confused cynic and represent what he felt at the time, but they are not to be taken as true for they are contradicted in other parts of Scripture.

We ought never to forget as Christians that unless we have a full biblical perspective on issues, we too can descend into making rash and heretical statements just as Solomon did. Cynicism numbs us spiritually and leaves us feeling downcast and disillusioned. A full view of Scripture, however, lifts us up and gives us God's perspectives. Cynicism confuses; Scripture clarifies.

FURTHER STUDY

Rom. 1:18–32;
Col. 3:5–10;
Eph. 5:3–5

1. How did Paul say man gives way to basic instincts?
2. Why did they become fools?

Prayer

O Father, how thankful I am that You have given me a Book which enables me to have the right perspective on all things. Teach me how to compare one scripture with another. To say not merely "it is written," but "it is written again." In Jesus' Name. Amen.

It's Lonely at the Top

"Better one handful with tranquillity than two handfuls with toil and chasing after the wind." (v. 6)

For reading & meditation—Ecclesiastes 4:1–6

*A*s we said yesterday, Solomon seems fine when his gaze is focused "above the sun," but he becomes filled with cynicism when he looks around at what is "under the sun." Today we see his gaze focused once again in the horizontal direction.

He "looks around," as he puts it, sees people caught in the grip of oppression, and his heart is filled with despair. His cynicism reaches new depths when he concludes that under these circumstances, those who had died were fortunate, and the unborn were in an even better position. Some commentators see these sentiments as marking the lowest point in the book. The savage rivalry and competitiveness that he sees all around causes him to say once again that life is meaningless. It's not healthy competition he is referring to here, but the savage, ruthless, brutal, dog-eat-dog mentality that rides roughshod over people's feelings. Those who get to the top by this method find when they get there they have everything they ever wanted—except friends. They pushed those aside on the way up, and thus they find it lonely at the top.

What's the answer—drop out of the system? No, that would be irresponsible, to say the least. Overreaction is rarely ever the right reaction. The answer, he says, is to decide that one handful of contentment is better than two handsful of competitiveness that gets you to the top, but leaves you feeling lonely at the top. Moffatt puts it beautifully when he translates verse 6 thus: "One handful of contentment is better than two hands full of toil and futile effort." It is.

FURTHER STUDY

Phil. 4:1–12;
Heb. 13:5;
1 Tim. 6:6–10

1. *What was Paul able to say?*
2. *What did the writer to the Hebrews exhort?*

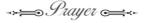

Prayer

Gracious Father, I come to You again to ask that You will touch my heart and deliver me from anything that might deter me from being the person You want me to be. Make me a truly contented Christian. In Jesus' Name I ask it. Amen.

85

A Threefold Cord

"A cord of three strands is not quickly broken." (v. 12)
For reading & meditation—Ecclesiastes 4:7–12

*S*ome people are lonely because of the oppression of others; some because their own competitiveness separates them from friends. In today's passage, however, we come face to face with a man who was lonely because he had no family connections. How does he handle it? He throws himself into an endless round of activity and buries himself in work. But money and possessions are not much good when you have no one to share them with. Life lived on this level, says Solomon, is also meaningless.

He then makes a statement which is often misunderstood: "Two are better than one . . . If one falls down, his friend can help him up . . . if two lie down together, they will keep warm" (vv. 9–11). Note the emphasis in these sayings is on two people. But at the end of the passage Solomon says something very strange: "A cord of *three* strands is not quickly broken." The point is: when you are in a close relationship with someone you love and who loves you, you have a third quality—a strength and power which unfolds from out of the relationship. In the fusion of friendship, you discover something you could never discover—except in a relationship. It is your strength, plus your friend's strength, producing an even greater strength.

Solomon's point, of course, in saying all this is that if you want to make it through days of disillusionment, the secret is friendship. There is no comfort quite like a friend when you are forced to live on "the ragged edge of time."

FURTHER STUDY

*John 15:1-14;
Prov. 18:24; 17:17*

*1. What has Jesus
called us?
2. How do we cultivate
friendship?*

Prayer

Father, I see that I am built for relationships, not only with You, but with others also. And in a relationship lies a power that is greater than the sum of its two parts. May I discover more of this.
In Christ's Name I ask it. Amen.

The Best Friend . . .

"Better a poor but wise youth than an old but foolish king who no longer knows how to take warning." (v. 13)

For reading & meditation—Ecclesiastes 4:13–16

Strange though it may sound, it is possible to have many friends and still be lonely. That's the point Solomon is making in the verses before us today.

Look again at the picture he presents in verse 13. It is a picture of two people: one a poor but wise youth, the other an old but rich king. Who would you think has the advantage? The king? Not so, says Solomon. He may have more experience of life, but something more than experience is needed if we are to walk effectively through the world. What we need is—wisdom. Experience without wisdom is of little benefit. It's not how many hours we have lived that counts, but what we have gained from those hours that is important.

The whole of chapter 4 has been taken up with the issue of loneliness, and Solomon ends by underlining the fact that it is not our circumstances that make us lonely, but our inability to apply wisdom to our situation. Take two people who are in exactly the same circumstances. Both are surrounded by agreeable and helpful companions. One enjoys the company of friends, but the other complains that he is lonely. Where lies the problem with the one who feels lonely? Not in the outer circumstances, but in the "innerstances"—his attitudes. He lacks the wisdom to see that no human being can provide him with the comfort which the soul so deeply craves. That is found only in God. The wise are those who understand that while human friends are important, the best friend to have is God.

FURTHER STUDY

James 2:18–24;
2 Chron. 20:7;
Exod. 33:7–11

1. What is said of Abraham?
2. How is Moses' conversation with the Lord described?

Prayer

My Father and my God, grant me the wisdom to understand that while the making and keeping of earthly friendships is important, the making and keeping of Your friendship is even more important.
In Jesus' Name. Amen.

Watch Your Step

"Guard your steps when you go to the house of God." (v. 1)
For reading & meditation—Ecclesiastes 5:1–3

*I*n this chapter, we catch Solomon in one of those rare moments when he breaks free of his cynical frame of mind—so let's make the most of it! He begins with a strong and positive declaration: "Guard your steps when you go to the house of God. Go near to listen . . ." The Living Bible paraphrases it thus: "As you enter the Temple, keep your ears open and your mouth shut!" God's people, Solomon is saying, are far too casual in their approach to worship. Familiarity may not breed contempt, but it certainly can breed insensitivity. The way we approach God's house will determine what we receive at God's house. When we make our way to God's house we ought to be spiritually alert, intent on hearing what God has to say to us, and spiritually expectant. "Bad preaching," said one famous Bible expositor, "is God's curse on an unexpectant congregation."

Generally speaking, there is far too much talking and not enough listening in church services. We come into God's presence with our minds bent on getting God to see things from our perspective instead of desiring to see things from His. We fill every silence with words. The words "Draw near to listen" ought, I think, to be emblazoned on the front of every church. If you are not hearing God when you go to church, the problem is not that God is not speaking; it is more likely that you have stopped listening. The next time you go to the house of God, say to your restless talkative spirit: "Shh! Listen!"

FURTHER STUDY

James 1:1–19;
Prov. 8:34;
Matt. 7:24

1. When is a man blessed?
2. What must we begin to do?

Prayer

Gracious God, forgive me that so often both in church and in my daily devotions I am more interested in letting You know what I want to say than in listening to what You have to say.
"Speak, Lord, Thy servant heareth." Amen.

Stand in Awe

"... do not protest to the [temple] messenger, 'My vow was a mistake.'" (v. 6)

For reading & meditation—Ecclesiastes 5:4–7

*D*id you know the more talkative you are, the more likely you are to fall into sin? If you have any doubt about that, read Proverbs 10:19. In the verses before us today, Solomon identifies another danger—making promises to God which we fail to deliver.

How many of us in the emotion of a church service have made promises to God that we have conveniently forgotten? The promises we make in haste we repent of at leisure. Perhaps we rationalize and say such things as "I didn't really mean it," or "I was carried away by the emotion of the moment." A vow made to God ought to be treated seriously. It is the seed plot of action. When we vow, we ought not to do it impulsively, but only after careful and prayerful consideration.

Solomon's advice on vows is quite simple: First, don't delay in delivering it (v. 5), and second, don't deny you said it (v. 6). Have you made a vow to God and never followed through on it? Ask God's forgiveness and the grace, if the vow is still capable of being undertaken, to do what you promised. We live in an age when vows and commitments do not seem as important as they once did. God keeps his vows; so should we. Let's heed this important message of Solomon: babbling, rambling, and ill-considered words, though found in many places, ought not to be found in church. It's no good opening your mouth wide and having a good sing if you only open half an ear and never get around to doing what you promised to God.

FURTHER STUDY

Matt. 5:33–37;
Num. 30:2;
Deut. 23:21;
James 1:8

1. What did Jesus teach about vows?
2. How can we avoid instability?

Prayer

O God, help me to see what tension I set up inside myself when I make vows to You that I do not keep. You keep Your word to me, may I also keep my word to You. Help me, where it is possible, to catch up on any unfulfilled promises. In Christ's Name I pray. Amen.

Money! Money! Money!

"Whoever loves money never has money enough . . ." (v. 10)

For reading & meditation—Ecclesiastes 5:8–12

Solomon is being cynical again. The rich tend to be the leaders, he says, and the poor the followers. Those with wealth are usually the most influential, and they are expert at appointing officials to watch over officials. In time, the "red tape" becomes so thick the poor have no hope of cutting through it. Solomon is not the only one who is cynical about bureaucracy. His main point, however, is to show us that wealth is not everything. As Derek Tidball puts it: "Money . . . increases your appetite but not your satisfaction."

There is nothing wrong with possessing money, of course; it is when money is allowed to possess you that trouble comes. My father wrote on the flyleaf of my Bible the day after I was converted: "Money is a universal provider for everything but happiness and a passport everywhere but to heaven." Wise words which I have never forgotten. Wealthy people, says Solomon, find it difficult to sleep because they are worried about their investments. The more money you have, the more you have to worry over. Someone put it like this: "More money, more worry, more worry, less sleep."

All this, of course, refers to those who have no sense of stewardship, for when money is surrendered to God, then money becomes a "trust"—a "trust" which is owned by God. We are not meant to be proprietors, but trustees of the Lord's money. God is the owner of everything on the face of the earth, and we are the owers. All giving ought to be out of gratitude for what He has given to us.

FURTHER STUDY

Matt. 6:19–34;
Deut. 8:13–14;
Mark 4:19;
1 Tim. 6:9

1. What is the danger of material increase?
2. What investment advice did Jesus give?

❖══ *Prayer* ══❖

Father, help me in relation to material things to see that I am a steward, not a proprietor; a servant, not a master; an ower, not an owner. Change my perspectives so that I look at everything from Your point of view. In Christ's Name I pray. Amen.

Gold—or God?

"Naked a man comes from his mother's womb, and as he comes, so he departs." (v. 15)

For reading & meditation—Ecclesiastes 5:13–17

olomon is still harping on about money. Pretty boring you might think. But isn't he putting his finger on the pulse of our problems? We try to find in gold what we ought to be finding in God.

Consider this, says Solomon: "Savings are put into risky investments that turn sour, and soon there is nothing left to pass on to one's son. The man who speculates is soon back to where he began—with nothing ... all his hard work has been for nothing; he has been working for the wind. It is all swept away. All the rest of his life he is under a cloud—gloomy, discouraged, frustrated, and angry" (vv. 14–17, TLB). Clearly, the soul's security cannot be found in money. When will people learn this?

Some of the ancients used to have their wealth put into their tombs alongside their bodies when they died, so that they could keep it with them in the afterlife. These days people have learned that you can't take the treasures of time into eternity; that's why you never see a trailer attached to a hearse.

When we consider material things we face this sharp issue: either we transform the material into the image of the spiritual, or the material will transform us into its own image. Those who allow the material to get the upper hand and begin to serve Mammon soon begin to look like their god. They become materialized. The light dies out in their eyes and the winter of materialism sets in.

FURTHER STUDY

1 Tim. 6:1–7;
Ps. 49:10;
Prov. 23:5; 27:24;
Jer. 17:11

1. What did Paul underline to Timothy?
2. What is the lesson of the partridge?

Prayer

O God, save me I pray from being transformed into the image of the material. Help me to keep my gaze
constantly on You so that I become more and more transformed into the image of Your Son.
This I ask in Christ's peerless and precious Name. Amen.

91

"Occupied with Gladness"

". . . God keeps him occupied with gladness of heart." (v. 20)
For reading & meditation—Ecclesiastes 5:18–20

*S*olomon does not allow us to stay too long in the darkness of his cynicism without seeking to throw some light across the road. He sets out in the verses before us today to give us a three-point sermon.

First, he says, set your face against the idea that happiness lies in the possession of material things, and refuse to put a priority on making money just for the sake of it. Take life as it comes, laugh a little bit more, and try to find pleasure in the simple things. Second, enjoy your work. It will not meet the deep needs of your soul, but it is good to be engaged in a task, however menial that task may be. Third, see everything God has given you as a gift rather than as something you have earned. Those who say "I made so much money this year" forget that if God had not given them the health and strength to achieve, they would never have made it. A grateful spirit ought not to be far from any one of us.

How blessed are those who, putting God first, find that He keeps their hearts "occupied with gladness" (v. 20). What a beautiful phrase Solomon chooses to describe the condition of those whose hearts are set on God. Can you think of anything more wonderful than to have a heart that is "occupied with gladness"? All the riches in the world, all the honors, all the accolades, all the applause, all the achievements, are as nothing compared to the joy of having one's heart occupied by the King of kings.

FURTHER STUDY

Eph. 1:1–18;
Prov. 10:22; 13:7;
James 2:5

1. What was Paul's prayer for the Ephesians?
2. What has God chosen the poor to be rich in?

Prayer

O God my Father, help me put a sign on my heart that says: "Occupied by the King of kings." Then, when lesser things seek to invade my soul, they will see that there is no more room, and leave to go on their way. Amen.

Source of Contentment

"God gives a man wealth, possessions and honor . . . but God does not enable him
to enjoy them . . ." (v. 2)

For reading & meditation—Ecclesiastes 6:1–2

In this chapter Solomon continues to focus on those whom we generally refer to as "well heeled." But he also draws our attention to the plight of those who have everything life can offer, yet are prevented from enjoying it, not by circumstances, but by God Himself.

Why would God do this? Is the Almighty an ogre who looks out for people who are enjoying themselves and then moves in at the crucial moment to sadistically deny them any feelings of pleasure? Surely such a cat-and-mouse game is unworthy of the Deity. Those who know God are aware that His purposes are always beneficent. In other words, nothing He does is done out of peevishness or caprice. When God acts to deny people enjoyment, it is because He wants to show them that He is the One who enables men and women to experience pleasure in things; the things themselves do not give pleasure.

That might sound manipulative to some, but divine love never exploits. It might look like exploitation to us because we are shortsighted and cannot see the end from the beginning. The point is that if people were able to find contentment in money, then they would become spiritually myopic and look no further—money would become their idol. So the issue when reduced to basics is this—those who make money their god will never find contentment. Any god that usurps the place of the true God puts the soul "out of joint," so to speak. The power to give contentment belongs to God alone.

FURTHER STUDY

Matt. 19:16–30;
Luke 12:33

1. What did the young man find difficult?
2. Which commandments were not mentioned?

Prayer

Gracious Father, I acknowledge with gratitude that You and You alone have the power to give contentment.
I want no other god to reign in my heart except You, the one true God.
Rule and hold sway, dear Father. Always. In Jesus' Name. Amen.

Shut Up to God

". . . [a man] cannot enjoy his prosperity . . . a stillborn child is better off than he." (v. 3)

For reading & meditation—Ecclesiastes 6:3–6

O bviously there are some advantages in having plenty of money. A wealthy man (a very wealthy man!) could afford to have a hundred children, says Solomon. With his money he could hire help to see to such everyday events as changing diapers and giving feedings.

Those who love lots of children and could afford to look after a hundred might think that this is the solution to the deep inner frustration that exists in their souls. Wealth can sustain a big family, but there comes a moment when those who live only for the family realize this is not where real life is to be found. There is nothing wrong in enjoying one's family (indeed Scripture encourages it). However, even the most loving family is powerless to quench the ache that resides deep in the human psyche. As Solomon reflects on this he becomes cynical again, and says that it is better to be a stillborn child than to be caught up in the meaningless nonsense of trying to find life outside of God.

Perhaps the guarantee of a longer life on earth might satisfy the soul. Not so, says Solomon. If life apart from God is marked by so much frustration, what benefit would a life of a thousand years twice over bring? In my experience, those who are honest enough to admit to this deep inner emptiness yearn for a shorter life rather than a longer one. In the end, to those who do not know God, it makes no difference whether they have been rich or poor.

FURTHER STUDY

Ps. 107:1–9;
Isa. 55:1–2;
John 7:37–38

1. What belief did the psalmist express?
2. What did Jesus promise?

Prayer

O God, I see now why this book is designed to silence me. For nothing can satisfy my soul except You. I need to take this lesson on board, for I tend to rely more on the visible than the Invisible.
Help me, dear Father. In Jesus' Name. Amen.

Where Is Your Identity?

"All man's efforts are for his mouth, yet his appetite is never satisfied." (v. 7)

For reading & meditation—Ecclesiastes 6:7–9

*I*f having a large family or living a thousand years does not meet the needs of the soul—then what does? Hard work perhaps? No, says cynical Solomon, not even that. Moffatt translates our text for today thus: "A man toils on to satisfy his hunger but his wants are never met."

Nothing brings satisfaction to a life where God is absent, not even hard work. Psychologists talk nowadays about A-type personalities, people who are obsessed with work and see their whole identity in terms of what they do. God help us if we see our identity in terms of our accomplishments rather than in being the objects of divine love. What will happen to us when we can't work any more, can't *accomplish*? It's interesting that the word "appetite" in our reading today is the Hebrew word *nephesh*, or "soul." What it is saying is this—the soul can never be satisfied with anything less than God. And, Solomon adds, both the fools and the wise end up in the same place if they do not know God.

If the soul could speak, it would say something like this: "I'm so hungry . . . so thirsty . . . why won't someone give me what I really long for?" And what does the soul long for? God. Far too many Christians try to make their souls work with *things* rather than God. When we get more satisfaction out of the things we do for God, rather than from God Himself, then we are in serious spiritual danger. Nothing fully satisfies the soul. Nothing, that is, apart from God.

FURTHER STUDY

Ps. 38:9;
Isa. 26:9;
Matt. 5:1–11

1. What did both the psalmist and Isaiah recognize?
2. What is the promise to those who hunger and thirst after God?

Prayer

O God my Father, forgive me if I seek my identity in the things I do rather than finding it in who I am. Show me even more clearly than ever that Your estimation of me is not based on my performance but on the fact that I belong to You. Amen.

Stop Arguing!

"... no man can contend with one who is stronger than he." (v. 10)

For reading & meditation—Ecclesiastes 6:10-11

$\mathcal{S}$olomon is "above the sun" now, putting the focus once again on God. "At life's core," says Dr. Larry Crabb, "the real issues are theological issues." When life is brought down to its irreducible minimum, the issue always is—God. What do we make of Him? How does He fit into our lives?

Have you not found that whenever you make sure God is in His place, everything around you falls into place too? You see things from a different perspective. God is sovereign, Solomon is saying here, and the sooner we recognize that the better. A purpose was written into the universe long before we arrived, and though at times it may look as if God is not in control, this is not so. And, he adds, because God is bigger than we are, it is useless to put ourselves in conflict with Him (v. 10). C. S. Lewis put it well when he said in *The Problem of Pain*: "To argue with God is to argue with the very power that makes it possible to argue at all."

How different life would be for us if we would get hold of the fact that God is sovereign and that we are His subjects. God is the Potter; we are the clay. God is omnipotent; we are impotent—relatively speaking, anyway. God is consistent; we are inconsistent. God has a crystal-clear perspective on everything; we more often than not are confused. What is all this saying to us? Arguing against the divine purpose is a waste of time. Better to trust the Almighty; He always knows what He is doing.

FURTHER STUDY

Job 9:1–14;
Isa. 45:9;
Rom. 9:20–21

1. What was Job's reasoning?
2. What question does Paul pose?

Prayer

O God, help me to have confidence in Your confidence. When I don't know what to do, help me see that that is a dilemma You never experience. I draw new strength and encouragement from Your sovereignty and power. Blessed Lord, I love You. Amen.

Accept Your Destiny

"For who knows what is good for a man in life . . . ?" (v. 12)

For reading & meditation—Ecclesiastes 6:12

*I*t doesn't do us any harm to see ourselves set over against the might and omnipotence of God, Solomon has been telling us. We are just a heartbeat away from eternity, and if God were to cause our hearts to stop at this very moment—we would die. We are very vulnerable people, and to try to go against the all-powerful Creator is about as effective as trying to shift the Rock of Gibraltar with a peashooter. Life functions best when we accept the destiny God has for us and close in with it.

This picture of God as all-powerful is not being presented to us (as Derek Tidball points out) in order to bring us to our knees in weak and helpless submission. It is simply a matter of fact, a matter of truth. God is stronger than we are and, for that matter, stronger than anything we might want to put our trust in—wealth and money in particular.

Solomon's last point in this chapter is the fact that we do not know the future, and his message, by implication, is that if we are wise we will get to know the One who knows the future. Knowing God means we come in touch with the only One who can really meet our soul's deepest needs. Contentment does not lie in a large bank balance, status, ambition, material possessions, or earthly success. It comes only when we are in a close relationship with God. Only He can give us the power to enjoy life. We would be wise to build on God, not on gold.

FURTHER STUDY

James 4:13–17;
Prov. 27:1; 19:21

1. What are we to say?
2. How does James describe our lives?

Prayer

O God, help me this day to stand before You with an open heart, an open mind, and an open being.
For I want to be changed not into the image of things, but into the image of You.
I will have no idols in my life. I own You as my only Lord. Amen.

"Better than Chanel No. 5"

"A good name is better than fine perfume . . ." (v. 1)

For reading & meditation—Ecclesiastes 7:1

*W*e are now at the halfway mark of the Book of Ecclesiastes, and one notices immediately a change of perspective. Solomon's cynicism does not altogether disappear, but a new note is being struck which rings out most clearly in this chapter and then continues to the end of the book. That new note is—wisdom. Solomon changes from a narrative to a proverbial style, and its effect is as dramatic as the sun breaking through the clouds on a dark and stormy day. He begins this chapter with a series of seven comparative proverbs, all built around the word *better.*

First, "A good name is *better* than fine perfume." A modern translation of that might read: "A good name is better than Chanel No. 5." A good name means a good character. It has been said that reputation is what others think of us, character is what we are deep down inside. Take care of your character and your reputation will take care of itself.

Second, "the day of death [is] *better* than the day of birth" (v. 1). Is this really so? Ought we to be mourning people's birth and celebrating at their deaths? Solomon seems to be turning life on its head. Why? Because the days that follow our deaths (for those whose hearts are right with God, that is) are more joyous and carefree than those that follow our births. It's good to feel "at home" with those who love us in this life, but much better, as the old hymn puts it, to be "at home with the Lord."

FURTHER STUDY

Prov. 1:1-33;
Ps. 111:10;
Mic. 6:9

1. What happens to those who turn to wisdom?
2. What do fools despise?

 *Prayer*

O God, You are the center of all my values, the center of my life. Can this life die within me? It cannot die any more than You can die. Death is the end of one life and the beginning of a new one.
I rest in glad assurance. Thank You, my Father. Amen.

Wise Advice!

"Do not be quickly provoked in your spirit, for anger resides in the lap of fools." (v. 9)

For reading & meditation—Ecclesiastes 7:2–10

W e continue looking at the rest of Solomon's comparative proverbs. Third, "It is *better* to go to a house of mourning than to go to a house of feasting" (v. 2). Remember, wisdom always sees beneath the surface of things. Solomon means that you are more likely to come face to face with reality in a funeral parlor than a restaurant. And being unwilling to face reality is to be ill-prepared for dealing with life.

Fourth, "Sorrow is *better* than laughter" (v. 3). Really? Yes, really. After a quick laugh, it's amazing how what we laughed about is so easily forgotten. It's not the same, however, with sorrow. Fifth, "It is *better* to heed a wise man's rebuke than to listen to the song of fools" (v. 5). We much prefer to listen to a song that's making its way up the charts than to listen to a rebuke, but in the long run the rebuke will do us the more good.

Sixth, "The end of a matter is *better* than its beginning" (v. 8). The way things end is reality. The whole picture is on display. Fantasies are over; truth is all that can be seen. We ought to learn from that and be more realistic in our projections and aims. Seventh, "Patience is *better* than pride" (v. 8). Are you one of those who prays: "Lord, give me patience . . . and give it to me right now!"? Beneath a patient spirit is a groundswell of wisdom. Pride pushes wisdom aside, and when that happens, then it is easy to play the role of a fool.

FURTHER STUDY

Prov. 2:1–3:35

1. What are we not to let out of our sight?
2. What do the wise inherit?

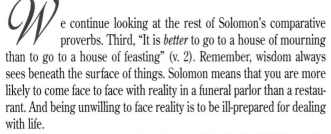

Prayer

My Father and my God, I have gathered some wisdom on my journey through life, but now I pray for the kind of wisdom that is greater and sharper than all earthly wisdom—Your wisdom. Make me a wise person, my Father. In Jesus' Name. Amen.

People of Destiny

"... the advantage of knowledge is this: that wisdom preserves the life of its possessor." (v. 12)

For reading & meditation—Ecclesiastes 7:11-14

Solomon now invites us to look at the benefits and advantages of wisdom. "Wisdom is a shelter," he says (v. 12). It protects us from pitfalls or from entering into foolish schemes and ideas. Wisdom protects us from being overtaken by an unexpected financial crisis, for example, by showing us the importance of "saving for a rainy day." Wisdom tells us that we should make sure our liabilities never exceed our assets; that it is better, whenever possible, to avoid temptation than to confront it; that to harbor resentment is like harboring a snake in your bosom, and so on. If you possess wisdom, then you won't fall apart under pressure. Wisdom won't stop you from experiencing problems, but it will protect you from unnecessary ones.

The second thing Solomon says about wisdom is that it gives us a clearer perspective on life. He asks: "Who can straighten what he has made crooked?" (v. 13). How we wish we could, but sometimes such a thing is beyond us. Wisdom will help us to focus only on the things that can be changed, and not to spend useless time and energy in trying to change the unchangeable. A divine thread of sovereignty runs through our lives, points out Solomon, so whether times are good or bad—be happy. Wisdom enables us to see that everything is under God's control—the up times and the down times, the "in" times and the "out" times. We are not the victims of blind fate or random chance. God is over all things and in control of all things. Thus we are people of destiny.

FURTHER STUDY

Prov. 4:1-27;
Ps. 51:1-19

1. Why are we to get wisdom?
2. What did David link wisdom to?

Prayer

O Father, help me trace Your hand in the whole of my life, not just the "good" bits. May I see that the setbacks as well as the successes are part of Your purpose for me, and thus praise You in everything. "Through good or ill You are with me still." Thank You, dear Father. Amen.

Keep Your Balance!

"The man who fears God will avoid all [extremes]." (v. 18)

For reading & meditation—Ecclesiastes 7:15–18

One perplexing situation for which wisdom and a divine perspective is needed, says Solomon, is when we see the righteous suffer and the wicked prosper. The psalmist struggled with this age-old problem (particularly in Ps. 73), and so have millions since.

A tyrant lives on, while a missionary family on their way to bring help and medical care to others is lost in a plane crash. You can't make sense of that unless you have an unshakable trust in God, and believe that one day (not now) He will answer every question to our satisfaction.

The second issue for which wisdom and a divine perspective is needed is the matter of spiritual balance. "Do not be overrighteous" is Solomon's advice (v. 16). He is thinking here, I believe, of those who (forgive the cliche) are too heavenly minded to be of any earthly good. I know people who think they are head over heels in love with the Lord, but who have no love for others. The apostle John called these people "liars" (1 John 4:20). Super-spirituality is out, says Solomon; it's an extreme. But lest we go to the other extreme he speaks out against this also: "Do not be overwicked" (v. 17). All of us, because of the Fall, have a wicked streak within us, and we should watch that we do not indulge that. He is not saying you can get away with a little wickedness. Far from it. He is saying don't give way to it. Solomon is pleading for moderation. Extremes and excesses are destructive. Keep your balance.

FURTHER STUDY

Pss. 73:1–28; 82:2

1. What conclusion did the psalmist come to?
2. What did he say he would do?

Prayer

O God, teach me how to avoid all excesses and extremes so that I might be a truly balanced Christian.
I would shun overspirituality as I would shun unbridled urges and lusts.
Help me, my Father. In Jesus' Name. Amen.

Wisdom—Only from God

"Whatever wisdom may be, it is far off and most profound—who can discover it?" (v. 24)

For reading & meditation—Ecclesiastes 7:19-24

*W*isdom provides us with an inner strength. That is the point Solomon is making in this passage. One who operates with wisdom possesses more strength than ten city officials. And those who have come up against officialdom and bureaucracy will know that this is some strength! When we have wisdom, we have the inner strength to cope with whatever comes—tensions, stresses, and problems that are not easily resolved.

Solomon goes on to point out, however, that the possession of wisdom does not mean we become popular. You will still get criticized, he tells us, but don't let that throw you. "You may hear your servant cursing you . . . many times you yourself have cursed others" (vv. 21–22). "When people criticize me," a friend told me, "I am thankful they don't know how bad I really am, or they would have much worse to say." As Chuck Swindoll puts it: "Give God thanks that people are just hitting the visible, not the whole truth."

Solomon's next statement about wisdom is: "'I [was] determined to be wise'—but this was beyond me" (v. 23). Solomon found in seeking wisdom that wisdom was not easy to find. Why is that? Because while we have an innate ability to gather knowledge, we cannot be wise without the help of God. Solomon did not make this next statement, but nevertheless, this is what he is saying: "If any of you lacks wisdom, he should ask God, who gives generously to all without finding fault" (James 1:5). You can find knowledge in the world, but wisdom—true wisdom, that is—comes only from God.

**FURTHER
STUDY**

*Job 28:1-28;
Prov. 3:13-14; 8:11*

*1. What are some of the
things Job compares
wisdom to?
2. What conclusion did
Job come to?*

-→===◉ *Prayer* ◉===←-

O God, I bow before You and acknowledge that the wisdom I need to handle life I just haven't got. I fail to see the things I ought to see and value the things I ought to value. Give me Your wisdom, dear Father—heavenly wisdom. In Jesus' Name I ask it. Amen.

What's Scarce?

"... I found one [upright] man among a thousand ..." (v. 28)

For reading & meditation—Ecclesiastes 7:25–29

Wisdom was something very important to Solomon. It was this that he prayed for when God said to him: "Ask for whatever you want me to give you" (1 Kings 3:5). In addition, Solomon had set out to discover all he could about earthly wisdom. When he put all his findings together, he concluded human wisdom was not all it was cracked up to be.

His next remark, one that some would say is extremely sexist, makes the point that while wisdom was elusive, so also was righteousness, and although he had found one righteous man in a thousand, he had not found one righteous woman at all. Does this mean that men are better than women? Of course not. Solomon is just making a comparison which in his culture would not have the connotation it has today. He is using what we call hyperbole—an exaggerated statement made for emphasis. Even if he was saying that men are better than women then, as R. Gordis points out: "When you work out his figures men are only one tenth of one percent better than women."

His real point is seen in verse 29—righteousness is scarce. Why? It's not God's fault, because in the beginning He made humankind pure and upright. But tragedy struck, and through the willful disobedience of Adam and Eve, sin invaded human nature. Our problems are not God's fault, but ours. They are not around us, but within us. We can't blame anyone other than ourselves for our lack of righteousness. The reason we are not righteous is because we don't want to be.

FURTHER STUDY

Jer. 23:1–6;
Pss. 34:15; 37:25; 97:2

1. What are the foundation elements of God's throne?
2. What is one of the Names of God?

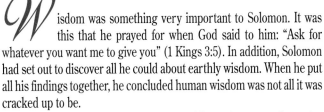

Prayer

Father, I am so thankful that although I cannot find righteousness in myself, I can find it in You. Through Christ's sacrifice for me on Calvary I have righteousness not merely imputed to me, but imparted to me. I am eternally grateful. Amen.

A Self-Portrait

"Who knows the explanation of things? Wisdom brightens a man's face . . ." (v. 1)

For reading & meditation—Ecclesiastes 8:1

A centuries-old saying goes: "Wise men are rarely academics, and academics are rarely wise men." Whether that is true I do not know, but I do know from reading Solomon's writings that wisdom is not something academic; it is designed to have a practical outworking in our lives. Many commentators believe that Solomon is giving us a self-portrait here, and is using himself as an illustration of how wisdom works in the lives of those who have a position of authority over others. In the text before us, two things are said about a wise man in authority: first, he has an understanding of the big picture, and second, he has a cheerful disposition.

First—*seeing the big picture*. Those who are not leaders concentrate on how to bring their skills to bear on the task in front of them—the "how"; those who are leaders, however, concentrate on the wider perspective—the "why." That is why, as someone put it: "the person who knows *how* will usually have a job but that person will usually work for the one who knows *why.*" The follower needs to know how; the leader needs to know why.

Second—*a cheerful disposition*. Nothing is more contagious than cheerfulness. Leaders are more often than not scared people—scared they might not lead well. Thus their faces become stern, hard, unsmiling, and intense. Wisdom, the kind that comes from God, that is, lights up the face. Thus the face more often than not radiates cheerfulness. A face that is always stern is not a face that reflects wisdom.

FURTHER STUDY

Prov. 15:1–33; 17:22; 12:25

1. What does the cheerful heart enjoy?
2. What does a cheerful look do?

Prayer

Father, whether I am a leader or not, give me a face that reflects Your wisdom. I know I am not responsible for the face I started life with, but I am responsible for the face I finish up with. May my face reflect Your face. In Jesus' Name. Amen.

More Leadership Qualities

"As no one is discharged in time of war, so wickedness will not release those who practice it."
(v. 8)

For reading & meditation—Ecclesiastes 8:2–8

We look at another three of Solomon's thoughts on the qualities of a wise leader.

Third—*a high regard for authority.* "Obey the king's command," (v. 2) says Solomon, or in other words, respect whoever is over you in authority. Those who have no respect for those higher than they will never get the respect of those under them. For those under them will sense they are not loyal to the ones above them, and the whole chain of command will be negatively affected. This is a major problem in industry and business today—a problem that could be solved by following Solomon's wise advice.

Fourth—*be willing to ride out the tough times without withdrawing your support* (vv. 3–4). If there are clearly sinful practices going on, that is another issue. But that apart, Solomon is telling us that you can't change authority unless you are higher than it, so the thing to do is to work effectively from beneath. Not by subversive or rebellious attempts, but by applying the fifth quality of leadership—*knowing when and how to appeal* (vv. 5–6). Timing is crucial. Many have ruined situations because they did the right thing but at the wrong time. "The wise heart will know the proper time and procedure" (v. 5).

The final words of this passage (vv. 7–8) remind us that everyone has their limitations, even those in the highest echelons of authority. There's a final bottom line from which all leaders must operate. It is the fact that all of us, bosses included, must one day die.

FURTHER STUDY

Rom. 13:1–6;
Titus 3:1–2

1. What did Paul teach about authority?
2. What are we doing when we rebel against authority?

Prayer

O Father, I see that no matter what position or power I have in life, I can do nothing to redirect the wind or change the fact that one day I will die. May this understanding evoke in me a continuous attitude of deep humility. In Jesus' Name. Amen.

How to Handle Mystery

"... joy will accompany him in his work all the days of [his] life ..." (v. 15)

For reading & meditation—Ecclesiastes 8:9–15

This section begins with a warning for those who are in positions of authority. Those who lord it over others in an unfair way will hurt themselves more than they hurt others. It might feel good to ride roughshod over people's thoughts and feelings, but in the end the one who acts in this way is demeaned as a person. He becomes less of a human being—a consequence every leader ought to work strenuously to avoid.

From here Solomon focuses on several mysteries, things we are all aware of, but for which we have no really clear answers. The first is this—wicked people being praised at their funeral (v. 10). Ever witnessed such a situation? It bothered Solomon so much he called it "meaningless." A second thing that mystified Solomon was why a sentence for a crime is not quickly carried out (v. 11). If Solomon was living in our day when rapists and psychopaths on remand are let out to re-enact their crimes, he would not simply say it is meaningless—he would go berserk.

A third thing that mystified the wise king is something he has mentioned once before—the mystery of how Providence seems to treat the good as though they were wicked and the wicked as though they were good. Solomon's way of dealing with mystery is quite simple: eat, drink, and put your trust in God (v. 15). In other words, continue the routines of life and keep going even though the mysteries remain unsolved. With God we can cope with anything that comes, even though we can't explain it.

FURTHER STUDY

Job 5:1–9; 11:7–9

1. How did Zophar describe the mysteries of God?
2. What's the difference between a mystery and a puzzle?

---✦═◇ Prayer ◇═✦---

Father, I see that if I can take this fact on board then I have one of the greatest keys of life. Help me to still serve You and love You even in the absence of explanations. This I ask in Jesus' Name. Amen.

It's Better to Trust

"Even if a wise man claims he knows, he cannot really comprehend [what goes on under the sun]." (v. 17)

For reading & meditation—Ecclesiastes 8:16–17

The sooner we come to terms with the fact that there are things which happen in life for which there is no adequate explanation, the better we shall be. I have seen people almost drive themselves insane by insisting that God was honor-bound to give them a clear answer or explanation for some dark or difficult situation into which they were plunged.

Now it is not wrong to desire answers from God, but as I have said before, when those desires escalate into a *demand*—we head for trouble. Some things that happen here on earth defy explanation. We must accept that and live with it. Life "under the sun" will always be a puzzle or, as Winston Churchill put it when trying to negotiate with Communist Russia: "a riddle wrapped in a mystery inside an enigma." Just remember that the missing pieces of every puzzle in your life are in the hands of the One who put this universe together in the first place.

Derek Tidball tells the story of a small boy who was bullied by some other boys because they said his father was a Frankenstein who put people to sleep, cut them open, took out parts and put in others. The boy's father, of course, was a surgeon. The little boy, however, was untroubled because he knew and trusted his father and was aware that even though he could not understand why his father did the things he did, he would not be involved in anything that was evil or bad. It is the same with God.

FURTHER STUDY

Isa. 40:1–31;
Rom. 11:33–36

1. What was Israel's complaint?
2. How did Isaiah address it?

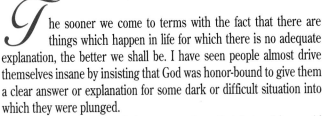

Prayer

O Father, help me drop my anchor into the depths of this reassuring and encouraging revelation—there is a good reason for everything You do. May I trust You even when I cannot trace You. In Jesus' Name I ask it. Amen.

Turning the Corner

"For the living know that they will die, but the dead know nothing ..." (v. 5)

For reading & meditation—Ecclesiastes 9:1–6

*I*n this chapter Solomon focuses our gaze more clearly on the issues that are "above the sun." Four facts that every believer should know and understand are laid out.

The first is *everything is in God's hands* (v. 1). When I think of myself as being in "God's hands" I feel tremendously reassured. Matters may seem out of control to me, but not to Him. It is true, as Solomon says, that "no man knows whether love or hate awaits him" (v. 1). But when we have God, then nothing will ever confront us that He and we can't handle together. The second fact is *the certainty of death* (vv. 2–3). Death is a common destiny for all. But how blessed are those whose goals reach beyond death, and who have a settled and assured eternal future with God. Anyone who lives only for time is a fool.

The third fact is *madness resides in the human spirit* (v. 3). Don't expect too much of humanity and you won't be disappointed. One of the best descriptions of sin I know is *insanity*. It is sheer insanity to think we can run our lives successfully without recourse to God. Yet most of humanity try to do it every day. Utter madness! The last fact is *where there's life there's hope* (vv. 4–6). "A live dog is better off than a dead lion!" says Solomon (v. 4). Why? Because the king of the jungle when dead has no hope. As long as there's life there's a chance dreams can come true, that plans can be realized, but, above all, that one's eternal destiny can be settled.

FURTHER STUDY

Ps. 89:1–13; 98:1;
118:15–16;
1 Pet. 5:6–7

1. What confidence does the psalmist express?
2. What is the exhortation in Peter's Epistle?

Prayer

Father, I see that along with life comes the presence of hope. Help me now, while I am alive, to know for certain that I will spend eternity with You. I yield myself to You today. In Jesus' Name. Amen.

"Go . . . with Gladness"

"Always be clothed in white, and always anoint your head with oil." (v. 8)
For reading & meditation—Ecclesiastes 9:7–10

G o, eat your food with gladness," Solomon says, "and drink your wine with a joyful heart" (v. 7). Hedonists reading these words might think: "Just what I want . . . freedom to go out and indulge myself." But hold on, read the next line: "Always be clothed in white, and always anoint your head with oil" (v. 8). That is a symbolic statement meaning—keep yourself clean. Solomon is not giving us permission to gorge ourselves, but to focus on one day at a time and enjoy every day as it comes. A paraphrase of what he is saying here which might be helpful is this: "The arguments for the meaninglessness of life are powerful—injustice, suffering, sudden death, criminals getting away with murder while the good die in penury and shame. My mind tells me to give up the search for meaning because there isn't any. But as I reflect on God, I find my heart beating again with the hope that I shall spend eternity with Him. Because of that I can go on, eating my food with gladness and drinking my wine with a joyful heart."

Solomon's counsel continues: husbands, enjoy your wives (v. 9). Enjoy, not put up with. You have a wife? Love her. Live it up and have fun in your marriage. Don't wait until you retire to enjoy life. Then Solomon adds: "Whatever your hand finds to do, do it with all your might" (v. 10). The only thing some people throw themselves into is their beds at night—weary, and utterly spent. They don't enjoy life; they simply endure it. You enjoy God; enjoy living too.

FURTHER STUDY

1 Tim. 6:1–21;
3 John 2;
Eph. 6:3

1. Why does God richly provide us with everything?
2. What was John's prayer?

 *Prayer*

Gracious loving heavenly Father, save me from thinking that I must wait until I die before I live. I will live more fully then, but help me to throw myself fully into life in the here and now also.
In Jesus' Name I ask it. Amen.

The Rat Race

". . . time and chance happen to them all." (v. 11)
For reading & meditation—Ecclesiastes 9:11–12

*A*n explanation is necessary for Solomon's reference to death in the verses we read yesterday: "In the grave, where you are going, there is neither working nor planning nor knowledge nor wisdom" (v. 10). Death, to Old Testament saints, was a mystery. They believed in life after death, but they were not sure of the quality of that life. Thus death is often spoken of in negative terms. Only since Christ came and defeated death have we been able to see it in its true perspective. This has to be kept in mind when reading the phrase I have referred to.

In today's section Solomon is concerned that his instruction to enjoy ourselves is not taken too far, and we get caught up in what is often described as "the rat race." "The race is not to the swift," he says, "or the battle to the strong . . ." (v. 11). The philosophy that drives most people nowadays is: if you want to get on, run faster than anyone else. That philosophy is for empty-headed rats, not people. People who love God and want to honor Him will resist that pressure. You can build a good business and be competitive without spending your life in the fast lane.

True success is walking with God. Keep in mind the fact that everything is in God's hands, Solomon once again reminds us. Things happen when you least expect them. Stock markets go down, somebody withholds a payment, and a business collapses. Nothing is certain in this world. God alone knows the end from the beginning—hence the need to put your entire trust in Him.

FURTHER STUDY

*Ps. 1:1–6;
2 Chron. 31:20–21*

1. What is the key to fruitfulness?
2. Why did Hezekiah prosper?

Prayer

Father, I see through new eyes the truth that the strong are not always the strongest, the clever are not always the cleverest. I am challenged to discover a new place of trust in my life. My trust, blessed Father, is in You. All in You. Amen.

A Tale of One City

"The quiet words of the wise are more to be heeded than the shouts of a ruler of fools." (v. 17)

For reading & meditation—Ecclesiastes 9:13–18

Solomon addresses avoiding getting caught in the rat race by putting it in a story. Imagine, he says, a small city with only a few people in it. Suddenly an invading army surrounds the city and besieges it. Inside it is a wise but poor man who comes up with an idea that saves the city. When the city was saved, the poor man was forgotten. The punch line is this: "Wisdom is better than strength" (v. 16). Strength is more impressive than wisdom, but in the long run wisdom is more effective. One writer says of this parable: "It is not a moral tale to show what people should do, but a cautionary tale to show what they are like." People easily forget or overlook the importance of wisdom, and Solomon is reminding us so that we are not surprised when it happens. The way of the world is this—be strong, be smart, be clever, be competitive. But when trouble strikes and people are under threat, they are ready to listen to wise words that get them out of trouble. Then, when the crisis is over, they forget what they heard and go back to being strong again.

Enemy forces surround us. We are under threat. Marriages are crumbling, and the moral ropes that once held us so fast and firm are now frayed or burning. We have a book called the Bible which contains the wisdom the world needs. We must draw more attention to it. People may listen, or they may not, but that is not our responsibility. We must speak so that God can work.

FURTHER STUDY

Josh. 1:8–9;
Pss. 119:1–40; 143:5

1. What was God's success plan for Joshua?
2. In what different ways did the psalmist describe God's Word?

Prayer

Father, I realize that if wisdom is to come through me then it must first reside in me. Make me a man or woman of the Book. May my mind be soaked in the wisdom of Scripture so that, when I speak, my words become Your words. In Christ's Name I ask it. Amen.

The Anatomy of a Fool

"Even as he walks along the road, the fool lacks sense . . ." (v. 3)

For reading & meditation—Ecclesiastes 10:1–3

This chapter offers us the anatomy of a fool. But when you see how a fool behaves, you might begin to think you are surrounded by fools. Remember, however, the old saying that when you point one finger at another person you are pointing three back at yourself.

Didn't our Lord warn us in Matthew 5:22 that we should not call anyone a "fool"? Yes, He did, but when Jesus talked of calling someone a fool, He was using a term which meant a "worthless" person. A person may do some silly things, but that does not make him worthless. No one who has been made in God's image should be called worthless. The Old Testament use of the word *fool* refers to someone who prefers going against the universe to going with it. Folly, points out Solomon in the opening verse of this chapter, is like dead flies in a costly perfume. A lot of extremely precious liquid is ruined by a very small thing. How many people do you know whose lives and reputations have been torn apart by just one foolish act of indiscretion? Fools are careless.

Then hear this, says Solomon—the wise go to the right, the foolish go to the left (v. 2). The text refers to walking in the right direction. You can spot a fool, Solomon tells us, as he walks down the street. It cannot be hidden. Fools have no sense. And everyone can see it.

FURTHER STUDY

2 Tim. 3:1–9;
Jer. 4:22;
1 Cor. 3:19

1. What did Paul point out to Timothy?
2. Why did God pronounce His people fools?

Prayer

Gracious God and loving heavenly Father, pour into my heart the wisdom that overcomes all folly, and enable me, I pray, to avoid the carelessness and senselessness that characterizes a fool. This I ask in Christ's peerless and precious Name. Amen.

Don't Take the Huff

"Fools are put in many high positions, while the rich occupy the low ones." (v. 6)
For reading & meditation—Ecclesiastes 10:4–7

A further characteristic of a fool, says Solomon, is that he cannot control his anger. If a boss is hot-headed then don't react in the same way, he instructs us (v. 4). A fool quits his job in a fit of temper, but a wise man remains calm. How many people reading these lines, I wonder, look back to difficulties that could have been avoided if only they had learned not to take the huff.

Solomon goes on to identify a problem that all of us have seen from time to time. It is the problem caused by putting a foolish and incompetent person in authority, who then, in turn, lords it over the ones who really ought to be in charge. "I've seen this evil," admits Solomon, and so, I am sure, have you too. The better qualified are put down, kept down, and mismanaged. Sadly I say it, but it is to be seen also in some parts of the Christian church.

Dr. Kenneth Gangel points out in his book *Thus Spake Qoheleth* ("Qoheleth" is a pseudonym for Solomon): "Certainly we see things every day in our own country and around the world which make us wonder whether there is a great deal more of foolishness than wisdom in every human government. Maybe God just wants us to see how foolish we are and how useless it is to trust in the vanities of mankind 'under the sun'." However much we might dislike it, the reality is this— fools cannot always be kept at a level where it is impossible for them to do much harm.

FURTHER STUDY

Luke 11:37–53;
Ps. 53:1;
Prov. 28:26

1. Why did Jesus call the Pharisees foolish people?
2. What is at the heart of a fool?

Prayer

O God, perhaps it is true, as is often said, that we get the government we deserve. Can it be that we are more party-political than prayerful over matters, and because of this we sometimes elect the wrong people. Forgive us. In Jesus' Name. Amen.

"Poetic Justice"

". . . skill will bring success." (v. 10)
For reading & meditation—Ecclesiastes 10:8–11

We begin a section now that most commentators regard as baffling and bewildering. Several dangerous activities are identified. In all of these, says Solomon, watch out because you can get hurt. Solomon uses graphic language to drive home the point that fools can't see further than their noses. They go blindly on and see only what they want to see—thus they come to grievous harm. Fools don't see danger, and it is these words of Solomon, I understand, which gave rise to the saying: "Fools rush in where angels fear to tread."

A "fool" digs a pit for someone to fall into, and falls into it himself. A "fool" breaks through a wall, and gets bitten by a serpent. A "fool" quarries stones and doesn't take proper precautions, so he gets hurt by the loose ones that fall on him. A "fool" splits logs without taking enough care, and an accident occurs. A "fool" wields an axe which doesn't have a sharp edge, and finishes up using more strength than he needed to. A "fool" handles a snake before it is charmed and it bites people, so he makes no profit because people avoid him. Such mishaps need not happen in any of these activities, Solomon is saying, if people operated from wisdom rather than foolishness.

A phrase that is often used to describe the situations Solomon has listed above is "poetic justice"—people get what they deserve. Fools, of course, do not understand this. They continue to live their lives doing foolish things, using and abusing people, and end up losers in the process. When will they learn?

FURTHER STUDY

Prov. 14:1–35; 12:23; 18:2; 20:3

1. List some of the contrasts between a wise and a foolish person.
2. How does your own life measure up?

--- *Prayer* ---

O Father, day by day it has become clearer and clearer that we cannot get through this life successfully without wisdom. And the best wisdom is Your wisdom. Again I pray, fill my heart and mind with the wisdom that comes from above. In Jesus' Name I ask it. Amen.

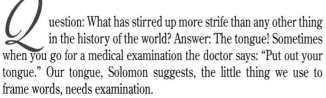

Put Out Your Tongue!

"At the beginning his words are folly; at the end they are wicked madness—" (v. 13)
For reading & meditation—Ecclesiastes 10:12-15

Question: What has stirred up more strife than any other thing in the history of the world? Answer: The tongue! Sometimes when you go for a medical examination the doctor says: "Put out your tongue." Our tongue, Solomon suggests, the little thing we use to frame words, needs examination.

Whereas the words of a wise man are gracious, Solomon tells us, the words of a fool consume him. The one who suffers the most consequences in life is the fool, not those he offends. The fool is "consumed" (v. 12). Strong word. It really means to be "swallowed up." The fool is the one who finishes up in difficulty, in police court, or even in prison. He speaks words that lead to his own undoing. Early in my ministry I learned to differentiate between people who are naive or silly and those who are just plain "fools." I learned also not to spend time trying to counsel a fool, but I would give all the time I could to help those who really wanted to be helped. Listen to this: "No one knows what is coming—who can tell him what will happen after him?" (v. 14). Those of you who are parents will, I imagine, have used similar words: "If you keep acting like that there's no telling where you will end up."

Then, continues Solomon, fools exhaust themselves by their inefficiency (v. 15). They can't even find their way to town or get from here to there. And it's not a matter of IQ. It is just plain stupidity. Fools are ever learning but never arriving.

FURTHER STUDY

Ps. 34:1–22;
Prov. 13:3;
James 1:26

1. What is the admonition of the psalmist?
2. When is our religion worthless?

Prayer

O Father, save me, I pray, from having the tongue of a fool. May my words be Your words, coming from thoughts that are Your thoughts. And help me not simply to learn, but to arrive.
In Jesus' Name I ask it. Amen.

"A Little Bird Told Me"

"Do not revile the king . . . because a bird of the air may carry your words . . ." (v. 20)

For reading & meditation—Ecclesiastes 10:16–20

*S*olomon draws attention to the picture of a land governed by an immature king. The NIV says "servant" (v. 16), but the real thought here is of immaturity. Moffatt translates verse 16: "Woe betide you, O land, when your king is a mere boy." In other words, woe betide you, O land, when you have a fool on the throne. In Isaiah 3:1–5 God predicted that if Israel did not listen to His word then mere children would govern them. In due course, that is what happened. Solomon's point is this—when foolishness in on the throne then chaos and disorder reign.

In verse 18 Solomon returns abruptly to the characteristics of a fool. Fools are senseless people, he points out once again (v. 18). Above them are sagging rafters and a leaky roof, brought about by idleness and procrastination. In such a situation fools talk a lot, and say things such as, "Money is the answer for everything," but wise people know it is not. Money helps, but responsible living is where the real answer lies. Just talking about things will not make them improve.

In fact, as verse 20 shows, mere talk can make matters worse. The saying "A little bird told me" comes from this very Scripture. Be careful how you talk about a fool, Solomon is warning, because the fool will surely find out what you have been saying about him. Then watch out! He will come at you with both guns blazing! So when dealing with a fool, take heed to Solomon's warning. Learn to keep things to yourself. Fools can be dangerous to your health.

FURTHER STUDY

Prov. 19:1–29; 6:6–11; 18:9; 24:30–34

1. What does a sluggard do?
2. What does Solomon recommend to the sluggard?

Prayer

O Father, help me discern the difference between what Your Word describes as a "fool" and a person who is simply naive or immature. I need this discernment if I am to relate to people in the way that honors and glorifies You. In Jesus' Name. Amen.

Be Generous!

"Give portions to seven, yes to eight . . ." (v. 2)
For reading & meditation—Ecclesiastes 11:1–2

S olomon's cynicism almost completely dissolves as we step into these last chapters. If you are like me, you are probably saying to yourself: "And not before time!"

He begins this chapter with a well-known saying: "Cast your bread upon the waters, for after many days you will find it again" (v. 1). What Solomon is conveying in these words is this: "Be generous, share yourself with others." I like Charles Swindoll's paraphrase of this verse, which reads thus: "Don't put the bread in the deep freeze—it'll dry out. Release it." The main thought underlying this statement is not simply to give, but to give boldly, enthusiastically, and energetically.

Are you bold in generosity? It is not the giving of money that is being emphasized here (although that is part of it), but the giving of oneself. When we give of ourselves generously we do not lose, for in this universe things have a way of coming back to us—both good and evil. Suppose the little boy had refused to let Jesus have the five loaves and two fishes, saying they were his and he would not let them go? He would have missed becoming the most famous little boy in history. The phrase "give portions to seven, yes to eight" is similar to our modern saying: "Give to the nth degree." It means throw away your calculators and clipboards. Give without measure. You never know when disaster is going to strike, so do your giving while you have the chance. God has opened Himself to us—generously. Ought we not to do the same to others?

FURTHER STUDY

*2 Cor. 9:1–11;
Prov. 25:21; 11:25*

1. What did Paul commend the Corinthians for?
2. What does God love?

Prayer

O God, help me to give of myself boldly, energetically, and enthusiastically. From now on I shall be the channel and not the stopping place of all Your generosity to me. In Jesus' Name I promise it. Amen.

Choose Life!

"Whoever watches the wind will not plant; whoever looks at the clouds will not reap." (v. 4)

For reading & meditation—Ecclesiastes 11:3-4

The verses before us today bring home to us our powerlessness to change certain things. Like the weather, for instance. When clouds are full of rain they drench the earth, says Solomon.

There is simply no point in focusing on the things that are unchangeable. Far better to get on with living and work at changing the things that can be changed. A sign on a rough road somewhere in northern Canada reads: "Choose your rut carefully. You'll be in it for the next 200 miles." Solomon's advice is that we should do everything in our power to stay out of ruts.

How many of you are stuck in ruts and have settled for a drab, predictable life when you could be using your God-given creativity to explore new things? Don't just drift through life—pursue it. Instead of thinking about the predictable things of life and giving all your attention to those, turn your gaze to new activities and new ideas. If you have retired, then come out of retirement. I don't mean go back to doing what you used to do, but take up new interests. Study for a degree, start helping a group of some sort to do something. You won't have the same energy that you had when you were forty, of course, but don't stop being creative. Don't get into a rut. William Gladstone, four times prime minister of Britain, was eighty-three when he was last appointed. Shame on you that you stand around and just watch the wind. Don't drift like a lazy cloud. Pursue something new and beautiful for God.

FURTHER STUDY

Deut. 30:1–20;
Josh. 24:15;
1 Kings 18:21

1. What challenge did Moses put before the people?
2. Is God putting any challenges before you?

⤜⇒ Prayer ⇐⤛

O God, forgive me that I spend so much time worrying about such things as whether it's going to rain or shine, instead of pursuing new things and new purposes. I'm through with all that, dear Lord. I'm choosing life. In Jesus' Name. Amen.

"Do Not Disturb!"

"... you cannot understand the work of God, the Maker of all things." (v. 5)

For reading & meditation—Ecclesiastes 11:5–6

*T*here are some things in life that, try as we might, we will never fully understand. This is Solomon's point in the verses before us today. We don't know which course the wind will take, or how bones are formed in a tiny fetus, but it happens anyway. And why? Because God is at work in everything, and the best thing we can do is trust Him. Modern-day science has cleared up many of the things that were mysteries to the people who lived thousands of years ago, but we are still faced with a good many unexplained phenomena. However, whether mysteries can be explained or not—we must carry on living.

"Sow in the morning and don't be idle in the evening" is Solomon's next word. He is not saying, of course, that we ought to work all through the day, or that it is wrong to have a time of leisure and relaxation; rather, he is pointing out the benefits of having other interests besides work. There is something wrong in the lives of those who, having finished their day's work, hang a sign on the door of their lives that says: "Do Not Disturb." If, after your day's work, you are too tired to focus on something else then perhaps you ought to re-evaluate your whole lifestyle. It's easy for me to tell you that because I've just done it myself. And I feel much better for it. Solomon's advice came to me at a crucial moment in my life, and unless I'm mistaken, today is going to be crucial and challenging for some of you too.

FURTHER STUDY

Col. 4:1–6;
Eph. 5:18

1. For what did Paul admonish the Colossians?
2. What does a drunk man do?

⟶ *Prayer* ⟵

O God, help me today to take a prayerful and careful look at my lifestyle. Am I really living—or just going through one dreary day after another? Teach me how to pursue life, not have it pursuing me. In Jesus' Name. Amen.

119

Day 115

It's Great to Be Alive!

"However many years a man may live, let him enjoy them all." (v. 8)
For reading & meditation—Ecclesiastes 11:7-9

D o you need permission to enjoy life? Then Solomon gives it to you in these verses. I love the Moffatt translation of verse 7, which reads thus: "Sweet is the light of life and pleasant is it for the eyes to see the sun." While Solomon is clearly talking about natural light, these words are also symbolic. God is often spoken of in terms of light. "The LORD is my light and my salvation—whom shall I fear?" (Ps. 27:1) is just one example. The light of God's love is ever present, and it is good for us to focus on it as often as we can.

The joy of living, Solomon continues, ought to permeate every period of our lives, right up to old age. "If a man lives many years, let him have joy throughout them all" (v. 8, Moffatt). This is not to ignore the fact, of course, that many have had some pretty rough experiences in life but with good Christian counseling these can be overcome. Indeed, Solomon recommends remembering the days of darkness, for when you experience the light and love of God you can look back at painful events without the loss of your soul. You are pained by the memories of them, but not overwhelmed. In fact, the dark days throw into even greater relief the brightness of the joy that comes from God.

The main theme of these two verses really is this—enjoy life now, not later. Don't miss enjoying life with God in the here and now also. Whatever your age, remember it's great just to be alive. Enjoy it!

FURTHER STUDY

Rom. 14:1-17;
Ps. 126:5;
Isa. 12:3;
Jer. 15:16

1. How does Paul define the kingdom of God?
2. Where did Jeremiah find his source of joy?

Prayer

O Father, I am thankful that whatever age I am, You lift the gloom and take the stinging pain of depression out of life. Help me focus more on the warmth and light of Your love than on the darkness of circumstances. In Jesus' Name I pray. Amen.

Have a Great Childhood

"... let your heart give you joy in the days of your youth." (v. 9)

For reading & meditation—Ecclesiastes 11:9–10

Solomon's final comments in this chapter are aimed at the young. Enjoy your days one by one, he is saying, because before you know it, you will be an adult.

The words that come next have sent some Christians into apoplexy: "Follow the ways of your heart and whatever your eyes see ..." (v. 9). I remember a youth leader in a church I pastored who set out to teach the Book of Ecclesiastes to the young people. But he deliberately left out these words. When I asked him why, he said: "That's bad advice for young people. They are inclined that way already so I thought it best not to draw attention to it." I drew his attention to the words that follow: "but know that for all these things God will bring you to judgment." This is what Solomon is really saying: "Relax and have a super time when you are young. There will be many impulses and many things that appeal to your eyes. Follow them, but keep in mind there will be a day of accountability. So don't let your impulses go wild."

Some believe that warning takes the joy out of living, but it shouldn't. If we ignore the God to whom we must all answer, then we leave ourselves open to experiencing not life but unrestricted liberty. And that kind of freedom is bad for us. So banish all worries, Solomon tells the young, and avoid those things that bring pain to your body. Young person, you are only young once. Stay close to God and you'll get the most out of it.

FURTHER STUDY

2 Tim. 2:14–22;
Ps. 103:1–5

1. What was Paul's advice to Timothy?
2. What is our youth renewed like?

Prayer

Thank you, my Father, for reminding me that there is no freedom without limitations. Help me see the wisdom that lies behind Your restrictions, and enables me to trust You and follow You all the days of my life. In Christ's Name I ask it. Amen.

No Greater Joy

"Remember your Creator in the days of your youth, before the days of trouble come . . ." (v. 1)

For reading & meditation—Ecclesiastes 12:1

*A*t long last we are introduced in the most clear terms to the only one who can give life meaning—God. Some people need to feel and experience the utter futility of trying to quench the deep thirsts of their souls in any other way but in God.

An Hasidic story tells of a man who went for a walk in a forest and got lost. He wandered around for hours attempting to find his way back home. Suddenly he came across another traveler who was also lost, and together they sat down to discuss what they could do. "I know," said one, "let's tell each other what paths we have tried and then it will be that much easier to find our way out." They did, and within a few hours both emerged safely from the forest. This is how many people find God—they try one meaningless path after another until, in the end, they find the Way.

The point Solomon makes in the verse before us today is that the best time to know God is when one is young. It is perilously possible that if the opportunity to open one's heart to God is not taken in youth, then procrastination can build strong resistance into the soul that makes it difficult (though not impossible) to respond in later life. I gave my life to God when I was in my midteens. Now, many years later, I thrill to the thought that not only have I known Him, but I have had the privilege of serving Him also. Believe me, there can be no greater joy.

FURTHER STUDY

2 Tim. 3:10–17;
Prov. 23:26; 8:32–36

1. What did Paul say of Timothy?
2. What is wisdom's call?

Prayer

O Father, I can testify to that too—there is no greater joy than knowing You and serving You. And as long as I am on this earth, may the wonder of both these privileges increase and abound. In Jesus' Name I pray. Amen.

The Plus of the Spirit

"... those looking through the windows grow dim ..." (v. 3)

For reading & meditation—Ecclesiastes 12:2–4

We are now drawn into a vivid picture of very old age. Solomon's purpose is to point out the advantages of serving God while young, and to convince us of his counsel to remember our Creator in the days of our youth. We can serve God in old age (as we have seen), but the reality is that very old age slows us down somewhat and we can't give as much energy to the work of God as we once did.

Verse 2 talks about mental aging. The sun and the light, which are symbols here of clarity and sharpness, recede, and darkness begins to descend on the mind. Verse 3 focuses on physical deterioration when "the keepers of the house tremble." It is thought that the words "keepers of the house" refers to our limbs which in very old age begin to tremble and become weak. We are left, also, with few teeth (at least of our own), and this is what is thought to lie behind the expression "when the grinders cease because they are few." Verse 3 speaks of the eyes growing dim, and verse 4 speaks of being shut in and of enforced inactivity: "the doors to the street are closed." The latter part of the verse reminds us that even sleep becomes difficult for those who are old. Some suffer a double denial—sleeplessness and deafness. Young people find it difficult to believe that is the way they will be one day (if, of course, they live long enough), but that is the reality. Therefore, young people, give God your best—while you can.

FURTHER STUDY

Mark 10:13–16;
Ps. 27:10;
Prov. 8:17

1. What did Jesus say to His disciples?
2. What was David's confidence?

 *Prayer*

Father, I know I have to face reality, but I know too that the touch of Your Spirit can be upon me when I grow old. Sustain me through all the years of my life so that I might know the plus of Your Spirit as well as the plus of the years. Amen.

Knowing How to Die

"Remember him—before the silver cord is severed . . ." (v. 6)
For reading & meditation—Ecclesiastes 12:5–8

C an you handle another day focusing on the characteristics of
old age? Remember the ability to face reality is one of the evidences of mental health! You don't have to dwell on the facts as they
relate to old age, but you do have to face them. That is all Solomon is
saying.

Four more characteristics are given in verse 5. First, fear—fear of
heights and being out in busy streets. Second, the appearance of gray
hair. Clearly, the phrase "the almond tree blossoms" is a reference to a
head of silver hair. Third, the difficulty of walking—"the grasshopper
drags himself along." One has a picture here of walking frames or walking sticks. As you know, it takes old people a little longer to get where
they want to go! Fourth, the waning of the sex drive. In verse 6
Solomon returns to the point he made in the opening verse of the chapter—remember Him. Remember God, he reminds us, before "the silver cord is severed, or the golden bowl is broken." These graphic word
pictures (and the ones that follow) all point to death.

Now to stop just there would be gloomy indeed, but Solomon gives
us something to lift our hearts: "the spirit returns to God who gave it"
(v. 7). Death, to those who love God, is not the end, but the beginning;
the majestic commencement of what life is all about—union with God.
To those who do not know God, however, death is a transition from
emptiness to even greater emptiness (v. 8). Those who know how to
live know also how to die.

**FURTHER
STUDY**

*1 Cor. 15:1–58;
Isa. 52:8;
2 Tim. 1:10;
Rev. 21:4*

*1. What is the victors'
shout?
2. Therefore what are
we to do?*

Prayer

O God, I am so thankful for the victory that Christ wrought for me over the grave. He "brought life and
immortality to light through the gospel." Help me to live in that victory from one day to another.
In Jesus' Name I ask it. Amen.

The Marks of a Preacher

"The Teacher searched to find just the right words . . ." (v. 10)

For reading & meditation—Ecclesiastes 12:9–10

*I*n these last few verses Solomon moves into a brief autobiographical section. These are a wise man's studied reflections and conclusions. The Preacher tells us what a preacher should be like. There are five characteristics.

First and foremost a preacher should be wise. He gets this wisdom not from his years, but from his communication with God. Second, he should be able to impart knowledge to others—help them understand the principles on which a godly life is built. Third, he must ponder things, reflect on them, and search them out. Fourth, he must then set those things in a logical order. In doing this he must pay particular attention to the use of proverbs, says Solomon—something we seem to miss out on in this day and generation. One Christian writer says: "Ours may be the first generation in civilized times that has not raised its young on proverbs." A sad comment, don't you think?

Fifth, a preacher should be able to search out and use the right words. A preacher depends on the Holy Spirit, of course, but he needs words to make his meaning clear. And not just words, but the right words. "The difference between the right word and the almost right word," said Mark Twain, "is the difference between a lightning flash and a firefly." The words of a good preacher are like windows through which the light of truth shines. Undoubtedly, Solomon exemplified all five of these characteristics. Would that there were more like him in the community of God's people today.

FURTHER STUDY

1 Cor. 1:1–23;
Rom. 1:15;
1 Cor. 9:16;
2 Cor. 10:16

1. What was Paul eager to do?
2. How did he work to do it?

Prayer

My Father and my God, give us more preachers, we pray, who know You and who know their craft. Work by Your Spirit in the hearts of those You have called to preach, so that the next generation might not be failed. In Jesus' Name we ask it. Amen.

Improving Our Adjectives

"The words of the wise are like goads, their collected sayings like firmly embedded nails . . ." (v. 11)

For reading & meditation—Ecclesiastes 12:11

Living as he did in an agricultural community, it is easy to see why Solomon likens words to goads. A goad is a long stick with an iron point that is jabbed against the tough hindquarters of an animal to make it increase its speed. Words motivate and urge us to action.

The New Living translation used a different picture to illustrate the same point: "A wise teacher's words spur students to action and emphasize important truths. The collected sayings of the wise are like guidance from a shepherd." Isn't this how Solomon used words?

Words and wise sayings are also like firmly embedded nails, says Solomon. Even that very phrase catches hold of the imagination. It recalls for me a vivid phrase I once heard Sir Winston Churchill use of one of his generals. "He reminds me," he said, "of an iron peg hammered into the frozen ground—firm, solid, immovable." And here's a personal confession—one of the reasons why I use so much alliteration (words with the same initial sound) is to help you remember them. This for example: "Eat enough to keep you fit and not enough to make you fat." I know people remember these statements because they sometimes quote them back to me. We must use the best and the most precise words we can when talking about Christ, remembering all the time, as C. S. Lewis said, that we are just adjectives striving to point others to the Noun. "And for people to believe that Noun," he added, "we must improve our adjectives."

FURTHER STUDY

Ps. 19:1-14;
Prov. 16:24

1. What was David's prayer?
2. What is the result of pleasant words?

Prayer

O Father, help me understand that it is not increasing my vocabulary that You are after, but doing the best with what I already have. You deserve nothing but the best. May I therefore be the best I can be. In Jesus' Name. Amen.

A Person of the Book

"Be warned, my son, of anything in addition to them." (v. 12)

For reading & meditation—Ecclesiastes 12:12

Solomon seems to have held off counseling his son until now. First, he counsels his son not to put too much trust in words or books that go beyond the Scriptures. I think Moffatt best captures the thought of Solomon in his translation of this verse: "My son, avoid anything beyond the scriptures of wisdom; there is no end to the buying of books, and to study books closely is a weariness to the flesh." The trouble with books is that you have to read a lot to get a little. That is not the same, however, with the Scriptures. "All scripture," said Paul to Timothy, "is inspired by God and profitable . . ." (2 Tim. 3:16, RSV). If we were to spend as much time in the Bible as we do in books about the Bible, we might be better off spiritually. Solomon is not saying that we ought to read nothing but the Scriptures; rather that we ought to make the study of the Scriptures our top priority.

In my time I have studied many subjects—psychology, sociology, communication, and so on. I found many of these subjects tiresome. The same cannot be said of Scripture, however. When I open the Book of books, the Bible, I come to it with an enthusiasm, an eagerness, and an expectancy that is not there with any other book. I hope you share that experience. *Every Day Light* may help you with your daily devotions (pray that it does), but don't let it take the place of Scripture in your life. I would be heartbroken if I thought it did.

FURTHER STUDY

*Josh. 1:1–8;
2 Kings 22:1–20*

1. What was God's command to Joshua?
2. Why did the king tear his robes?

Prayer

O God my Father, while I am thankful for all the books that help me learn of You and know about You, help me never to put these ahead of Your Word, the Bible, but always behind it. Make me a person of the Book. In Jesus' Name. Amen.

127

The End of the Search

"For God will bring every deed into judgment . . . whether it is good or evil." (v. 14)

For reading & meditation—Ecclesiastes 12:13–14

*T*oday our exploration of Ecclesiastes comes to an end. We have traveled with Solomon over many roads, and have listened to a wide variety of reflections. The world does not have the resources to meet the needs of the soul, he has been saying, and any attempt to try to find meaning in life apart from God is utterly futile. Meaning comes only when we attach ourselves to God.

It all boils down to this, is his penultimate statement—"Fear God and keep his commandments" (v. 13). To "fear God" means we must reverence Him and put Him first. To "keep his commandments" means we obey Him whether we feel like it or not. Some see Solomon's concluding words as an anticlimax. No graphic word picture, no impressive or catchy sayings. But then this is the art of evangelism. Winning souls does not mean forcing the gospel down people's throats, but going with them down one road after another and showing them that this is not where life is found, then quietly bringing them back without fuss to the inescapable conclusion that the one true reality is God.

Solomon's last statement is simple yet quite staggering: "God will bring every deed into judgment . . . whether it is good or evil." Why such a solemn note to end? Because we can't live irresponsibly and get away with it. We can't buck the universe. God always has the last word. How do we sum up the message of Ecclesiastes? Like this: fear God and serve Him because one day you are going to stand before Him. I'm ready. Are you?

FURTHER STUDY

2 Cor. 5:1–10;
Jer. 17:10;
Matt. 16:27;
1 Pet. 1:17

1. How are we to live
our lives?
2. What are we to make
our goal?

Prayer

My Father and my God, if I am not ready then let Your Spirit be in my heart, and help me make the decision
to turn my life over to You today. I do so now in humble repentance and simple trust.
Take me, cleanse me, and make me Your child. In Jesus' Name I ask it. Amen.

DEUTERONOMY 11:11

Section Three
The Twenty-Third Psalm

The Twenty-Third Psalm

Selwyn Hughes writes that the Twenty-third Psalm towers over the others like Mt. Everest. The visual imagery in that comparison captures the majesty and importance of King David's words. David was a man of action who spoke plainly and from the heart. This psalm is a masterpiece of simplicity and clarity, just like a lone mountain peak shimmering in the clear air of a winter sunrise or a field of bluebonnets in the Texas hill country not far from where Larry Dyke lives.

Many children memorize this psalm in Sunday school before they are even old enough to read it. It was the first chapter of the Bible that they really felt inside of them. Along with a couple of other passages—the first few verses of Genesis and John 3:16—the Twenty-third Psalm is more familiar than any other writing in the world. Yet after all these years we never get tired of it. Every time we run across it, or turn to it during our devotional times, it is as fresh and refreshing as it was the week before, or last year, or twenty years ago. We all change a little every day. We're all different people every time we encounter this text, and it helps us understand God's love for us and His provision for us in a new way.

Great painters put some special creative spark in their work that makes us want to look at it again and again. Most people have seen photographs of the Sistine Chapel and the Mona Lisa and van Gough's swirling stars hundreds and hundreds of times. The artwork itself doesn't change, but as we change it says something to us that we didn't hear before. Dyke goes back to Cumberland Falls in Kentucky time and time again. The falls are just the same, but he sees them differently. Every time he paints them, he paints them differently. Like this psalm, no matter how familiar they are to him, he never tires of them because they always show him something new.

The message of the Twenty-third Psalm is timeless and all-embracing. As Hughes says, it turns stumbling blocks into stepping stones. It reminds us that no matter what our life is like at the moment, God is watching over us as a shepherd watches over his sheep—familiar, welcoming, every vigilant, meeting every need with patience and love.

L.G.G.

"A Nightingale among Birds"

"The LORD is my shepherd . . ." (v. 1, RSV)
For reading & meditation—Psalm 23:1–6

We begin today a phrase-by-phrase exposition of one of the most beautiful and best-loved passages in the whole of God's Word—*The Twenty-third Psalm*. This serene and sacred psalm towers over the others as does Mount Everest over the Himalayas. The great preacher C. H. Spurgeon said of it: "What the nightingale is among birds, this psalm is among others; it has sung sweetly in the ear of many a dejected soul, and in the night of his weeping has given him hope for a morning of joy."

Commentators believe that this psalm was written during the time when David's son Absalom rebelled against him, causing him to flee into the wilderness of Judea. Outlawed and hunted, David solaced himself with images drawn from his more peaceful days as a shepherd.

Psalm 23 is a passage that particularly speaks to people who, like David, are experiencing a major upheaval in life. Do you feel let down by someone who has been extremely close to you? Have the skies suddenly become overcast and gray? Then this psalm is for you. Begin today by memorizing it and repeating it out loud to yourself. Roll every word around on the tip of your spiritual tongue and suck every precious drop of refreshment from it. Let it lie upon your mind until you feel its peace and serenity invading and penetrating every cell of your being. I promise you that if, day by day, you will make the effort to absorb the truths that lie buried in this matchless psalm, you will never again be overwhelmed by life's difficulties and problems.

FURTHER STUDY

Pss. 3:1–8; 30:1–12;
42:5

1. What is the psalmist's testimony?
2. What is his response?

Prayer

Gracious and loving Father, I am so grateful that Your Word is tailor-made to meet my every need.
Day by day, make this psalm come alive in a way that I have never known before.
For Your own dear Name's sake. Amen.

Putting Problems in Context

"For who is God besides the LORD? And who is the Rock except our God?" (v. 31)

For reading & meditation—Psalm 18:1–50

*P*salm 23 has a special application to people who, like David, are experiencing a major upheaval in life. David begins by putting his problems in their proper context—he focuses his gaze directly upon God: "*the LORD is my shepherd.*" Have you learned yet how to get your spiritual focus right when caught up in a crisis? If you don't immediately bring God into the problem, then you have no proper frame of reference. Someone has said, "If we haven't that within us which is above us, we will soon yield to that which is around us."

I feel immensely sorry for those who do not know God and have to face their troubles alone. An agnostic professor spoke for all who share his agnosticism when he wrote: "I am not sure whether my doings have anything cosmic at the back of them, whether I am working with anything significant, or just working meaninglessly alone, with no one to back my work or care." No wonder someone described both agnostics and atheists as "people who have no invisible means of support."

How different even desperate situations look when God is brought into the picture. Instead of being tossed about on wave after wave of inane existence, we have a star by which we can steer our boat—and a safe and certain harbor. David puts his problems in the right context by saying, "Look at who my Shepherd is—the Lord of glory!" When we pause in the midst of our problems to reflect on *who* is guiding us, we will say, like David: "The Lord! *He* is my Shepherd."

**FURTHER
STUDY**

*Isa. 26:1–9;
Pss. 37:5; 118:8*

1. What is part of the
process of learning
to trust?
2. What results from trust
in God?

Prayer

O Father, teach me more about the art of putting my problems in the proper context by immediately bringing
You into the situation. It seems amazingly simple. Help me not to complicate it by my unbelief.
For Jesus' sake. Amen.

Hearsay — or Heartsay?

"'Come now, let us reason together,' says the Lord . . ." (v. 18)

For reading & meditation—Isaiah 1:10–20

*D*avid goes on to focus on his relationship with God: the Lord is my Shepherd. Obviously David has no doubts about his personal relationship with the divine Shepherd, and is thrilled to belong to Him. Permit me to ask: do you know the Lord in an intimate way? Can you say, as did David: the Lord is my Shepherd?

Perhaps one of the saddest situations in life is to hear so many who recite the Twenty-third Psalm, yet have no personal relationship with the one of whom it so tenderly speaks. A great actor was once asked to recite something in a small social gathering, and he decided upon Psalm 23. He recited the words with perfect diction and tone, and his performance was followed by great applause. An old minister who was present asked if he, too, could be permitted to recite the same psalm. Although it soon became obvious that he lacked the skill and professionalism of the actor, and though he stumbled and faltered over some of the words, there was not a dry eye in the audience by the time he had finished.

Someone who was there described the difference in the audience's reactions in this way: "The actor knew the psalm, but the minister knew the Shepherd. "So I ask you again: do you really belong to Him? Do you live under His daily direction and control? Knowing the psalm is one thing—hearsay—but knowing the Shepherd is quite another—heartsay. If you do not know Him in this personal way, then I urge you—surrender your life to Him this very moment.

FURTHER STUDY

Phil. 3:1–14;
Heb. 8:11;
1 John 2:3

1. What was Paul's great desire?
2. What is the main goal of your life?

Prayer

O God, I see that we all stand before You with one need that is above all others—the need to know You personally. I am grateful that You are throwing open to me the gates of eternal life. I acknowledge my sin, humbly repent of it and enter in—now. Amen.

Our Primary View of Him

"Hear us, O Shepherd of Israel, you who lead Joseph like a flock . . ." (v. 1)
For reading & meditation—Psalm 80:1–19

Why did David choose to think of God as his Shepherd? The picture of God we carry deep in our hearts is the one we relate to whenever we find ourselves surrounded by trouble or difficulties. But perhaps what is more important is this—we will interpret every event of our lives in accordance with the inner picture that we have of Him.

I have referred before to the fact that, when I have asked people during counseling to describe to me their *primary* view of God, I have been surprised that so often they see Him, not as a loving Shepherd but as an austere and stern Judge. God *is* a Judge, of course—as David discovered when he committed adultery with Bathsheba—but that is not His *primary* relationship to His children. Someone has pointed out that the two most beautiful illustrations of God's relationship to His people given in Scripture are those of a Father and a Shepherd. It is interesting also that the two best-known passages in the whole of God's Word—the Lord's Prayer and Psalm 23—use these analogies.

What kind of picture of God, I wonder, do you carry deep down in your heart? If your *primary* view of God is as a Judge, then you will tend to interpret your problems as God's judgment upon you, rather than an opportunity to experience in your troubles His tender love and care. Make no mistake about it—the image of God that you carry deep in your heart is the one that you will relate to in a moment of crisis.

FURTHER STUDY

Col. 1:1–15; 2:9;
John 1:1–2

1. How has God revealed
   Himself to us?
2. What is your picture
   of God?

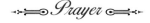

Prayer

O Father, help me develop a true image of You in my heart: a picture that is exposed, not from my own feelings and ideas about You, but from the principles that lie hidden in Your precious Word.
In Jesus' Name I ask it. Amen.

Whistling in the Dark?

"... we are the people of his pasture, the flock under his care ...." (v. 7)

For reading & meditation—Psalm 95:1–11

*D*avid, in the midst of his trials, consoled himself with the thought that God was not his Judge, but his Shepherd. This was his *primary* view of God, and thus the image of the divine Shepherd's tender love and care filled his heart.

Someone once said: "You will never rise higher in your Christian life and experience than your image and concept of God." How true. You see, you can recite the words of Psalm 23 all day, but it will not have much effect if the picture of God you carry deep in your heart is that of a tyrant or a despot. Your wrong image of God will negate the impact of the words. Archbishop William Temple put it like this:—"is not so much the words we say with our lips that produce inner peace, but the thoughts that we carry deep within our heart. It is down there—in the heart—that the real changes take place. If the thoughts in our hearts do not really correspond with the words on our lips, then we are just *whistling in the dark*" (italics added).

So before we go any further into this simple, yet profoundly beautiful psalm, check on how true to Scripture your primary picture of God is. Is He tender—or tyrannical? Caring—or condemning? A negative view of God is rarely changed overnight, but I am confident that as we meditate day by day upon this transforming psalm, we shall finally come to the same conclusion as David—that everything that a good shepherd is to his sheep, God is to His people.

FURTHER STUDY

Pss. 100:1–5; 79:13;
Isa. 40:11;
Zech. 9:16

1. Where does the divine Shepherd lead us?
2. What is the psalmist's response?

Prayer

O Father, I am so grateful that my feet are on the staircase and I am on an upward way. Lead me day by day to a new awareness and a new understanding of Your infinite love and care.
For Your own dear Name's sake. Amen.

"Divine Diligence"

"I am the good shepherd. The good shepherd lays down his life for the sheep."(v. 11)

For reading & meditation—John 10:1–18

O ver the past few days, we have seen the importance of gaining a clear concept of who God is, or, as someone once said, "The clearer your concept of God, the more vital will be your relationship with Him." How clear is your concept of God? Can you say, as did David, "the Lord is my *shepherd*"?

Psalm 23 has been described by someone as "David's hymn of praise to divine diligence." The entire passage recounts the way in which the divine Shepherd spares no pains for the welfare of His sheep. No wonder David, previously a shepherd himself, took pride in being a member of God's flock.

The Christian writer, Phillip Keller, tells how he spent some years working as a shepherd in East Africa, and makes reference to a shepherd he knew who was completely indifferent to the needs of the sheep. "The man," he says, "gave little or no time to his flock, letting them pretty well forage for themselves as best they could, both in summer and winter. They fell prey to dogs, cougars and rustlers. They had only polluted, muddy water to drink. In my mind's eye I can see them still standing at the fence, huddled sadly in little knots, staring wistfully through the wires at the rich pastures on the other side."

That shepherd ignored the needs of his sheep—he couldn't care less. How different is the divine Shepherd. For Him there is no greater joy, no richer reward, no deeper satisfaction than that of seeing His sheep safe, contented and flourishing under His care.

FURTHER STUDY

Matt. 18:1–14;
Heb. 13:20–21;
1 Pet. 2:25; 5:4

1. How did Jesus reveal the character of a true shepherd?
2. How did He demonstrate this in His own life?

Prayer

My Father and my Shepherd, how can I ever sufficiently thank You for drawing me into Your fold. Help me to realize that hour by hour, and day by day, I am the special object of Your tender, loving care. I am so deeply grateful. Amen.

No Matter What . . .

"He tends his flock like a shepherd: He gathers the lambs in his arms . . ." (v. 11)

For reading & meditation—Isaiah 40:1–11

We turn now to the next phrase which David utters as he encourages himself in God: "The Lord is my shepherd, *I shall not want.*" What a bold and positive statement to make! At first glance, however, the words seem quite absurd. Here is David in the midst of intense privation, hunted and hounded by hostile enemy forces, deserted by many of his former supporters—yet quietly affirming, "I shall not want." In the past I have known many Christians who have had great difficulty in understanding this phrase. They have said, "How can I recite this verse with any meaning when I want so many things? I want a happy family/better living conditions/an adequate supply of money/employment/a wife/a husband" and so on.

David's meaning becomes clear when we dig a little deeper into the original Hebrew words that are used. One translation says: "I shall lack nothing." Another puts it like this: "I shall not lack any good thing." "The main thought," says one commentator, "is that of not lacking—not being deficient—in proper care, management or husbandry."

So what David is really saying is this: no matter what hardships or privations come my way, I am confident of this one thing—that *I shall not lack* the expert care and tender supervision of my Master and my Shepherd. There were many things that David lacked—he lacked the comforts of life, family affection, physical security, and so on. What he did not lack, however, was the assurance that God was with him in his difficulties, managing his affairs and turning all his stumbling blocks into stepping stones.

FURTHER STUDY

Matt. 6:25–34;
2 Cor. 9:8;
Phil. 4:19

1. What did Jesus teach the disciples?
2. What is God's promise?

Prayer

My Father and my God, I see that although I lack many things, I shall never lack Your expert management and care. You are my unfailing Companion, my constant Guide, my Good Shepherd . . .
I am so grateful. Amen.

139

"God Should Treat Me Better"

"But even so, you love me! You are holding my right hand! You will keep on guiding me all my life . . ." (vv. 23–24, TLB)

For reading & meditation—Psalm 73:1–28

*I*f we accept that Psalm 23 was written during the time of David's sojourn in the wilderness of Judea, then when he said "I shall not lack any good thing" he could not have been referring to material or physical benefits, for quite clearly he was bereft of them. David is boasting in the fact that no matter what hardship he might endure, he would never *want*—never *lack*—the expert care and management of his tender, loving Shepherd.

It is at this point that we must take a long, hard look at reality, for there are many who believe that once we become Christians, we ought to be exempt from the ordinary ills that afflict humanity. Those who adopt this attitude go down like bowling pins when trouble strikes. A woman who had been overtaken by a series of difficult problems said to me: "Why should this happen to me? I'm a Christian. God should treat me better." I pointed out that the attitude she was adopting was highly dangerous, but I am afraid my words did not make much of an impression. She finished up in a serious nervous condition which required several months of hospital treatment.

Richard Baxter wrote of the Great Plague, "At first so few religious people were taken away that they began to be puffed up and boast of the great differences which God did make. But quickly after that they all fell alike." What, then, is the difference between a Christian and a non-Christian? The difference is not in what happens to us, but what we are able to do with what happens.

FURTHER STUDY

Isa. 41:1–10;
Deut. 33:27;
Ps. 18:35–36

1. What was God's assurance to the children of Israel?
2. What was the psalmist's affirmation?

Prayer

Dear Lord Jesus, You who took everything that men threw at You and made it work toward Your ends—teach me how to do the same. Impress this truth deeply upon my spirit: that it is not what happens to me, but what I do with it, that determines the result. Amen.

"Putting Back the Perspective"

"He will not let your foot slip—he who watches over you . . . will neither slumber
nor sleep." (vv. 3–4)
For reading & meditation—Psalm 121:1–8

We said yesterday that difficulties and problems come to all of us—Christians and non-Christians alike. But while the same things happen to us all, they do not have the same effect upon us all. The same thing happening to two different people may have an entirely different effect. It all depends on our inner attitudes. As someone has said: "What life does to us in the long run depends on what life finds in us."

During a counseling session, a man said, "I have found a verse in the Bible that describes my life perfectly." He picked up a Bible that was lying on the desk and opened it to Job 5:7. "Here, read that—aloud," he said to the counselor. The counselor read: "Man is born to trouble as surely as sparks fly upward." "I was born to trouble," complained the counselee. "I *live* in trouble and I'll probably *die* in trouble. There's always a new burst of sparks, and they are burning me something awful."

The counselor, with a flash of divine insight, said, "There's another verse which accurately describes your life also: it's 1 Peter 5:7." Then, handing him the Bible, he said: "Now *you* read it—aloud." The man read these thrilling words: "Cast all your anxiety on him because he cares for you." He was silent for a time, and then, with a tear trickling down his cheek, said, "Thank you for putting the perspective back into my life. I needed a word from God and He has given it to me through you today." I wonder—is this also His word to you?

FURTHER STUDY

2 Cor. 1:1–11;
Luke 12:6–7;
Isa. 25:4

1. How did Jesus illustrate God's care?
2. Why does God allow us to go through trials?

Prayer

O Father, You know the tendency I have to let troubles change my perspective. Help me to keep in clear focus the fact that You will never allow anything to happen to me without providing me with the grace to turn it from a trial into a testimony. I am so grateful. Amen.

"Listening Posts"

"And after the earthquake a fire, but the Lord was not in the fire; and after the fire
a still small voice." (v. 12, RSV)

For reading & meditation—1 Kings 19:1–18

Comb the record of the Scriptures and you find, time and time again, that when God's servants were caught up in periods of great difficulty and distress, they knew that the Shepherd had not abandoned them but was working out His purposes with infinite tenderness and skill.

Take, for example, the apostle John. He says: "I . . . found myself in the island called Patmos, for adhering to God's word and the testimony of Jesus . . . I found myself rapt in the Spirit and I heard a loud voice . . ." (Rev. 1:9–10, Moffatt). He was isolated and bereft of human companionship and care—but was he bereft of the care and companionship of his Master? Assuredly not! Listen again to what he says: "I found myself in the island called Patmos . . . and I *heard*." Shut off from men, he was more open to God.

Islands of isolation are good "listening posts." Shut off from the clamoring voices of the world, you can hear God more easily. Just recently I leafed through an old Bible which I had discarded, and I was intrigued to see that I had written a date against certain Bible verses. Only the Lord and I know what happened on those dates, but I can tell you that they were times when I felt utterly barren and isolated. Today I can bear witness to the fact that the Good Shepherd, with characteristic skill, used those moments to speak to me in a way that I have never forgotten. My prayer is that He will do the same for you—today.

**FURTHER
STUDY**

Ps. 29:1–11;
John 10:4;
Rev. 3:20

1. When do we often hear
the Shepherd's voice?
2. Why do Christ's sheep
follow Him?

Prayer

O Father, so often my isolations get me nowhere and bring me nothing. Help me to turn my islands of isolation into "listening posts," so that from out of the silence I may hear Your unmistakable voice.
For Your own dear Name's sake. Amen.

There — I Saw!

"They bruised his feet with shackles, his neck was put in irons, till what he foretold came to pass . . ." (vv. 18–19)
For reading & meditation—Psalm 105:1–22

We saw yesterday how away from the clamoring voices of the world, the apostle John was able to hear God's voice more easily.

Much later in the Book of Revelation we read: "So he bore me away rapt in the Spirit to the desert, and there I saw . . ." (Rev. 17:3, Moffatt). John is now in a *desert* on the island. In addition to the isolation—there was barrenness. Sometimes our isolations are more than we can bear, but when they are accompanied by barrenness—life borders on the intolerable. Let us not forget, however, that our Shepherd will never allow us to get into any position in which He cannot work for our good and for His own eternal glory.

Listen to the words again: "So he bore me away . . . to the desert . . . and there I *saw* . . ." "Saw" what? The downfall of the empires of the world! In the isolated and barren periods of life we may be able to do or contribute little, but we can see God do much—indeed everything. And in the end, does it matter all that much whether we do things, or see God do them? Our work *is* important—but dispensable. Union and fellowship with God are what really matter. John might have thought to himself, as he was left alone on Patmos—"There's not much future in this place!" Yet he finished up by seeing the whole future of mankind. Take it from me, when your present offers you little on your island of isolation, your Master will see that the future will offer you everything.

FURTHER STUDY

Isa. 54:1–10;
1 John 1:3; 5:20;
1 Cor. 1:9

1. What is the Lord's answer to barrenness?
2. What is the central purpose of life?

Prayer

Father, I see that if I am "in the Spirit" then I am fulfilling my life purpose—whether I am in a desert or elsewhere. And help me to grasp the fact that when the present offers me little, the future offers me everything. I am so thankful. Amen.

The Shepherd Is Near

"... you will fill me with joy in your presence, with eternal pleasures at your right hand." (v. 11)

For reading & meditation—Psalm 16:1–11

*W*e turn now to focus on the next phrase of this beautiful and exquisite psalm: *"He makes me lie down in green pastures."* Phillip Keller, the Christian writer and one-time shepherd to whom I referred earlier, explains that sheep are extremely timid animals by nature, and cannot be made to lie down unless four requirements are met. They will not lie down until they are (1) free from all fear; (2) free from friction with the other sheep; (3) free from torment by flies and parasites, and (4) free from the pangs of hunger. Obviously, it depends on the diligence of the shepherd as to whether or not his flock is free from these disturbing influences.

The very first thing a shepherd does in order to calm and reassure his sheep is to make them aware of his presence. The *Handbook of Bible Times and Customs* states: "Nothing puts a flock of sheep more at ease than to see their shepherd walking in the field." Isn't it just the same in the Christian life? I don't know about you, but whenever I am beset by troubles and trials the thing that quietens and reassures my spirit is the keen awareness that my Shepherd is nearby. There is nothing like Christ's presence to dispel the tension, the panic, and the terror of the unknown. Perhaps at this very moment you are facing a tragedy or a crisis that threatens to send shock waves of fear through your whole being. Take heart—your Shepherd is not far away. His presence in the situation makes a world of difference.

FURTHER STUDY

Pss. 139:1–14; 4:8;
Ezek. 34:14;
Rom. 14:17

1. What was the psalmist's question?
2. What was his conclusion?

Prayer

Blessed and gentle Shepherd, help me to be keenly aware of Your presence in my life throughout every minute and hour of every day. For I can face anything if I know that You are there. Thank You, dear Lord Jesus. Amen.

"Where Love Is, Fear Is Not"

"There is no fear in love. But perfect love drives out fear . . ." (v. 18)

For reading & meditation—1 John 4:9–21

One of the ways in which the Good Shepherd delivers us from fear is by making us keenly aware of His loving presence. When I was young, I was terrified of thunder. If I was out on the street when a thunderstorm occurred, I would hide in a doorway, terror-stricken. When a thunderstorm came in the night, however, I had little fear because I knew that automatically my mother would come to me and stay all night to make me feel safe. Now, whenever I read "perfect love drives out fear," I cannot help but think of my mother slipping into bed with me during a thunderstorm. Her loving presence made all the difference between calmness and fear.

When we are conscious that we are deeply loved, then fear dissolves as readily as the morning mist before the rising sun. Fear can come only where love is not—and where love is, fear is not. Some try to get rid of their fears by drowning themselves in alcohol. But the next morning the fears are back—multiplied. Others try to push their fears down into the subconscious and pretend they are not there. This, too, is ineffective. The way to deal with fear is to focus more on Christ than you do on your fear. You see, you become like the thing on which you focus. Focus on fear—and you cannot help but become perturbed. Focus on Christ and you cannot help but be at peace. Keep your eyes fixed on your Shepherd—and you will soon be convinced that there is really nothing to fear.

FURTHER STUDY

Isa. 12;
Ps. 118:5–6;
Prov. 3:24

1. What was the psalmist's assurance?
2. What is the antidote to fear?

Prayer

O Father, if the light of God surrounds me, the love of God enfolds me, the presence of God encourages me, the power of God defends me—why should I be afraid? Today all my fears shall be dissolved " in the great quiet of God." Amen.

Friction in the Flock

"Therefore this is what the Sovereign LORD says . . . I myself will judge between
the fat sheep and the lean sheep." (v. 20)

For reading & meditation—Ezekiel 34:11–24

oday we look at the second source of conflict from which a
good shepherd seeks to deliver his sheep—tension, rivalry,
and competition within the flock itself. I am given to understand that
just as there is a "pecking order" among chickens, so there is a "butting
order" among sheep. This thought is brought out very vividly in the
passage that is before us today. Rival tension, competition for status,
and self-assertion can produce a great deal of friction in a flock—the
sheep are unable to lie down and rest in contentment.

Unfortunately, there are many churches like this. Men and women
fight and compete among themselves for position or status and thus
create conflict in the Christian community. The apostle James says of
them that they "want what you don't have, so you scheme and kill to
get it. You are jealous for what others have, and you can't possess it, so
you fight and quarrel to take it away from them" (Jas. 4:2, NLT). Many
are prevented from enjoying the blessings of corporate fellowship
because of the competitiveness and status-seeking of a few.

How does a shepherd deal with friction among his sheep? He does
it by walking among them to discipline the offenders and reassure
those that are alarmed. A good shepherd has great compassion for the
sheep that get butted and pushed around by the more domineering
ones. Is your church or fellowship in conflict because of over-competi-
tive and status-seeking Christians? Then make sure your eyes stay
focused on the divine Shepherd. He will discipline them and reassure
you.

**FURTHER
STUDY**

Ps. 133:1–3;
1 Pet. 3:8;
1 Cor. 1:10;
John 17:20–21

1. What was the prayer of
the Good Shepherd?
2. What will invoke
God's blessing?

Prayer

Gentle and loving Shepherd, forgive us that by our competitiveness and status-seeking, we so easily turn
Your flock into a feud. Walk among us in love—to discipline and to encourage.
For Your own dear Name's sake. Amen.

Overcoming Irritations

"But he said to me, 'My grace is sufficient for you, for my power is made perfect in weakness.'" (v. 9)

For reading & meditation—2 Corinthians 12:1-10

Sheep, especially during the hot season, can be driven almost to distraction by marauding insects. At such times it is quite impossible for the shepherd to make them lie down: they remain on their feet, stamp their legs, shake their heads, and are ready to rush off in any direction to find relief. A diligent shepherd can make sure that they are regularly dipped, so that their fleeces are cleared of ticks. And he can see to it that they are put out to graze in areas where there is plenty of shade.

We now ask ourselves: how does our Good Shepherd go about the task of helping His sheep overcome the irritations that beset them? What is the remedy He uses to help us come to a place of quiet contentment and repose? The answer is this—divine grace! The apostle Paul, in the passage before us today, tells of experiencing a "thorn in the flesh." What it was nobody quite knows. Eye disease, epilepsy, an unrelenting satanic attack—each has been suggested. But still nobody is certain. One writer, commenting on this, says: "Paul had a thorn in the flesh but nobody knows what it was: if we had a thorn in the flesh everybody would know what it was." Paul tells us he sought three times for its removal—yet it remained. At last, however, came the comforting word: "My grace is sufficient for you." God's grace enabled Paul to cope with his irritation and, believe me, that same grace will enable you to cope with yours.

FURTHER STUDY

1 Tim. 1:1–14;
2 Tim. 2:1;
Eph. 2:7

1. What was Paul's testimony?
2. What was his exhortation to Timothy?

Prayer

O God my Father, I know that You can either free me from life's irritations, or give me sufficient grace to cope with them. Help me to come to terms with the fact that You allow only what can be used for Your glory and my good. Help me to trust that design. For Jesus' sake. Amen.

Hungry Sheep Don't Lie Down

"... Listen, listen to me, and eat what is good, and your soul will delight in the richest of fare." (v. 2)
For reading & meditation—Isaiah 55:1-13

*T*he fourth and final condition which is necessary before a sheep can lie down contentedly is freedom from hunger. This fact, of course, is clearly implied in the words: *"He makes me lie down in green pastures."*

Nothing delights a shepherd as much as seeing his sheep well and truly fed, for it is only then that they will lie down to rest and ruminate. One eastern shepherd comments: "Whenever I see one of my sheep moving around discontentedly, always on its feet, looking here, there and everywhere, I know that sheep is hungry. And hungry sheep do not thrive. I make it my goal to immediately try to ascertain what is wrong, for I know that unless the matter is soon rectified, the sheep will languish and lack vigor and vitality."

A shepherd sometimes has to work extremely hard to bring his sheep into "green pastures." He has to go ahead of his sheep and reconnoiter the best grazing areas, then plan how to get them safely to the spot he has selected—all of which requires unrelenting energy and determination. Sometimes, when the sheep are safely settled in "green pastures," a shepherd will spy one or more of the sheep nibbling at inferior forage instead of enjoying the lush pasture that he has provided. Every shepherd says that it is a disappointing and frustrating moment. How does the divine Shepherd feel, I wonder, when, after having supplied the "green pastures" of His Word on which we may feed, we attempt to live day by day off the barren ground of the world around us?

FURTHER STUDY

*John 6:32–58;
Ezek. 34:14;
Jer. 3:15; 15:16*

*1. What did Jesus declare?
2. What is your current diet?*

Prayer

O Father, forgive me that so often I attempt to draw my nourishment from the dry and barren ground of the world, when You have supplied me with such rich and verdant pastures in Your Word. Help me to begin today to reverse this situation. For Jesus' sake. Amen.

"Still Waters"

"Jesus stood and said . . . 'If anyone is thirsty, let him come to me and drink.'" (v. 37)
For reading & meditation—John 7:28–44

We move on now to consider the next phrase that occurs in "David's hymn of praise to divine diligence"—*"He leads me beside still waters."* One cannot help but notice how the varied needs of the sheep and the many-sided care of the shepherd are pictured with consummate skill in the short sentences of this psalm.

A small booklet entitled "The Song of the Syrian Guest" is a brief analysis of Psalm 23 from the viewpoint of a Syrian shepherd. In it the writer makes this illuminating comment: "So many things familiar to us are strange to you who come from the West. When you read the words, 'He leads me beside still waters', you think of quietly flowing streams, but streams are few and far between in the Middle East and the shepherds do not rely upon them. Sheep are afraid of fast-running water; they will drink only from a quiet pool. The 'still waters' are the wells and cisterns, and the shepherd leads his sheep to these still waters so that he may draw water and quench their thirst."

What a deeply impressive and suggestive picture this is of the way in which the divine Shepherd leads us day by day to the quiet waters of spiritual refreshment. Before you begin this day, pause for a moment now, close your eyes if possible, and focus again on the passage you have just read. Allow the Good Shepherd to prepare you for the day that lies ahead, to slake your spiritual thirst, and refresh your soul with His eternal Word.

FURTHER STUDY

*Isa. 55:1–7; 44:3;
Ps. 36:8;
Matt. 5:6*

1. What is God's promise to the thirsty?
2. How thirsty are you today?

Prayer

Divine Shepherd, help me to drink this moment from the clean and clear springs of Your eternal Word so that the world will be astonished at my serenity and joy. This I ask for Your own dear Name's sake. Amen.

Replenishing Our Resources

". . . his compassions never fail. They are new every morning; great is your faithfulness." (vv. 22–23)

For reading & meditation—Lamentations 3:19–40

*W*e continue meditating on the phrase, "He leads me beside still waters." Today we ask ourselves: what is the spiritual parallel in all this? How, in an age of turmoil and strife, can we discover those "still waters" of which the Bible so eloquently speaks? The answer is found in the quiet time—a concept that unfortunately seems to be missing in the lives of many modern-day Christians—a time, preferably at the beginning of the day, when we meet with God in prayer and the reading of the Scriptures.

One of the things that concerns me about many young Christians today is the fact that they are not taught to begin the day with God. Much of this, I know, is a reaction against the legalism that pervaded the church a couple of decades ago, when many Bible teachers suggested that if you missed your daily quiet time—for any reason at all—you were in danger of losing your soul. Nowadays—generally speaking—we seem to have swung to the other extreme, regarding a daily quiet time as unimportant and irrelevant.

The simple truth is that if we do not provide for a quiet time at the beginning of the day, we will most likely have to provide for an unquiet time throughout the day. A diver who is too busy to make sure his air supply is working before he descends into the depths is no more foolish than the Christian who descends into the murky waters of today's world without getting his spiritual breathing apparatus connected up with the pure air of the kingdom of God.

FURTHER STUDY

*Ps. 46:1–11;
1 Pet. 3:4;
Eccl. 4:6*

*1. What is very precious to God?
2. How can we "know that He is God"?*

Prayer

Gracious Father, help me to realize that the quiet time is not only quieting, but quickening. It produces in me a quiet heart, which becomes a quiet confidence and ends in a quiet power. It makes sense, dear Lord. Help me to maintain it. Amen.

"The Morning Watch"

Day 142

"... in the morning I lay my requests before you and wait in expectation." (v. 3)

For reading & meditation—Psalm 5:1–12

*I*f you are too busy to have a daily quiet time, then you are too busy. Probably you will have to take time off during the day to deal with issues that you might have more easily foreseen had you begun the day with God. I am not advocating a legalistic attitude to this issue, for there are some days when circumstances make it impossible to keep to a routine. But as far as possible, begin every day by spending a little time with God in prayer and the reading of His Word.

One shepherd described his feelings of exasperation when, taking his sheep to a clean, quiet stream to be watered, he found many of them stopping to drink from small pools beside the trail. "The water in these pools was filthy and polluted," said the shepherd, "but the sheep were quite sure it was the best drink obtainable." How sad that so many Christians are like those stubborn sheep—they stop to drink at any stream except the pure waters of God's eternal and inerrant Word. From what source do you draw your spiritual strength?

I asked a man who was living a defeated Christian life if he kept a daily quiet time and he replied: "Yes, I spend ten to fifteen minutes every day reading Shakespeare." A couple said that their idea of a quiet time was to quietly read the newspaper for half an hour after breakfast. These sincere but defeated souls found release and victory when they set up real quiet times, in which they took on board the quieting and quickening resources of God.

FURTHER STUDY

John 4:1–30;
Jer. 2:13;
Rev. 22:17

1. What lesson can we learn from the woman at the well?
2. Are you drinking from a broken cistern?

Prayer

Forgive me, dear Father, that so often I stop and drink at the muddy pools of the world when You are seeking to lead me to the pure water of Your Word. Help me to take "the pause that refreshes" to drink from the clear springs of Your eternal truth. In Jesus' Name I pray. Amen.

"An Island Within"

"I rise before dawn and cry for help; I have put my hope in your word." (v. 147)
For reading & meditation—Psalm 119:137–152

*W*e continue meditating on the phrase, "He leads me beside still waters." Some Bible teachers say: "If you are filled with the Spirit, then you can draw from God's resources, not just at the beginning of the day, but every hour of the day. Better a fountain in the heart than a fountain by the way."

This confuses two quite separate issues. It is perfectly true that by reason of the Spirit's indwelling, we can draw upon His resources moment by moment, but that does not do away with the need for a daily quiet time. One writer puts it like this: "Those who say they can live in a state of prayer without stated times for prayer will probably find themselves without both. It is as futile as thinking that you can live in a state of physical nourishment without stated times for nourishment."

I believe with all my heart that the divine Shepherd seeks daily to lead His sheep to the "still waters" of His Word, and how sad it is that so many Christians prefer to drink from the polluted pools of the world. The poet says:

> What a frail soul He gave me, and a heart
> Lame and unlikely for the large events.

I wonder if, more often, we haven't given ourselves "a heart lame and unlikely for the large events." God has given us infinite resources through prayer and the reading of the Scriptures. They are ours for the asking and the taking. The quiet time creates an island of quiet within us, and that becomes the atmosphere of the day.

FURTHER STUDY

1 Sam. 9:11–27;
Isa. 30:15;
Num. 9:8;
Job 37:14

1. What was Samuel's word to Saul?
2. How is God's strength made known?

Prayer

Loving Father, teach me how to make the best use of my daily quiet time, and help me to saturate my thinking with Your thinking so that I cannot tell where my mind ends and where Yours begins.
In Jesus' Name I ask it. Amen.

The Inexhaustible Book

"For the word of God is living and active. Sharper than any double-edged sword . . . it judges the thoughts and attitudes of the heart." (v. 12)

For reading & meditation—Hebrews 4:1–13

W e spend one more day meditating on the phrase, "He leads me beside still waters." I feel constrained to say again that in my view, it is God's desire to daily lead His sheep to the "still waters" of Scripture so that He might slake their spiritual thirst and prepare them for the day ahead.

The Bible should be at the heart of every quiet time. I knew a Christian who believed in the importance of a quiet time but unfortunately had a very low estimate of Scripture and saw no necessity for its use in his meditations. He thought he could get to God directly—through the medium of his own conceptions. His conceptions, however, were man's thoughts about God—not a good enough medium for communication with the Eternal. He finished up by going off on a tangent and getting involved in a false cult.

Unless our thoughts are constantly corrected by God's thoughts, they will either go off on a tangent or become sterile and unproductive. The Bible is God's revelation of Himself, and the more we meditate on it the clearer our minds will become concerning the nature of God and His purpose for our lives. I consider the content of *Every Day with Jesus* to be exhausted after it has been read through once—hence the continuous supply. But you can never exhaust the meaning of the Scriptures. Let the Lord lead you daily to the "still waters" of His Word. Then, and only then, will you know a serenity of soul in the midst of life's turmoil and difficulties.

FURTHER STUDY

Jer. 15:1–16;
Deut. 8:3;
Job 23:12;
Ps. 119:103

1. What was Jeremiah's experience?
2. What did the children of Israel have to learn?

Prayer

O Father, help me come to the quiet time with quiet expectancy—expectancy that here my weakness shall become strength, my doubt becomes faith, my fears become courage and my sin becomes redemption. I ask this for Your own dear Name's sake. Amen.

"Cast Down?"

"A bruised reed he will not break, and a smoldering wick he will not snuff out." (v. 3)

For reading & meditation—Isaiah 42:1–16

*T*he next phrase in this exquisite psalm is: *"He restores my soul."* What a comforting and encouraging statement this is! Here again, it points to the constant care of the Good Shepherd who is set on providing the fullest security for His sheep.

David is not speaking here as a shepherd, though he was one, but as a sheep. He knew from firsthand experience that the welfare of any particular sheep depended to a great degree on the shepherd who owned it. But what does David have in mind when he exclaims: "He restores my soul"?

Some believe it has reference to the way in which God comes to us when we feel cast down and sets us up on our feet again, so to speak. It's interesting that the phrase "cast down" is an old English shepherd's term for a sheep that has turned over on its back and can't get up again by itself. If this happens, and the shepherd does not arrive on the scene within a reasonably short time, the sheep panics and can easily die of fright.

Are you feeling "cast down" at this moment? Well, take heart—the author of this psalm knew that experience too. In Psalm 42:11 he cries out: "Why are you cast down, O my soul, and why are you disquieted within me? Hope in God . . ." (RSV). Notice that last phrase—*"hope in God."* That's the secret. The divine Shepherd will not let you down. Look up—for even now He is moving toward you. He will pick you up and put you back on your feet again.

FURTHER STUDY

*Heb. 13:1–6;
1 Pet. 1:3;
Ps. 40:17;
Isa. 41:10*

1. What has God promised?
2. What should be our confident response?

⇒ *Prayer* ⇐

Blessed and gentle Shepherd, I do indeed look to You. To whom else can I go? I look to You now with the eyes of faith and I take from Your hand the power, the release, and the healing I so deeply need. Thank You, dear Father—thank You. Amen.

Restored—by a Look

"The Lord turned and looked straight at Peter." (v. 61)
For reading & meditation—Luke 22:47–62

We said yesterday that the phrase "cast down" is an old English shepherd's term for a sheep that has accidentally turned over on its back and cannot get up again by itself. "A 'cast' sheep is a very pathetic sight," says Phillip Keller. "Lying on its back, its feet in the air, it flays away, frantically struggling to stand up without success. Sometimes it will bleat a little for help, but generally it lies there lashing about in frightened frustration."

He goes on to say that whenever a shepherd finds that a sheep is missing, his first thought is this: my sheep may be cast down somewhere—I must go in search of it and set it on its feet again. "Some of my most poignant memories," he continues, "are wrapped around the co-mingled anxiety of keeping a count of my flock and repeatedly saving and restoring cast sheep."

The care and concern that Phillip Keller had for his sheep pales into insignificance, however, beside that of our Lord Jesus Christ. Many Christians hold the view that when they fall by the way in their Christian experience, God becomes extremely angry with them. Not so. The revelation of Scripture is that the Almighty, the Lord of all creation, has a shepherd's heart. He is infinitely more compassionate toward the sheep of His fold than any human shepherd could ever be. Reflect again on the tender manner in which Jesus restored Peter after he had three times denied Him. The tenderness, the compassion, and the patience He showed him are just the same as He will show in restoring you.

FURTHER STUDY

Luke 24:13–35;
John 10:11;
Heb. 13:20;
1 Pet. 5:10

1. How did Jesus reveal
His shepherd's heart to
these disciples?
2. What was the result?

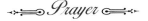

Prayer

Gracious, loving Father, I am so relieved to know that when I am "cast down," You do not become disgusted or furious with me, but You restore me with infinite tenderness and care. How can I ever sufficiently thank You? All honor and praise be to Your wonderful Name. Amen.

"Draws Me Back into His Way"

"... do not give the devil a foothold." (v. 27)

For reading & meditation—Ephesians 4:17–32

We move on to consider another interpretation of the phrase, "He restores my soul." The Syrian shepherd we mentioned on Day 142, Faduel Moghabghad, claims that the statement has reference to the fact that in shepherd country there are many private gardens and vineyards, and if a sheep wanders into one of these private plots, it is forfeited to the owner of the land. In his view, therefore, the phrase "he restores my soul" has reference to the way the divine Shepherd brings us back and rescues us when we stray into forbidden and dangerous places. One of our hymns, you might remember, contains some lines that reinforce this view:

> Put His loving arms around me
> Drew me back into His way.

How encouraging to know that when, by our heedlessness and inattention to God's ways, we stray into Satan's domain, the divine Shepherd does not leave us to our own devices, but constantly seeks our deliverance and restoration.

We must be careful at this point not to press the analogy of a sheep too far, or else we will come out believing that when we wander from the fold, it is solely the Shepherd's responsibility to seek us out and bring us back. We have some responsibility too—the responsibility to confess our sin and to be willing and ready to be restored. We can be assured of this—God will always be willing to restore if we are willing to be restored.

**FURTHER
STUDY**

*John 6:1–13;
Matt. 9:36;
Ezek. 34:6;
1 Pet. 2:25*

1. How did Jesus see
   the crowd?
2. What was His
   response?

Prayer

Father, I confess that at times I am just like a stubborn, foolish sheep that turns and wanders from Your way.
Help me, whenever that happens, to be as ready to be restored as You are to restore.
For Your own dear Name's sake. Amen.

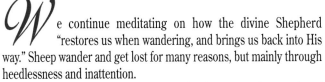

"Little Tufts of Worldliness"

Day
148

"Do not love the world or anything in the world. If anyone loves the world, the love of the Father is not in him." (v. 15)

For reading & meditation—1 John 2:1–17

We continue meditating on how the divine Shepherd "restores us when wandering, and brings us back into His way." Sheep wander and get lost for many reasons, but mainly through heedlessness and inattention.

Some of us get lost the same way. Like sheep, we take a series of steps, none of them seemingly important, but each one increasing our distance from the Shepherd. We go with the crowd to the hinterland of evil, expecting to stay inwardly aloof while being outwardly near. Soon, however, the temptation becomes too great for us, our defenses crumble, and we rationalize the issues until evil, which before looked hideous, becomes first bearable, then inviting, then desirable. How many times have we said to ourselves: "But everybody does it—what's the point of being different?" Or a series of neglects takes place: "I'm too busy now to have a quiet time—I'll begin next week." Or: "This duty is pressing—but I'll make sure it is done tomorrow." "Action turns into attitude, attitude turns into habit, habit turns into character."

A Christian once said to me: "I didn't intend to get into this mess spiritually. I just let things slip, and now that I need my faith it seems to have gone." How easy it is to find ourselves in Satan's territory, not because of deliberate intention, but through a series of inattentions. "The descent to hell," said someone, "is so gradual that many do not suspect the road they are following is a downward path." The little tufts of worldliness that lure us on will, unless we are careful, leave us lost and forlorn.

FURTHER STUDY

Luke 21:7–36;
Matt. 16:26;
Col. 3:2;
Titus 2:12

1. How would you define "the world" in this sense?
2. On what should we set our affections?

Prayer

O God my Father, help me to resist the appeal of those little tufts of worldliness that, as I partake of them, lead me back to the territory of Satan from which I was once delivered. Help me not to get lost through careless inattention. For Jesus' sake. Amen.

157

Run-Down Souls

"' . . . I will restore you to health and heal your wounds,' declares the LORD . . ." (v. 17)

For reading & meditation—Jeremiah 30:12-22

*T*oday we examine another interpretation of the phrase: "He restores my soul"—one which claims that these words have reference to the way God ministers to us when we become spiritually debilitated. Personally, this is the view I find most satisfying.

A sample of the kind of thing I mean is found in a letter which arrived today: "I'm worn down by my circumstances . . . tired of the pressures . . . wearied by the constant demands that are being made upon me. Can God do anything for me in this situation?" I was happy to respond that He can! The Good Shepherd can step into our lives when we feel tired and jaded, and provided we let Him, quickly restore our spiritual zest and enthusiasm.

In one place in the New Testament, our Savior is described as a stimulator: "By all the stimulus of Christ" (Phil. 2:1, Moffatt). Those who know nothing of Christ's stimulus—His ability to restore tired and jaded souls—are forced to turn to other stimulants to tide them over. Listen to the way that a famous missionary to India describes Christ's ministry of spiritual restoration: "He is like the first rainfall of the monsoon in India—the dry, dusty ground, so barren and so hard, the very next day has a green film of vegetation over it. The moisture apparently touches the dead soil, and lo, it is alive. So Jesus touches our parched and barren lives, and lo, they sprout with life, with vitality and with hope." May you know the wonder of His restoring touch this very moment.

FURTHER STUDY

Heb. 4;
Ps. 51:12;
Isa. 57:18

1. *Why can we come boldly to the Lord?*
2. *What will we find?*

Prayer

Blessed Lord Jesus, help me to feel the tingle of Your Spirit upon my spirit this day, turning my drabness into delight, my grief into glory, and my jadedness into jubilation. Restore to me the joy of my salvation. In Your dear Name I pray. Amen.

"All We Like Sheep . . ."

"The path of the righteous is like the first gleam of dawn, shining ever brighter till the full light of day." (v. 18)

For reading & meditation—Proverbs 4:10–19

We focus now on the next phrase in David's "hymn of praise to divine diligence": *"He leads me in paths of righteousness for his name's sake."* One translation puts it: "He leads me in the paths that are right." Another says: "He leads me in the right way."

The Hebrew word for *paths* means "well-defined or clearly-marked trails." Sheep, as everyone knows, are stubborn and self-willed creatures. If left to themselves, they will almost invariably wander off in a direction of their own choosing. An experienced shepherd, of course, is well aware of this, and tries to offset this tendency by going ahead of his sheep and making himself as visible as possible.

We, too, are stubborn and self-willed creatures—we prefer to do our own thing. "All we like sheep have gone astray; we have turned every one to his own way" (Isa. 53:6, RSV). As someone has said: "It is by no mere whim on God's part that He has called us sheep. Our behavior patterns and life habits are so much like those of a sheep that it is well-nigh embarrassing."

Our desire for self-determination, however, has to be curbed or else the results will be disastrous. The prophet Micah said: "O shepherd, guide thy people, thine own flock, so lonely, lonely like a wild patch within a garden" (Mic. 7:14, Moffatt). The universe around us is orderly because it obeys God and follows the will of its Creator—it is a garden. When we obey ourselves, rather than God, then we are a wild patch of disorderliness within that garden of orderliness.

FURTHER STUDY

*Phil. 1:1–11;
Pss. 48:10; 145:17;
Jer. 23:6*

1. *What should we be filled with?*
2. *Write out a definition of righteousness.*

Prayer

O God, I see so clearly that one of the reasons You want to be my Shepherd is to deliver me from self-dominance and self-determination. Experience tells me that a self-centered life is futile. Give me the power to overcome it. In Jesus' Name I pray. Amen.

Having Your Own Way

"There is a way that seems right to a man, but in the end it leads to death." (v. 12)

For reading & meditation—Proverbs 14:1–15

We saw yesterday that although our divine Shepherd seeks to lead us in the paths that are right, we are so stubborn and self-centered that we decline to follow. We prefer our own way even though it may lead us straight into trouble.

When challenged about this issue, many of us, of course, strongly deny it. Yet in actual fact, comparatively few of God's people follow continually in His path. We say: "I want to do God's will and be led by Him in all that I do"—and then promptly proceed to follow our own self-determined desires. We sing beautiful hymns and choruses that contain such words as: "The Lord knows the way through the wilderness, all I have to do is follow"—then take the path that we think is best.

This is an issue that we must come to grips with right now, for unless we learn how to give up our self-centeredness, we will fall into serious trouble—no matter how loving and concerned is our Shepherd. I recognize that this is a difficult issue for many Christians, for our civilization teaches us self-interest as the primary motivating force in life—"every man for himself and the devil take the hindmost." Actually if self-interest is primary, then the result is self-destruction, for the self-centered soon become the self-disrupted. They are making themselves God, and they are not God, so the universe won't back their way of life. They are like the ones we referred to yesterday—". . . so lonely, lonely like a wild patch within a garden."

FURTHER STUDY

Luke 12:13–40;
Rom. 8:13–14;
Gal. 5:24

1. Why was the rich man a fool?
2. What does the Spirit enable us to do?

ᎢᎢᎢ Prayer ᎢᎢᎢ

Father, it is becoming clearer day by day that when my life is centered in You, it is fruitful: when it is centered in myself, it is frustrated. Help me to shift the center of my life from myself to You—today.
In Jesus' Name I pray. Amen.

A Way Which Is Not the Way

"I desire to do your will, O my God; your law is within my heart." (v. 8)
For reading & meditation—Psalm 40:1–17

When we try to follow our own way instead of God's, we finish up self-defeated. As one writer puts it: "If you won't live according to God's way, you can't live with yourself."

A cartoon shows a doctor taking the pulse of a very sick world. He shakes his head and says: "You are in a bad way—you are allergic to yourself." If you insist on going your own way, and self-concern becomes the driving force of your being, then you will eventually be driven into conflict with yourself. You will find yourself with all kinds of problems and complexes—you will be allergic to yourself.

A woman once said to me: "I've insisted upon having my own way all my life, but now that I am middle-aged it has caught up with me. I'm empty, incapable of accomplishing anything." You can get away with having your own way for a while, but in the end it will catch up with you—that which is whispered in the ear will be shouted from the housetops (Matt. 10:27). A Christian who has never learned to go God's way rather than his own way gets nowhere—and everybody can see it. Jesus penetratingly said: "Whoever wants to save his life will lose it" (Luke 9:24, Moffatt). Notice, He did not say, "whoever saves his life will lose it," but "whoever *wants* to save his life will lose it." Why? Because the law of the universe decrees it. Life will not back the person who refuses to take God's way—for his way is not *the* Way.

FURTHER STUDY

1 Sam. 15:1–31;
Acts 5:29;
James 1:25

1. What was Samuel's message to Saul?
2. What was the early disciple's attitude?

Prayer

O God my Father, I see how You have wrought Your laws into the texture of my being. I cannot center on myself without that self going to rack and ruin. Lift me out of myself into Yourself—out of my ways into Your Way. For Jesus' sake. Amen.

"Only One Way"

"... My Father, if it is possible, may this cup be taken from me. Yet not
as I will, but as you will." (v. 39)

For reading & meditation—Matthew 26:36-46

O ne of the characteristics of a radiant Christian," says Oswald
J. Smith, "is a willingness to put his personal life and affairs
into the hands of Jesus Christ—without qualification and without reser-
vation." This is what Christ refers to when He talks about taking up the
cross *daily*. It means being prepared day by day to put self-interest to
death and to say, "No longer my will, but yours be done."

When the urge toward self-assertion, self-aggrandizement and self-
pleasing gives way to the desire to please God, much of the strain goes
out of life. Dr. William Sadler, the psychiatrist, tells of a lady he once
treated who said to him, "You know, I am a very sensitive person."
"Yes," said Dr. Sadler, "I know you are a very *selfish* person." "But I did-
n't say 'selfish'," protested the woman. "I did," replied the doctor. She
went away angry but ten days later came back, chastened, and confessed it was true. Her self-centeredness was the basis of her illness.

The Man who was the healthiest person who ever lived on our planet, a Man who radiated health—only to touch Him was to be made
whole—followed the way of His Father right to the very end. When
confronted by the cross, He was greatly tempted to follow His own
desires and take the way that seemed best to Him, but He came
through the struggle to say: "Father ... not as I will, but as you will."
God's way is not just a way, or even the best way—it is *the* Way.

**FURTHER
STUDY**

Col. 3;
Gal. 2:20;
Rom. 6:11

1. What was Paul's
confession?
2. List some characteris-
tics of the unselfish life.

⊷⊷⊸⊜⊸ *Prayer* ⊸⊜⊷⊷⊷

Blessed Lord Jesus, You show me how to truly live—help me to live Your way. I want to abound, not drag
leaden feet to dead tasks. Purge me of self and make me a committed follower of Your Way.
For Your own Name's sake. Amen.

"Kicking Up Our Heels"

"... when he, the Spirit of truth, comes, he will guide you into all truth." (v. 13)

For reading & meditation—John 16:1-15

We spend one last day meditating on the phrase: "He leads me in paths of righteousness for his name's sake." The reward of following the Lord's path is that we shall be led from one good pasture to another.

An efficient shepherd always tries to keep his sheep on the move, thus avoiding over-use of the land and enabling his sheep to continually enjoy wholesome, fresh forage. Phillip Keller says: "... whenever the shepherd opens a gate into fresh pasture, the sheep are filled with excitement. As they go through the gate even the staid old ewes will often kick up their heels and leap with delight at the prospect of finding fresh feed. How they enjoy being led on to new ground."

Do you experience a similar delight as the Good Shepherd leads you to wholesome, fresh forage? Are you one of those Christians who want to continually feed on just one doctrine or truth, and never go on to enjoy the other delights which God has for you in His Word? Be assured of this—God wants us to move with Him day by day to discover new insights and fresh revelation as He opens up to us the glories of His precious Word. Every Christian should meet the day with as much delight as a sheep that is being led into new pasture. Spiritually, we should kick up our heels and leap with delight at the prospect of finding fresh forage. Expect God to show you some new insight day by day. Faith is expectancy—according to your expectancy, be it unto you.

FURTHER STUDY

Heb. 5;
1 Cor. 3:2;
1 Pet. 2:2

1. What should we desire?
2. What should we move on to?

Prayer

O Father, help me to come to Your Word each day with faith and expectancy. Lead me from one fresh green pasture to another, and enable me to wake up each morning tingling with anticipation at the new vistas that are opening up before me. For Jesus' sake. Amen.

The Valley of the Shadow of Death

". . . and free those who all their lives were held in slavery by their fear of death." (v. 15)

For reading & meditation—Hebrews 2:5–18

*W*e come now to the phrase which many commentators see as marking the halfway stage of this psalm: *"Even though I walk through the valley of the shadow of death, I fear no evil; for thou art with me."* The scene is evening, when the shepherd leads his sheep down the mountainside into the valley, where long flickering shadows lie across the trail. The sheep, because they are so timid and defenseless, are usually frightened by this experience. But they follow the shepherd and therefore are comforted. They will not fear evil because the shepherd is with them.

Millions of Christians have been greatly comforted by this verse. It underlines the fact that although death may be a dark valley, it is not something to fear. The Good Shepherd is well aware of our fear of death and constantly seeks to reassure us that, for the Christian, death is but a dark valley opening out into an eternity of endless delight. He has told us: "Surely I will be with you always—yes, even in the valley of the shadow of death." What a comfort—what a consolation.

Many Christians fail to enjoy life because of a morbid fear of death—it overshadows all they think and do. Look at how Moffatt translates our text for today: "And release from thraldom those who lay under a life-long fear of death." Note the terror in some of the words: "thraldom," "lay under," "life-long fear of death." Can there be a release from such fears? Thank God—there can!

FURTHER STUDY

Rom. 5:1–14;
2 Sam. 14:14;
Eccl. 8:8;
Heb. 9:27

1. What is the most certain thing about life?
2. Why has the believer no fear of death?

-+-==◉ *Prayer* ◉==-+-

O God my Father, I am grateful that in relation to death, I need not be in thraldom. I can be free, gloriously free—and free now. You are not the God of the dead, but the God of the living. In You I live, not just for time, but for all eternity. I am so thankful. Amen.

The Three Elements of Fear

"When you pass through the waters, I will be with you . . . For I am the LORD, your God . . ." (vv. 2–3)

For reading & meditation—Isaiah 43:1–13

*M*any people, some Christians included, see death as an intruder. Gandhi, the great Indian leader and politician, said that he started his Swaraj movement to help people overcome the fear of death. Politics was only a minor part of his purpose. "My aim," he said, "was the abandonment of the fear of death. So long as we let ourselves be influenced by the fear of death, we can never attain freedom."

When we come to analyze the fear of death, three elements can be seen to be present: the fear of the physical act of dying, the fear of finality, and the fear of judgment. Let's look first at the fear of the physical act of dying. This is very real to some people. Perhaps they have suffered and know, through bitter experience, how pain lacerates and hurts.

Doctors assure us that what people normally call "the agony of death" is felt much more by those who are watching than by the one who is passing away. Sir Frederick Treves, the eminent surgeon, said, "A last illness may be long, wearisome and painful, but the closing moments of it are, as a rule, free from suffering. There may appear to be a terrible struggle at the end, but of this struggle the subject is unconscious. It is the onlooker who bears the misery of it." Add to this natural phenomenon the supporting power of God's never-failing grace, and it is possible to look even this physical aspect of death quietly in the face and say, "My enemy—you are not really the terror that you seem."

FURTHER STUDY

Luke 16:19–31;
Num. 23:10;
Ps. 116:15;
Prov. 14:32

1. What did Jesus teach about death?
2. What sustains the righteous in death?

Prayer

My Father and my God, when the inevitable moment comes for me to walk through the valley of the shadow of death, help me to remember that Your grace and power can support me, not only spiritually, but physically too. I take great confidence from that. Thank You, Father. Amen.

"My Father Will Be Waiting"

"... I will come back and take you to be with me that you also may be where I am." (v. 3)
For reading & meditation—John 14:1–14

*N*o Christian need fear that death is equivalent to extinction, for Christ has said: "I go to prepare a place for you . . . that where I am *you may be also*" (vv. 2–3, RSV, italics added). Dr. W. E. Sangster tells how, as a young boy living in the heart of London, he went for a walk one day and got lost. A kindly policeman took him by the hand and led him to the police station. After waiting for what seemed like several hours in a dingy room, an officer came and took him down a dark passage where he saw his father waiting for him. Sangster said, "It will not be different, I think, when I die. *At the end of the dark passage my Father will be waiting.*" Though we shrink in the frailty of our human nature from what some refer to as "the Grim Reaper," death really has but one mission—to bring us into God's more immediate presence and give us an eternal place in our Father's house.

Finally, let us take the fear of judgment. Some research conducted a few years ago showed that this third component is not as common as it was half a century ago. Fewer people now attend church, and those who do, generally speaking, rarely hear a sermon on the fact of future judgment. No man or woman, however, who knows Christ should fear judgment. And why? Because, as Paul so beautifully puts it in his letter to the Romans: "There is therefore now no judgment for those who are in Christ Jesus." In Christ, judgment is in the past tense.

FURTHER STUDY

*Heb. 11:1–16;
Phil. 1:21;
Rom. 14:8*

*1. How did the Old Testament saints die?
2. How did Paul view death?*

Prayer

Blessed Lord Jesus, I listen to Your words and they breathe hope and inspiration into my heart. Take from me every doubt and fear this day. Help me to realize each day that I live in a resurrected Christ, and since You cannot die, neither can I. Amen.

"The Vocabulary Is Changed"

Day
158

"When he had said this, he fell asleep." (v. 60)

For reading & meditation—Acts 7:54–60

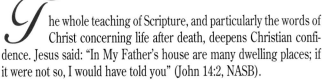

The whole teaching of Scripture, and particularly the words of Christ concerning life after death, deepens Christian confidence. Jesus said: "In My Father's house are many dwelling places; if it were not so, I would have told you" (John 14:2, NASB).

Jesus says, in effect: "If about seventy years of life were all that you could expect, I would be open with you and encourage you to make the most of the time you spend on this earth . . . *but in my Father's house . . .*" Take again the way Jesus and the New Testament use the words *death* and *sleep*. To the mourners standing around the lifeless body of a little girl, Jesus said: "The child is not dead but asleep" (Mark 5:39). He used the same word also when talking of the death of Lazarus: "Our friend Lazarus has fallen asleep; but I am going there to wake him up" (John 11:11).

One commentator makes the daring assertion that in the New Testament, after Jesus' death and resurrection, no one who was a Christian was ever said to have died. He claims that when sin had done its utmost in nailing Christ to the tree and hiding His tortured body in a sepulchre sealed by a huge stone, it was still powerless to destroy the Life which used His flesh. Death was dead—not He! Now everything "in Christ" is alive, and thus the vocabulary has to be changed to fit the facts. What we call "death," and Jesus called "falling asleep," is simply the transition from one plane of life to another—from earth's gloom to heaven's glory.

FURTHER STUDY

1 Cor. 15:1–21;
John 11:11;
Acts 13:36

1. Of what is Christ the first fruits?
2. What is the difference between sleep and death?

Prayer

Lord Jesus, You who are Master of life and death, I am so grateful that in You I see the death of death and the defeat of defeat. In You everything is alive—alive with meaning, destiny, goal—alive forevermore. Hallelujah!

167

"Just Getting Fit to Live!"

"But thanks be to God! He gives us the victory through our Lord Jesus Christ." (v. 57)

For reading & meditation—1 Corinthians 15:42–57

The Christian faith is the only faith that lights up death. "And it lights it up," says E. Stanley Jones, "not merely with a word but with a Word become flesh." Jesus went through the dark experience we call death, and resurrection became flesh in Him. Anyone who lives in Him is as deathless as He is.

It was said of Emerson, the great writer and debater: "He did not argue; he let in the light." The same can also be said of Jesus: "He did not argue immortality, *He showed Himself alive.*" The greatest evidence for the fact that there is life after death is, as we said, the resurrection of Jesus Christ. One of Tennyson's biographers wrote: "He laid his mind upon the minds of others with the result that they believed his beliefs." Jesus does the same. He not only believed in immortality, but demonstrated it. His living guarantees our living.

A woman was teaching a group of Japanese children on the island of Hawaii about the life and death of Jesus, when one of the children jumped up and cried out: "Ah . . . this no fair . . . Him one swell guy." One little girl who knew the story urged him to sit down. "Don't get upset," she said. "He didn't stay dead." Well, if He didn't stay dead, nor shall I stay dead. William James, when asked if he believed in personal immortality, said: "Yes—and the more strongly as I grow older." Why?—"Because I'm just getting fit to live." I, too, am just getting fit to live. How about you?

FURTHER STUDY

1 Cor. 15:22–42;
Isa. 25:8;
2 Tim. 1:10

1. What is the last enemy?
2. What has Christ done to death?

Prayer

Lord Jesus, the more I reflect on the wonder of Your resurrection from the dead, the more I realize that my soul will not die at death, but dance its way through to life eternal. In You I am free from death. I know it. Glory!

168

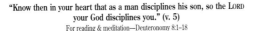

No Discipline— No Disciples

Day

160

"Know then in your heart that as a man disciplines his son, so the LORD
your God disciplines you." (v. 5)

For reading & meditation—Deuteronomy 8:1–18

*W*e move on now to consider the phrase: *"Thy rod and thy staff, they comfort me."* Shepherds, in Bible days, carried very little equipment with them when they tended their sheep, but invariably they carried a rod and a staff. The rod was a club which was used for a number of purposes, but mainly to drive off wild animals or catch the sheep's attention. If a shepherd saw a sheep wandering from the path or approaching a potentially dangerous situation—such as poisonous weeds, or the edge of a precipice—he would hurl his rod slightly ahead of the sheep, thus startling it for a moment and causing it to scurry back to the safety of the flock.

The rod therefore became *an object of discipline*, not to hurt or injure the sheep, but to direct it back into the way. Young shepherds would train for hours and compete with each other to see who could throw his rod with the greatest accuracy and across the greatest distance. The rod was what a shepherd relied on to protect both himself and his sheep whenever there was the threat of danger.

How many of us, I wonder, can go through the Christian life day after day without the need for some discipline? I can't—and I'm sure that is true of you also. Someone described the Christian life in this way: "Dependence plus discipline equals dependable disciples." Notice—dependence *plus* discipline . . . You can't be a dependable disciple without discipline. No discipline—no disciple. It's as simple as that!

FURTHER STUDY

*Prov. 3:1–12;
Ps. 94:12;
John 15:1–2*

1. What motivates God to discipline?
2. What is God's purpose in discipline?

Prayer

Divine Shepherd, help me to see that the reason You discipline me is because You delight in me. You love me too much to let me get away with things that are not good for me. I am so thankful. Amen.

169

Day 161

"Discipline's Divine Design"

"... the aim of the Christian discipline is the love that springs from a pure heart, from a good conscience, and from a sincere faith." (v. 5, Moffatt)

For reading & meditation—1 Timothy 1:1–17

Observing the way in which a shepherd in Bible days used his rod to discipline his sheep gives us a glimpse into the character of God. Some Christians have such a distorted view of God that they interpret His disciplines as punishment, and fail to see that our heavenly Father disciplines us not because He is angry with us, but because He loves us.

To understand God's purpose in disciplining us, it is necessary to observe the difference between fear and respect. The Bible uses the word *fear* in two ways: as a form of anxiety, and as a form of respect. As Christians, it is right that we have a deep respect for the Almighty, but we must see also that God does not want us to live out our days in anxiety, apprehension, and dread.

Some parents attempt to influence and discipline their children through the use of anxiety, but God does not deal with His children on that basis. One woman, wanting to teach her daughter the rules of the road, took her down to a busy crossroads and shouted to her as the cars approached: "Look out—here comes a car!" The child soon learned how to keep out of the way of approaching cars, but she also developed a morbid fear of traffic. One of the goals of parenthood is to so train children that they develop respect without fear. Our text says: "The aim of the Christian discipline is the love that springs from a pure heart . . ." The aim of God's discipline is not fear—but love that springs—and sings!

FURTHER STUDY

Heb. 12:1–11;
Prov. 13:24;
Rev. 3:19

1. What is discipline a mark of?
2. What does it produce in our lives?

Prayer

O God, what release this concept brings into my life as I ponder its implications. Your disciplines are intended not to leave me with a sigh but with a song. I am grateful beyond words. Thank You, dear Father. Amen.

Punishment vs. Discipline

"My Son, spurn not the Eternal's schooling, never be weary of his discipline" (v. 11, Moffatt)

For reading & meditation—Proverbs 3:1–12

God's rod of discipline is designed to help us: "Thy rod and thy staff, they comfort me." Rarely should we use the word *punishment* in relation to the disciplines which God effects in our lives as Christians. Although there is a sense in which God is bound to punish sin, in the life of a Christian as well as a non-Christian, the thought uppermost in God's mind when disciplining a Christian is not retribution for past misdeeds, but the development of future maturity. Bruce Narramore, a Christian psychologist, believes that the word *punishment* should be reserved for non-Christians only. He says, speaking of the relationship that God has with His children, that "as Christ took our punishment on the cross, we are no longer sinners, but saints. Thereafter the focus of God's dealings with us is not retributive, but remedial. We Christians are not under punishment, but under discipline—and the difference is vital."

I find it difficult to believe that God's disciplines do not contain an element of punishment, but I see the point Bruce Narramore is making—namely, that when we do wrong or wander from the pathway, God does not pounce upon us so as to even the score; His disciplines follow a divine design that is calculated, not merely to punish our wrongdoing, but to promote our spiritual growth and maturity. How consoling this thought is—that when we disobey, God intervenes to correct us, not in anger, or with a desire to get even with us, but out of the deepest concern and interest for our spiritual development and well-being.

FURTHER STUDY

Prov. 22:1–15;
Jer. 5:3;
Heb. 12:5

1. What did Jeremiah say about the children of Israel?
2. What is God's "rod of discipline"?

Prayer

Loving heavenly Father, help me to see that the hand which holds the rod of discipline is a nail-pierced hand. The love that led Jesus to die for me is the same love that leads You to discipline me. Thank You, dear Father. Thank You. Amen.

"Hand in Hand"

"I, even I, am he who comforts you." (v. 12)
For reading & meditation—Isaiah 51:1–16

*I*t is the staff," says Phillip Keller, "that identifies a shepherd
as a shepherd. No one in any other profession carries a
shepherd's staff. It is uniquely an instrument used for the care and
management of sheep. It will not do for cattle, horses or hogs. It is
designed, shaped and adapted especially to the needs of sheep."

The staff was a slender pole with a little crook on the end, used for
a variety of purposes. It was used to gently lift a newborn lamb and
bring it to its mother when it had become separated (a ewe will sometimes reject her offspring if it has the smell of human hands upon it).
It was used also to reach out and draw a sheep to the shepherd's side
for physical examination, as timid and nervous sheep tend to keep as
much distance as possible between themselves and the shepherd.

The main use of an ancient shepherd's staff, however, was to guide
the sheep. The tip of the staff would be laid against the animal's side,
and the gentle pressure applied would guide the sheep in the way the
shepherd wanted it to go. One observer of the ways of a shepherd with
his sheep says: "Sometimes I have been fascinated to see how a shepherd will actually hold his staff against the side of a nervous or frightened sheep simply so that they are 'in touch.' They will walk along the
way almost as though they were 'hand in hand.' To be treated in this
special way by the shepherd is to know comfort in a deep dimension."

FURTHER
STUDY

Matt. 9:18–26;
Ps. 86:17;
Isa. 66:13;
2 Cor. 1:3–4

1. What were Jesus' words
to the woman?
2. Why does God
comfort us?

⊷⊶⟹ *Prayer* ⟸⊷⊶

Gentle and tender Shepherd, I long for a closer and more intimate contact with You than I have ever experienced before. Let me feel the gentle pressure of Your staff against my side as I walk with You
through this day. In Jesus' Name I pray. Amen.

"Called Alongside"

"... the Counselor, the Holy Spirit, whom the Father will send in my name, will teach you all things ..." (v. 26)

For reading & meditation—John 14:15–27

The Shepherd's rod and staff were used not to intimidate the sheep, but for their welfare and support. I hesitated to use the shepherd's staff as a type of the Holy Spirit, but as I considered the caring and comforting ministry of the Good Shepherd, my mind ran immediately to the passage before us today. Jesus said: "And I will pray the Father, and he shall give you another Comforter, that he may abide with you for ever" (v. 16, KJV). Notice that Jesus used the pronoun "He," indicating that the Holy Spirit is a person. He is a person who counsels, comforts, guides, empowers—but most of all abides. An impersonal influence—an "It"—doesn't do that!

Modern translations substitute for the word "Comforter" such words as "Helper," "Counselor" or "Strengthener." But the Greek word is *parakaleo*: *para*, meaning "beside," *kaleo*, meaning "to call"—one who is called alongside us. Why is He called alongside? For counsel? Yes. For strength? Yes. For everything? Yes. There isn't a single thing needed for life that He isn't there to provide. Just as a shepherd walks alongside his sheep to comfort and to guide, so the Holy Spirit has come among us to bring the reality of Christ's word and presence to our hearts. It is through Him that we are in touch with Christ, and it is through Him also that there steals over us the assurance that we are one with Him and that we "belong." Oh, the security of being under His constant supervision and care. Too good to be true? Too good not to be true.

FURTHER STUDY

John 15; 16:13; Rom. 8:13–14

1. What did Jesus say the Comforter would do?
2. Has the Comforter come into your life?

Prayer

Loving divine Shepherd, can I ever get over the wonder of Your love and care for me? Help me to pass it on to others in just as gracious a way as You give it to me. You care for me, not grudgingly but graciously. I am so very, very thankful. Amen.

"He Has Gone Ahead"

"On this mountain the LORD Almighty will prepare a feast of rich food for all peoples . . ." (v. 6)

For reading & meditation—Isaiah 25:1-9

*A*s we turn to focus on the next phrase in the "Shepherd Psalm," we cannot help but notice that David appears to change the metaphor—from the good shepherd to the gracious host: *"Thou preparest a table before me in the presence of my enemies."*

Many commentators claim that the psalm is written in two parts: the first using a shepherd and his sheep, and the second using a banquet with the host and the guest. One writer says: "It's a pity that David didn't finish his psalm by staying with the one figure of a shepherd, rather than bringing in the concept of a banquet and a host. It seems to me to lose the sweet simple melody and to close with strange heavy chords when it changes to a scene of banquet hospitality."

That conclusion is quite wrong, for despite the seeming change of metaphor, David actually keeps the shepherd figure right to the end. When David referred to a "table," he was thinking of the high, flat-topped plateaus where the sheep were taken to graze in the summertime. Prior to taking his sheep on to this higher ground, a caring shepherd would go up alone to see if there were any wild animals or any poisonous weeds and, if so, plan his grazing program to either avoid them or take whatever steps were necessary to eradicate them. The sheep arriving on the high tableland would not realize it, but they owed their safety and security to the fact that the shepherd had gone before them to prepare for them a "table" in the presence of their enemies.

FURTHER STUDY

*Matt. 22:1-14;
Pss. 31:19; 68:10*

1. *What is the message of this parable?*
2. *What does it illustrate?*

--⊹══◈ *Prayer* ◈══⊹--

O Father, what comfort and security I derive from knowing that no situation or circumstance will ever come about in my life which You have not anticipated and foreseen. You have surveyed every path ahead—so lead on; I will follow. Amen.

Kept—by the Power of God

". . . who are protected by the power of God through faith . . ." (v. 5, NASB)

For reading & meditation—1 Peter 1:1–9

Those who have studied ancient Bible customs and the ways of eastern shepherds state: "There is no higher task for a shepherd than to go from time to time to study places, examine the grass and find a good and safe feeding place for his sheep." There are many poisonous plants in the grass and the shepherd must find and avoid them. It has been known for a shepherd to lose hundreds of sheep in one day by failing to take the necessary precautions in this matter.

Another observer of eastern customs says: "There are vipers' holes from which the poisonous snakes emerge to bite the noses of the sheep. The shepherd must burn the fat of hogs at the holes to bring out the snakes and then either kill them or drive them away." In addition to these dangers around the feeding ground, there are holes and caves in the hillside in which wolves and jackals live. The bravery and heroism of the shepherd reaches its highest point as he works to close up these dens with stones, or confront and kill the beasts with his long-bladed knife.

The way God protects and cares for His children as they go out into the world is a grander and more wonderful thought than that of seating them at an indoor banqueting table. If it is not apparent already, it should be quite clear by now that in those quaint and beautiful lines "Thou preparest a table before me in the presence of my enemies," the shepherd figure is as real as in the previous section of the psalm.

FURTHER STUDY

2 Tim. 4:1–18;
Gen. 28:15;
Deut. 33:27;
Prov. 2:8

1. What was Paul's testimony?
2. What did God promise Jacob?

Prayer

Father, I am so thankful that Christianity is not a "hot-house religion." You provide for me, not only in the safe and secure confines of my home, but also out there in the midst of a cold and cruel world. I am truly grateful. Thank You, Father. Amen.

Staying Close to the Shepherd

"Simon, Simon, Satan has asked to sift you as wheat. But I have prayed for you . . .
that your faith may not fail." (vv. 31–32)
For reading & meditation—Luke 22:24-33

A classic example of the way in which the divine Shepherd ministers to His children is seen in the passage before us today. Jesus tells Simon Peter that Satan has sought to tempt him and sift him like wheat, but that He has prayed that Peter's faith might not fail in that moment of overwhelming testing. Where would I have been, where would you have been, but for that blessed ministry of the divine Shepherd—going before us, anticipating our circumstances and supportively working and praying for us, so that we might not be overtaken by the enemy of our souls? If He did not minister to us in this way . . . where should we be?

This does not mean, of course, that the responsibility for our safety and security rests entirely on our divine Shepherd. We, too, have a responsibility—a responsibility to make sure that we keep as close to Him as we possibly can. This is the one sure place of safety. "It is always the distant sheep, the roamers, the wanderers," says one shepherd, "which are picked off by predators in an unsuspecting moment. Sometimes the sheep is so overtaken by fear that it is too frightened to even cry out. It might give a plaintive bleat before its blood is spilled." The divine Shepherd wants to forestall every calamity that would come our way, and strives to keep our lives free from serious dangers and hazards. And, of course, our lives will be danger-free if we stay close to Him, where He can provide for us and protect us.

FURTHER STUDY

Heb. 2; 7:25;
1 Cor. 10:13;
James 4:7;
Rom. 16:20

1. What does Christ do in our times of temptation?
2. What should we do?

Prayer

My Father and my God, thank You for reminding me that although You make Yourself responsible for my safety and security, I also have a responsibility—to stay as close as I possibly can to You. Help me to do just that—today and every day. For Jesus' sake. Amen.

Blessings – Not Just for Now

"... They also brought ... flour and roasted grain, beans and lentils, honey and curds ... for David and his people to eat." (vv. 28–29)

For reading & meditation—2 Samuel 17:20–29

Some commentators believe that when David wrote the words, "Thou preparest a table before me in the presence of my enemies," he had in mind the events about which we have read in today's passage. Driven into the wilderness by his son Absalom's rebellion, David and his followers became desperately hungry, thirsty, and weary. God came to his aid, however, and directed to him three men who "brought bedding and bowls" (so that David could wash and refresh himself) as well as "articles of pottery ... wheat and barley, flour and roasted grain, beans and lentils, honey and curds, sheep, and cheese ..."

How David must have rubbed his eyes in astonishment as he saw God provide for him a "table in the presence of [his] enemies." Can you cast your mind back at this moment to something "special" that God did for you to demonstrate His tender love and care? I can. Every Christian has these times—how sad that we forget them so soon.

God never does anything "special" in our lives just for the sake of the passing hour—it is done also as a pledge for the future. It is as though God is saying: "I'll do this for you now, not only to meet your need, but also that you might *always* know you are the object of my love."

If new dangers startle us with fear, we have forgotten the past mercies. I believe that David's confidence in God was due to the fact that whenever he faced a new problem, he remembered vividly the past hour of deliverance.

FURTHER STUDY

1 Kings 17;
Ezek. 34:14;
Isa. 25:6;
John 6:51

1. How did Elijah experience God's provision?
2. What are we to feed on?

Prayer

O Father, forgive me for taking so much for granted—rather than taking it with gratitude. I recall the words of Your servant John Newton and make them my own this day: "His love in time past forbids me to think, He'll leave me at last in trouble to sink." Thank You, Father—thank You. Amen.

Someone Had to Suffer . . .

"This is how we know what love is: Jesus Christ laid down his life for us." (v. 16)
For reading & meditation—1 John 3:11–24

*W*e spend one more day meditating on the phrase: "Thou preparest a table before me in the presence of my enemies." A shepherd may have to go through a good deal of personal sacrifice and danger in order to prepare the "table," or feeding ground, for his sheep. He may have to endure loneliness, privation, hunger, and sometimes even physical injury to make the feeding ground safe for his sheep. Many a shepherd comes back from such an expedition covered in cuts and bruises.

Just as a good shepherd sacrifices himself for the sake of his sheep, so has Christ, the Good Shepherd, gone to the utmost lengths possible to bring His sheep into a place of spiritual contentment and security. Unfortunately, we forget all too easily just what was the personal cost to Christ in preparing the table for His redeemed people. When next you come to the Table of Communion—which is really a feast of thanksgiving in remembrance of His tender love and care—ask yourself: do I fully appreciate what it cost my Lord to prepare this table for me? And what did it cost? It cost Him His *life*.

As Christmas Evans, one of our great Welsh preachers, picturesquely put it: "Never did any shepherd climb a mountain as dangerous and as challenging as Mount Calvary. There on its summit the Good Shepherd drew sin to battle, overcame all its forces, silenced forever the voice of the archenemy of our souls—and by so doing has prepared for us a table in the presence of our enemies. Come and be fed . . ."

FURTHER STUDY

Titus 2;
John 15:13;
Gal. 1:4;
Eph. 5:1–2

1. *What is the greatest act of personal sacrifice?*
2. *How are you demonstrating this in your life?*

Prayer

My Father and my God, how can I thank You enough for the grace that turns a tabletop of isolation like Calvary into a place where I can find life for my soul. I am so grateful. Thank You, dear Father. Amen.

Those Stupid Flies!

"I myself will tend my sheep and have them lie down, declares the Sovereign LORD." (v. 15)

For reading & meditation—Ezekiel 34:1–16

*W*e turn to focus on the next phrase in this beautiful and inspired psalm: *"Thou anointest my head with oil, my cup overflows."* Sheep, we are told, are especially irritated by flies and other winged parasites which buzz around their heads and make their lives a misery. *The Handbook of Bible Times and Customs* lists over twenty varieties of flies that can be found in the Middle East—warble flies, deer flies, black flies, nose flies, and so on. "Sheep are especially troubled by nose flies," says one shepherd, "for they buzz around the head of a sheep attempting to alight on the damp mucous membranes of the sheep's nose." So irritating can be the effect of nose flies that sometimes a sheep will beat its head against a tree or a rock in order to find relief. An alert shepherd, when he sees this taking place, goes to the sheep that is in trouble and bathes its head in olive oil. This results, almost immediately, in a dramatic change in the sheep's behavior. Gone is the frenzy and restlessness and soon the sheep begins to graze or lie down in peaceful contentment.

Perhaps at this very moment you are facing an endless bombardment of irritations and difficulties that are causing you to become downcast and fainthearted. Draw near to Jesus—your heavenly Shepherd. Spend some moments in quiet prayer and contemplation. Let Him bathe your hurts in the soothing oil of the Spirit. Then rise and go your way in the knowledge that no matter how frustrating life's circumstances and situations the Divine Shepherd is only a prayer away.

FURTHER STUDY

Luke 10:30–37;
Jer. 8:22;
Ps. 92:10;
Isa. 61:3

1. How did Jesus illustrate God's compassion?
2. What was Jeremiah's question?

Prayer

O Father, what a comfort it is to know that You are always ready to minister to me whenever I am driven almost to the point of distraction. Help me not to try and struggle through but to avail myself of your inexhaustible resources. Amen.

When Evil Thoughts Molest

"Thou wilt keep him in perfect peace, whose mind is stayed on thee . . ." (v. 3, KJV)

For reading & meditation—Isaiah 26:1–12

We saw yesterday how flies and other winged parasites buzzing around the head of a sheep can often drive it to distraction. Relief comes only when the shepherd is able to bathe the sheep's head with the soothing oil which he carries with him for this purpose.

What a striking picture this presents of the way in which God ministers to us in the midst of life's irritations. A motto on the desk of a high school principal reads:

> For every irritation under the sun
> There is a remedy, or there is none.
> If there be one, try to find it,
> If there be none, never mind it.

The suggestion, regarding an irritation for which there is no remedy, to "never mind it" is good, but not quite good enough. The irritation may be so present and insistent that you cannot help but mind it.

Take, for example, the evil or lustful thoughts that sometimes buzz around in our heads. It is impossible not to mind them. What is to be done? Several things are possible. First build a strong picture of Christ in your mind. In your reading, meditation, and personal prayer time, seek to develop a clear picture of your Savior. Then, when a wrong thought strikes, focus your mind, not on the thought, but on Him. Wrong thoughts can be outwitted by swiftly directing the mind to a more absorbing theme. And what better theme is there in the whole realm of thought than Christ?

FURTHER STUDY

Rom. 8:1–9; 12:2;
Phil. 4:8

1. On what things should we focus our thoughts?
2. List some items in each category.

Prayer

My Father and my God, help me to develop a strategy that will assist me in dealing with the wrong thoughts that sometimes buzz around in my mind. I know You are eager to help me—make me eager to be helped. For Your own dear Name's sake. Amen.

Outmaneuvering Wrong Thoughts

". . . if anything is excellent or praiseworthy—think about such things." (v. 8)

For reading & meditation—Philippians 4:1–9

*W*e said yesterday that the first thing we should do about wrong thoughts is to learn how to build a clear picture of Christ in our minds. The minute a wrong or obsessive thought comes into the mind and is recognized, we should look immediately to the Lord. Our victory depends on the skill we develop in quickly turning from the wrong thought to focus on Christ.

A second way in which some Christians have learned how to outwit the power of evil thoughts is to use also, as lesser helps, any wholesome subject in which they have a keen interest. A university graduate tells how, once he realized that the battle against evil thoughts had to be won where it had begun—in the mind—he could quickly shut off a train of wrong thoughts by anticipating the graduation ceremony at which he hoped to receive his degree. He said he focused also on other wholesome things—such as his hobbies, or an intriguing sermon he had heard—and he proved by experience that with practice and determination he could divert his mind into interesting and clean channels.

As you can see, much of the success in overcoming wrong thoughts depends on how one prepares for the conflict—for conflict it is. When Paul encourages us to reflect upon things which are true, noble, right, pure, lovely, and admirable, he is giving us good advice. To think and keep on thinking of these things, with a picture of Jesus at the center of them, is the only adequate preparation for the fight against evil thoughts.

FURTHER STUDY

Job 37:1–14;
Pss. 48:9;119:59;
1 Sam. 12:24

1. What was the advice given to Job?
2. List some of the "great things" God has done for you.

Prayer

Father, I see that in this matter of dealing with wrong thoughts, prevention is better than cure. Fire me with a resolve to meditate in the Scriptures until my thoughts become Your thoughts and my attitudes Your attitudes. For Jesus' sake. Amen.

Ask, Man, Ask!

"... Ask and you will receive, and your joy will be complete." (v. 24)

For reading & meditation—John 16:16–33

e have seen that the mind bent on overcoming the irritation of evil thoughts can find many a ruse to outmaneuver them. But the supreme Helper is Christ:

> When evil thoughts molest,
> With this I shield my breast—
> May Jesus Christ be praised!

We must not only focus our gaze upon Christ when worn down by the thoughts that buzz around inside our heads, but we must ask Him to help us. In talking over the years with people who were plagued with evil thoughts, I have been surprised at the number who have told me that they have never actually come to God and asked directly for His help. James reminds us that one of the reasons we do not receive is simply because we do not ask (James 4:2).

How, then, do we ask? It can be done in your own words or in the words of an appropriate hymn. You can say something like this: "Father, lay Your consoling hand on this forehead which is oppressed with irritating and evil thoughts. Help me now by breaking their hold upon me, and release me from their grip. In Jesus' Name." It must be understood, of course, that as well as praying, you, too, must accept some responsibility in this matter. It's no good praying, "Lord, deliver me from this evil thought," and then wallowing in it in your imagination. God will do His part, but you must also do yours.

FURTHER STUDY

*1 Cor. 2;
Matt. 15:19;
Ps. 94:11; 1:1–2*

1. *What is available to us?*
2. *In what do the righteous delight?*

Prayer

Father, I see so clearly that Your ability to give is limited only by my capacity to receive. Help me to be as eager as You are in bringing about deliverance and release in my thought life. For Your own dear Name's sake. Amen.

"O Lord, Help Me . . ."

". . . the anointing you received from him remains in you . . ." (v. 27)

For reading & meditation—1 John 2:18–29

How does our Lord go about the task of responding to our petitions to be delivered from wrong thoughts? He does it through the gentle, yet powerful ministry of the Holy Spirit.

The words *oil* and *anoint* are used in Scripture to depict several things, not the least being comfort, gladness and consolation (Ps. 45:7). It is this thought which the psalmist had in mind when he wrote, "Thou anointest my head with oil, my cup overflows." When a Christian is driven almost to distraction by the obsessive or evil thoughts that buzz around in his head, the most important thing he can do is to approach the Shepherd and say: "O Lord, help me—apply the soothing oil of Your Spirit to every area of my mind." And He will! It will surprise you how speedily and efficiently He complies with such a request when it is made in deadly earnest.

Some Christians make it their *daily* petition to ask God for the anointing of the Spirit upon their minds. Coolness in place of heat, and peace instead of torment are the rewards of those who are swift to turn to the Shepherd and invite Him to minister to them in this way. So when thoughts seem to almost drive you up the wall, draw close to the Shepherd and let Him apply the oil of the Spirit to your troubled and anxious mind. And you need have no fears that His supply of oil is limited in any way. He draws from a cup that never runs dry: "You anoint my head with oil, *my cup overflows.*"

FURTHER STUDY

1 Sam. 16:1–13;
Ps. 133:2; 20:6;
2 Cor. 1:21–22

1. What was the purpose of anointing with oil?
2. Where was the oil applied?

Prayer

Father, I see yet again that You alone can minister to me in those moments when irritating or evil thoughts crowd into my mind. So I rest in glad assurance—for "You anoint my head with oil, my cup overflows." Thank You, dear Father—thank You! Amen.

"The Hound of Heaven"

"... Does he not leave the ninety-nine in the open country and go after the lost sheep
until he finds it?" (v. 4)

For reading & meditation—Luke 15:1-7

W
e move on now to consider the phrase: *"Surely goodness
and mercy shall follow me all the days of my life."*
Throughout this psalm, David has placed a continuous emphasis on
the care and diligence of the divine Shepherd. He has made it abundantly clear that all the benefits enjoyed by the believer are due in no
small measure to the skill and management of the Good Shepherd.
With such a Shepherd, we need never fear, for no matter what difficulties and problems we may encounter, He follows hard on our heels to
redeem every single event and situation.

The word *follow* in this phrase literally means "pursue"—thus it
could just as well be translated: "Goodness and mercy shall pursue me
all the days of my life." David is saying that although his enemies are
pursuing him to dethrone and destroy him, God is following even harder on his heels to dispense the twin qualities of goodness and mercy.
Francis Thompson, in his memorable poem entitled "The Hound of
Heaven," put the same thought in this way:

> ... those strong Feet that followed, followed after.
> But with unhurrying chase
> And unperturbed pace
> Deliberate speed, majestic instancy
> They beat—and a Voice beat
> More instant than the Feet
> "All things betray thee, who betrayest me."

**FURTHER
STUDY**

*Rom. 8:28–39;
Luke 15:8–10; 19:10*

*1. What was Paul's
conviction?
2. What is the message of
the parable of the coin?*

Prayer

O Father, how can I ever thank You enough for "those strong Feet that follow after," and the love that constantly dogs my footsteps, seeking nothing but my eternal good? I run out of words, dear Lord—
but not out of gratitude. I am so deeply, deeply thankful. Amen.

Blocks Become Blessings

"Now I want you to know, brothers, that what has happened to me has really served
to advance the gospel." (v. 12)

For reading & meditation—Philippians 1:12–30

Many consider that when David uttered the phrase,
"Surely goodness and mercy shall follow me all the days
of my life," he was simply being poetic and not proclaiming a solid fact.
They say: "It's easy to repeat this statement and believe it when everything is going well, but what about those times when health fails, or
income falls and troubles come 'not in spies but in battalions'?" And
what about those times also when we have to watch a loved one writhe
in the agonies of unrelieved pain, or when close friends prove false and
disloyal? Can we really say at such times: "Surely goodness and mercy
shall follow me all the days of my life"? I believe we can.

As I look back over my life, I can recollect one particular occasion—
during 1968—when, as I looked forward to the future, things looked so
black that I considered leaving the ministry. Now, with hindsight, I can
see that the hour of darkness was one of the great turning points in my
life, and moved me toward a wider ministry. Goodness and mercy followed me, and turned what looked like despair into a door of greater
opportunity.

It is my belief that God does not engineer what we might describe as
"calamities" or "disasters," but that they happen as the consequence of
sin, ignorance, or carelessness. Such is His skill, however, at turning
tragedy to triumph and loss into gain that I can understand why some
believe *He* sent the tragedy and devised the disaster—so marvelously
does He bring good out of evil.

FURTHER STUDY

2 Cor. 4;
Prov. 30:5;
Isa. 43:1–2

1. What was Paul's testimony?
2. What is God's promise?

⇢⇒ *Prayer* ⇐⇠

Father, help me to realize that whenever anything "bad" happens to me, Your goodness and mercy soon
follow in its tracks, to turn the blocks into blessings, and the interruption
into an interpretation. Thank You, Father. Amen.

The Sinking of the Titanic

"So do not fear, for I am with you . . . I will strengthen you and help you; I will uphold you wi
th my righteous right hand." (v. 10)

For reading & meditation—Isaiah 41:1–16

*M*any people saw the loss of the *Titanic* in 1912 as an act of God's judgment because of the proud boast of its owners that it was "unsinkable." I do not see it in that light. The loss of the *Titanic* was due to reckless racing through an icefield, and the death toll was greater than it needed to have been because she only carried lifeboat accommodation for 1,200 people, though the passengers and crew totaled 2,293. The great ship went down due to a compound of pride and criminal folly. "Many a life," says one writer, "has been saved by the *Titanic*. The track of westbound ships across the Atlantic was shifted further south, away from the dangerous ice-fields. The obsolete Board of Trade requirements with regard to emergency boat accommodation were stringently revised."

This is often the way it is in life—disappointment, tragedy, and grief teach people a great deal. In the Christian life, however, this is not *often* the way it is—but *always* the way it is. God follows hard on the heels of every event and circumstance in our lives, not only teaching us a great deal, but working to turn every loss into a gain. Look back over your life. Have there not been times when you questioned God's wisdom? Have you not had moments when you thought you could survive better on your own? But what is your view now? Are you not convinced that He followed you in goodness and mercy? Did not good come out of the evil, light out of darkness, and faith out of despair?

FURTHER STUDY

*2 Cor. 12:1–10;
Ps. 34:19–20;
1 Pet. 4:12–13*

*1. How did Paul view his setback?
2. Why should we rejoice in these things?*

Prayer

Gracious God and loving Father, I see I need not whine or complain when things don't go the way I planned.
Assured of Your constant mercy and goodness, I can make music out of every misery, and a song out
of every sorrow. All glory and honor be to Your wonderful Name. Amen.

What a Difference!

"When all kinds of trials and temptations crowd into your lives . . . don't resent them as intruders, but welcome them as friends!" (v. 2, J. B. Phillips)

For reading & meditation—James 1:2–18

*I*t probably goes without saying that this phrase of David's— "Surely goodness and mercy shall follow me all the days of my life"—is an utterance of faith. It can be said only by someone who looks beyond the events and circumstances of life and has implicit confidence in the One who is ultimately in control. David believed that nothing could happen to him, no difficulty or dilemma could come into his life without eventual good emerging from the chaos. Most of us, when we look back over our lives, can see the truth of this, but the challenge is to believe it when we are going through the circumstances. Ah—then it is not so easy.

Phillip Brooks was one of the great preachers of a previous generation. He began his career as a schoolteacher, but he was a failure. In the midst of his depression, there came to him a clear call to the Christian ministry. At first he pushed it aside, but the call grew louder and louder. He was led on step-by-step to become a preacher of amazing influence, gaining a position of high esteem on both sides of the Atlantic.

He says in one of his sermons on the Twenty-third Psalm: "In the hours of my humiliation, if anyone had said to me that 'God's goodness and mercy' were following hard on my heels, I would have considered them an imbecile. *But they did!* How differently I might have responded if I had believed then, as I believe now, that His goodness and mercy are my constant companions." How differently indeed!

FURTHER STUDY

Lam. 3:22–36;
Pss. 103:17–18; 108:4;
Titus 3:5

1. What are "new every morning"?
2. Write out a definition of mercy.

Prayer

Father, I see that what I believe makes, not just a difference, but a world of difference. Help me to be as ready to praise You when trouble comes as I am when it goes. In Jesus' Name I ask it. Amen.

"But God"

"But God raised him from the dead . . ." (v. 30)
For reading & meditation—Acts 13:13–31

*T*he thought which has been quietly shaping itself in our minds is the powerful and transforming one that the goodness and mercy of God follow hard on our heels to turn every tragedy into a triumph and every loss into a gain. It is easy to affirm this as we look back—the challenge is to affirm it with equal conviction as we look ahead.

If you can get hold of this truth and absorb it into your life as a working principle, then it will transform your attitude toward everything. Never again will you be at the mercy of circumstances. In Acts 5:40–41 we read an astonishing statement: "When they had called in the apostles, *they beat them* . . . Then they left the presence of the council, rejoicing . . ." (RSV, italics added). Rejoicing? Over injustice? How is it possible to rejoice over an injustice? Because they believed, with David, that the last word was not with men, but with God—"goodness and mercy" would follow them and turn the situation to their advantage. When you can rejoice over injustice, you are indomitable.

Another verse from Acts that always intrigues me reads thus: "Because the patriarchs were jealous of Joseph, they sold him as a slave into Egypt. But God . . ." (Acts 7:9). That phrase, "but God," is at the end of every injustice—He has the last word. And just as God used the injustice done to Joseph to feed the Egyptian people and his own family, so He transforms every sorrow, every bereavement, every tragedy. Christianity may not explain everything, but it most certainly transforms everything.

FURTHER STUDY

*Rom. 2:1–4;
Ps. 34:8;
Nahum 1:7*

*1. To what should God's goodness lead us?
2. How would you define goodness?*

Prayer

Gracious Father, help me to be brave and to face up to everything that comes, knowing that if the worst should happen, we can turn it into the best. I say "we," for I cannot do it alone. Only in You can I be truly invincible. Amen.

"I'll Never Leave This Outfit!"

"How lovely is your dwelling place, O LORD Almighty! My soul yearns, even faints, for the courts of the LORD . . ." (vv. 1-2)
For reading & meditation—Psalm 84:1-12

We come now to the final phrase in David's "hymn of praise to divine diligence": *"I shall dwell in the house of the Lord forever."* As we said when we began our meditations on this psalm, David is speaking here as a sheep—one of God's flock.

David knew, better than anyone, that a sheep's welfare depended to a great degree on the love and care of its shepherd. Having begun with the proud boast, "The Lord is my shepherd"—or, "Look at who my shepherd is—my owner, my manager—the Lord is!"—he finishes on an equally positive note: "I shall dwell in the house of the Lord forever." The thought that comes through is clearly this—I am so utterly contented with being under the care of my loving Shepherd that I have no wish to have my circumstances changed—I want things to stay this way forever!

Some commentators have expressed disappointment at David's use of the word *house* in the closing phrase of his psalm, believing it to detract somewhat from the imagery of a shepherd and his sheep. But the word *house* has a much wider meaning than most seem to attach to it. It means, in fact, the "household" of God, the "flock" of God—or, as the Amplified Bible translates it—the "presence" of God. Phillip Keller's rugged translation of this final phrase may offend the purists, but to me it states fairly accurately what was in the psalmist's mind. "Nothing will ever make me leave this outfit! It's great!" And to that I add a hearty *Amen*!

FURTHER STUDY

Pss. 122:1-9; 26:8; 27:4; Eph. 2:19-22

1. What was the psalmist's attitude toward God's house?
2. What is your attitude toward it?

Prayer

Father, I too want to add my "Amen" to this tremendous and exciting fact. I am so content with the way You care for me and the way You manage my life that I, too, "wouldn't change this outfit for anything." Amen.

189

Life – Not Mere Existence

"Now this is eternal life: that they may know you, the only true God, and Jesus Christ, whom you have sent." (v. 3)

For reading & meditation—John 17:1–19

*D*avid's words in the final part of this psalm reflect the idea that, as one of God's flock, he is so satisfied with the care of his Shepherd that he wants things to stay that way—forever. He has no wish or desire to change, and his words ring with positive assurance: "I shall dwell in the house of the Lord forever."

A Harvard University professor once lectured on the theme: "Is eternal existence desirable?" and came to the conclusion that it is not. If all that eternity offers is just existence, then I would tend to agree with the professor's conclusion. Who can bear mere existence eternally? But if it's eternal *life*—that's different. "Life has to be eternal or else it is not worth living."

Dr. E. Stanley Jones, when referring to the subject of life after death, remarked: "Only life that is eternal is really life: every other kind of life has the seeds of death in it." George Bernard Shaw once said, "I don't want to have to live with George Bernard Shaw forever." We can hardly blame some people for not wanting to live with themselves forever, because they are poor companions to themselves now. To spend eternity with a self you dislike is not a happy prospect. But suppose you have a self that is transformed into the image of Christ, and joined to Him inseparably—what then? Ah—that is different! That is more than existence—that is *life*. Remember, eternity is not just living forever—it is living with *Jesus* forever. That's what makes the difference.

FURTHER STUDY

1 John 5:1–12;
John 6:27;
Rom. 2:7;
Titus 1:2

1. What is eternal life?
2. Do you have the assurance that you have eternal life?

❦ *Prayer* ❦

O Father, I am so thrilled to realize that the life which You have given me is not just a matter of quantity, but quality. I am not just going to exist forever, I am going to live forever. Thank You, Father. Amen.

"An Assurance Was Given Me"

"The Spirit himself testifies with our spirit that we are God's children." (v. 16)

For reading & meditation—Romans 8:1–17

We continue meditating on the final phrase of Psalm 23—"I shall dwell in the house of the Lord forever." David feels so secure in the flock of God that he has no hesitation in affirming that this is the way it will be forever. Do you, I wonder, feel as safe in your Christian life as David did in the Shepherd's fold?

This is not the time or place to debate the issue of "eternal security"—or, as it is sometimes described, "once saved, always saved"—but it is right to focus here on that most blessed of all earthly experiences—*assurance*. The question is often raised in Christian circles: can a person have, in this life, the assurance of personal salvation? One denomination gives this answer: "It is not possible to know in this life, with any degree of certainty, that one is a recipient of the grace of God."

What utter nonsense! John Wesley wrote in his *Journal* on May 24, 1738, after hearing a reading from Luther's *Preface to the Book of Romans*: "I felt my heart strangely warmed. I felt I did trust in Christ, Christ alone, for salvation, and an assurance was given me that He had taken away my sins, even mine, and saved me from the law of sin and death." Wesley had the assurance of salvation. And so, I might humbly add, do I. But what is more important, as far as you are concerned, is that if you surrender your life fully to Jesus Christ and trust Him alone for your soul's salvation, then so can you.

FURTHER STUDY

1 John 4:1–13; 3:24; Gal. 4:6; 8:38–39

1. Who brings assurance to our lives?
2. Do you have complete assurance of salvation?

Prayer

Gracious and loving heavenly Father, I am so thankful that You have made it possible for me to have now, on this earth, the assurance of personal salvation. Help me not just to realize it, but to rejoice in it. For Your own dear Name's sake. Amen.

"Mightily Assured"

"Most assuredly, I say to you, he who believes in Me has everlasting life." (v. 47, NKJV)
For reading & meditation—John 6:35–51

We said yesterday that one section of the Christian church affirms that it is not possible for a person to know with certainty that he or she is a recipient of God's grace. Another section of the church says: "We can state that we hope to be saved, or that we are trying to be saved, or that we are being saved, but no one can say, 'I am saved,' until he arrives safely over on the other side."

Ian MacPherson, in *This Man Loved Me*, tells how a woman said to him, "I think it is great presumption for a person to say they are saved." He asked her if she was saved. "I belong to a church," she said. "But are you saved?" he continued. She replied: "But I believe it would be presumptuous for me to say that I am saved." "Well," said the preacher, "I think it is greater presumption for anyone professing to believe in Jesus not to say that he is saved—for Christ Himself declares: 'He who believes in Me has everlasting life.'"

The Bible makes it clear that we can be assured of salvation in this life, certain that when we die we will go straight into the immediate presence of the Lord, *and* fully assured that we have eternal life. An old Welsh miner used to put after his name the letters M.A. I knew he did not have a Master's degree and I asked him what it meant. "Oh," he said, "it means that in relation to being with Christ in eternity, I am Mightily Assured."

**FURTHER
STUDY**

*2 Tim. 1:1–12;
Ps. 27:1;
Isa. 12:2;
Rom. 10:9*

1. What was Paul's
   confession?
2. What are the two
   requirements for assurance of salvation?

 *Prayer*

O Father, I am so grateful that You are the center of my life. Can this life within me die? Never—for it is deathless and immortal. I rest in this glad and glorious assurance. Thank You, Father. Amen.

Nostalgia for Heaven

"We . . . would prefer to be away from the body and at home with the Lord." (v. 8)

For reading & meditation—2 Corinthians 5:1–15

*T*rue Christians not only have an assurance that when they die they will go to heaven, but they also have a nostalgia for it. The word *nostalgia* comes from two Greek words: *nostos*, meaning "return home"; and *algos*, meaning "pain."

An old legend tells of a seal king who desired the company of a human being. One day he heard, from his cavern under the sea, a baby's cry—and he rose to the surface to discover a tiny infant in a derelict boat. Just then a rescue party intervened, and he lost his prize. But as the boat was towed away, the seal king threw into the heart of the child a little salt wave, saying as he submerged, "The child is mine. When he grows, the salt sea will call him and he will come home."

It is only a legend, of course, but it underlines the timeless truth that when God comes into our lives we have not only the assurance that we belong to Him, but a deep, insatiable longing for home. One preacher claims there are two things you notice about a Christian who is head over heels in love with Christ. You notice first how natural and "at home" he is, and the next thing you say to yourself is, "This man is an exile; he doesn't belong here at all." You can observe this in the apostle Paul. How busy and concerned he was for Christ's affairs on earth, and yet he sighs, as in our text today, to be "at home with the Lord." Do you have a nostalgia for heaven?

FURTHER STUDY

2 Tim. 4:1–8;
John 17:4;
Acts 20:24

1. What was the reflection of Jesus and Paul?
2. What was Paul "ready" for?

Prayer

Gracious and loving Father, help me never to forget that, as far as this world is concerned, I am not a resident but a sojourner. You are preparing for me in eternity, not a mere habitation, but a Home. I just can't wait to see it. Amen.

No Separation — Forever

"My sheep listen to my voice . . . and they shall never perish; no one can snatch them out of my hand." (vv. 27–28)

For reading & meditation—John 10:22–38

We come now to our final day together in meditating on the sublime phrases of what someone has described as "the sweetest religious song ever written—the Twenty-third Psalm." It began with a positive note of assurance: "The Lord is my shepherd, I shall not want," and it ends in the same joyous and exhilarating way: "I shall dwell in the house of the Lord forever."

This psalm, as we have seen, pictures a sheep so fully satisfied, so utterly content and so much "at home" with the shepherd that there is not the slightest desire for change. Conversely, of course, on the shepherd's side, such a relationship has developed that he would never think of parting with one of his sheep. So strong are the bonds between them that nothing can separate them—ever.

I first entered the ministry in Wales. Many of the farmers in the area were deeply caring of their sheep, but there was one who was notorious for his disinterest and neglect. When one looked at his scraggly sheep, huddled together in the corner of the field, one could almost see in the eyes of these abused creatures a longing to find themselves under the care of a gracious shepherd.

Aren't you glad you don't belong to a shepherd like that? As a Christian, you belong to the *Good Shepherd*. Rejoice in that fact! His care for you will last not only through time, but will go on into eternity also. You will dwell forever . . . *forever* . . . in the constant care and loving presence of the Lord.

FURTHER STUDY

Phil. 1:1–6;
Isa. 43:4;
Luke 12:7;
1 Pet. 5:7

1. Of what can we be confident?
2. Write your own psalm today about your relationship with the Shepherd.

Prayer

Lord Jesus, how good and secure it feels to be under Your personal care. And to think that this same care will be extended into eternity is more than I can comprehend. May the wonder of this stupendous fact break more and more into my life, day by day. For Your own dear Name's sake. Amen.

Section Four
The Spirit-Filled Life

The Spirit-Filled Life

*E*very art form has a rhythm to it. Music produces a pattern of sound and silence, dance gives us a visual composition of movement and rest; painting is a play of light and shadow, architecture and sculpture alternate mass and space. We often talk about art having a particular "spirit" or emotion. These creative rhythms are emotional sparks from the all-encompassing fire of the Holy Spirit that inspires everything made by human hands.

In this section of commentaries, Selwyn Hughes wisely reminds us that our only hope of safety and happiness is in our surrender to the Holy Spirit. Like the rhythmic flow of a musical accompaniment, the Spirit is always present and always moving in our lives. We need to live Spirit-filled lives. In fact, to follow in Jesus' footsteps we must live with the Spirit of his Father inside us. It's a spiritual state we as God's children long for.

A lot of people, particularly new Christians or people seriously considering Christianity for the first time, shy away from the thought of a Spirit-filled life because they insist they're not worthy to live a life like that. Selwyn's message to them is, nobody is! If God rewarded us based on what we deserved, none of us would have a chance of getting anything. There is no way any of us can earn the blessing of a Spirit-filled life. It's only by God's grace that we receive the Holy Spirit. But that grace isn't something to push away from. Rather, it's a gift we should embrace with open arms and thankful hearts.

In his second letter to the Corinthians, Paul writes, "Where the spirit of the Lord is, there is freedom." As one who was frequently a prisoner himself, Paul knew the value of freedom. It's a rare and delicate state, always subject to change, threatened by worldly conflict, and the enemies of righteousness. A Spirit-filled life frees us to live with the confidence that the very essence of God glows within us. Nothing else in all of creation is so pure or so powerful.

L.G.G.

A Command to Be Obeyed

"Do not get drunk on wine . . . Instead, be filled with the Spirit." (v. 18)

For reading & meditation—Ephesians 5:1–20

Our next theme is both challenging and life-changing—*the Spirit-Filled Life*. We begin by focusing on a well-known text which in the Amplified Bible reads: "And do not get drunk with wine . . . but ever be filled and stimulated with the (Holy) Spirit."

However we view the doctrine of the Holy Spirit, or whatever experience we may have had of Him in the past, if we do not enjoy an ever-present flow of His power in our lives, then we are living below the New Testament standard. This text, as many commentators have pointed out, is a command to be obeyed. If we are not experiencing what the Bible commands, then our lives are not in harmony with God's purposes. I meet many Christians who are sighing over lost ecstasies, mourning over lost victories, and who are downcast because they have lost touch with God. It is largely because they are living, not "the life of the Spirit," but the life of following an ideal with their own resources, stirred by emotion through a special sermon or something they read in a book. They grow tired and are on the point of giving up.

A translator in India, working on an early edition of *Every Day Light* on the Holy Spirit, wrote: "I'd like another subject. I'm tired of working on the Holy Spirit." A lot of Christians have that problem—they grow tired of working on the Holy Spirit, instead of letting the Holy Spirit work on them. Let's stop working on the Holy Spirit, and allow Him to work on us!

FURTHER STUDY

Rom. 8:1–17;
Ezek. 36:27;
John 14:17;
Heb. 10:15–16

1. *What is the result of "the law of the Spirit of life" in Christ Jesus?*
2. *What is Paul teaching about the Holy Spirit?*

Prayer

Blessed Holy Spirit, help me as I thread my way through the maze of thoughts and attitudes about your Holy Spirit. Help me to come out with Your thoughts and attitudes. I want to be filled with the Spirit—today and always. For Jesus' sake. Amen.

United on One Thing

"May . . . the fellowship of the Holy Spirit be with you all." (v. 14)

For reading & meditation—2 Corinthians 13:5–14

The Christian church is greatly divided over the issue of how the Holy Spirit operates in the lives of believers. One section of the church believes that when we admit Christ into our lives at conversion, we also receive the Holy Spirit in all His fullness, and then we should go on to appropriate His presence and power in our hearts day by day. Another section claims that at conversion Christ *alone* enters our lives, and then we need, on some subsequent occasion, to invite the Holy Spirit in also. A third group says that both Christ and the Holy Spirit come into our lives at conversion, but there are different *operations* of the Spirit (sanctification, baptism in the Spirit, etc.) which we ought to experience as we grow in our Christian lives. However, the church is united on one thing—Christianity is a religion in which the Holy Spirit plays a prominent part.

The benediction most used in Christian circles is the one before us today, for it is the most complete: "The grace . . . of the Lord Jesus Christ and the love of God and the presence and fellowship (the communion and sharing together, and participation) in the Holy Spirit be with you all" (Amplified Bible). Grace introduces you to the love of God which eventuates in participation in the Holy Spirit, and that participation is for *all*. It is the destiny of every Christian to participate in the Holy Spirit, and the only thing that can block that participation is our unsurrendered will.

FURTHER STUDY

1 John 4;
Rom. 8:16;
Gal. 4:6;
1 John 3:24

1. How is error exposed?
2. What is the result of the Holy Spirit's work?

Prayer

O Father, if it is my destiny to participate in the Holy Spirit, then over these next weeks, turn all my anticipations into participations. In Jesus' Name I pray. Amen.

Refined Ineffectuality

"... The Spirit Whom He has caused to dwell in us yearns over us—and He yearns for the Spirit
[to be welcome]—with a jealous love." (v. 5, Amp. Bible)

For reading & meditation—James 4:1–10

The practical-minded James gives us a picture in our text for today of God yearning over us, eager to dwell within our lives through His Holy Spirit; more eager than we are to be indwelt. If this is true then it is immensely encouraging, for it means that God is willing to do everything in His power to enable us to live a Spirit-filled life.

Suppose there had been no Holy Spirit? Just what kind of Christianity would have faced the world? It would be like having a New Testament with just the four Gospels, no Acts, and no Epistles. If the New Testament had ended with the four Gospels, it would not have been a gospel that would have conquered the world!

We see a picture in the Acts of the Apostles of a Holy Spirit-less type of Christianity. When Paul arrived in Ephesus, he sensed a central lack in the lives of certain disciples, so his first question was: "Did you receive the Holy Spirit when you believed?" And they said, "No, we have not even heard that there is a Holy Spirit" (Acts 19:2). There were about twelve men in that group, and without the Holy Spirit, what were they doing? Apparently holding their own—but their faith was non-contagious and without dynamic power. There are many in today's church who, although they have heard about the Holy Spirit and are well-versed in the Scriptures, know only the formality and ritualism of the services the church offers. The disciples at Ephesus knew the outer baptism, but not the inner one. The result? Refined ineffectuality.

**FURTHER
STUDY**

*Acts 19:1–20;
Joel 2:28;
Matt. 3:11;
Luke 11:13*

1. What events followed the coming of the Holy Spirit to Ephesus?
2. How did this relate to evangelism?

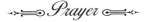

Prayer

O God, save me from this refined emptiness that lacks the anointing and power of the Spirit. I'm through with emptiness. I want fullness. Thank You, Father. Amen.

The Blasphemy against the Spirit

"... but the blasphemy against the Spirit will not be forgiven." (v. 31)
For reading & meditation—Matthew 12:22-37

We are seeing that the command to live a Spirit-filled life applies to all Christians—with no exceptions. Unfortunately, however, there are those within the Christian church who think they are exceptions. They have become so obsessed with the notion that they have blasphemed against the Holy Spirit that they live under a cloud of perpetual self-condemnation. This problem is one of the devil's most popular devices in trying to hinder God's children from experiencing the continuous flow of the Spirit in their lives.

What does it mean to "blaspheme" against the Holy Spirit? In my view, it is *willfully* attributing to the Holy Spirit the filthiness of Satan. It is more than just a passing thought entering the mind; it is a continued stance of resistance which refuses to face the truth. And that sin is seldom committed. In all my ministry, I have never met anyone who I thought had committed this sin. I have met many who believed they had done so, but close questioning revealed that it was not so much deliberate rebellion as obsessive thoughts—and that really is another problem.

This sin is so distinctive that anyone troubled about committing it shows, by the very fact that they are troubled, that they have not committed it. If they had, the Holy Spirit would have departed and they would not be troubled. Don't let Satan bully you into believing that obsessive thoughts or unclean desires are evidences that you have gone too far to be forgiven. If you *want* to be forgiven, your very wanting is a sign of the Spirit's presence in your life.

FURTHER STUDY

1 John 1;
Ps. 103:3;
Eph. 1:7;
Acts 13:38

1. How much sin does God forgive?
2. How is God's forgiveness appropriated?

Prayer

O Father, help me not to listen to Satan's taunts, but to recognize that my longings to be better are a sign of Your life within me. How could I seek You if, in a measure, I had not already found You? Thank You, Father. Amen.

The Spirit—Outraged

"How much more severely do you think a man deserves to be punished . . .
who has insulted the Spirit . . ." (v. 29)
For reading & meditation—Hebrews 10:19–39

*W*e said yesterday that one of the devices Satan uses to keep some Christians from experiencing all the fullness of the Spirit is to persuade them that the obsessive or unclean thoughts they might have in connection with the Holy Spirit are direct "blasphemy" against the Spirit. Such thoughts are usually due to deep emotional and psychological problems, and not deliberate disobedience against the Holy Spirit. They can be forgiven.

Another verse which seems to cause problems for some Christians is the one before us today. In the days of the early church, there were some Jews who, after embracing Christianity, decided to abandon it and return to their old religion—Judaism. Before being readmitted to the faith of their fathers, they were required to renounce the Christian gospel by figuratively trampling on the blood of Christ, at the same time saying words to this effect: "I renounce the blood of Jesus as unworthy and ineffectual." In the religion of the Jews, trampling on blood was a sign of contempt. What greater effrontery, then, to the Christian faith than to tread under foot the blood of the Son of God, and openly state that it was ineffectual and unworthy. Such an act, said the writer to the Hebrews, not only insulted the Holy Spirit, but outraged Him (Heb. 10:29, RSV). Such an action is seldom committed in modern times. Take it from me, most upsets in connection with the Holy Spirit are caused by the Spirit of grace calling us to repentance and forgiveness.

FURTHER STUDY

*Heb. 9;
Matt. 26:28;
Rom. 5:9;
1 Pet. 1:18–19*

1. Why is Christ's shed blood so precious?
2. How does it apply to accusing thoughts?

Prayer

O Father, release me, I pray, from all Satan's attempts to influence my thinking, and enable me to enjoy, from this day forward, the freedom of "life in the Spirit." For Jesus' sake. Amen.

Don't Dampen the Spirit

"Do not put out the Spirit's fire . . ." (v. 19)

For reading & meditation—1 Thessalonians 5:12–24

The sin described in Scripture as "blasphemy against the Holy Spirit" rarely occurs in the life of a Christian. It is a conscious resistance, and anyone worrying about it has not committed it. There is, however, a more frequent sin. It is one which almost all Christians have committed, and is known as "quenching the Spirit."

How do we "quench" the Holy Spirit? We can do this in many ways, but the chief way is by refusing to let Him have full control of our lives. The Amplified Bible says: "Do not quench (suppress or subdue) the (Holy) Spirit." You see, it is possible for you to possess the Holy Spirit without the Holy Spirit possessing you. Dr. Handley Moule, the great Anglican bishop of a past generation, used to say: "The difference between someone who is quenching the Spirit and someone who is allowing the Spirit to have free course in their life, is the difference between a well in which there is a spring of water choked, and a well in which the obstruction is removed so that the water springs up and fills the well."

If we are choked by fears, resentments, indecision, self-centeredness, then we are suppressing the Holy Spirit who resides in us in order to free us. I know that many are afraid to surrender completely to the Spirit, afraid that they will become what some people call "hot-pots." But the danger to the present church is not from "hot-pots" but from "cold fish"! Unless I am greatly mistaken, our churches are more in danger of freezing up than burning up.

FURTHER STUDY

Acts 10:34–48;
2 Cor. 3:17;
Rom. 8:2;
Luke 4:18

1. What happened while Peter was preaching?
2. What liberty did this bring?

 Prayer

O God, forgive me, I pray, for not allowing Your Holy Spirit to have full sway in my life and experience. Let Your divine fire burn within me, and help me not to dampen it. For Jesus' sake. Amen.

"Not As Good As Your Book"

"No one else dared join them, even though they were highly regarded by the people." (v. 13)

For reading & meditation—Acts 5:12–16

A Hindu said to a missionary in India: "Sir, I do not want to appear presumptuous, but have you found out what the Acts of the Apostles records? I see there a strange power, making weak, ineffective men into strong, effective, radiant men. That seems new and central—have you found that?" And that is the central question we must ask ourselves. We are taken up with so many little and marginal things in church life that we miss the central power.

Some children, on the way to see the ocean, got occupied with a pond one of them had made by blocking a tiny stream. One little fellow, seeing the ocean in the distance, said, "Come on, Billy, that ain't the ocean—that's only a pond." Sometimes I feel like calling to the thousands of Christians who are gathered around their little denominational pools, thinking them to be the ocean: "Come on, brothers and sisters, that isn't the whole thing. Look over there. The ocean awaits us—God's ocean of power and plenty. I'll race you to it!" A Christian, who gave a Bible to an acquaintance, asked him some time later if he had read it. "Yes," said the man, "and what is more, I have found you out. You are not as good as your Book! The Book says there is power for human weakness, joy instead of sorrow, victory instead of defeat—but I see little of this in you." What an indictment! Could the same be said of you and me?

FURTHER STUDY

John 6:44–71;
Rev. 2:4; 3:16;
Matt. 24:12

1. How did some of Jesus'
   disciples respond?
2. What did Simon
   Peter say?

Prayer

O Father, help me to be as good as the Book. Show me the way to power and poise, so that I will represent the highest qualities of life to those I live with or work with. For Jesus' sake. Amen.

Who Is the Holy Spirit?

"... he will guide you into all truth: for he shall not speak of himself ..." (v. 13, KJV)

For reading & meditation—John 16:12-16

*W*e have seen that the Christian faith is a religion of the Spirit, and unless we are continually filled with His divine resources, then our lives are largely ineffective. If the Scripture places so much emphasis on being possessed by the Holy Spirit, then it follows that we ought to find out everything we can about the one who seeks to indwell us. I say "who," for the Holy Spirit is not just an impersonal influence, nor is He just a sense of fellowship when we get together, nor an enthusiasm over ideas or causes. It is evident from the personal pronouns used of Him in the Scriptures that the writers viewed Him as a member of the Trinity, equal in honor and status to the Father and the Son.

However, the Holy Spirit does not like to draw attention to Himself. In the Old Testament, the Spirit turns the spotlight fully upon the face of the Father. In the New Testament, He turns it fully upon the face of the Son. Never does He focus attention on Himself.

We owe a great deal of our understanding of the Holy Spirit to what Christ said of Him in the Gospels, for there Jesus returns the compliment, and occasionally turns the spotlight upon the Holy Spirit, revealing His nature and His ministry. Jesus, in fact, put His disciples through a deliberate course of mental and spiritual training to prepare them for the reception of the Spirit; and if we are to understand the Spirit's ministry in our lives, then we must enroll in this course too.

FURTHER STUDY

John 14:16–31;
15:26–27;
Luke 24:49; 11:13

1. What did Jesus teach about the Holy Spirit?
2. What does the word "comforter" mean?

Prayer

Gracious Father, this week, as I seek to understand who the Holy Spirit is and what He wants to do in my life, give me an eager mind and a receptive spirit. In Jesus' Name I pray. Amen.

The Birth of the Spirit

" . . . no one can enter the kingdom of God unless he is born of water and the Spirit." (v. 5)

For reading & meditation—John 3:1-16

*J*esus prepared His disciples for the reception of the Holy Spirit. This course of training is best revealed in John's Gospel. There are six lessons:

(1) *The birth of the Spirit.* It is through the ministry of the Holy Spirit that we are born again into the kingdom of God. John makes clear what the new birth is not: "Children born not of natural descent, nor of human decision or a husband's will, but born of God" (1:13). The new birth is brought about by the Holy Spirit, and unless He is involved in it, then it is not a new birth at all. Someone has described the new birth: "It is the change, gradual or sudden, by which we, who are the children of the first birth, through a physical birth into a physical world, become children of the second birth, through a spiritual birth into a spiritual world." Just as you have to have brains to enter into the kingdom of knowledge, an aesthetic nature to enter the kingdom of beauty, a musical sensitivity to enter the kingdom of music, an emotional nature to enter the kingdom of love, so you have to have a spiritual birth to enter the kingdom of God.

Jesus, in His first reference to the Holy Spirit in John's Gospel, put His finger on the first step of the Spirit's ministry in human life—the birth of the Spirit. Jesus said these words, not to a down-and-out, but to a member of the Jewish ruling council, a Pharisee. If Nicodemus, a morally upright religious leader, needed the Spirit, then we all need Him.

FURTHER STUDY

Gal. 5;
John 1:13;
Titus 3:5;
1 Pet. 1:23

1. What are the characteristics of those born of the Spirit?
2. What does it mean to "walk in the Spirit"?

Prayer

O Father, I am grateful for this new life within—the new birth—and now I want more. This that I have experienced sets my heart on fire for life in all its fullness. Amen.

Intake — and Outflow

"Whoever believes in me, as the Scripture has said, streams of living water will flow
from within him." (v. 38)
For reading & meditation—John 7:37-44

*W*e continue examining some of the lessons Jesus taught His disciples, when preparing them for the reception of the Holy Spirit.

(2) *The outflowing of the Spirit.* When the Holy Spirit comes in, He also wants to get out. This is the rhythm of the life of the Spirit—intake and outflow. If there is more intake than outflow, then the intake stops; if there is more outflow than intake, then the outflow stops. Jesus is teaching His disciples here that when the Holy Spirit is given, they would enter into a phase of becoming outgoing and creative. This is not only spiritually but psychologically healthy. We are made for creative activity, for contribution, and unless we contribute, we get in conflict with ourselves. Those in a family who are always demanding and not donating become tied-up people. The world's philosophy (and I beg you not to heed it) is: "How can I *get?*" The Christian's philosophy is: "How can I *give?*" The Christian is the healthier personality.

John, in commenting on the words of Jesus here, says: "By this he meant the Spirit, whom those who believed in him were later to receive. Up to that time the Spirit had not been given, since Jesus had not yet been glorified" (v. 39). Why couldn't the Spirit be given until Jesus was glorified? Because before there could be attunement (man being right with himself), there had to be atonement (man being right with God). The death of Jesus on the cross cleared the way between man and God, and the coming of the Spirit cleared the way between man and himself.

**FURTHER
STUDY**

*1 Kings 17:1–16;
1 Cor. 2:12;
Matt. 10:8;
2 Cor. 9:7*

*1. What was Elijah's
instruction?
2. What principle does
the widow's action
illustrate?*

⊸⇒ *Prayer* ⇐⊷

O Father, help me not to be a tied-up person—receiving but never giving, demanding but never donating.
Flow in and flow out of me this day—and every day. For Jesus' sake. Amen.

The Spirit—a Permanent Guest

"... he will give you another Counselor to be with you forever—the Spirit of truth" (vv. 16–17)
For reading & meditation—John 14:1–17

We come now to the next lesson Jesus gave His disciples when preparing them to receive the Holy Spirit.

3. *The Spirit's coming would not be a temporary visitation—He would abide in them forever.* In the Old Testament, the Holy Spirit provided temporary supplies of power to individual people for certain tasks. When these purposes were accomplished, He returned to heaven. The disciples were no doubt aware of this aspect of the Spirit's ministry, but now Jesus gives them the breathtaking news that the Holy Spirit's coming would be permanent: "He will abide in you and be with you *forever*." What a revelation this must have been to the disciples. The occasional would give place to the permanent; the special give way to the general. Jesus was saying, in effect, that the Holy Spirit would not come and go—a kind of "hide-and-seek" experience—but He would move within the inner recesses of their beings and abide with them forever.

This is probably one of the most important truths we can grasp from the Scripture, for there are many Christians who think of the possession of the Holy Spirit as tentative and momentary. However, that would defeat the very point and purpose of redemption, for as someone said: "The Holy Spirit is the applied point of redemption." In other words, the Spirit is the cutting edge of the Christian life. His coming into our lives must be permanent or our redemption (at least its application) will be temporary. The Holy Ghost becomes a Holy Guest! And, thank God, a permanent guest!

FURTHER STUDY

Gen. 1;
Ezek. 36:27;
1 John 3:24;
Heb. 9:14;
Rev. 22:17

1. What was the Holy Spirit's ministry in the beginning?
2. What is His ministry since Pentecost?

Prayer

Blessed Holy Spirit, I am so grateful that You are willing to take up a permanent abode within my heart. With You abiding in me, I want for nothing and am equipped for every task. I am so thankful. Amen.

"With"—or "in" and "upon"

"... he dwells with you, and will be in you." (John 14:17, RSV)
"But you shall receive power when the Holy Spirit has come upon you ..." (Acts 1:8, RSV)

For reading & meditation—John 14:16-21 and Acts 1:8

Here is another lesson Jesus taught His follows about the Holy Spirit:

(4) *The Holy Spirit is a resident counselor.* The Greek word here is interesting: *parakletos—para* (beside), *kletos* (call)—one who is called alongside to help. There isn't a single thing needed in the Christian life that He isn't there to provide. Note the difference in the prepositions that are found in the passages before us today. Jesus said that the Spirit was "with" them, but later would be "in" them and "upon" them. I take these prepositions to mean that the Holy Spirit was "with" them prior to Pentecost, but was "in" them and "upon" them subsequent to Pentecost. Prior to Pentecost their lives lacked character and consistency. They cast out devils, but, on other occasions, they seemed to be somewhat influenced by them.

Simon Peter is a case in point (Matt. 16:23). The disciples were loud in their assertions of loyalty, and loud in their blunderings and misunderstandings. The Spirit was most certainly "with" them—helping, encouraging and revealing—but He was most certainly not "in" them or "upon" them. When the Spirit came "in" and "upon" them at a later date, then fitful living became faithful living; erratic loyalty became everlasting loyalty.

Today, in the lives of many Christians, the Holy Spirit seems to be working on the outside rather than on the inside. Actually, of course, the Holy Spirit is resident "in" every Christian, but He wants more than just to be resident—He wants also to be president! How is it in your life and experience? Is the Spirit a passing guest or a permanent guest?

FURTHER STUDY

*Eph. 1;
John 15:6; 16:7-8*

*1. How are we "sealed with the Holy Spirit"?
2. What is "the earnest of our inheritance"?*

Prayer

O God, forgive me for not utilizing the resources of the Holy Spirit whom You have placed within me. Help me to see that the Spirit within makes for adequacy without—if I avail myself of Him. Amen.

The Whole Truth

"... the Holy Spirit ... will teach you ... and will remind you of everything
I have said to you." (v. 26)

For reading & meditation—John 14:22-31

*A*nother lesson given by Jesus to His disciples when preparing them to receive the Holy Spirit was:

(5) *The Holy Spirit would teach them and remind them of all that Jesus had said.* A famous agnostic once said that the irreconcilable conflict between science and religion is that science is never fixed—it is open and progressive: religion, on the other hand, is fixed on absolutes and dogmas.

Well, it is true that Christianity is fixed, but it also provides for a continuing revelation: "The Holy Spirit will teach you all things." Jesus is God's final and complete revelation, but because of the limitations in us, that revelation must be gradually unfolding. Notice, however, that the teaching of the Spirit is according to a fixed pattern: "He will ... bring to your remembrance all that I have said to you" (v. 26, RSV). He will teach us *more* than Jesus taught, but not other than Jesus taught. Someone said of this approach that it is both conservative and radical; because it conserves all that Jesus taught, and because it applies to new areas of life the universal aspect of Jesus.

"He will ... bring to your remembrance all that I have said." Note that word *all*. When we are not under the Holy Spirit's tutelage, we tend to focus on just one thing Jesus said and neglect the "all." Then what happens? We produce a lopsided type of Christianity, with an overemphasis on one thing and an underemphasis on another. Some Christian communities, who concentrate on one truth, miss the whole truth. Christians, under the Spirit's control, give heed to the "all."

FURTHER STUDY

1 Cor. 2;
Neh. 9:20;
Luke 12:12;
1 John 2:27

1. What has God revealed to us by His Spirit?
2. What does the Holy Spirit bring to us?

Prayer

O Father, I don't want to live on a truth, or even a cluster of truths—I want to live on the Truth.
In Jesus' Name. Amen.

The Final Emphasis – Jesus

"He will bring glory to me . . . (v. 14)
For reading & meditation—John 16:5–16

We come now to another lesson that Jesus taught His disciples about the Holy Spirit:

(6) The Holy Spirit will glorify Jesus. The promise of today's verse was fulfilled after the Holy Spirit came on the disciples at Pentecost, for we read: "We are witnesses of these things, and so is the Holy Spirit, whom God has given to those who obey him" (Acts 5:32). This shows that the divine Spirit and human spirits were working together for the same end—the glorification of Jesus.

The statement that the Holy Spirit would glorify Jesus was one of the most important lessons in the process of spiritual education. The whole purpose of the Spirit's coming was not to glorify Himself or the person who receives Him, but to glorify Jesus. That puts the emphasis in the proper place. If the Holy Spirit glorified the person who received Him, then that would make Christianity an eccentric religion—off center. If He glorified Himself, then it would make Christianity Spirit-centered rather than Christ-centered. Christianity, that is not linked to the Incarnation, can have no fixed idea as to what God is really like. Spirit-centered Christianity would leave us going off at a tangent into all kinds of weird areas of subjectivity.

There are some Christians who are more Spirit-oriented than Christ-oriented. They hear what they describe as the "voice of the Spirit" telling them to do strange and unseemly things. Every "voice" we hear must be tested against the character of Jesus, and if it doesn't come up to His standard, then it has to be rejected. The Holy Spirit will always glorify Jesus.

FURTHER STUDY

Matt. 3;
Isa. 11:2; 42:1; 61:1;
John 1:32;
Acts 10:38

1. What did Isaiah prophesy?
2. How was this fulfilled?

---⟫═◦ *Prayer* ◦═⟪---

O God, my Father, I am conscious that I am thinking through a delicate issue here. Give me such a clear vision of Jesus, so that I shall always decide according to Him. Amen.

The Upper Room

"... they went up to the upper room, where they were staying ..." (v. 13, RSV)

For reading & meditation—Acts 1:1–14

We have examined some of the lessons Jesus taught His disciples as He sought to prepare them for the coming of the Holy Spirit. Now we consider the significance of what occurred in the place called "the upper room." The upper room has been described as "the birthplace of the Church." Certainly it was there that power was loosed which changed the world.

Some commentators believe that the upper room was part of someone's home—someone sympathetic to Jesus and His ministry. Why did the Holy Spirit come upon the disciples in a home and not in a sacred place such as the Temple? If the Holy Spirit had come upon them in the Temple, then His coming would have been associated with a sacred place, sacred services, and sacred occasions. The Holy Spirit came in the most common of all places—a home. It was as if He was saying, "I am here not just for 'sacred' occasions, but for all occasions, for all of life."

One writer said in commenting on the ordinariness of the upper room, "The Holy Spirit is not a spiritual luxury to be imported into the unusual, but a spiritual necessity for the usual." He is to be the pulse-beat of all we do—the usual as well as the unusual, the ordinary as well as the extraordinary. In the coming of the Holy Spirit, the ordinary and seemingly insignificant things of life are touched with a divine significance: every bush is aflame with the glory of God, every moment is packed with eternity, and every contact we make is part of His perfect purposes.

FURTHER STUDY

Joel 2:18–32;
Isa. 32:15; 59:21;
Ezek. 39:29

1. What had God promised would follow the coming of the Holy Spirit?
2. What is the Lord exhorting the Israelites to do?

Prayer

O God, I am so thankful that I don't have to wander from sacred place to sacred place in search of Your power and Your glory. You come to me just where I am until my heart glows with Your shekinah glory. Amen.

Day 201

All Places Sacred

"When they arrived, they went upstairs to the room where they were staying." (v. 13)

For reading & meditation—Acts 1:12–26

We make a great deal of "the upper room" now, but in the days of Jesus it was just one room in a home where some of the disciples were staying. Just think of it! God's most precious promise—the promise of the Father (v. 4)—was fulfilled in one of the most ordinary places on earth—a home. This puts Christianity into a different mold from other world religions with their emphasis on places, rites, ceremonies, etc.

Whenever I visit places with a sacred history, I am saddened when I see so many pilgrims trying to get a special touch from God through touching a sacred place. Weary pilgrims trudge from one spot to another, trying to obtain something of the sacred place to keep for themselves. It is unnecessary to make a special trip to a sacred spot in order to get a special touch from God, for the Almighty cannot approve of only giving Himself in a special place. There's nothing wrong in visiting these places, of course, providing one does not believe that God is limited to them. If God were confined to such places, how would the poor, or those who are busy bringing up their families, find Him?

The most freeing thing that ever happened in religious history was when God, in the power of His Holy Spirit, came upon His waiting disciples in a home. In this age, God can be found anywhere in the world, providing He is found in Christ; and He comes to all, wherever they may be, when they lift up a surrendered and trusting heart to Him.

FURTHER STUDY

Matt. 18:1–20;
Ps. 139:8;
Prov. 15:3;
Acts 17:27–28

1. What did Christ teach about His presence?
2. What was David's conclusion?

 Prayer

O God, I am so thankful that I do not need to move from where I am, except in my attitude, to find You coming in all Your fullness and power. Here, right now, where I am, I reach up to You; and I know that You are reaching down to me. Thank You, Father. Amen.

214

All Becomes "All"

"They all joined together constantly in prayer . . ." (v. 14)
For reading & meditation—Acts 1:14–26

The upper room was associated in the minds of the disciples with the *Last Supper*, for it was in this room that Jesus unfolded for them the meaning of redemption. As He broke bread with them, He said, "This is my body which is given for you: do this in remembrance of me." Taking the cup of communion, He said, "This cup is the new covenant in my blood, which is poured out for you" (Luke 22:19–20).

The upper room had a double content—the cross and the Spirit. These are more closely connected than we might realize, for if we do not bear the spirit of the cross, we will not bear the Spirit of God. We are to be crucified followers of a crucified Lord.

Did that upper room stand in the minds of the disciples as a symbol of Christ's self-giving? And would the whole atmosphere of the place remind them that, just as He had offered His all, so must they offer their all? I cannot help but believe that the connection between the Last Supper and the promised descent of the Holy Spirit would be much upon their minds. In that room, God, in the person of His Son Jesus Christ, had offered His all. Now the 120 disciples were being confronted with the same challenge. Out of Christ's offering came power, for God answers self-giving by the giving of Himself. We can only conclude that something significant happened in the lives of those disciples in that ten-day waiting period, for out of that "all" offering came "all" power.

FURTHER STUDY

Matt. 26:17–30;
Eph. 2:14
Col. 1:20; 2:14

1. What was abolished by the cross?
2. What is the relationship between "Passover" and "Pentecost"?

Prayer

O God, in this "upper room" where I am right now, I offer my little "all," and I take instead Your almighty "all." I exchange my poverty for Your riches, my emptiness for Your fullness, my weakness for Your strength. Amen.

215

All Persons Sacred

"In those days Peter stood up among the believers (a group numbering about
a hundred andtwenty) . . ." (1:15)

For reading & meditation—Acts 1:15 and 2:1–4

We continue meditating on the various aspects of the upper room. The next interesting thing we notice is that the Holy Spirit came, not just on the twelve, but on the one hundred and twenty.

Suppose the Spirit had come on the twelve and had bypassed the others who were waiting in that room—what would that have done to Christianity? It would have limited the Spirit's power and presence to special people, called to a specially sacred task. Someone has remarked that the addition of a zero to the twelve, making one hundred and twenty, is one of the greatest additions in history. It is! The coming of the Holy Spirit on the one hundred and twenty meant that all distinctions, based on a special class or group, were gone. Some have different gifts, of course, such as are described in Romans chapter 12, 1 Corinthians chapter 12 and Ephesians 4:11. However, as far as receiving the gift of the Holy Spirit is concerned, then *all* who are redeemed are eligible.

If we think this through carefully, it might enable us to regain a sense of mission in life. Some occupations are considered sacred and some secular. This produces a sag in every so-called secular occupation—the layman is in a secular occupation, and so is excused if he lives a second-rate Christian life. This impoverishes life because it removes any sense of divine calling. A minister can be holy and a layman can be holy—all on the same conditions with no special favors. Sacredness is found in character, not in a collar; in values, not in vestments.

**FURTHER
STUDY**

Acts 10; 11

*1. What problem did
some of the early
Christians have?
2. How did God
overcome this?*

Prayer

O Father, I am grateful that I, as a person, can receive the greatest gift of all—the Holy Spirit—and live out
my life where You have placed me, with a sense of divine vocation. Thank You, dear Father. Amen.

Men and Women—Equal

Day 204

"All these with one accord devoted themselves to prayer, together with the women . . . they were all filled with the Holy Spirit . . ." (1:14 & 2:4, RSV)

For reading & meditation—Acts 1:12–14 and 2:4

The Holy Spirit came in a home, thus lifting Christianity out of the tyranny of sacred places. He came upon *all* those who were waiting, not just the Twelve, thus making clear that the Holy Spirit is available for a person, as a person. Another interesting thing we observe is that the Holy Spirit fell upon the women as well as the men.

What would have happened if the Holy Spirit had bypassed the women and had come only on the men? Some, no doubt, would have been pleased with such a distinction, particularly those who were steeped in Judaism—but the Holy Spirit made both sexes equal. Until this moment there had been in Israel a specially sacred sex—the male sex. "Every male that opens the womb shall be called holy to the Lord" (Luke 2:23, RSV). That is as far as the Jewish faith went, but Christianity goes farther—women received the glorious gift of the Holy Spirit.

This fact overwhelms all the arguments about man's superiority, and places men and women on an equal basis before God. This has nothing to do with the role of a woman in marriage, as described by Paul in Ephesians 5:22–24—that is another issue entirely. Paul's teaching, that a woman has a certain role in marriage, however, must not be construed as meaning that she is not equal with her partner. God sees both men and women as equal, and on that great Day of Pentecost, He clarified the issue for all by demonstrating that women, as well as men, were temples of the Holy Spirit.

FURTHER STUDY

Rom. 16;
Matt. 27:55–56;
Luke 7:37–38; 10:38–42

1. How did Paul commend women in the church?
2. How significant were women in the life and ministry of Christ.'

Prayer

O Father, I am so thankful that the coming of the Spirit breaks all barriers down. Help me to look out at life through Your eyes, for when I do then all things drop into focus. Amen.

217

"The Ground Is Level"

"They all joined together constantly in prayer, along with the women and Mary the mother of Jesus, and with his brothers." (v. 14)

For reading & meditation—Acts 1:12-14

*T*he coming of the Holy Spirit made not only all places and persons equal, but canceled out all distinctions based on blood or special privilege.

Today's passage says that among those who devoted themselves to prayer were "Mary the mother of Jesus, and his brothers." How easy it would have been to have established a privileged line through those who were closely related to the Lord. If the Holy Spirit had set these people aside in a certain way, and had come to them and them alone, then Christianity would have merely followed the family line for all succeeding generations. However, Mary, blessed though she was, waited, together with the others for the coming of the Holy Spirit. And when she received Him, she received Him on the same basis as the others—faith in Christ as Savior and Lord. At the great moment of the Holy Spirit's coming, no one was singled out for special favor, no distinctions were made based on blood and no one was identified as being superior or inferior. All were equal.

"At the foot of the cross," said Dr. Abernathy, when a judge and a Chinese laundryman stood before him to be received into the membership of his church, "the ground is level." In Islam, the descendants of the prophet Mohammed are greatly honored. In Christianity, no such hierarchy was ever attempted. Why? Because it was canceled out by the coming of the Spirit. A new hierarchy came into being. The blood of God's Son has made it possible for us all to become sons of God. Human blood is no longer important.

FURTHER STUDY

Luke 1:38–55; 2:51; John 2:3–5; 19:25

1. List some of the characteristics of Jesus' mother.
2. Does she have a special place within the church?

Prayer

O God, my Father, in giving Your Holy Spirit to me, You have opened the Highest to the lowest, the Greatest to the least. I belong to the twice-born nobility! Hallelujah!

The Young and the Old

". . . I will pour out my Spirit on all people . . . your young men will see visions, your old men will dream dreams." (v. 17)

For reading & meditation—Acts 2:14–21

*A*nother barrier that went down in the upper room was that between the young and the old. Peter pointed out that what had happened in the upper room was the fulfillment of Joel's prophecy, in which the prophet had declared that the day would come when young and old alike would receive the gift of the Holy Spirit. "This is the day the prophet spoke about!" said Peter. "It's arrived!"

"There has always been a sacred age," said someone, "— old age." In almost all religions, power and sanctity have been associated with the old. This is why many religions tend to be backward-looking rather than forward-looking. In the upper room there were young men (I think we can assume this) who received the gift of the Holy Spirit in the same way as their elders. What a dynamic this produced. Young and old moving together in the power of the Spirit. The old would naturally want to conserve the values and good things they had come to love and respect, while the young would want to move these values into greater realms and make them more widely operative.

One writer said, "The Christian faith demands radicalism as well as conservatism to fully express itself." Young and old combine to fully express the nature of the Christian faith, for conservatism or radicalism on their own are weak. Together, however, they become strong and powerful. The Holy Spirit in the old would lead them to hold onto the good things of the past; the Holy Spirit in the young would push them toward greater conquests and discoveries.

FURTHER STUDY

*1 Tim. 5; 4:12;
1 John 2:13–14;
1 Pet. 5:5;
Rom. 12:10*

1. What was Paul teaching Timothy?
2. What is "preferring one another"?

Prayer

Heavenly Father, I am thankful that both young and old can be used in the kingdom. Blend the conservatism of the old with the radicalism of the young, so that this generation might see a new Pentecost. For Jesus' sake. Amen.

219

The Feast of Pentecost

"When the day of Pentecost came, they were all together . . ." (v. 1)

For reading & meditation—Acts 2:1–12

The occasion of the Feast of Pentecost was extremely fitting for the descent of the Holy Spirit, for the Feast of Pentecost was also called the Day of the Firstfruits—the festival when the first fruits of the harvest were offered to God in thanksgiving and prayer.

On that first Day of Pentecost, Jerusalem was doubtless crowded with people gathered from all parts of the nation. As the people outside the upper room offered to God the firstfruits of the natural harvest, those inside were offering to God the gift of themselves—the firstfruits of a spiritual harvest, which Christ would reap in that generation and the generations to come. At a divinely ordained moment—nine o'clock in the morning—the Holy Spirit fell upon those waiting disciples and transformed them, in a matter of minutes, from men and women who were timid and hesitant into fearless and fiery disciples. Instead of cowering behind closed doors for fear of the Jews (John 20:19), they stepped out into the crowded streets of Jerusalem, and rallied around Peter as he declared the truth of what had happened. And what a sermon Peter preached that day! Three thousand people were converted! Today we have to preach three thousand sermons to get one person converted!

The first Day of Pentecost ended, as far as the nation was concerned, in a religious festival. However, for the disciples it ended in a religious fervor that set the world on fire. The former concluded with a strong community spirit; the latter concluded in an eternal fellowship, the deepest on earth—the church.

FURTHER STUDY

Lev. 23:1–21;
Deut. 16:10;
Acts 20:16;
1 Cor. 16:8

1. What did the Feast of Pentecost signify?
2. How did it relate to the Passover Feast?

Prayer

O God, give us another Pentecost! Make this day the beginning of new things for me and for Your church. Fill me now—to overflowing—with Your blessed Holy Spirit. For Jesus' sake. Amen.

Steps to the Divine Infilling

"Check up on yourselves . . . Do you feel Christ's presence and power
more and more within you?" (v. 5, TLB)

For reading & meditation—2 Corinthians 13:5-14

*H*ave you found yourself longing to know more of the
Spirit's quickening power in your life? If so, you will be
gratified to know that I intend now to focus on the steps you need to
take in order to help you open yourself more widely to the power and
presence of the Holy Spirit. Before you begin to focus on these steps,
pray that you will not stumble on them, for to miss your way here could
mean the difference between defeat and victory. The steps are simple
but important.

1. *Examine yourself to see how much of the Spirit is lacking in your life.*
Although the Holy Spirit came into you at conversion (John 3:6), there
is a great deal of difference between you possessing the Spirit and the
Spirit possessing you. Andrew Murray said, "We want to get possession of the Holy Spirit and use Him: the Holy Spirit wants to get possession of us and use us."

Make an inventory of your needs. Is it power to witness that you
lack? Is it purity of thought that is your greatest need? Is it strength to
overcome temptation? Identify the area of need before you go any further. Once you identify a need, you can then focus your prayers on
meeting it. Whatever your views concerning the doctrine of the Spirit,
and whatever experiences you may have known in the past, ask yourself: Am I filled to overflowing with the Spirit right now? If not, pinpoint
your greatest area of need, and prepare for it to be met.

FURTHER STUDY

*Eph. 5:1–20;
Ps. 139:23–24;
Rom. 8:27*

1. *What was the prayer
of David?*
2. *Make it your
prayer today.*

Prayer

Father God, my heart is eager to know You in all Your fullness. I am ready to take the steps: I stand upon the
threshold with my hand on the doorknob. I know the door will open. Thank You, Father. Amen.

Day 209

The Spirit of Holiness

"... put on the new self, created to be like God in true righteousness and holiness." (v. 24)

For reading & meditation—Ephesians 4:17–32

We continue to focus on the steps toward greater openness to the work of the Holy Spirit in your life:

(2) Ask yourself: Is there any unresolved conflict, unrepented sin, or any thing I must put right in order that God can flood my life with His Holy Spirit? We must not forget that the Spirit of God is called the Holy Spirit. Holy symbolizes purity; Spirit symbolizes power. The Holy Spirit is completely holy, searching, convicting, cleansing, yet at the same time immensely powerful to support, strengthen and sustain. If there is anything in our lives that need to be put right, then talk to God about it now. Remember, at this point, that you are not just reading a page— you are ridding yourself of a plague. You cannot have the Holy Spirit flowing through your life and hold onto unrepented sin. One or the other must go.

(3) *Remind yourself that God is more eager to give you His Holy Spirit than you are to receive.* Jesus called the giving of the Spirit "the promise of the Father" (Acts 1:4, RSV). This is the promise of promises. For God to go back on a promise would be the very reverse of His nature; it is impossible. The character of God is behind this promise. You can bank on it. If you could part the clouds for a moment and look into heaven, you would see in the heart of God such an intense longing and yearning for you to be filled with His Spirit that it would completely overwhelm and overawe you. He aches to give you the fullness of His Spirit—He really does.

FURTHER STUDY

*Acts 2:14–38;
Pss. 51:17; 34:18;
Isa. 66:2*

1. How did Peter exhort the people to receive the Holy Spirit?
2. What was the result?

Prayer

O Father, what You want for my life, I want too—my will and Your will to coincide. Make me as eager to be filled as You are to fill me. For Jesus' sake. Amen.

222

Proper Priorities

"... how much more will your Father in heaven give the Holy Spirit to those who ask him!" (v. 13)

For reading & meditation—Luke 11:1–13

*I*n the passage before us today, Jesus spends some time sharing with His hearers that God is both a Father and a Friend. It is vitally important that we realize that God *wants* to give us the Holy Spirit, for if we are not absolutely sure of this, then our asking will be shot through with indecision and uncertainty. The great Archbishop Temple said, "We ask for the Holy Spirit, yet in the depth of our heart we are not sure whether He wants to give it to us, and this one single doubt negates the object of the exercise." So stop wishing to receive the Spirit in all His fullness and start expecting. You can be positive in asking because God is positive in giving.

(4) *Bring the whole matter to a crisis.* One great preacher said that "the soul grows by a series of crises." Make it a matter of priority to spend some time in prayer to receive more of His Spirit and become desperate over the issue. Treat it as if God dropped a letter into our mailbox this morning which said, "I would like to see you as soon as possible over a matter of a very important gift I want to give you." If that happened, I wonder how you would handle your schedule over the next few days? Things you thought were top priority would become of secondary importance. When you decide to give God top priority in your plans, then, believe me, God will give you His top priority—the Holy Spirit.

FURTHER STUDY

Matt. 6:1–15; 14:23;
2 Kings 4:33;
Luke 6:12

1. *What did Jesus teach about prayer?*
2. *What was His example?*

Prayer

Lord, I wonder, am I thirsty or desperate enough to make this matter of being filled with the Spirit my top priority? Help me face up to the challenge—now. For Jesus' sake. Amen.

Day

211

The Art of Self-Giving

"Your attitude should be the same as that of Christ Jesus . . ." (v. 5)

For reading & meditation—Philippians 2:1–11

We continue examining the steps we must take to open ourselves to a deeper experience of the Holy Spirit.

(5) *Match God's self-giving with your own self-giving.* Since God, in the giving of His Holy Spirit, is giving Himself to us—flowing into every area of our being to live alongside our imperfections—then we must be willing to give ourselves to Him. God holds nothing back; and when we give ourselves to Him, we must hold nothing back. When I say "ourselves," I mean our total personality, the central, fundamental self. But, you ask, how shall I know when I have given myself? Silence the heart before Him and see if anything unsurrendered rises to the surface. If nothing arises after a reasonable time, then you must take it for granted that there is nothing left behind. To be sure that everything is covered, however, tell God that you surrender all you know and all you don't know. Let Him know also that if anything unsurrendered is shown to you in the future, then that belongs to Him also.

In asking God for the Holy Spirit, you are really asking God for Himself. It becomes part of what Martin Luther calls "the divine exchange." God gives Himself, and you give yourself. Conversion, of course, is a "divine exchange," but now, in your surrendering to the Holy Spirit, God is going to come into your personality deeper than before. Just as a canvas surrenders to the painter, you must put yourself fully and completely in the hands of God. In surrender, you don't just have Him; He has you.

FURTHER STUDY

*Phil. 3;
Rom. 12:1;
Exod. 32:29;
Prov. 23:26*

1. What was Paul's testimony?
2. Where does dedication start?

Prayer

Gracious Father, help me now to bring this wandering and recalcitrant will of mine into firm and positive commitment to You. I'm glad to do it, for my will was made for Yours. Amen.

224

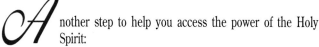

Believing—We Receive

Day 212

"... the Father will give you whatever you ask in my name." (v. 16)

For reading & meditation—John 15:1–17

*A*nother step to help you access the power of the Holy Spirit:

(6) *Now reach out in faith and receive the fullness of all that God has for you.* We enter into all God's blessing by faith. As a child of God, you are heir to all that the Father has—Himself. So reach out and take Him now. Jesus said, "if anyone is thirsty, let him come to me and drink" (John 7:37, italics added). Are you thirsty? Then drink. "And this is the confidence which we have in him, that if we ask anything according to his will he hears us. And if we know that he hears us in whatever we ask, we know that we have obtained the requests made of him" (1 John 5:14–15, RSV).

Here are the principles again: *Confidence*—"the confidence which we have in Him"; confidence in the character of God as seen in Christ. *Conversing*—"we ask anything." *Condition*—"according to his will." *Conviction*—"we know that he hears us in whatever we ask." *Consequence*—"we know that we have obtained." Follow the principles one by one. Have confidence in the character of God. Converse with Him and tell Him your need—to be filled to overflowing with His Holy Spirit. Believe that the condition is met, and your asking is in harmony with His will. Remind yourself that He hears your request, and that He is flooding your whole being with His power. Have the boldness to take what is there. Faith will turn it to fact; fact will turn it to feeling. Now welcome His coming in whatever manner He comes. You are thirsty—so drink . . . and drink . . . and drink.

FURTHER STUDY

Acts 7:42–56;
John 20:22;
Eph. 5:18; 3:19

1. What was said of Stephen?
2. What is Paul's exhortation?

Prayer

O Father, how can I thank You enough for bringing me to this moment. It is an end, yet it is a beginning. I know that life is ahead of me for life is within me. I am grateful beyond words. Amen.

225

A Life Set to Obey

"... the one who sows to please the Spirit, from the Spirit will reap eternal life." (v. 8)

For reading & meditation—Galatians 6:1–10

Here is another principle to follow to open your life to the power of the Holy Spirit:

(7) *Set your life to obey the Holy Spirit.* Today's verse gives the right attitude: "... he who sows for the Spirit will reap life eternal from the Spirit" (Moffatt). You surrender a seed to the earth trusting that something will happen, and the thing that happens is that it grows and changes. If you sow your life in the Spirit and respond every moment to the Spirit, as the sowed seed responds to the gentle caressing of the earth, then you reap eternal life, here and in the hereafter. Eternal life is a new quality of life which you possess now and will enjoy forever. When you come under the law of the Spirit, you are under the law of creation—what is sown will also be reaped.

Although we receive an infilling of the Spirit through faith, we retain that experience by obedience: "The Holy Spirit, whom God has given to those who *obey* him" (Acts 5:32, italics added). The emotions become a by-product of our obedience. So learn to walk in obedience to His will from now on, and whenever you fall into sin, or feel that the Holy Spirit is not in your life, then go through the same steps once again. Remember, too, that even though you might enjoy a close fellowship with God, you will need, on occasion, to ask Him to fill you to overflowing. Someone heard Billy Graham pray to be filled with the Spirit. "I thought you had been filled," said the person. "I have," said Billy, "but the trouble is, I leak!"

FURTHER STUDY

Acts 1:1–11; 5:29;
James 1:25;
1 Sam. 15:22

1. What did Christ command?
2. In what did their obedience result?

Prayer

O God, my Father, now that I have seen how to open my life to more of Your Spirit, help me to live day by day in utter obedience to Your commands. This I ask in Jesus' Name. Amen.

What Does His Coming Mean?

"... every city or household divided against itself will not stand." (v. 25)

For reading & meditation—Matthew 12:22–37

*W*hat are some of the evidences of the Spirit-filled life? How do we know when we are fully indwelt by the divine Paraclete?

I am not going to begin where you might expect in the area of spiritual gifts (that will come later), but in a realm I believe to be equally important yet seldom mentioned. I refer to the area of the subconscious. The longer I live, the more I feel the church has missed its way here. We have talked much about the work of the Spirit on the conscious level, but little of His work at a subconscious level. We have failed to see, generally speaking, that part of the work of the Holy Spirit in the life of a Christian is to project His Power and presence into the depths of the personality—even the subconscious.

We are told that about one-tenth of the mind is conscious and the other nine-tenths subconscious. Like the iceberg, which is nine-tenths submerged, life is largely lived in the submerged part of our being. Now, if this is so, then it becomes evident at once that if the submerged nine-tenths is not working with the conscious purposes in the one-tenth, then there is going to be a serious division; a division so serious becomes divisive. Whatever controls the nine-tenths greatly influences the one-tenth. The Holy Spirit wants to project Himself into that submerged part of our being in order to harness those untamed forces, and make them work for us and not against us. Then the subconscious is no longer an enemy, but a friend.

FURTHER STUDY

Joel 2:18–32;
Rom. 12:2;
1 Cor. 14:3;
2 Tim. 1:7

1. What did Joel prophesy?
2. What is the difference between dreams and visions?

Prayer

O God, my Father, I am grateful that You have provided for my deepest need—the need of unifying and controlling the depths within me. My heart tingles at the thought that I can be unified— on the inside. Thank You, Father. Amen.

Is There an Answer?

**"I love to do God's will . . . but there is something else deep within me . . .
that is at war . . ." (vv. 22–23, TLB)**

For reading & meditation—Romans 7:21–25

A devoted Christian man I knew married a widow who had a teenage son. The son was deeply rebellious, and the man, now his stepfather, grew very resentful toward him. One night, while the mother was away, they shared the same bedroom, and the man woke up in the middle of the night, finding himself trying to push the young man out of the bedroom window. Another push, and he would have fallen and been seriously injured.

What had happened? The man told me that he had gone to sleep that night with great bitterness in his heart toward his stepson. The subconscious mind is very receptive at the moment one drops into sleep, and the resentment his subconscious mind received precipitated an act which would have horrified him when conscious.

A little girl said, "I want to be good, but I don't want to be obedient." Her conscious mind wanted her to be known as good, but her subconscious mind, where self-centeredness was the driving urge, did not want to obey anything except itself. The minister who preaches full surrender to God, yet yearns to be praised and complimented, is suffering from a division between the conscious and the subconscious mind. The person who works hard at helping others, but does it to meet some inner need, rather than truly giving themselves to the needs of others, is inwardly divided. The question is: Can the subconscious be reached by the Holy Spirit? With all my heart, I say it can. In the Holy Spirit, we are provided with a divine presence that redeems and unifies the whole personality.

**FURTHER
STUDY**

*James 1;
Rom. 8:6;
Isa. 26:3;
Phil. 4:8*

*1. What makes a man
unstable?
2. What brings stability
and peace?*

Prayer

O Father, I am tired of inward division that threatens to tear me apart. Tame these wild horses within me so
that I might know Your perfect peace in every part of my being. For Jesus' sake. Amen.

"Ablaze with Light"

"... if your whole body is full of light, and no part of it dark, it will be completely lighted ..." (v. 36)

For reading & meditation—Luke 11:33–36

A minister once said: "Without the Holy Spirit, the Christian religion would have to work purely with the historical, in the presentation of the historic Jesus." If it wasn't for the Holy Spirit, then our faith would focus only on what Jesus did for us in the past, and not what He can do for us in the present. The Spirit is the link that applies the redemption of Jesus Christ to every area of our lives, and makes the cross and the resurrection contemporary. The power of Christ's redemption must be in us as continuously and as permanently as the subconscious itself.

Someone once asked me if I could point them to a Scripture that supported my view that Christ, through the power and presence of the Holy Spirit, could unify the conscious and the subconscious. I pointed him to Ephesians 1:10: "[He planned] ... to unify all things and head them up and consummate them in Christ"(Amp. Bible). I know Paul is talking here about the final consummation of the age, but I also believe that the principle of unifying things (for which Christ died) is not just something that we will experience on a cosmic scale in the future, but something that we can experience on a personal level in the present. Another verse, of course, is the one before us today. When the conscious and subconscious are unified, and work together toward positive ends, then this verse is fulfilled: "If then your whole body is full of light having no part dark, it will be wholly bright" (Luke 11:36, RSV).

FURTHER STUDY

2 Cor. 3;
Eph. 5:8;
Phil. 2:15;
2 Pet. 1:19

1. How is the "veil" removed?
2. What does this bring?

⤳ Prayer ⤲

O God, my Father, I want my inner being to be bright with Your light, with no part remaining unredeemed. Take away the dark part so that I am ablaze with light. For Jesus' sake. Amen.

"Life in Him"

"... all things were made through him, and without him was not anything made that was made.
In him was life ..." (vv. 3-4, RSV)

For reading & meditation—John 1:1-14

Today we come to the crux of this matter of the coordination of the subconscious. How does the Holy Spirit unify our deepest instincts?

The stream of energy that flows through our beings breaks up into three main channels: self, sex, and the herd. The self-instinct is at the basis of all our actions. It is the drive we have to assert ourselves—to be prominent. Sex is the creative urge, the drive to reproduce. The herd instinct is the one that causes us to follow the crowd. We say, "Everybody does it," and that decides life for us. These instincts were built into us by God, but sin has perverted them. They function now (except when they are surrendered to the Holy Spirit) in a self-centered framework.

The verses before us today show that God made our instincts. His stamp is upon them. Note two things: (1) God made our instincts—"without him was not anything made that was made," and (2) they are made to work in His way—"That which has been made was life in him" (RSV, footnote). When our urges and drives are surrendered to Him, they become "life in Him"—they live. But when we surrender the instincts to themselves, they are death. Outside of God there is nothing but death and inside of Him there is nothing but life. A schoolboy I read about quoted a statement of Jesus this way: "I am come that you might have life and have it *moribundantly*." That's what happens when the Holy Spirit does not have control of our driving urges. We live life "moribundantly."

FURTHER STUDY

*Rom. 1; 8:7;
Eph. 4:17*

*1. How did man
become "vain in his
imaginations"?
2. What happened when
God gave man up to his
own desires?*

Prayer

O Father, I don't want to live life "moribundantly," but more abundantly. I want that which has been made—
my body, my mind, my spirit—to be life in You. May it be so to the glory of Your Name. Amen!

The Way Is—Surrender

"Do you not know that your body is a temple of the Holy Spirit, who is in you . . ." (v. 19)

For reading & meditation—1 Corinthians 6:9–20

*H*ow do we go about controling our strong urges? Do we push them under? No, for as Hadfield said, "Repressed instincts are like bad boys who, when put out of class, retaliate by throwing stones at the windows." It's better to keep the bad boys in class, and teach them to direct their energies to better ends.

If the answer is not to be found in repression, then is it to be found in expression? Shall we give free rein to the urges within us? No, for that would lead us into deeper bondage. Shall we try to eliminate them? By no known process can these driving urges be eliminated. Put them out of the door and they will climb back in through the window, often in disguise. The philosophies of Buddhism are built on the idea that we can eliminate instincts and wipe out desire. A Buddhist monk was asked by a missionary: "What is your desire?" "Nothing." "Where are you going?" "Nowhere." "Where have you come from?" "Nowhere." He wanted to be a blank—but not quite. He ardently desired to be a blank, so desire was still there, turned toward the absence of desire.

If we can't eliminate the driving urges, and we shouldn't repress or suppress them, or express and release them, then what can we do? We must allow the Holy Spirit to take them over. Our urges are properly fulfilled only when they are surrendered to the will of God. When we allow the Holy Spirit to get into the driving seat of our personalities, then we are in safe hands.

FURTHER STUDY

Num. 11:1–9;
Eccl. 6:7;
1 Cor. 10:6;
Eph. 2:3

1. What was the problem of the children of Israel?
2. What did they fail to see?

Prayer

O Father, help me to move over and let Your Holy Spirit do the steering. These urges that are within me are too strong for me to handle. From now on, You be the driver. Amen.

Full Surrender

"Now the Lord is the Spirit, and where the Spirit of the Lord is, there is freedom." (v. 17)
For reading & meditation—2 Corinthians 3:7–18

*M*odern approaches to the subconscious can do no more than throw the pale light of information into it. The message of the Bible, however, is not merely information but transformation: "where the Spirit of the Lord is, there is freedom." So if the Spirit of the Lord is within us, there is freedom from the conflict between the conscious and the subconscious.

If such a freedom is possible, why do so many live out their lives in conflict? Because they have never appropriated the power and presence of the Spirit available to them, and channeled Him into the deeper regions of their personality through self-surrender. God, Christ, or the Holy Spirit will never barge their way into any area of the personality. They come in when we put up the white flag of surrender, and, by a conscious act, agree to their residing and presiding within us.

It's surprising how many Christians say with the conscious mind, "I surrender all," and yet with the subconscious say, "I want some areas for myself." We must take ourselves in hand, and decide whether or not we want the Holy Spirit simply to evangelize certain areas of our personality, or whether we want Him to occupy our entire being. If you haven't properly settled that issue, then ask yourself today: Am I just kidding myself when I say I want to be filled with God? Is there a part of me that says, "Come in," while another part of me says, "Keep out!"? The Holy Spirit only comes into the areas where He is freely admitted.

**FURTHER
STUDY**

*James 4;
Gal. 2:20;
Rom. 6:6;
2 Tim. 2:11*

1. *Where does strife
come from?*
2. *What was Paul's
testimony?*

Prayer

O Father, I think You have put Your finger right on my problem. Perhaps the reason I have never felt the
Holy Spirit's full control is because deep down I never wanted it. But now I do. My whole being
cries out for its rightful Lord. I surrender now. Amen.

Driving in the Right Direction

"We proclaim him, admonishing and teaching . . . with all wisdom, so that we may present everyone perfect in Christ." (v. 28)

For reading & meditation—Colossians 1:21–29

*I*n the Spirit-controlled life, self is still there, but now it is not self-centered but God-centered, and, therefore, rhythmic and harmonious. "Perfect function," said a famous doctor, "is perfect health." The self functions perfectly and is, therefore, perfectly healthy—a self you can live with. The sex drive is still there, but now, being God-centered, it functions as God intended it to function. If one is married, then it can be expressed in a physical relationship, but if one is unmarried, then it can be sublimated and channeled into creativity in other directions. The herd instinct is still there, but now it is fastened on the kingdom of God, and one moves with the rest of the church toward the unity of the faith and the unity of the Spirit.

The life in the Spirit is not one of asceticism but one of assertion. We get rid of unacceptable desires in the only way possible, by replacing them with higher desires. We get rid of self-centeredness by God-centeredness, through surrender. We get rid of sex domination by surrendering the drive to God, and the controls He places upon it. Then what happens? Sex serves us, and makes us creative in the whole of life—not just within the physical relationship of marriage. We get rid of the herd dominance by surrender to God, and, when surrendered, the herd instinct comes back to us. But what do we find? We love people more because we are no longer dominated or intimidated by them. The expulsive power of a new affection casts out "lower loves" by focusing them on higher objectives.

FURTHER STUDY

Heb. 6;
Matt. 5:48;
2 Cor. 13:11

1. What did Paul mean by "perfection"?
2. What was Paul's desire?

Prayer

Holy Spirit, I am beginning to learn that when You have control, then everything is a perfect cosmos—when I have control, it is chaos. As life is for living, I want to live it to the brim. Help me not just to surrender, but to stay surrendered. Amen.

233

Another Comforter

"... he will give you another Comforter ..." (v. 16)
For reading & meditation—(John 14:15–18)

*W*e have examined the work of the Holy Spirit in the subconscious mind, and we saw that when He is allowed to fully penetrate our personalities, the inner conflicts subside. We become inwardly unanimous for God. The Holy Spirit *coordinates* the inner forces of our being and directs our lives toward one great purpose and end.

Today (and over the next six days) we are going to examine another aspect of the Spirit's ministry which He seeks to apply in our lives—the ministry of *comforting*. We have discussed earlier the special word which Jesus used to describe the Holy Spirit—*Paraclete*—which, we said, was made up of two Greek words, *para* (alongside) and *kaleo* (call). This word is translated in many modern Bibles as "Counselor," but in older versions the word *Comforter* is used. This is an emphasis which, I believe, can easily be missed.

The Holy Spirit is not just a counselor, who dwells within us to give good counsel and advice, but He is there also to minister to our hurts and bind up our wounds. Being filled with the Spirit doesn't mean that you suddenly become immune to life's hurts, or that there will not be times when you feel overwhelmed by life's difficulties. How comforting it is to know that when we hit rough times in life, the divine Paraclete comes alongside to *comfort* as well as advise. A schoolteacher, who had opened himself to the Holy Spirit, said, "Now that I am fully in His hands, I may be shaken, but I cannot be shattered." *That* is comforting!

FURTHER STUDY

*John 14:1–18;
2 Cor. 1:3–4;
1 Thess. 5:11–14;
Isa. 66:13*

1. How did Jesus comfort the disciples?
2. How can we comfort one another?

Prayer

Gracious Holy Spirit, I am deeply grateful that You are within me, not only to heighten my powers, but to heal my hurts. Blessed Comforter! I am so grateful. Amen.

"Help"

"... the Spirit helps us in our weakness ..." (v. 26)
For reading & meditation—Romans 8:18-27

*W*hat comfort this verse brings to all those who, at this moment, may be engulfed by huge problems. The Holy Spirit helps us in our infirmities. Thank God He doesn't leave us alone; we are not abandoned to our paltry resources, to somehow struggle through—He comes to heal our wounds and minister to our hurts.

One of the most exciting words in the Greek language is this word *help*. It is a combination of three words: *sun*—"along with," *anti*—"on the opposite side," and *lambano*—"to take hold of." All together: *sunantilambanotai*. It means "to take hold of, together with us, over on the other side." Doesn't this throw a new and illuminating light on the work and ministry of the Spirit in our lives? The words of Jesus in John's Gospel could be paraphrased thus: "I will send you a Helper who comes alongside when you call, and who will take hold of any burden or problem and carry it with you." Oh, how we ought to thank God for this great ministry of the Holy Spirit—He is with us to take hold of and help us carry our infirmities, our weaknesses, our heavy loads, and give us the comfort we need.

The Greek experts tell us that the more technically we look at the word, the more exciting it gets. It is in the indicative mood and represents a fact. It is in the middle voice, indicating that the Holy Spirit is doing the action only with our cooperation, and it is in the present continuous tense, speaking of continuous action. He is always there!!

FURTHER STUDY

Heb. 4;
Pss. 28:7; 40:17;
Heb. 13:6

1. How do we enter into God's rest?
2. Why can we come to Him boldly?

~→≈ *Prayer* ≈→~

O God, the more I learn about the Holy Spirit, the more I see how much I owe to Him. Forgive me, I pray, for failing to recognize His presence and ministry in my life. For Jesus' sake. Amen.

235

The Hurt of Rejection

"He was despised and rejected by men . . ." (v. 3)

For reading & meditation—Isaiah 53:1–12

We continue meditating on the fact that one of the ministries of the Holy Spirit within our lives is that of a Comforter. During my ministry, I have observed that there are five main hurts which people experience in life.

The first is the hurt of *rejection*. Can the Holy Spirit comfort us when we feel rejected? He most certainly can. Sooner or later in this mixed-up world everyone feels rejected. Indeed, some go through so much rejection, they cease to expect anything else. Rejection often happens in childhood: the child may have been unwanted by his parents, or may have been the wrong sex, or for some reason doesn't please her parents. These feelings of rejection are recorded in our system on a kind of tape recorder, and later in life, whenever we feel rejected, we not only experience the present rejection, but in some strange way it triggers the "tape recorder" inside us, and we play back all the feelings of rejection we felt in earlier years.

Past feelings of rejection that have never been healed may put a weight on the personality that is too heavy for it to bear, and this is why, as we say, a person breaks down. People rarely break down because of one event; it is usually the one event that becomes the last straw. Have you deep feelings of rejection within you that you are carrying from the past? Or have you been rejected in recent days or weeks? Then draw near to God. The Spirit is with you to heal your hurts—right now.

FURTHER STUDY

Luke 15:11–32;
Eph. 1:6;
2 Cor. 5:9;
Acts 10:35

1. What is the message of the parable?
2. What three things did the younger son receive to verify this?

Prayer

Gracious Holy Spirit, I am so thankful that You come alongside to help in my hour of need. I offer You every feeling of rejection and hurt that lies within my heart. Heal me now in Jesus' Name. Thank You, Father. It's done. Amen.

False Accusation

"Blessed are you when people . . . falsely say all kinds of evil against you because of me." (v. 11)

For reading & meditation—Matthew 5:1–12

*T*oday we examine another hurt that often arises within the human heart—*false accusation.*

Has someone accused you of a wrong for which you were not responsible, and though you try to explain or defend yourself, no one seems to believe you? It hurts, doesn't it? I have known many Christians who, when faced with the hurt of false accusation, turn away from the Christian life altogether. How sad! I have a friend who was falsely accused by fellow Christians in a church and, although I and many others knew the accusation was not true and passionately defended him, he broke down and was placed in a mental institution.

People (even Christians) have their own ways of trying to cope with the feelings that arise when they are falsely accused. Some turn to liquor. They want to dull the pain inside them, and so they take what seems to them to be an easy way to that end. But it doesn't work, for there is always the morning after. Some turn to books. That was the advice Edmund Gosse gave to his friend Robert Ross when he became involved in the Oscar Wilde scandal at the end of the last century. "Turn for consolation to books," he said. But it didn't work. Others might turn to nature, to art, or to music. There is, however, a better way. If you are a Christian, and your heart is heavy because of a false accusation, then I assure you that the blessed Comforter is alongside you even now. Offer the hurt to Him. He delights to heal.

FURTHER STUDY

James 3;
1 Pet. 3:16; 2:1
Luke 6:7

1. What is the hardest thing to tame?
2. For what should we use our tongues?

Prayer

Blessed Lord Jesus, You who knew the hurt of being falsely accused, draw near in the power of Your Spirit and heal me now. I take—and You undertake. Thank You, Savior. Amen.

The Hurt of Disappointment

"For you are God, my only place of refuge. Why have you tossed me aside?" (v. 2, TLB)

For reading & meditation—Psalm 43:1-5

*A*nother deep hurt that may come is *disappointment*. We expect things to happen in a certain way, and when they don't, then we feel let down. We can be disappointed by people, or even by God, if He chooses to direct our lives in a way other than we had hoped.

A woman wrote to me that during a meeting, where I spoke on "The Healing of Life's Hurts," the Lord had ministered to her deep feelings of disappointment. Her disappointment was with God, for, as she put it, "not healing my husband, and taking him to be with Himself." On the way home from the meeting, she narrowly missed being involved in a serious accident, and the Lord whispered to her heart: "And you have been doubting my love for you?" Within hours the bitter pain of disappointment was healed—pain that she had been carrying for a number of years.

Are you in the throes of disappointment at this moment? Have others let you down? Or perhaps you feel God has let you down and, because He is God, you feel you ought not to feel that way; therefore, you are repressing your disappointment and pushing it down into your subconscious. Bring it to Him—now. God is not going to get mad at you for telling Him that you are disappointed with Him. If you feel upset with God, then confess the hurt, tell Him exactly how you feel. Then, when it is all out and you admit you were wrong—not He—surrender the hurt into His hands and experience the healing the divine Comforter brings.

**FURTHER
STUDY**

*John 11:6–22;
Pss. 13:1–6; 69:3;
2 Pet. 3:9*

*1 . How did David
express his
disappointment?
2. What did Martha
do about her
disappointment?*

Prayer

Heavenly Father, I am so thankful that I can bring all my hurts and disappointments to You. Some earthly fathers won't permit their children to be upset with them, but You accept me as I am. I am so grateful. Heal every disappointment in me now. For Jesus' sake. Amen.

The Hurt of Failure

"But Peter followed him . . . to see the outcome." (v. 58)

For reading & meditation—Matthew 26:57–68

*A*nother hurt that produces great pain is *failure*. A missionary said to me, "I just can't go back to the mission field because everything I have tried to do has crumbled. I am a failure." I pointed out to her that the story of Jesus on this earth is one of apparent failure. He was rejected by His nation and ended His life on a cross. Those who looked on as He died saw in His death the failure of His cause. But was it? Three days later the failure turned into triumph, as He rose from the dead and proved Himself victorious over all His enemies.

I explained to her that to say, "I am a failure," is to believe a lie. The fact that you have failed in something does not make *you* a failure. You are a child of God and a joint heir with Christ—a son or daughter of heaven in whom dwells resurrection life. How then can you say you are a failure? Some things you do may not work out the way you would like, but is that so terrible? *Success or failure is not so important as being true to what God has asked you to do.*

When I uttered the last sentence, she said, "You have resolved the biggest tension of my life." As we prayed together, the Holy Spirit completed the healing, and she stood up with a new sparkle in her eyes. May God use these words to minister to your hurts too—success or failure are secondary to being true to what God has asked you to do.

FURTHER STUDY

Matt. 26:33–35;
26:69–75;
Luke 15:7; 24:12;
John 21:15–19;
Acts 2:14

1. How did Peter seek to rectify his failure?
2. How did the Holy Spirit help Peter through failure?

Prayer

Gracious Father, thank You for showing me that when things fail that does not mean I am a failure. Heal the inner hurts I have experienced through failure, and help me to be true to You—in everything. For Jesus' sake. Amen.

The Hurts of Deep Trauma

"... God has made me forget all my trouble ..." (v. 51)

For reading & meditation—Genesis 41:46–52

We come now to examine the fifth and final hurt—the hurt that comes through having experienced some deep horror, such as physical beating, sexual abuse, serious injury. There are many "walking wounded" in the Christian church. The Holy Spirit yearns to heal you of those hurts, but He can only do so when you let Him.

For the Holy Spirit to be able to heal our deep hurts, we must be willing to part with the resentment that is often mixed up in them. When something traumatic happens to us, more often than not, we respond to it with a measure of self-pity, and say, "Why should that have happened to me?" However you might justify the bitterness at the time, there must be a willingness to abandon all resentment before there can be a deep healing. This is what I mean when I say that the Holy Spirit will heal your hurts—if you let Him. He can't bring healing where there is bitterness—that would be like healing over a boil. When you part with the bitterness, then, I assure you, a deep healing will begin.

Have you heard the story of Joni Eareckson? Young, beautiful, vivacious, she had a diving accident which resulted in paralysis. She is now a quadriplegic. She paints pictures with a brush held between her teeth. Her witness has become worldwide. At first she was angry and bitter, but one day she let go of the bitterness and experienced inner healing. Outside she remained the same, but inside she was made anew.

FURTHER STUDY

Job 42;
Heb. 12:15;
Eph. 4:31;
Deut. 32:32;
Acts 8:23

1. What was Job's confession?
2. When did God bring good out of Job's calamity?

Prayer

Blessed Holy Spirit, I see that when I hold onto bitterness and resentment, I succeed only in blocking Your healing power. I surrender every resentment, every ounce of self-pity, into Your hands, and receive in its place complete healing. Amen.

The Divine Contributor

"But the fruit of the . . . Spirit, [the work which His presence within accomplishes]—is love, joy (gladness), peace . . ." (v. 22, Amp. Bible)

For reading & meditation—Galatians 5:16–23

*A*nother aspect of the Spirit's activity in our lives is His ministry of *contributing* to our growth in Christlikeness. The Holy Spirit is not just a coordinator, unifying the conscious and subconscious, or a comforter, ministering to our deep hurts, but He is also a contributor—He assists us in becoming more like Jesus.

Have you ever considered what is God's chief goal for your life? It is not to make you like Billy Graham, or any other Christian celebrity. God's chief goal for you is to mold you into the image of His Son, Jesus Christ. I like the way the Living Bible paraphrases Romans 8:29, "For from the very beginning God decided that those who came to him . . . should become like his Son." Isn't that beautiful? And the Holy Spirit has come within you in order to contribute to that great goal.

How does He achieve such a tremendous task? By dispersing in our personalities the ingredients of Christ's nature, the characteristics of which are seen in what Paul describes as "the fruit of the Spirit." The nine ingredients of the fruit of the Spirit were exemplified in the life of Jesus, and it is part of the Holy Spirit's work to diffuse them in, and through, our personalities. When Paul refers to the flesh, he talks about "works," but when he refers to the Spirit, he talks about "fruit." "Works" indicate something manufactured, not natural. "Fruit" points to something that is a natural outcome. As someone said, "When we are in Christ, evil is alien, but goodness is natural." It is!

FURTHER STUDY

Ps. 1:1–6;
James 3:17;
Eph. 5:9;
Rom. 14:17

1. What delights the godly man?
2. What fruit is found in righteous people's lives?

Prayer

Father, help me to keep all my channels open so that the fruit of the Spirit may grow and grow in me. I ask this for the praise and honor of Your wonderful Name. Amen.

Love and Joy

"... he predestined us to be adopted as his sons through Jesus Christ, in accordance
with his pleasure and will ..." (Eph. 1:5)

For reading & meditation—Galatians 5:22–23 and Ephesians 1:3–14

*T*he first quality the Holy Spirit seeks to develop in us is love. Paul emphasizes love in 1 Corinthians 13:13: "And now these three remain: faith, hope and love. But the greatest of these is love." The more we allow the Holy Spirit to have His way in our hearts, the more we grow in love. If we don't grow in love, then we don't grow—period. We remain immature without love, for as Dr. Karl Menninger put it: "If love is ingrown, centering on itself as the focus of its love, then the result is an immature personality. If the love is selective, applied to certain groups, classes or races, again the result is an immature personality."

Ephesians 1:5 in the Moffatt translation reads: "... destining us in love to be his sons through Jesus Christ." We are destined to be God's children, through love—"destining us in love." If that destiny came out of love, it must hold within it a destiny to love. When you allow the Holy Spirit to develop God's love in you, you are deciding to live with the grain of the universe. You are fulfilling your own destiny.

The second ingredient in the fruit of the Spirit is *joy*. Many Christians know little of *joy*—they live under the lash of duty. Are you such a one? It is no accident that joy follows love, for joy is a by-product of love. If you seek joy first, it will elude you. But when you love with Christ's love, joy will seek you out. You will be automatically joyful.

**FURTHER
STUDY**

*1 Cor. 13;
Rom. 8:35; 5:8;
2 Cor. 5:14;
Eph. 2:4*

*1. List the characteristics
of God's love.
2. How are these
characteristics applied
in your life?*

Prayer

O Father, I want Your Holy Spirit to dwell so deeply in me that my life will be like an artesian well, springing
up to carry Your love and joy into all my relationships. For Jesus' sake. Amen.

Joy and Peace

Day
230

"Jesus then repeated, 'Peace be with you! . . .' with these words he breathed on them, adding, 'Receive the holy Spirit!'" (John 20:21–22, Moffatt)
For reading & meditation—Galatians 5:22–23 and John 20:19–22

*M*any Christians don't expect joy to flow through their personalities, and because they don't expect it, they don't get it! A lady said to me once, "I prayed for God to fill me with His Spirit, and I didn't experience a single thing." "And what did you expect to happen?" I asked. "Nothing," she replied. "Then," I said kindly, "you got what you expected, didn't you?" Walk through life expecting God's love and joy to break through, and it will. "Whatever you ask for in prayer, believe that you have received it, and it will be yours" (Mark 11:24).

The third fruit of the Spirit is *peace*. This is a truly inspired order: first, love—love is pre-eminent; then joy—joy comes as a result of love; and then peace—peace is joy deepening into firm confidence. "Peace," says one writer, "is joy with its arms folded in deep assurance." How lovely!

A great number of Christians believe that life is a struggle and, through fighting life's forces, we develop. But that is only half the story. It is true that as we grapple we grow, but it is also true that, no matter how difficult our circumstances, or however stormy things may be, it is possible to enjoy in the inner depths of our spirits a deep, settled peace. Paul said that God's peace passes understanding, and someone added, "and misunderstanding also!" Once a mob stoned a building where John Wesley was preaching, and, when all the people fled, Wesley lay down and went to sleep with the stones all around him. He was at peace with God, and, therefore, had a peace that passed understanding.

FURTHER STUDY

John 16:19–33;
Rom. 8:6;
Col. 3:15;
Phil. 4:7

1. *What disrupts our peace?*
2. *What does the word rule mean?*

Prayer

Gracious Father, it gets better and better. In You, and through Your Holy Spirit, I have not just love and joy, but inner calmness and tranquility. I am eternally grateful. Amen.

Patience and Kindness

". . . as God's chosen people . . . clothe yourselves with . . . kindness . . . and patience." (Col. 3:12)

For reading & meditation—Galatians 5:22–23 and Colossians 3:12:14

The fourth fruit of the Spirit is *patience*. The King James Version uses the word "longsuffering." Someone has suggested that longsuffering is "love stretched out." It is so elastic and tough that it doesn't break up into impatience. It maintains a patient attitude amidst the flux of human events. Patience, however, must not be confused with indifference. A group of people in ancient history called Stoics made indifference a virtue, and some people in the early centuries of the church tried to Christianize this characteristic; but it couldn't be done. A Christian is someone who cares. Because we care, we suffer, but in the midst of suffering, we discover the Spirit's enabling patience.

A woman, after finding Christ, went through a time of great persecution from her family. She said, "I have never been a patient woman, but since Christ and the Holy Spirit came into my life, He has turned me upside down and inside out. I always had to have the last word in any family argument. I still have the last word, but my last word is silence." Now, whenever she says something, her family listens, because she speaks out of the depth of silence. The Amplified Bible presents Galatians 5:22 as, "But the fruit of the . . . Spirit, [the work which His presence within accomplishes]—is . . . patience."

The next fruit is *kindness*. This may seem a very ordinary virtue, but yet, without it, the other virtues are incomplete. It is not by chance that this virtue is in the middle of the nine, for it puts flavor in all the others.

FURTHER STUDY

1 Thess. 1;
Rom. 5:3; 12:12;
Luke 21:19;
James 1:4

1. How did Paul relate patience to tribulation?
2. In what did Paul rejoice?

Prayer

Father, I want all the other virtues to be flavored with kindness, so that the spirit of kindness pervades everything I do and everything I am. For Jesus' sake. Amen.

Kindness and Generosity

". . . your generosity will result in thanksgiving to God." (2 Cor. 9:11)
For reading & meditation—Galatians 5:22–23 and 2 Corinthians 9:6–15

We continue meditating on the fifth fruit of the Spirit—*kindness*. In the unforgettable description of a model wife in Proverbs 31, there is this statement: "She openeth her mouth with wisdom; and in her tongue is the law of kindness" (v. 26, KJV). Note: "the *law* of kindness." A model wife passes an inner law in the legislature of her personality, that everything she says and does will be in accord with the "law of kindness." Kindness is not something set in her emotions; it is set in her will, and thus becomes a life attitude. May we, on bended knee, this day pass that same law in the legislature of our own hearts, and so come under its sway forever.

The sixth fruit of the Spirit is *goodness*. The Greek word *agathosune* means, according to the experts, "kindness at work." This is why the word is best understood, as it is sometimes translated, as generosity. This leads us to an interesting statement which Jesus once made: "If your Eye is generous, the whole of your body will be illumined" (Matt. 6:22, Moffatt). If your "Eye" (your outlook on life, your whole way of looking at things) is generous, then your whole personality will be illumined or lit up. Jesus was generous toward everyone—the poor, the meek, the sinful and the unlovely—and His whole personality was full of light. By the ministry of the Holy Spirit that characteristic of Jesus is generated in us—if we let it. And when we do, then we begin to see everyone with "the generous Eye."

FURTHER STUDY

2 Pet. 1;
Rom. 12:10;
1 Cor. 13:4;
Eph. 4:32;
Col. 3:12

1. From what does kindness flow out?
2. How can you show kindness today?

Prayer

Lord Jesus, Your generous Eye saw in me something that wasn't there—and then it was there! Help me to thus create what I see in others. For Your own dear Name's sake. Amen.

Faithfulness and Meekness

"... Let him show it by his good life, by deeds done in the humility that comes from wisdom."
(James 3:13)

For reading & meditation—Galatians 5:22–23 and James 3:13–18

*T*he seventh fruit of the Spirit is *faithfulness*. A Christian, in whom this fruit has developed, will be completely dependable. Someone has said: "The ultimate test of a man's character is this: Are there any circumstances under which he will not speak the truth? If so, the rest of his character is worthless, for basically he is unsound." Strong words. How many of us, I wonder, could pass that test? I knew a Christian worker who worked herself almost to a standstill in the cause of Christ, but she couldn't refrain from telling lies; and those lies cancelled out a lot of her life's work.

Is it is ever right to lie? "God is not a man, that he should lie" (Num. 23:19). If God cannot lie, then He won't delegate to us the privilege of doing it for Him! How faithful are you as a Christian? Let's go over our lives today in the light of the Holy Spirit's presence, and check to see if there are any loose ends, unfulfilled promises, or half-fulfilled tasks; and if there are, let's decide to complete them.

The eighth fruit of the Spirit is *gentleness* or *meekness*. This word is greatly misunderstood in Christian circles, for meekness is seen by many as weakness. It brings to mind (for many) the cringing spirit of Uriah Heap who said, "I am so very 'umble, Master Copperfield, so very 'umble." I once saw a powerful steam hammer come down so gently on an egg that it just cracked its top. That is meekness. It is divine strength and power projected in the gentlest manner.

FURTHER STUDY

Luke 19:1–28;
Rev. 2:10;
Heb. 10:23;
1 Pet. 4:19;
1 Cor. 4:2

1. What was the master's response to the faithful steward?
2. How did he deal with the unfaithful one?

Prayer

O Father, how I long for this quality to be seen in my life. Too often I am either too assertive or too unassertive. Give me, by the Spirit, a meekness that lets others know I am a follower of You. For Jesus' sake. Amen.

Self-Control

"But the fruit of the . . . Spirit . . . is . . . self-control (self-restraint, continence) . . ."
(Gal. 5:22–23, Amp. Bible)

For reading & meditation—Galatians 5:22–23 and Matthew 10:37–39

*T*he last of the nine fruits of the Spirit is *self-control*. It is interesting that Paul puts self-control last. Other religions would put it first. Confucianism taught that self-control would help produce the "superior" man. Hinduism thinks self-control will produce the "realized" man. Stoicism thought self-control produced the "detached" man. Modern cults believe self-control produces the "happy" man. They all go about it the wrong way. We do not gain Christ through self-control; we gain self-control through Christ. This is the only place the word is used in the New Testament, and it is used here as a by-product of love. When you begin with love, you end up with self-control. If you attempt it the other way around, then you end up with a nervous breakdown.

The self-control that comes by the Spirit is not a nervous, anxious self-control; it is a control that is unstrained, therefore beautiful. No wonder a great thinker said, "Love Christ and do what you like," for when you do, then you will like what He likes. That's the kind of self-control the Spirit gives. We delight to control what needs to be controlled because we desire to please Him.

As we come to the last moments of thinking through these beautiful fruit of the Spirit, may I remind you that all the qualities belong together. Moffatt translates Galatians 5:22 thus: "But the harvest of the Spirit is ..." It is *one* harvest; where love leads, and joy and peace find their home; where longsuffering and kindness have their spring; where goodness, faithfulness, gentleness, and self-control abide—there the likeness of Jesus appears.

FURTHER STUDY

Matt. 27;
Prov. 16:32;
Rom. 6:12;
2 Pet. 1:5–6

1. In what ways did Jesus display self-control?
2. In what ways do you show self-control?

 Prayer

Blessed Holy Spirit, I am so thankful that You are working in me to produce the image of the Lord Jesus
Christ. May the lineaments of His nature show through me more and more every day.
For His Name's sake. Amen.

247

The Mantle of Power

"But you shall receive power when the Holy Spirit has come upon you . . ." (v. 8, RSV)

For reading & meditation—Acts 1:1–8

*W*e look now at the way in which the Holy Spirit clothes His people with supernatural power. It is one thing to be unified on the inside; it is another to be fortified to meet whatever happens on the outside. The Holy Spirit—if we let Him—can do both. Jesus, when speaking of the Holy Spirit in John's Gospel (14:17), used two different prepositions to describe His work. He said, "He lives *with* you and will be *in* you (italics added)." In the passage before us today He uses a different preposition: He shall come *upon* you. The word *upon* gives us a picture of the Holy Spirit wrapping a mantle of divine omnipotence around the shoulders of His disciples, which would enable them to do great exploits in His Name.

The story of Elijah and Elisha in the Old Testament illustrates this particular aspect. Elijah, you remember, wore a mantle that was invested with supernatural power. Elijah's servant Elisha, no doubt, greatly coveted that supernatural mantle. Elijah promised him that if he saw him when he returned to heaven, the mantle (double share of his spirit) would be his. On the day of Elijah's departure to heaven, Elisha fulfilled the condition, kept his eyes on the ascending Elijah, and received the desired mantle. He then went out and performed twice as many miracles as his master.

The mantle of power Jesus used when He was here on earth, He has now given to us. Now, hold your breath, for this is what Jesus said of those who have faith in Him: "Greater works than these shall he do" (John 14:12, KJV).

FURTHER STUDY

2 Kings 2;
Zech. 4:6;
Luke 4:14;
Acts 19:11–12

1. What characteristics did Elisha show in obtaining the mantle?
2. What is said of Jesus when He returned from the wilderness?

Prayer

O Father, what a challenge this puts before me, and everyone else in the church today. We are hardly performing a tenth of what You did, let alone twice as much. Something is wrong. Show me how to put it right over these next few days. In Jesus' Name. Amen.

Purity and Power

Day 236

" . . . because our gospel came to you not simply with words, but also with power, with the Holy Spirit and with deep conviction." (v. 5)

For reading & meditation—1 Thessalonians 1:1–10

We ended yesterday by saying that although Jesus told us that through the Holy Spirit's power, we would do greater works than He had performed, the truth is that we are just not availing ourselves of the divine resources. There are notable exceptions to what I am saying but, by and large, this is the way it is in today's church. Paul could say: "Our gospel came to you . . . in power and in the Holy Spirit and with full conviction" (RSV). At the center of that "power" and "full conviction" was the Holy Spirit. That is lacking in much modern Christianity—it lacks power and conviction because it lacks a full encounter with the Holy Spirit.

Some years ago, when I was a pastor in the north of England, another minister in the town (a good friend of mine) said, "You preach about the Spirit's power and I'll preach about the Spirit's purity. That way we will keep a balance in the lives of Christians in this town." I pondered what he said, and came to the conclusion that such a procedure would produce lopsided Christians, for both congregations needed to hear of the Spirit's purity and power.

Today's churches can be divided into two camps, those where the purity aspect of the Spirit is emphasized and those where the power aspect of the Spirit is emphasized. If every church focused with equal emphasis on both these characteristics of the Spirit, then we would witness a healthier and more powerful body of believers. Onesidedness produces lopsidedness. Purity is essential, but so is power. The Holy Spirit supplies both.

FURTHER STUDY

Acts 5:1–16;
1 Cor. 12;
Gal. 5:22–26

1. How did the early church learn about the Holy Spirit's power and purity?
2. What was the result?

Prayer

O Spirit of purity and power, live in Your church as both. For I need purity to see my destiny, and power to follow it. Give me equal measure. In Jesus' Name. Amen.

249

"It's Coming!"

" . . . by the power of signs and miracles, through the power of the Spirit." (v. 19)

For reading & meditation—Romans 15:13–19

I believe, with all my heart, that God wants to clothe His people in this generation with a supply of the Spirit's power that will enable them to produce the same degree (if not more) of signs, wonders, and miracles that the early church experienced. However, most of us are afraid to give ourselves to Him for that purpose.

Peter Wagner, a highly respected minister in the United States, and a writer on church growth, says, "I was a dispensationalist (someone who believed supernatural signs were just for the early church) who carried a Scofield Bible everywhere I went. When a healing evangelist came to our city, I warned believers to stay away. Then God began to work on me, not by some flash of lightning that changed me in ten minutes, but gradually over the last five years of my missionary travels." He goes on to say that he has no leading to become a charismatic or a Pentecostal, and though he still carries his Scofield Bible, and preaches from it, he is convinced that in the years that lie ahead, the church, if it is not to be ignored, must face up to the need for it to expect and demonstrate a ministry of signs, wonders, and miracles.

Almost every letter I get from ministers these days contains a reference to their deep desire for greater power in their preaching and teaching. I believe the Holy Spirit is whetting our appetites for a greater display of power than the world has ever seen. And, believe me, it's coming!

FURTHER STUDY

Acts 4:23–37;
Zech. 4:6;
Mic. 3:8;
Luke 4:14

1. What was the result of the Acts 4 experience of the Holy Spirit?
2. Ask God to fill you with more of His power today.

⤚⟶ *Prayer* ⟶⤙

O Father, I am on the tiptoe of expectation as I realize that You are getting Your church ready to witness a revival of New Testament Christianity. Let it happen soon, dear Lord, soon. Amen.

"It Lacks That"

"My message and my preaching were not with wise and persuasive words, but with a demonstration of the Spirit's power . . ." (v. 4)

For reading & meditation—1 Corinthians 2:1–12

We continue meditating on the Spirit as power. We said yesterday that this is what is lacking in much of modern-day Christianity. It lacks power and it lacks conviction because it lacks a close encounter with this aspect of the Spirit's resources. If we are to experience the fullness of the Spirit in our lives, then we must open ourselves to everything He wants to give us. We must not pick and choose and say, "I'll take this, but not that," for in order to be God's true representatives in this world, we must know Him in all His fullness.

I watched a man on television one day examine a beautiful painting. He studied it for a few moments, and said, "Its perspective is good, the coloring is fine, the tones are excellent, the idea behind it is to be commended," but then, snapping his fingers, he said, "It lacks *that*."

The same can be said of a lot of Christian activity in this generation. Our preaching is correct, our services well-structured, our music is fine, our organization is superb, but it lacks one thing—the throbbing power of the Holy Spirit. Without the power of the Spirit in our midst, we are preaching unquickened truth—truth that doesn't fall upon the soul with convicting, sobering, awakening, converting power. Our Christianity is not bad—it is just dull. The Holy Spirit, *when accepted and obeyed*, turns insipidity into inspiration, dullness into dancing, and mediocrity into magnificence. If we are not careful, we may find ourselves in court one of these days accused of contravening the Trade Descriptions Act!

FURTHER STUDY

*Acts 19:21–41;
Eph. 5:18; 3:19*

1. How did the Holy
Spirit give Paul
holy boldness?
2. What was Paul's
exhortation to the
Ephesian church?

Prayer

Ouch, Lord, this hurts! But I know from experience that You hurt me in order to heal me. Begin with me today, and set me on fire that others may catch it too! Amen.

251

Day
239

Every Christian — a Charismatic

"With great power the apostles continued to testify to the resurrection . . ." (v. 33)
For reading & meditation—Acts 4:31–37

A friend of mine shared with a group of others in his week-
ly Bible study that he believed their church lacked visible
evidence of the Holy Spirit's supernatural power. One of the group
remonstrated with him and said, "Don't use that word 'supernatural'
here—it frightens me and upsets me." Isn't it sad that a Christian (and
there are many others who share his dislike) can be afraid of one of the
most valid and needed ministries in the church today—*supernatural*
power.

The word *supernatural* means "beyond the powers of nature or
miraculous." How much of that which goes on in today's church can be
explained by this word? If you are saying to yourself, "Selwyn seems to
be strongly supporting the charismatic movement," then let me make
clear my views on that subject. I believe every Christian is a charismatic, for the word *charisma* simply means "gifts of grace," and every
Christian has at least one basic gift—hence every Christian is a charismatic. The reason why the charismatic movement came into promi-
nence was because of the reluctance of many to face up to the fact that
supernatural signs and wonders are part of God's program for His
church in this present day. I know the movement has caused divisions,
and there are signs that the emphasis is now diminishing, but whether
it diminishes or not, one thing remains sure—God wants His people to
demonstrate to the world that the signs, wonders, and miracles the
early church experienced are still part of His purposes for today.

FURTHER STUDY

Rom. 15;
Mark 16:17–20;
Acts 4:29–30

1. What was Paul's testimony?
2. What is recorded of the early disciples?

Prayer

O Father, help me to think this through, and take away any fears I might have of the supernatural. Show me
that a church that can be explained only in natural terms is a million miles from the mark.
In Jesus' Name I ask it. Amen.

252

Channels of Blessing

"... how God anointed Jesus ... with the Holy Spirit and with power; how he went about ...
healing all that were oppressed ..." (v. 38, RSV)

For reading & meditation—Acts 10:34–48

*W*e continue meditating on the importance of being clothed with power from on high. "It is at the place of power," says one writer, "that religion is either vitiated or made vital." How much spiritual power is projected from our lives, both individually and corporately, into a lost and dying world? If we are honest, we will be compelled to say—very little.

A sign on the door of the electricity company stated: "The electric bell is not working—please knock." All our signs, making great claims for the gospel, are cancelled out if power is not apparent in our everyday lives. The Holy Spirit's power is not confined to delighting the saints with manifestations of the gifts of the Spirit in our church gatherings, but in empowering them for effective witness in the world. We must watch that we do not degenerate into being simply consumers of blessing rather than channels of blessing.

Recently I have had a stream of letters telling me how God has been leading different people to pray for healing from sickness for their non-Christian friends—and remarkable things have happened as a result. Some would regard it as doctrinally incorrect to pray for a person's healing if that person is *not* a Christian. Jesus did it; and so did Paul. I feel that the Holy Spirit is nudging me to say that, in the future, one of the ways by which we will see multitudes won to Christ is when we allow the Holy Spirit to work through us in supernatural signs and wonders. God is calling us to launch out into the deep.

FURTHER STUDY

Acts 3:1–13;
Isa. 53:5;
Luke 4:18;
1 Cor. 12:9

1. What were Peter and John doing following the coming of the Spirit?
2. How did they respond to the lame man?

Prayer

O Father, something within me seems to draw back at the borders of the supernatural. Give me the faith and expectancy, however, to step over that line, and demonstrate to others that I am not just a consumer, but a channel of Your blessings. Amen.

Step Out in Faith

"... they will place their hands on sick people, and they will get well." (v. 18)

For reading & meditation—Mark 16:14–20

*B*ecoming intimately acquainted with the power aspect of the Holy Spirit's ministry is vital if we are to move out into the world and share with people the message of new life in Christ.

We have usually taken the words, "You shall receive power when the Holy Spirit has come upon you" (Acts 1:8, RSV), as power to talk about Jesus. It is—but it is much more. It is power in general. Under that general power is the specific power to witness; but the power itself is for the total personality—the strengthening of faith, the heightening of expectancy, the flushing out of fear, the daring to believe. And one of the ways in which God seems to be leading His children to witness to their non-Christian friends in these days is by praying, in the power of the Spirit, for their *physical* as well as spiritual needs. Our aim in doing this should not be to try to convince those who have a "prove-it-to-me" mentality, as many of those who were eyewitnesses of Christ's healing ministry were not persuaded. It is rather to show to them that the Christian faith is concerned about the physical as well as the spiritual needs of people.

If you have not experienced the empowering work of the Holy Spirit, then be assured that such an experience awaits you as you take a step of faith toward what, up until now, has been a vast spiritual unknown. Just one more step—and you are there!

FURTHER STUDY

*Matt. 8:1–13;
9:29–30; 17:20;
Heb. 11:1;
John 6:28–29*

1. How did the centurion show faith?
2. What did Jesus exclaim?

Prayer

O Father, I've come too far to go back now. Take me in Your arms today, and empower me in such a way that my life of worship and witness will be entirely transformed. For Jesus' sake. Amen.

The Master's Voice

"The Spirit himself testifies with our spirit that we are God's children." (v. 16)

For reading & meditation—Romans 8:9–17

We now examine one more characteristic of the Holy Spirit's ministry in our lives. The Spirit not only coordinates, comforts, contributes, and clothes, but He also *convinces*. The word *convinces* has a wide range of meaning. It means "to persuade, to win over, to bring around, to assure and to satisfy."

We consider today the ministry of the Spirit whereby He assures us that we are members of the divine family, and that we hold a valid passport into heaven. One Bible scholar suggests that the word *with* (rather than *to*), in the text before us today, implies that there is a double witness—the Spirit witnessing downward, and our own spirit witnessing upward. It could be regarded as a mere play upon words, but I think he has an interesting point here. All of life is one piece. There are no dualisms, no compartments. The laws that govern the universe have one source—God.

Some of you will be old enough to remember the famous advertisement for "His Master's Voice" records, which pictured a dog sitting before a phonograph, pricking up its ears at hearing its owner's voice. Is not that a picture of what goes on in a Christian's heart after conversion? The Spirit speaks and says, "You belong to God," and our own spirit answers back and says, "My heart recognizes the voice of its rightful Lord." We know that voice because it is the voice of the one who created us and designed us. The facts from above, and the facts written in our own spirits, kiss each other, and are wedded henceforth and forevermore.

FURTHER STUDY

John 16:1–11; Acts 2:37; 24:25

1. How does the Holy Spirit convict?
2. What is the difference between "convict" and "convince"?

Prayer

O Father, I am so grateful that as Your Spirit presses down, my spirit presses upward—and both say the same thing: I belong to You. What assurance! I am so thankful. Amen.

Safe and Sealed

"In him you also, who have heard . . . were sealed with the promised Holy Spirit, which is the guarantee of our inheritance . . ." (vv. 13–14, RSV)

For reading & meditation—Ephesians 1:3–14

*I*n the verse before us today we see that those who "heard" were "sealed." Does the "sealing" take place at conversion, or at some point beyond it? I believe it takes place at conversion. A seal is a mark of ownership, and when the Holy Spirit comes in to regenerate our beings at conversion, He produces the assurance in our hearts that we are heirs of God and joint heirs with Christ. I know that some believe that the "sealing" takes place subsequent to conversion, such as at one's baptism by total immersion, or at a crisis point of sanctification, or, as some would describe it, when we are baptized in the Holy Spirit. But how insecure life would be if we had to wait for "this" or "that" experience in order to know that we are safe in Christ.

One historian says that it was customary in Ephesus for certain traders to send their slaves into the marketplace to make purchases for them and, once the transaction was completed, the slaves would mark the item with their master's seal, whereupon it was delivered to the master's home. In something of the same way, the Holy Spirit in our hearts seals, once and for all, the question of His ownership over our lives, and also acts as a pledge, or guarantee, that one day we will be safely delivered to our Father's home in glory. In Wales, many years ago, I heard a frail old Christian say: "The envelope (meaning his body) may be a bit tattered, but the letter inside is quite safe." It is!

FURTHER STUDY

John 5;
Rom. 8:16;
Gal. 4:6;
1 John 4:13

1. How does the Holy Spirit "bear witness"?
2. What confidence does this give us?

 *Prayer*

O Father, what endless blessings follow the coming of Your Spirit into my life. I am saved by grace, sealed by the Spirit and supported by eternal love. What more could I ask for this side of glory! Amen.

The Spirit Guides

"... those who are led by the Spirit of God are sons of God." (v. 14)

For reading & meditation—Romans 8:14–27

The Holy Spirit seeks to bring us around to accepting God's guidance for our lives. "For all who are led by the Spirit of God are sons of God" (Rom. 8:14, RSV).

This is a stage in life which many Christians never attain—they are not Spirit-led Christians. They are led by self-interest, physical impulses, or by the opinions of others. They have not put themselves at the disposal of the Spirit to be led of Him in the details of their lives. Hence they lack direction and, therefore, a goal. When Christians say to me, "The Holy Spirit never seems to guide me," I usually reply, "But how well do you listen?" The problem we face over guidance is not because the Spirit fails to lead us, but because we are not listening.

We must be prepared to stop talking and wait before Him so that He can talk to us. In this frenzied age, many Christians have lost the art of listening. They are willing to spend time in prayer talking to God, but are not willing to spend some of the time listening to God. We must stop, wait, and tune ourselves into the Spirit's wavelength if we are to hear His voice and feel His gentle impressions. A Quaker woman inquired of a young man, "Hast thou heard God speak lately?" "No," said the young man. "Then thou hast forgotten to be still," said the woman. "Be still, and know ..." says the Scripture (Ps. 46:10). Be unstill and you will not know. God guides everyone who wants to be guided.

FURTHER STUDY

Acts 16; 10:19–20; 13:2;
John 16:13

1. How did the Holy Spirit guide Paul?
2. What was the result?

Prayer

O Spirit of the living God, help me tune my heart so that I can hear Your voice, for without Your guidance my life lacks mission and direction. Take the reins of my life and guide me. For Jesus' sake I pray. Amen.

The Conscience Corrected

"I am speaking the truth in Christ . . . my conscience bears me witness
in the Holy Spirit . . ." (v. 1, RSV)
For reading & meditation—Romans 9:1–16

*A*nother way in which the Holy Spirit exercises His *convincing* ministry in our lives is by addressing our consciences, and prevailing upon them to take the way of Christ in every issue. Today's verse brings together the objective standard, "the truth in Christ," and the subjective standard, "my conscience bears me witness in the Holy Spirit."

Some people say, "I'm living in accordance with my conscience—isn't that enough?" No, for conscience by itself is not a safe guide. Conscience is the capacity to distinguish between right and wrong—according to the standards you uphold. It can be taught to approve directly opposite things. A missionary intervened to stop an Indian woman throwing her child into the Ganges as a human sacrifice. "But my conscience tells me to do it," she said. "And my conscience tells me to stop you from doing it," said the missionary.

Conscience is not an infallible guide unless it has in it the highest content possible—the Holy Spirit. The Holy Spirit can be relied upon to act as Jesus would act in every situation, for the Holy Spirit is a Christlike Spirit. I am bold to say that there is not one of you reading these lines (if you are a Christian) who, by the mercy of God, doesn't know something in your conscience of the work of the Holy Spirit as Convincer. He pleads in you and with you to bring your conscience to the highest place possible "a conscience void of offense toward God" (Acts 24:16, KJV).

**FURTHER
STUDY**

Rom. 14; 15:1–13;
Acts 24:16;
2 Cor. 1:12;
1 Tim. 1:5

1. What is Paul teaching
about our conscience?
2. How does he relate it
to the ministry of the
Holy Spirit?

Prayer

O Father, I surrender myself and my standards to You for cleansing and correction. Teach me the standards
of Christ so that my conscience may bear a true witness. For Jesus' sake. Amen.

Not the End—a Beginning

Day
246

"... stay in the city until you have been clothed with power from on high." (v. 49)

For reading & meditation—Luke 24:36–49

*W*riting on the subject of the Holy Spirit has whetted my appetite for more of His fullness and His power. I can never be the same again. I hope something similar happens to you.

We have seen how the Holy Spirit coordinates and unifies the conscious and the subconscious, how He comforts and contributes, how He clothes and convinces. There is much more that could be said, of course, about His ministry in our lives, but let me draw your attention to something I have emphasized already—*God is willing to give you as much of His Spirit as you are willing to receive.*

If you believe that you received all of the Spirit at conversion, then the question for you is this: How much is He ruling and reigning in my life at this present moment? If you believe that the Holy Spirit is given subsequent to conversion, then permit me to ask you this: What steps have you taken to open your being to Him in order that you might be filled with all His fullness? Don't, I beg you, remain stagnant because of some doctrinal position you might hold. Seek Him afresh today, that He might flow through your life in the fullness of His power. And don't just focus on being filled for the blessing you might enjoy. Remember, the Holy Spirit is like electricity—He won't come in unless He can get out. Tell Him you want to be a channel, not just a consumer, and today will be, not an end, but a beginning.

FURTHER STUDY

John 7:32–44;
Matt. 5:6;
Isa. 55:1;
Rev. 22:17

1. What was the promise of Jesus?
2. How thirsty and hungry are you today?

Prayer

O God, now as I take all barriers down, come in by Your Holy Spirit's power, and flood my life with Your divine glory. May the receiving flow out in giving. This I ask for Your own dear Name's sake. Amen.

259

Section Five

Strong at the Broken Places

Strong at the Broken Places

There are times when we seriously question why God lets something happen to us that we don't think should happen. We are disappointed, defeated and overwhelmed. What is He thinking? Doesn't He know how I hurt?

This is a crisis of faith we all face at one time or another. If we sincerely love God and try to obey Him, why does he allow suffering and brokennes in our lives? In the pages that follow, Selwyn Hughes takes up this question with confidence, walking boldly where it would be far easier to tiptoe along using standard generalities.

Hughes reminds us that after a broken bone heals, the point where the break occurred is actually stronger than the rest of the bone. In the same way, God uses brokenness to strengthen our weak spots. When we want things that draw us away from Him, He corrects us by taking those things away. Maybe it's money, power, publicity, or praise. From our perspective we can't see that these things we love so much are driving a wedge between us and our Creator. But of course God sees everything. He knows, even when we don't, the difference between what we want and what we need. God satisfies our true needs, and separates us from the wants that threaten to separate us from Him.

Dealing with brokenness also gives us a chance to show the world how to respond to disappointment or failure from a Christian perspective. We have God's grace to sustain us, and His hand to guide us. Every setback is a chance to understand God's plan for our lives more fully, and to see Him transform a weakness in life into a strength for His glory.

It isn't what happens to Christians that sets them apart from the world, but how they react to it. To stay strong in the face of failure, to hold on to a biblical perspective no matter what happens, is to feel the power of God in your life as you've never felt it before. "I can do all things through Christ who strengthens me." For peace of mind and stress-relief in today's culture, there's no better cure.

L.G.G.

Out of Weakness — Strength!

"... out of weakness were made strong ..." (v. 34, KJV)
For reading & meditation—Hebrews 11:30–40

When I first felt the urge to write on the theme: "Strong at the broken places," I had great difficulty in tracing its origin. Then someone wrote to me, quoting the full phrase from the writings of Ernest Hemingway, who said: "Life breaks us all . . . but many are made strong at the broken places." I felt this to be a gentle nudge from the Holy Spirit, and began at once to put my thoughts together on this thrilling theme.

It is a principle of life that the place in which a bone breaks and then heals will be so strong that, generally speaking, it will never break there again. In the same way, when the skin is cut and scar tissue forms, the healed part becomes tougher than the surrounding skin. If this happens in the natural, why not in the spiritual? The writer to the Hebrews tells us, in the passage before us today, that God is expert at taking the weaknesses of His children and turning them into strength. What an encouraging truth! A traveler in the Netherlands tells how his guide pointed out an historic site. "This is where the sea broke through," he said, "causing thousands to drown. But see—it is now so strongly reinforced that it will never break through there again."

Have you been broken by life to such an extent that you feel an overwhelming sense of weakness? Then take heart—God specializes in matching His ability to your disability. By His transforming grace, your frustration can become fruitful. You can be strong at the broken places.

FURTHER STUDY

*Pss. 34:1–22; 147:3;
1 Cor. 11:24*

1. What is promised to the brokenhearted?
2. Why was Jesus broken?

Prayer

O Father, this sounds fine as theory, but can it really become a fact? Your Word says it can. I am ready and eager to learn. Teach me, my Father. In Jesus' Name. Amen.

The "Inner-Stances"

"We are handicapped on all sides . . . we may be knocked down but we are never
knocked out!" (vv. 8–9, J. B. Phillips)

For reading & meditation—2 Corinthians 4:1–15

*W*hy is it that while the same things can happen to us all, they may not have the same effect upon us all? The same thing happening to two different people may have entirely different effects. Why should this be so? It depends not so much on the circumstances, but on the "inner-stances"—or, in other words, our inner attitudes. As someone has said, "What life does to us in the long run depends on what life finds in us." Life's blows can make some people querulous and bitter, others they sweeten and refine; the same events, but with opposite effects.

The Gospels tell us that there were three crosses set up on Calvary on the first Good Friday. The same event happened to three different people, but look at the different results. One thief complained and blamed Jesus for not saving Himself and them; the other thief recognized his own unworthiness, repented of it and found an open door to Paradise. Jesus, of course, saw it as the climax of His earthly achievements and made it the fulcrum on which He moved the world.

What counts, therefore, is not so much what happens to us, but what we do with it. The same sunshine falling on two different plants can cause one to wither and die, while the other will blossom and flourish. And why? It all depends on the response the plants make. Although, of course, they both need water, one plant is more suited to hot sunshine than the other, and therefore responds with more life and growth, while the other shrivels up and dies.

FURTHER STUDY

2 Cor. 11:21–29;
2 Tim. 4:7;
Ps. 37:28;
Prov. 2:8

1. What was Paul's testimony?
2. How did he sum up his life?

Prayer

Gracious heavenly Father, write this precept upon my heart so that I shall never forget it: it's not so much what happens to me, but what I do with it that is important. Thank You, Father. Amen.

Are Christians Exempt?

". . . He causes his sun to rise on the evil and the good, and sends rain on the righteous
and the unrighteous." (v. 45)

For reading & meditation—Matthew 5:38–48

W e are meditating on the theme, "Strong at the broken places," and we are discovering that although life deals blows to us all, those who meet life with the right responses and the right inner attitudes are those who turn their weaknesses into strengths.

I know some Christians who believe that they ought to be exempt from the cruel blows of life. A young man who was stunned after failing his examination said, "I cannot understand. I prayed very hard before the examination, and I lived an exemplary life for the Lord. Why, oh why, should He fail me at this important moment?" Later he confessed to a friend, "As a result of God letting me down, my faith in Him has been shattered."

I can sympathize with the young man's feelings, of course, but I cannot agree with his conclusions. Suppose prayer alone could enable us to pass examinations—what would happen? Prior to examination time, classrooms would be deserted, and everyone would flock to the churches for prayer and meditation. Not a bad situation, you might think. But what would happen to the minds of young people if prayer *alone* brought success? They would become blunted by lack of study. I suspect the young man I have just referred to was depending more on prayer than on diligent and painstaking study. Now prayer *and* study make a good combination, but prayer without study never helped anyone pass an examination. Christians are not exempt from the natural laws that govern the universe. We may through prayer be able to overcome them, but we are not able to avoid them.

FURTHER STUDY

James 2:14–26;
1 Tim. 4:9–16;
2 Tim. 2:15

1. What is James teaching us?
2. How does Paul apply this to Timothy?

Prayer

Father, thank You for reminding me that even though I am a Christian, I am still governed
by natural laws that apply equally to everyone. I cannot be exempt,
but through You I can overcome. I am so grateful. Amen.

How Do You Respond?

"Be careful that none of you fails to respond to the grace which God gives, for if he does there
can . . . spring up in him a bitter spirit . . ." (v. 15, J. B. Phillips)

For reading & meditation—Hebrews 12:4–15

*T*oday we must examine an issue that may be extremely challenging to us Christians, but we must face it nevertheless. Why is it that many non-Christians, though broken by life, succeed in becoming "strong at the broken places," while many Christians go through similar experiences and come out crippled and bitter?

A few years ago I watched a television program in the United States in which a famous Jew, Victor Frankl, talked about his experiences in a concentration camp in Nazi Germany. When he was brought before the Gestapo, they stripped him naked and then, noticing that he was still wearing his gold wedding ring, one of the soldiers said, "Give it to me." As he removed his ring, this thought went through his mind: "They can take my ring, but there is one thing nobody can take from me—my freedom to choose how I will respond to what happens to me." On the strength of that, he not only survived the Holocaust, but also developed his whole psychiatric system called *Logotherapy*, which states that "when you find meaning in everything, then you can face anything."

Frankl, a non-Christian, survived the horrors of the Holocaust because he was sustained by an inner conviction that he would come through it, and be able to use the suffering to good effect. His system of Logotherapy is now being used to help thousands who have mental and emotional problems. If a non-Christian, bereft of redemptive grace, can respond to life in this way, then how much more those of us who claim to be His children?

**FURTHER
STUDY**

*Heb. 4;
2 Cor. 12:9–10;
Lam. 3:22–23*

*1. Why can we come
boldly to God?
2. What was Paul's inner
attitude to his problem?*

Prayer

O Father, whenever You corner me like this, You know my tendency to wriggle and try to get off the hook.
Help me to face this issue and take my medicine, however bitter it tastes. For Jesus' sake. Amen.

Two Men – Different Reactions

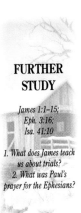

"... 'My grace is sufficient for you, for my power is made perfect in weakness.'" (v. 9)

For reading & meditation—2 Corinthians 12:1–10

We must spend another day examining this very important issue of why it is that some non-Christians seem to respond better to life's problems than many Christians.

Just recently I heard of two different people whose business ventures collapsed. One was a Christian and the other an agnostic. The agnostic responded to the situation by saying, "I cannot determine what happens to me, but I can determine what it will do to me. It will make me better and more useful." He struck out in another direction, and his new venture prospered to such a degree that he won an award. The Christian responded to the collapse of his business by saying, "Life is unjust. What's the point of trying? I shall withdraw from the cut-throat world of business and concentrate on my garden." He had to undergo some in-depth counseling before he was on his feet again, and after six months he felt strong enough to rebuild a new and now prosperous business.

What can explain the different reactions of these two men? We could explain it in terms of temperament, upbringing, and so on, but there is one thing that must not be overlooked—the Christian had access to the grace of God which, if utilized, should have enabled him to view the situation even more positively than the non-Christian. As a counselor, I understand why people respond wrongly to life's situations. However, my understanding of it does not prevent me from recognizing that the true biblical response to life's problems is to take full advantage of the grace of God and turn every setback into a springboard.

FURTHER STUDY

James 1:1–15;
Eph. 3:16;
Isa. 41:10

1. What does James teach us about trials?
2. What was Paul's prayer for the Ephesians?

Prayer

Gracious Father, help me to respond to everything in the way a Christian should. Help me to see that not only do You lift the standard high, but You also supply the strength for me to attain it. For Jesus' sake. Amen.

Doing What Is Right

"... continue to work out your salvation ... for it is God who works in you to will and to act according to his good purpose." (vv. 12–13)

For reading & meditation—Philippians 2:5-16

*W*e ended yesterday by saying that the biblical response to all of life's problems is to take advantage of the unfailing grace of God, and turn our setbacks into springboards. I know that some will respond to that statement by saying, "It sounds good in theory, but it's hard to put it into practice. What about the hurts that some people carry inside them, that make it difficult or sometimes impossible for them to make use of God's grace to turn their problems into possibilities?"

I do understand and sympathize with the wounds that people have, which sometimes militate against their desire to respond to life in a biblical way. I know from firsthand experience the arguments that people can put forward to avoid doing what God asks in His Word. However, I must take my stand, and so must you, on the authority of Scripture, and affirm that God never asks us to do what we are incapable of doing.

Much of evangelical Christianity, I am afraid, is man-centered. We need a return to a God-centered position which does exactly what God asks, whether we feel like it or not. I freely confess that there are times when I don't *feel* like obeying God. I know, however, what is right—that God has redeemed me and that I belong to Him—and I do what He wants me to whether I feel like it or not. What controls you in your Christian life—your feelings or what you know God asks and expects you to do? Your answer will reveal just who is in the driver's seat!

FURTHER STUDY

John 14:15–31;
Luke 12:11–12;
1 Cor. 2:13

1. *How do we express our love for Christ?*
2. *How are we enabled to do this?*

Prayer

Gracious and loving heavenly Father, teach me the art of responding to life, not with my feelings but with a clear mind and a clear resolve. Help me to do what is right—
whether I feel like it or not. For Jesus' sake. Amen..

Get Hold of This!

"... we know that in all things God works for the good of those who love him, who have been called according to his purpose." (v. 28)

For reading & meditation—Romans 8:28–39

*B*efore going on to examine some of the major ways in which life breaks us, we pause to review what we have been saying over these past few days. We said that while the same things may happen to us all, they do not have the same effect upon us all. Life's blows make some people querulous and bitter; others, they sweeten and refine.

We also saw that the reason some respond to life positively and turn their problems into possibilities is because of right inner attitudes. There are many non-Christians who put us to shame when it comes to the question of rightly responding to life, and it is high time, therefore, that we Christians got our philosophy of living sorted out once and for all.

If, as the Scripture teaches, God will let nothing happen to one of His children without supplying the necessary grace to turn the stumbling block into a stepping stone, then we ought to be ahead of the world in demonstrating how to meet whatever life sends us with confidence and faith. Be quite clear about this: no one can fully represent the Christian way of living until they commit themselves to believing that, though God may allow what appears to be a disaster in the life of one of His children, He does so only if He can turn it to good effect. If transformation is not possible, then God would never have allowed it to happen in the first place. So let this truth sink deep into your spirit—God only allows what He can use.

FURTHER STUDY

1 Pet. 4;
Pss. 30:5; 40:1–3;
Isa. 43:2

1. What is God's promise during trials?
2. How does Peter encourage us to respond to them?

Prayer

Father, I come to You now to ask that this truth be so impressed upon me during the weeks ahead that never again will I have to be reminded of it. For Your own dear Name's sake. Amen.

"*Never Soar as High Again?*"

"These have come so that your faith . . . may be proved genuine and may result in praise, glory and honor when Jesus Christ is revealed." (v. 7)

For reading & meditation—1 Peter 1:3–9

e turn now to examine some of the ways in which our lives become fractured, and what we can do to become "strong at the broken places."

We begin by looking at the brokenness which comes about through *failure*. Probably someone reading these words is caught up in a vortex of gloom due to a failure. You may be feeling like the man who said to me: "I am stunned by my failure. My life is shattered into smithereens. I read somewhere that 'the bird with the broken wing will never soar as high again.' Does that mean I can never rise to the heights in God which once I knew?"

I reminded him of Simon Peter—a man with one of the worst track records in the New Testament. He was prejudiced, bigoted, stubborn, and spiritually insensitive. Again and again he got his wires crossed, such as the time when he attempted to divert Christ from going to His death in Jerusalem (Matt. 16:22), or his insistence that they should stay on the Mount of Transfiguration (Matt. 17:4). Then, on the eve of Christ's crucifixion, he denied and even cursed his Lord. I can imagine Satan whispering in his ear: "Now you're finished. Burned out. A failure. You'll be forgotten . . . replaced." But by God's grace, Peter rose from failure to success. He became "strong at the broken places." Because he refused to live in the shadow of his bad track record, his two letters are enshrined forever in the Scriptures. Failures, you see, are only temporary tests to prepare us for more permanent triumphs.

FURTHER STUDY

Exod. 2; 3

1. How did Moses fail God?
2. How did God deal with him?

Prayer

O Father, I see so clearly that no failure is a failure if it succeeds in driving me to Your side. All things serve me—when I serve You. Amen.

Incisive Questions

"So I turned my mind to understand, to investigate and to search out wisdom . . ." (v. 25)
For reading & meditation—Ecclesiastes 7:21–29

What steps must we take, when broken by failure, to ensure that we become strong at the place of weakness? Keep in mind that the principles we are considering are not only corrective, but also preventative.

The first thing we should do, whenever we have failed in anything, is to *analyze the reason for the failure*. These are some of the questions you should ask yourself: Have I contributed in any way to this failure by such things as inattention to detail, lack of preparation, naiveté, wrong timing, disregard of moral principles, or insensitivity to other people's feelings? Another question is: What does God want me to learn from this failure? It is difficult, of course, to sit down and question yourself like this when failure strikes; but, as soon as possible after the event, try to assess the lessons that can be learned by honestly facing your emotions—such as hurt, anger, anxiety. Remember, when we stop learning, we stop living.

Yet another question to ask yourself is this: Has God allowed this failure so that His purposes for me might be made clear? I know a man, well-known in evangelical circles, who, when he was in his teens, mapped out a career for himself. Although a brilliant student, he failed the entrance examination into his chosen profession. When the news was broken to him, he simply said, "Lord, I just know You are involved in this: what do You want me to do?" This was the moment God had been waiting for, and He showed him a new path that has made him Christ's ambassador to millions.

FURTHER STUDY

James 3 and 1:5;
Prov. 2:1–5; 3:13–14

1. What are the characteristics of earthly wisdom?
2. How are we to obtain wisdom?

Prayer

Father, help me to face my failure in the knowledge that some good can be wrested from even the most depressing circumstances. Show me that incisive questions can bring incisive answers.
In Jesus' Name. Amen.

Day 256

Looking Failure in the Face

"... 'Now is the Son of Man glorified and God is glorified in him.'" (v. 31)

For reading & meditation—John 13:12–32

*T*he second thing we should do when failure strikes is to *face it in the knowledge that with God something can be made out of it.*

The account before us today tells of Christ's betrayal by Judas. Notice how Jesus first accepted the situation before He went on to make something out of it. The Master said: "What you are about to do, do quickly." He made no attempt to ignore the situation, sweep it under the carpet, or pretend it was not there—instead He calmly and deliberately faced reality. Before we go any further, make up your mind to face up to all of life's problems, because if you try to ignore them, you will become inwardly demeaned. The account continues: "As soon as Judas had taken the bread, he went out. And it was night. When he was gone, Jesus said, 'Now is the Son of Man glorified and God is glorified in him.'"

Not only did Jesus accept the situation, but He moved on to turn it into victory. No self-pity, no egotistical concern—He took charge of the situation and made the betrayal contribute to His victory. Was Jesus hurt by Judas' betrayal? I should think so. But instead of spending the night wallowing in self-pity He looked at the situation from God's point of view and quietly affirmed: "Now is the Son of Man glorified." It may take you a little while to be able to respond to difficult situations in the way Jesus did, but remember this—the resources on which the Master drew are yours for the asking.

FURTHER STUDY

Matt. 26:58–75;
Luke 24:12;
John 21:15–19;
Acts 2:14

1. What was the progression of Peter's failure?
2. How did he face his failure?

Prayer

Father, I see that my life will be made or broken at the place where I acknowledge and deal with my failures. Help me not to run away from them, because in You I am more than a match for anything. Thank You, Father. Amen.

272

A Biblical Mentality

"You know, brothers, that our visit to you was not a failure." (v. 1)
For reading & meditation—1 Thessalonians 2:1–12

Today we examine yet another principle which we must develop in our lives if we are to become strong at the broken places of failure: *cultivate a biblical perspective on everything.* You may be familiar with the passage before us today, but I want to emphasize several points from it which help us to see how effectively Paul believed and practiced spiritual principles.

Firstly, his words and preaching, despite strong public opposition, were not the result of his own thinking—they were the result of the gospel of God (v. 2). Secondly, the very foundation of his life and character were based on the truth of the gospel (v. 3). Thirdly, he considered God's Word as something "entrusted" to him, and it gave him such security that he didn't feel the need to compromise or become a "people pleaser" (v. 4).

It may sound old-fashioned and naive to some, but I believe with all my heart that the secret of surviving life's crushing defeats and blows is to develop a spiritual and biblical perspective on everything. "It is blessed," wrote C. H. Spurgeon, "to eat into the very soul of the Bible until, at last, you come to talk in Scriptural language, and your spirit is flavored with the words of the Lord, so that your blood is *Bibline* and the very essence of the Bible flows from you." Descriptive, isn't it? I find this idea of being committed to a biblical mentality so rare among modern-day Christians that I sometimes tremble inwardly with concern. Someone said, "Time spent with the Bible knits up the ravelled sleeve of care." It does.

FURTHER STUDY

Ps. 119:97–104;
Josh. 1:8;
2 Cor. 10: 1–5;
Rom. 12:2

1. How can we cultivate a biblical perspective?
2. How is our mind renewed?

 Prayer

O Father, help me, also, "to eat into the very soul of the Bible . . . until my spirit is flavored with the words of the Lord." Give me a biblical mentality. For Jesus' sake I pray. Amen.

"I Didn't"

"Let us fix our eyes on Jesus . . . who for the joy set before him endured the cross . . ." (v. 2)
For reading & meditation—Hebrews 12:1–13

*A*nother principle in coping with failure is this: *If the thing in which you failed is clearly the right thing for you to do, then dedicate your energies to God, try again, and don't give up.*

A father, trying to encourage his teenage son after he had failed an examination, said, "Don't give up, try again." "What's the use?" said the son. "It's easier to quit." His father remonstrated with him, saying, "The people who are remembered in life are the people who, when they failed, didn't give up, but tried again." He went on, "Remember Churchill? Remember Thomas Edison? They didn't give up!" The boy nodded. His father went on, "Remember John McCringle?" "Who is John McCringle?" the boy asked. "You see," said the father, "you don't remember him—he gave up."

A poster showed a picture of a man sitting on a park bench looking depressed and disconsolate. His arms were folded across his chest, and there was a look of resignation on his face. The caption read, "I give up." When I first saw this poster, I looked at it for a few moments and turned away, but then my eye was attracted to something in the right-hand corner of the poster. It was a picture of a black hill and on it a very tiny cross. These words, barely perceptible, were printed beneath it: "I didn't." Feel like giving up at this moment? Then lift your eyes to the cross. The one who triumphed over all obstacles holds out His hands toward you. Take His hand, and in His strength and power— try again.

FURTHER STUDY

*Phil. 3;
James 1:6–8;
Matt. 6:22*

*1. What was Paul's attitude?
2. What happens when our eye is single?*

Prayer

O God, help me to link my littleness to Your greatness, my faintheartedness to Your boldness,
my fear to Your faith. Then nothing can stop me. Amen.

274

"Grace – Greater than Failure"

"... God is able to make all grace abound to you, so that in all things at all times ... you will abound in every good work." (v. 8)

For reading & meditation—2 Corinthians 9:6–15

*A*nother principle we must develop in our lives if we are to cope with failure is this: *However disappointing and discouraging our failures, grace covers them all.* No fears need creep in today from yesterday's failures, for grace has wiped them out and works to turn them to good effect. This does not mean that we evade the consequences of our failures, but providing we respond correctly and with honesty, grace flows in to take over and transform. Emerson says: "Finish every day and be done with it. You have done what you could. Some blunders, some failures, some absurdities will have crept in. But forget them. Tomorrow is a new day."

This is good advice, but not quite good enough. We cannot just "forget them," especially if our failures have brought distress to others also. However, when we face things honestly and determine to learn from our failures, then God transforms those failures by His grace. He wipes away the burning memories of shame and self-disgust so that our failures, seen through grace, do not paralyze us but propel us forward.

The Old Testament ends with a curse (Mal. 4:6), but the New Testament ends with grace (Rev. 22:21). What does this suggest? It suggests that grace does not simply look back at past deeds; it looks forward to hold that future steady. You are under grace today, and you will be under grace tomorrow. What a prospect! The past can't hurt you, and both today and tomorrow are secure. Our failures, therefore, make us sing—sing at the redemption that grace draws from them.

FURTHER STUDY

Rom. 5 and 3:23–24;
2 Tim. 2:1;
Titus 3:7

1. What are the characteristics of grace?
2. What is the result of being justified through grace?

Prayer

O Father, I am so thankful that grace holds the keys of yesterday and tomorrow. You lock the one—and open the other. And there is grace for today too! I am eternally grateful. Amen.

Hallelujah –
the Pressure's Off

"Now it is God who makes both us and you stand firm in Christ ." (v. 21)

For reading & meditation—2 Corinthians 1:12–22

A further principle is this: *Strive not so much to succeed but to do the right thing.*

I remember addressing a group of ministers in Atlanta, Georgia, on "Pitfalls in the Ministry." I told them the story of my own failures, which at that time amounted to a great many, and I said, "The lesson I have learned from my failures is that I don't have to succeed. I have to do the right thing under God's guidance, and leave success or failure in His hands." One of the ministers came to me afterwards and said, "I am a pastor of one of the largest churches in this area, and regarded by my peers as one of the most successful ministers in my denomination. But today you have helped me overcome the greatest pressure in my life—the pressure to succeed."

In the early years of my ministry, I was extremely success-oriented; when I succeeded, I felt good, and when I failed, I felt devastated. Then God said to me quite bluntly one day, "Are you willing to be a failure?" The question shook me rigid. It was a whole week later before I found sufficient grace to answer that question with a "Yes," and when I did, I was instantly released from the two things that had crippled my life and ministry—the pressure to succeed and the fear of failure. Now, what matters is not succeeding or failing, but being true to Him. Success and failure are in His hands. I am not on the way to success, I am on the Way. What a difference!

FURTHER STUDY

Rom. 7; 8

1. What brought Paul through his despondent struggle?
2. Write down the number of times "I" occurs in chapter 7 and "Spirit" in chapter 8.

Prayer

O Father, set me free today from these two crippling disabilities—the pressure to succeed and the fear of failure. Help me to do the right thing, and to leave success or failure in Your hands. For Jesus' sake. Amen.

"Men Cry Out Against the Heavens"

Day 261

"he [God] . . . cares for the helpless.
He does not ignore those who cry to him for help" (v. 12, NLT)

For reading & meditation—Psalm 9:1-20

Having learned something about how to cope with failure, we turn now to face the issue of what to do when life breaks us with *unmerited suffering and affliction.* I get more letters on this subject than on almost any other. People write and say, "My suffering is so great that I sometimes doubt the existence of a God of love. Can you say something that will help me regain my faith in this tragic hour?"

One of the most poignant elements in suffering is that there often seems to be no meaning in it. One great writer said that anyone who was undisturbed by the problem of unmerited suffering was a victim of either a hardened heart or a softened brain. He was right. Everyone who is mentally alive, especially if he believes in a God of love, finds this problem difficult to solve. No wonder the poet cried out:

> My son, the world is dark with griefs and graves
> So dark that men cry out against the heavens.

I suppose there is nothing that makes people cry out against the heavens so much as the anguish which comes unbidden and unmerited. Some of our sufferings are the result of our own crassness and stupidity. But what about when life breaks us with sufferings that are not directly related to us? Does God remember us then? Our text today says that He does. This in itself should be enough to keep us brave, if not blithe; in peace, if not in happiness. Write it on your heart. God remembers you in your suffering. He really does!

FURTHER STUDY

Rom. 8:17–26;
2 Cor. 1:7; 4:11–18;
1 Pet. 5:10

1. What is God's purpose in suffering?
2. What are some of the ways in which Christ suffered?

Prayer

Lord Jesus, You who experienced suffering in a way I will never know, hold me close to Your heart so that my sufferings will not demolish me, but develop me. For Your own dear Name's sake. Amen.

Suffering Is Inevitable

"Yet man is born to trouble as surely as sparks fly upward." (v. 7)
For reading & meditation—Job 5:1–18

*H*ow do we, as Christians, cope with the problem of unmerited suffering? The first thing we must do is to recognize that in a universe whose balance has been greatly upset by sin, undeserved suffering is bound to come. Face this, and you are halfway to turning the problem into a possibility.

In an Indian palace, many years ago, a child was born whose parents decided to keep all signs of decay and death from him. When he was taken into the garden, maids were sent before him to remove all the decaying flowers and fallen leaves, so that he would be protected from all signs of suffering and death. One day, however, he left his home and, while wandering through the streets, came across a corpse. His reaction was so strong that he set about establishing the teaching that, as life is fundamentally suffering, the only thing to do is to escape into Nirvana, the state of extinction of self.

The young man was Guatama Buddha, whose beliefs are shared by millions of his followers, not only in India but around the world. His philosophy is a dramatic and tragic result of trying to protect oneself from the realities of life, one of which is suffering. The Christian faith is the opposite of that: it exposes us to the very heart of suffering—the cross. Then it takes that suffering, and turns it into salvation. This is why Christians should not be afraid to face the worst that can happen—because with God it can be turned into the best.

FURTHER STUDY

Isa. 53;
Luke 22:40;
Heb. 2:9–10; 5:8; 8:1

1. Why was it necessary for Christ to suffer?
2. How can suffering become positive?

 Prayer

Father, I am so thankful for the cross—what is my suffering compared to that? And even if I have to bear similar suffering, I know that out of it will come to me what came to You—a resurrection. Blessed be Your Name forever. Amen.

The Best Out of the Worst

"Live such good lives among the pagans that, though they accuse you of doing wrong,
they may see your good deeds and glorify God . . ." (v. 12)

For reading & meditation—1 Peter 2:11-25

*Y*esterday we said that the first attitude we should adopt toward unmerited suffering is to accept that it is bound to come. Sin has unbalanced the universe, and suffering is one of the inevitable results. To deny this is to deny reality, and the denial of reality is the denial of life. Arising out of this comes our second principle: *God is able to turn all suffering to good and glorious ends.*

J. B. Phillips translates today's verse: ". . . although they may in the usual way slander you as evildoers, yet when disasters come they may glorify God when they see how well you conduct yourselves." Note the phrase, "when disasters come." They are bound to come to everyone—it's foolish to think that, just because we are Christians, we are exempt. We are part of a universe that has been unbalanced by sin, part of a mortal, decaying world. However, though we may fall victims to life's disasters, we are able, through the redemptive purposes of God, to turn them into doors of opportunity and step through them into richer, more abundant living.

A woman who was converted from one of the cults said in a testimony meeting in her church: "They taught me that the first thing I should concern myself about is my happiness. You have taught me that the first thing is to 'belong.' That makes me feel safe." Since she was safe, her happiness was safe too. Others are baffled by life's tragedies. Only the cross has an answer. Out of the worst, Christ brings the best, and makes life's victims victorious.

FURTHER STUDY

John 10:1–10;
2 Cor. 9:8;
Eph. 3:20

1. What does the thief seek to do?
2. What does Christ bring us?

⌘ Prayer ⌘

Father, the more I think about this, the more excited I get. You have given me such security.
I can stand anything because I can use everything. Oh glory! Amen.

279

Not Comfort – But Character

"... Shall we accept good from God, and not trouble?" (v. 10)

For reading & meditation—Job 2:1–10

*W*e come today to one of the most difficult principles to understand in relation to suffering—but it must be grasped nevertheless. It is this—*Accept suffering as a gift from God.*

This principle flows out of today's verse—a verse which one commentator describes as "the most profound verse in the Bible." It is obvious from reading this passage that Job's God is not a celestial Being who sits on the parapets of heaven, dropping nice little gifts into the laps of His children, at the same time saying, "There, that will make you happy; that will surely please you." There is much more to God than that. The God of the Bible dispenses the things that bring most glory to His Name. If, in achieving glory, He sees that suffering is the best means to that end, then that is what He will give. So mark this well—God is not under an obligation to make you comfortable.

Can you see the truth that is contained in the words of our text today? "Shall we indeed accept good from God and not accept adversity?" (NASB). You are ready to accept good, but are you just as ready to accept adversity? You see, God's goal is not our comfort, but our character. That is why it is wrong to tell a non-Christian, "Trust God, and your troubles will all be over." It's unfair, dishonest, and downright unbiblical. In fact, becoming a Christian may mean that you will have more troubles than before. And why? Because character is formed in the furnace of affliction—no suffering, no character.

FURTHER STUDY

1 Pet. 1:1–9;
Pss. 66:10; 119:67;
Isa. 48:10

1. What analogy does the Scripture draw?
2. What is the result of enduring suffering?

Prayer

Father, if ever I needed Your help I need it now. It's easy for me to accept good from Your hand; help me also to accept adversity. Etch these words, not merely into my mind, but into my spirit.
In Jesus' Name I ask it. Amen.

The Agony of God

"... he ... carried our sorrows, yet we considered him stricken by God, smitten by him, and afflicted." (v. 4)

For reading & meditation—Isaiah 53:1–12

*D*r. E. Stanley Jones said: "Christianity is the only religion that dares ask its followers to accept suffering as a gift from God, because it is the only religion that dares say God too has suffered."

Surely it must mean something to us, as Christians, to know that though living in this world is costing us pain, it is costing God more. But how much has God suffered? Some Christians think that the full extent of God's sufferings were the hours in which He watched His Son die upon the cross, but it means much more than that. The Bible tells us that Christ was "the Lamb slain from the foundation of the world" (Rev. 13:8, KJV). That means that there was a cross set up in the heart of God long before there was a cross set up on the hill of Calvary.

God's sufferings began at the moment He planned the universe, and tugged at His heartstrings from the moment that He laid the foundations of the world. The pain of the cross must have pierced right through Him as He waited for that awful moment when His Son would die on Calvary. How long did He wait? Centuries? Millennia! Then finally it came—the awful screaming agony of crucifixion. Was this the end? No. Now His sufferings continue in the world's rejection of His Son, and in the indifference of His children. So doesn't it mean something, even everything, to know that, though living in this world is costing us pain, it is costing God more? I find this thought deeply comforting. I pray that you will too.

FURTHER STUDY

Matt. 26:36–42 and 27;
Isa. 50:6;
Luke 22:44;
Heb. 2:10

1. List five aspects of the sufferings of Christ.
2. What was the "cup" Jesus had to drink?

Prayer

Father, I realize that now I am looking into the heart of the deepest mystery of the universe—Your sacrificial love. Help me to understand this fully, for when I see this I see everything. Amen.

281

God Is in Control

"... I am God, and there is none like me. I make known the end from the beginning ...
My purpose will stand, and I will do all that I please." (vv. 9–10)

For reading & meditation—Isaiah 46:3–13

*R*ecognize that because you are finite you will never be able to fully understand the ways of God.

It was a wonderful moment in my life when I was delivered from the torment of trying to figure out the reasons why God behaves the way He does. I was reading the Scripture at the top of this page when these thoughts hit me like a bolt from the blue: God is in control of the world. Don't try to grasp all the ramifications of this truth; just accept it. I have never spent a single moment since in trying to figure out why God does what He does. I accept His sovereignty without question—and I am all the better for it.

"One of the marks of maturity," says Charles Swindoll, "is the quiet confidence that God is in control ... without the need to understand why He does what He does." "He does according to his will in the host of heaven and among the inhabitants of the earth; and none can stay his hand or say to him, 'What doest thou?'" (Dan. 4:35, RSV). There are, of course, many more Scriptures that make the same point—the Almighty is in charge. If you are in a turmoil of fear trying to figure out the reasons why God does what He does, then stop. You can't anyway. Feverishly trying to unravel all the knots can bring you to the edge of a nervous breakdown. The finite can never plumb the infinite. Face the fact that God's ways are unsearchable and unfathomable. Then you will start to live—really live.

FURTHER STUDY

Isa. 55 and 40:28–31;
Rom. 11:33;
Job 11:7

1. What has God promised instead of thorns and briers?
2. How are God's ways different to ours?

⤟⟶ *Prayer* ⟵⤞

My gracious Father, set me free today from the tyranny of trying to fathom the unfathomable. Quietly I breathe the calm and peace of Your sovereignty into my being. No longer will I struggle to understand: I shall just stand. Thank You, Father. Amen.

God Tests before He Entrusts

"... those who suffer according to God's will should commit themselves to their faithful Creator and continue to do good." (v. 19)

For reading & meditation—1 Peter 4:12–19

*G*od seldom uses anyone unless He puts that person through the test of suffering and adversity.

Jesus, you remember, began His ministry in the wilderness of temptation, but it culminated in a garden in Jerusalem on Easter morning. Our lesser ministries, too, need the test of suffering. An ancient proverb says: "He who is born in the fire will not fade in the sun." If God lets us suffer in the fire of adversity, depend on it—He is only making sure that we will not fade in the sun of smaller difficulties. Has life broken you by suffering and affliction? Are you feeling weakened and drained by the things that have happened to you? Take hold of the principles we have been examining this week, and I promise you that never again will life break you at the point of suffering.

This does not mean that you will never again experience suffering, but it does mean that you will respond to the suffering with a new and positive faith. Let me draw your attention once more to the text we looked at the other day: "Although they may in the usual way slander you as evildoers, yet when disasters come they may glorify God when they see how well you conduct yourselves" (1 Pet. 2:12, Phillips). Make no mistake about it—the world is watching how we Christians react to suffering. What do they see? People who struggle on in continual weakness, or people who have been made "strong at the broken places"?

FURTHER STUDY

Rom. 5:1–11;
2 Thess. 1;
Matt. 5:10–12

1. What are some of the results of suffering and affliction?
2. Are these being evidenced in your life?

Prayer

O Father, I am one of Your followers, but so often I am afraid to follow You all the way. Yet I see that Your way is right—nothing else is right. I know You will stand by me; help me to stand by You. For Jesus' sake. Amen.

When Riches Take Wings

"Do not wear yourself out to get rich. . . . Cast but a glance at riches . . . for they will surely sprout wings and fly off . . ." (vv. 4–5)

For reading & meditation—Proverbs 23:1–8

*W*e move on now to consider yet another way in which life can break us—*through financial disaster or material loss.* Some Christians speak scornfully against money. I have heard them quote Scripture in this way: "Money is the root of all evil." They forget that the text actually reads: "The love of money is the root of all evil" (1 Tim. 6:10, KJV).

Money in itself is not evil. It feeds the hungry, clothes the naked and succors the destitute, and through it many errands of mercy are performed. Some years ago the recorder at the Old Bailey made a statement which was reported in almost every newspaper. He said, "A couple of pounds very often saves a life—and sometimes a soul." It may be true that money cannot bring happiness but, as somebody said, "It can certainly put our creditors in a better frame of mind." Perhaps nothing hurts more than when life breaks us through a financial crisis, and we experience something of what the writer of the Proverbs describes—"riches taking wings."

Can we be made strong at the broken place of financial failure? We can. I think now as I write of a man I knew some years ago who lost all his assets. Such was his financial crisis that he lost everything—literally everything. Life broke him. He came out of it, however, with a new philosophy that changed his whole attitude toward money. I am sure of this: life will never break him there again. He was made strong at the broken place. And so, my friend, can you be.

FURTHER STUDY

Matt. 6:19–34;
10:29–31;
Luke 12:15

1. What did Jesus teach about possessions?
2. What is to be our priority?

Prayer

O Father, help me to settle once and for all my attitude toward this complex problem of money. If it is a weakness, then help me make it a strength. For Jesus' sake. Amen.

Transferring the Ownership

"... because you ... have not withheld your son, your only son, I will surely
bless you ..." (vv. 16–17)

For reading & meditation—Genesis 22:1–19

*W*e referred yesterday to the man who was broken by a
financial disaster, but came out of it enabled to say, "Never
again will I be broken by material loss." And why? Because he built for
himself a biblical framework which enabled him to see the whole issue
of finances from God's point of view.

Here are the steps my friend took in moving from financial bondage
to financial freedom. (1) *In a definite act of commitment, transfer the
ownership of all your possessions to God.* Whether we acknowledge it or
not, we do not in reality own our possessions. We are stewards, not
proprietors, of the assets which God puts into our hands. After reading
the story of Abraham and his willingness to sacrifice his son, my friend
got alone with God and offered every single one of his possessions to
the Lord. He said, "I continued in prayer until every single item I had
was laid on God's altar, and when it was over I was a transformed man.
That act of dedication became the transformation point in my
finances."

If, in reality, we do not own our possessions, then the obvious thing
to do is to have the sense to say to God: "Lord, I'm not the owner, but
the ower. Teach me how to work out that relationship for as long as I
live." When you let go of your possessions and let God have full control, the whole issue of stewardship becomes meaningful. You are handling something on behalf of Another. Money is no longer your master—it becomes instead your messenger.

FURTHER STUDY

1 Kings 17;
1 Cor. 4:1–2;
Rom. 14:12

*1. What can we learn
from the widow at
Zarephath?*
*2. What is the character-
istic of a steward?*

Prayer

Father, I'm conscious that, once again, You have Your finger on another sensitive spot. I wince, but I know I
can never be a true disciple until I make this commitment. I do it today—gladly.
For Your own dear Name's sake. Amen.

"Hitched to a Plough"

"Set your minds on things above, not on earthly things." (v. 2)
For reading & meditation—Colossians 3:1–17

We continue to consider the steps that can move us from financial freedom:

(2) *Streamline your life toward the purposes of God's kingdom.* Livingstone said, "I will place no value on anything that I have or possess, except in relation to the kingdom of Christ. If anything I have will advance that kingdom it shall be given or kept, whichever will best promote the glory of Him to whom I owe all my hopes, both for time and eternity." Another missionary said, "That first sentence of Livingstone's should become the life motto of every Christian. Each Christian should repeat this slowly to himself every day: *I will place no value on anything I have or possess, except in relation to the kingdom of Christ.*" If it advances the kingdom it has value—it can stay. If it is useless to the kingdom it is valueless—it must be made useful, or go.

John Wanamaker, a fine Christian businessman, visited China many years ago to see if the donations he had made to missionary work were being used to their best advantage. One day he came to a village where there was a beautiful church, and in a nearby field, he caught sight of a young man yoked together with an ox, ploughing a field. He went over and asked what was the purpose of this strange yoking. An old man who was driving the plough said, "When we were trying to build the church, my son and I had no money to give, and my son said, 'Let us sell one of our two oxen and I will take its yoke.' We did so and gave the money to the chapel." Wanamaker wept!

FURTHER STUDY

James 4:8–17;
Rom. 14:8;
Ps. 24:1;
Hag. 2:8

1. How should we approach life?
2. Is your value system biblical?

Prayer

Father, I feel like weeping too when I consider how little of my life is streamlined for kingdom purposes. Help me to be willing to be hitched to a plough and know the joy of sacrifice. For Jesus' sake. Amen.

Riches or Poverty – So What?

"I know what it is to be in need, and I know what it is to have plenty. I have learned the secret of being content in any . . . situation . . ." (v. 12)

For reading & meditation—Philippians 4:4–13

*H*ere is another step that can move us from financial bondage to financial freedom.

(3) *Recognize that you are only free when you are free to use either poverty or plenty.*

There are two ways in which men and women try to defend themselves against financial disaster. One is by saving as much as possible in an attempt to avert it. The other is by renouncing money or material things entirely in order to be free from their clutches. Both methods have disadvantages. The first, because it can cause miserliness and anxiety, and tends to make a person as metallic as the coins they seek to amass. The second, because it seeks to get rid of the difficulty by washing one's hands of it entirely. In each case, there is a bondage—one is a bondage to material things, the other a bondage to poverty. The man who is free to use plenty *only* is bound by that, while the man who is free to use poverty *only* is also bound. They are both bound. But the person who, like Paul in the text before us today, has "learned the secret of being content . . . whether living in plenty or in want" is free, really free.

While waiting for a train in India, a missionary got into a conversation with a high-caste Indian. "Are you traveling on the next train?" the missionary asked. "No," he replied, "that train has only third-class carriages. It's all right for you, because you are a Christian. Third class doesn't degrade you and first class doesn't exalt you. You are above these distinctions, but I have to observe them." *Lifted above all distinctions!*

FURTHER STUDY

James 2:1–10; 5:1–8

1. Where does favoritism come from?
2. What does James say about selfish living?

Prayer

O Father, what a way to live—lifted above all distinctions. Plenty doesn't entangle my spirit, and poverty doesn't break it. No matter how I have lived in the past—this is how I want to live in the future. Help me, dear Lord. Amen.

A Need or a Want?

"And my God will meet all your needs according to his glorious riches in Christ Jesus." (v. 19)

For reading & meditation—Philippians 4:14–23

Today we look at yet another step that will help us overcome financial disaster: (4) *Learn to differentiate between a need and a want.* Your needs are important, but not your wants. God has promised to supply all your needs, but not all your wants.

What are our needs? Someone defined it like this: "We need as much as will make us physically, mentally, and spiritually fit for the purposes of the kingdom of God. Anything beyond that belongs to other people's needs." If this is true, then how do we decide what belongs to our needs? No one can decide that for you; it must be worked out between you and God. Go over your life in God's presence and see what belongs to your needs, and what belongs to your wants. Let the Holy Spirit sensitize your conscience so that you can distinguish the difference.

A fisherman tells this story: "Yesterday on the lake I let my boat drift. As I looked at the water, I could see no drift at all. Only as I looked at the fixed point of the shoreline could I see how far I was drifting." It is a parable! It is only as you fix your eyes on Christ, and watch for His approval, that you will know whether you are staying on God's course—or drifting away from it. One more thing: keep your needs strictly to needs, not luxuries disguised as needs. If you eat more than you need, you clog up your system. It is the same with other things. Needs contribute; luxuries choke.

FURTHER STUDY

*Exod. 16;
Pss. 23:5; 33:18–19;
37:25*

*1. How did God supply the needs of the Israelites?
2. List some of the needs God has supplied in your life.*

⇢ *Prayer* ⇠

Gracious Father, bring me under the sway of Your creative Spirit. Sensitize my inner being so that I might hear Your voice when I am about to go off course. This I ask for Your own dear Name's sake. Amen.

Promises! Promises!

"...'it's no good!' says the buyer; then off he goes and boasts about his purchase." (v. 14)

For reading & meditation—Proverbs 20:1–22

*W*e continue following the steps that help us become strong at the broken place of financial disaster: (5) *Ask God to help you resist the powerful pressures of this modern-day consumer society.*

I once listened to a sermon in which the preacher likened Satan's conversation with Eve in the Garden of Eden to the subtle tactics of modern advertising. The main point he made was that if Eve could become discontent with all she had in that lush garden called Paradise, there is little hope for us unless we identify and reject modern methods of alluring advertising. What exactly is alluring advertising? One definition puts it like this: "Alluring advertising is a carefully planned appeal to our human weakness, which is designed to make us discontented with what we have so that we can rationalize buying things we know we do not need and should not have."

Not all advertising, of course, falls into this category, but much of it does. Charles Swindoll, an American author, claims that some advertising is not just alluring, but definitely demonic. I agree. He says that he and his family have developed a simple technique to overrule television commercials that attempt to convince us that we need a certain product in order to be happy. He describes it like this: "Everytime we feel a persuasive tug from a television commercial, we simply shout at the top of our voices: 'Who do you think you're kidding!'" He claims it really works. God expects us to discipline ourselves in relation to many things, and not the least is the discipline of spiritual "sales resistance."

FURTHER STUDY

1 John 2:12–17;
Gen. 3:6;
James 1:13–16

1. What are the three avenues which advertising exploits?
2. What is John's admonition?

Prayer

Father, help me, I pray, to see right through the alluring advertising of today's world, and develop within me the wisdom and strength to build up a strong spiritual "sales resistance."
For Your honor and glory I ask it. Amen.

"Be a Generous Person"

"Command them . . . to be generous and willing to share. In this way they will
lay up treasure for themselves . . ." (vv. 18–19)

For reading & meditation—1 Timothy 6:6–19

We have been discussing the steps we need to take to become strong at the place where life breaks us through a financial disaster.

The sixth and final principle the friend I previously referred to used, and which we need to practice too, is this: (6) *Become a generous person.* Look again at the text at the top of this page. It is so clear that it hardly needs any explanation. Woven through the fabric of these verses, as well as in many others in the New Testament, is the thought: give, give, give, give, give. When you have money, don't hoard it, release it. Let generosity become your trademark. This is not to say that you have to give all your money away, but give as much as you can, and as much as you believe God would have you give. Jesus once said, "If your eye is generous, the whole of your body will be illumined" (Matt. 6:22, Moffatt).

What does this mean? If your eye—your outlook on life, your whole way of looking at things and people—is generous, then your whole personality is illumined, lit up. Jesus had little to give in terms of finances, but He was generous toward all—the sick, the needy, the maimed, the sinful, and the unlovely. His whole personality was full of light. So be like Jesus—begin to see everybody and everything with a generous eye. Don't be a mean person. One of the greatest definitions of Christianity I have ever heard is simply this: "Give, give, give, give give. . . ."

FURTHER STUDY

Luke 21:1–4; 6:38;
Eccl. 11:1;
Acts 4:32–35;
Matt. 5:42

1. What did Jesus teach about giving?
2. How did the early church work this out?

Prayer

Lord Jesus, help me this day and every day of my life from now on, to make generosity the basis of all my dealings with people. Make me the channel and not the dead end of all Your generosity to me.
For Your dear Name's sake. Amen.

When Evil Thoughts Oppress

"For out of the heart come evil thoughts . . ." (v. 19)
For reading & meditation—Matthew 15:1–20

*W*e turn now to focus on yet another place where life can break us—through *the affliction of evil thoughts*. I am thinking not simply of an occasional wrong thought popping into one's mind, but of those situations where people become oppressed by thoughts which are obsessive and repetitive. A letter I received some time ago said, "My private discussions with Christians of all denominations has led me to believe that more are afflicted and oppressed by evil thoughts than we might imagine."

When the late Dr. Sangster, the great Methodist preacher, once visited Bexhill-on-Sea, he found a lovely avenue of trees. A nature lover to the core, he walked admiringly up and down the avenue, and then noticed a strange thing. Two of the trees were dead, and not only dead, but dismally and evilly offensive. Frost could not account for it; their neighbors were all healthy. He made inquiries, and found out that the gas main which ran underneath them had been leaking! Everything on the surface had been in their favor—the sea breezes, sunshine, rain . . . but they had been poisoned from beneath.

There are many Christians like that. Perhaps you are one. The circumstances of their lives all seem in their favor—a good job, a happy family, a pleasant environment, a fine church, yet their lives are mysteriously blighted by evil thoughts. Who can help us when our lives are spoiled by continual and oppressive evil thoughts? Jesus can! Christ can not only heal the brokenness but also make you strong at the broken place.

FURTHER STUDY

Matt. 5:27–28; 6:19–34;
2 Cor. 10:5;
Eph. 4:22–24

1. List eight ways in which Satan seeks to attack our minds.
2. What is the Christian antidote?

Prayer

O Father, I am so grateful that You are showing me Your indomitable way. You can do more than sustain me in my weakness; You can turn my weakness into strength. Make me strong in this area. For Jesus' sake. Amen.

"Be Careful, Little Eyes"

"And if your eye causes you to sin, pluck it out." (v. 47)
For reading & meditation—Mark 9:42–50

*W*hat are the principles we must follow if we are to move from weakness to strength in relation to this matter of evil thoughts? The first is: *Take steps to ensure that you are not contributing to the problem by the literature you read or the things you watch.*

One great philosopher said that if you want to evaluate the moral tone of a society, just examine its literature. These days it is hardly possible to pick up a newspaper that does not contain a picture or an article that is calculated to inflame our passions. We live in an age which is preoccupied with sensuality and hedonism (the pursuit of pleasure). Any discussion on this subject must inevitably be linked with sex, as this is one of the main ingredients in the problem of evil thoughts. Although sex is not evil in itself, few topics can so engross the mind or kindle our curiosity. People with a passionate nature, however high their ideals, often fight a battle in their mind and imagination with sexual fantasies. These, in turn, make them the kind of people of whom Montaigne speaks with much contempt: "Men and women whose heads are a merry-go-round of lustful images."

Fix it firmly in your mind that the first step to victory over evil thoughts is to cut off the supply at the source. Burn any books or magazines in your possession that others might describe as "really hot." Turn off the TV when it violates biblical standards. Avoid newspapers that go in for nudity. Saying "no" to sensuality is the same as saying "yes" to God.

**FURTHER
STUDY**

*2 Sam. 11:1-17;
1 John 2:16;
Luke 11:34;
Eph. 1:18*

*1. What was the source of
David's downfall?
2. List six ways in which
Satan tempts us through
our eyes.*

Prayer

Father, help me to realize that although Christianity is a privilege and not a prohibition—it does have prohibition in it. Today I am going to make up my mind to say a firm "no" to the things that are not of You. Strengthen me in this resolve. Amen.

The Pathway to Sin Is Short

"To set the mind on the flesh is death, but to set the mind on the Spirit is life and peace." (v. 6, RSV)

For reading & meditation—Romans 8:1-17

*A*lthough it may be impossible to prevent evil thoughts from entering your mind, make a conscious decision not to entertain them. A well-worn phrase puts the same thought in this way: you can't stop the birds from flying into your hair, but you can prevent them from building nests.

Burns, the famous poet, said that when he wished to compose a love song, his recipe was to put himself on "a regimen of admiring a beautiful woman." He deliberately filled his mind with pictures that were extremely dangerous to his passionate nature. Shairp, his biographer, said of him, "When the images came to be oft repeated, it cannot have tended to his peace of heart or his purity of life."

Augustine, one of the great early Christians, also trod this dangerous path. He came to Carthage with its tinseled vice and began at once to coax his own carnal appetites. He said: "I loved not as yet, yet I loved to love; and with an hidden want I abhorred myself that I wanted not. I befouled, therefore, the spring of friendship with the filth of concupiscence, and I dimmed its lustre with the hell of lustfullness; and yet, foul and dishonorable as I was, I craved, through an excess of vanity to be thought elegant and vain. I fell; precipitately then."

Augustine's experience, like that of many others, goes to show the folly of entertaining evil thoughts and desires. Make up your mind, then, that although you may not be able to stop evil thoughts crowding into your mind, you will not play host to them.

FURTHER STUDY

Pss. 119:1-11;
139:23-24;
Prov. 23:7;
Matt. 22:37;
Phil. 4:8

1. When do evil thoughts become sin?
2. How can we use our thought life productively?

Prayer

Father, although I know what I should do, it is often hard—though not impossible—to do it. I give my will to You again today. Take it and strengthen it, so that it will do Your bidding. In Jesus' Name I pray. Amen.

The Law of Reversed Effort

"But we see Jesus ..." (v. 9)
For reading & meditation—Hebrews 2:5–18

Yesterday we said that we must make sure we do not entertain evil thoughts. How does it work in practice? *Build within your mind a strong picture of Jesus, and when an evil thought comes into your mind, turn and look at Him.*

Those who study the mind tell us that evil thoughts are not driven out by dwelling on them, even prayerfully. It is bad tactics to direct sustained attention to them, even in penitence, for then you experience what is called the law of reversed effort. This law states that "the more attention you focus on avoiding something, the more likely you are to hit it." A simplified form of this happens when a cyclist sees a pothole ahead of him, and concentrates on avoiding it—only to run into it.

The longer things are held in the focus of attention, the deeper they are burned into the memory and the more mental associations they make. The way to overcome them is to outwit them by swiftly directing the mind to some other absorbing theme. It may be difficult to dismiss them, but they can be elbowed out by a different and more powerful idea. What better idea than to hold a picture of Jesus in your mind, reinforced by daily Bible meditation and prayer, so that in the moment of overwhelming testing, the mind is turned toward Him. One who developed this technique into a fine art said: "Christ in the heart and mind is the safeguard. To think of Him is to summon His aid. Evil thoughts dissolve in the steady gaze of His searching eyes."

FURTHER STUDY

James 4:1–8;
1 Pet. 5:8–9;
Eph. 6:11

1. What are the three steps James gives for overcoming Satan's attacks?
2. How does this apply to wrong thoughts?

Prayer

O God, my Father, help me develop in my mind and imagination such a powerful picture of Jesus that it will become the saving focus of my being. Help me turn to Him immediately whenever evil thoughts crowd my mind. For Jesus' sake. Amen.

The Word to the Rescue

"I have hidden your word in my heart that I might not sin against you." (v. 11)
For reading & meditation—Psalm 119:1–16

*A*nother important principle to follow in developing a plan to overcome oppressive and evil thoughts is this: *Store up the Word of God in your mind so that it becomes readily available in times of need.*

This is one of the most powerful and successful principles of Christian living. Sometimes people write to me and say: "Your practical suggestions are very interesting and intriguing, but do they work?" I have one answer: try them and see! They most certainly work for me, and I am absolutely sure that if you apply them in the way I am suggesting, they will work for you, too.

A minister who was away from home on a preaching visit was provided by the church with accommodations in one of the city's large hotels. One night, while going up in the elevator, a woman accosted him and suggested that they should spend the night together. "This was more than an evil thought," said the minister, "it was an evil thought clad in the most beautiful and attractive woman I have seen for a long time. I was lonely and she was available." He went on, "But do you know what immediately flashed into my mind? Not my wife and four children—at least not at first. Not even my position and reputation. No, and not even the thought that I might be found out. The thing that immediately rose up within me was an instant visual replay of Romans 6:11-12, 'Count yourselves dead to sin but alive to God in Christ Jesus.'" The memorized verse came to the rescue—right on time.

FURTHER STUDY

Ps. 119:17–40;
Jer. 23:29;
Eph. 6:17;
Heb. 4:12

1. How can we hide God's Word in our hearts?
2. How can we use the weapon God has given us?

Prayer

Gracious Father, help me to have Your Word so deeply hidden in my heart that it triggers an automatic reaction within me whenever I am threatened by evil. For Jesus' sake. Amen.

The Last Thought at Night

"I will lie down and sleep in peace, for you alone, O LORD, make me dwell in safety." (v. 8)
For reading & meditation—Psalm 4:1–8

*L*et your last thought at night be a thought about your Lord and Savior Jesus Christ.

The last thoughts that lie on our minds at night are powerful and determinative, for the door into the subconscious is opening and they drop in to work good or evil. It's bad enough struggling with evil thoughts while you are awake; don't let them take control while you are asleep. Your conscious mind may be inactive while you are asleep, not so the subconscious. The last thoughts lying in your mind as you go to sleep usually become the "playthings" of the subconscious, and it works on these during the hours you are asleep.

If it is true that your mind is active while you are asleep—and there certainly seems to be plenty of evidence to support this theory, then make your mind work in a positive and not a negative way. Satan delights in dropping an evil thought into your mind during the moments immediately prior to sleep, because he knows that it will work destructively all through the night, influencing your attitudes and most likely preventing you from enjoying a peaceful night's sleep. Then when you wake, you find that not only do you have to face the problems of another day, but you also have to face them without having drawn fully on the resources available to you through sleep. Thus begins a recurring pattern which cannot help but drag you down. So learn to elbow out any evil thought that enters your mind just before sleep, and let your last thought be a thought of Christ.

FURTHER STUDY

*Gen. 1; 24:63;
Pss. 1:1–6; 63:6*

*1. When does God's day start?
2. Why is it important to meditate on God's Word at night?*

⟿ Prayer ⟿

Father, if it is true that my mind works when I am asleep, then help me to make it work for good and not for evil. Teach me the art of holding a thought about You on my mind immediately prior to going to sleep. I shall begin tonight, Lord. Amen.

Moving Together into Victory

". . . make every effort to add to your faith . . . self-control . . ." (vv. 5–6)

For reading & meditation—2 Peter 1:3–11

od is willing to do His part in helping you in this battle with evil thoughts—but you must be willing to do yours.

There is a teaching in some Christian circles that if we discover a need for change in our lives, we should passively wait upon God until He accomplishes it. It sounds so spiritual, but actually it borders on profound error. A Christian man once said to me: "I would like to be free from a certain sin I am involved in, but I find I am powerless to break away from it." I asked him what he expected to happen in order for him to find deliverance. He said, "I expect God to take away the desire for this sin and thus set me free." He was saying, in effect, "God is responsible for delivering me, and my task is to wait passively until He does so."

That view is unbiblical—and what is more, it doesn't work. Although deliverance comes from God, *we are the ones who carry it out.* Let that sink in! The principle is this—you supply the willingness, and He will supply the power. Do you really want to win this battle against evil thoughts? If so, you can. Show God you mean business by putting the principles you have learned this week into practice, and you will pave the way for His miraculous power to work in and through you. Once you have done this, life's oppressive and evil thoughts will never be able to break you again. Here, too, you can become strong at the broken places.

FURTHER STUDY

Dan. 1;
Rom. 6:13;
Eph. 6:13

1. How did Daniel and his friends deal with temptation?
2. What were the results of their resisting temptation?

Prayer

Gracious Father, thank You for reminding me that deliverance is a team effort. It involves the Holy Spirit and me. I supply the willingness: You supply the power. So let's team up, Father, and move together into victory. Amen.

Coming Back from Doubt

"Thomas said to him, 'My Lord and my God!'" (v. 28)

For reading & meditation—John 20:19-31

*W*e consider another important place where some Christians are broken—the area of deep and disturbing doubts. Some men and women have received Christ as their Savior and Lord, but yet are afflicted with paralyzing doubts. Some of these people go through deep agony of soul as they wrestle inwardly with doubt, ending up spiritually exhausted.

Someone like this told me that she was a scientist and had serious doubts about certain parts of the Scriptures. "I'm afraid that one day I will wake up," she said, "and discover that science has disproved large chunks of Scripture." I could sympathize with her problem, but really her doubts were quite unfounded. *Real* science will never disprove Scripture, only confirm it. Half-baked science may appear to discredit the truth of God's Word, but real science can only validate it.

I suppose the classic example of doubt is found in the disciple Thomas. We call him "doubting Thomas"—an unfair label if ever there was one. It's sad how we pick out a negative in a person and label him for that one thing. Thomas had his moment of doubt, but he came back from that place of weakness to become strong at the broken place. How strong? Let history judge. A well-authenticated tradition has it that Thomas went to India and founded a church there. Even today there are Christians in India who call themselves by his name—the St. Thomas Christians. They are some of the finest Christians I have ever met. Thomas had his doubts allayed in one glorious moment of illumination—and then he went places. So can you!

FURTHER STUDY

Ps. 37:1-40;
Isa. 12:2;
Luke 12:29

1. List seven steps of trusting given in verses 1-9 of this psalm.
2. What are five results of trusting?

 *Prayer*

O my Father, just as You took Thomas and changed him from a doubter to a man of amazing faith and achievement—do the same for me. For Your own dear Name's sake I ask it. Amen.

Truth – in the Inner Parts

"Surely you desire truth in the inner parts . . ." (v. 6)

For reading & meditation—Psalm 51:1–19

W hat do we do when we find ourselves assailed by honest doubts? Firstly, *we must learn to distinguish between honest doubts and defensive doubts.*

Many of the doubts that trouble Christians concerning aspects of the Christian faith are made half-consciously into a screen to hide some moral weakness or failure. I am not denying that some people experience acute intellectual problems in relation to their faith, and it would be arrogant to suggest, or even hint, that everyone troubled by doubts is consciously or unconsciously using them as a screen. But because experience has shown that some do, this issue has to be faced. Ask yourself now: am I using my doubts as a "defense mechanism" to cover up some weakness or personal defect? A "defense mechanism" is a device employed by our minds to prevent us from facing up to reality.

Adam used a defense mechanism when he blamed Eve for his sin. It is called *projection*—refusing to face up to personal responsibility, and projecting the blame onto someone else. Could it be that some of your doubts may be due to this? I am not suggesting, of course, that they *are*, but they *could be*. If you are willing to look at this issue objectively, or perhaps with the help of a wise and responsible Christian friend, then, I assure you, God will not withstand your plea. One hymnwriter said:

Jesus the hindrance show,
Which I have feared to see
Yet let me now consent to know
What keeps me out of Thee.

FURTHER STUDY

Gen. 3;
2 Cor. 2:11; 10:1-6;
11:3, 14

1. What was Satan's approach to Eve?
2. How could Eve have overcome his strategy?

Prayer

Gracious Father, You know how difficult it is for me to see myself as I really am. Help me to be honest with myself—even ruthlessly honest. For I want to be as honest as You. Help me in this hour of challenge. For Jesus' sake. Amen.

Dealing Positively with Doubt

"... they ... examined the Scriptures every day to see if what Paul said was true." (v. 11)

For reading & meditation—Acts 17:1–15

*W*hat do we do when we find ourselves assailed by honest doubt? Well, first we must recognize that *doubts can be valuable if they motivate us to search deep and long for the answers.* Perhaps it was this thought that led Samuel Coleridge to say, "Never be afraid of doubt . . . if you have the disposition to believe."

Unfortunately, there is very little sympathy given to those who doubt in most evangelical churches. Doubters are about as welcome in some congregations as a ham sandwich in a synagogue! It was because of the lack of concern shown in many churches toward those with honest doubts that two American missionaries, Francis and Edith Schaeffer, set up their ministry in a remote Swiss village. They established a center for those with doubts about their faith and called it *L'Abri*, which is French for "The Shelter." Hundreds made their way there over the years, and came back with their doubts resolved.

Have you ever heard of Frank Morrison? He was an agnostic who, many years ago, set out to demonstrate the validity of his doubts about the resurrection of Christ. The more he looked into the facts, however, the more convinced he became that Christ actually did rise from the dead. He finished up writing a book entitled *Who Moved the Stone?*, which is one of the greatest evidences for the resurrection I have ever read. There are clear answers to all the doubts you may have concerning the Christian faith. Search for these answers, and the more you struggle, the stronger will be your faith.

FURTHER STUDY

Matt. 14:22–36;
21:21–22;
Luke 12:29;
Heb. 11:6;
James 1:6–8

1. What did Jesus teach about doubt?
2. What causes doubt, and how should it be dealt with?

Prayer

Father, help me today to understand that all things can contribute to my faith, including my doubts. When I realize this, then I will go far. Thank You, Father. Amen.

John's Doubts about Jesus

"... 'Are you the one who was to come, or should we expect someone else?'" (v. 3)

For reading & meditation—Matthew 11:1–11

*A*lthough God would prefer us to believe, He is exceedingly loving and gracious toward those who struggle with honest doubts. Did you notice, when we were looking at Thomas the other day, that Jesus did not reject his doubting attitude, nor did He refuse his request for physical evidence that He was truly the Christ? Instead, Jesus said to him, "Put your finger here; see my hands. Reach out your hand and put it into my side. Stop doubting and believe" (John 20:27).

The passage before us today tells of another occasion when one of Jesus' followers became oppressed by doubt. John was in prison, and probably suffering great discomfort and disillusionment. John's messengers came to Jesus, wanting to know whether He really was the Messiah, or whether they should be looking for somebody else. John, you remember, had baptized Jesus and had introduced Him to the world with these words: "Look, the Lamb of God, who takes away the sin of the world!" (John 1:29).

Does it not seem strange that John, who witnessed the descent of the Holy Spirit upon Jesus at His baptism, should now have doubts about who He was and the validity of His mission? How did Jesus respond to this situation? With tenderness and sensitivity, He said, "Go back and report to John what you hear and see: The blind receive sight, the lame walk, those who have leprosy are cured, the deaf hear ..." (Matt. 11:4–5). Our Lord could have rebuked the doubting disciple with strong words of reproof, but He didn't. Although He cares about problems, He cares more about people.

FURTHER STUDY

Rom. 8:18–39;
John 8:1–11; 3:16–17;
Rev. 12:10

1. Who condemns us?
2. How did Jesus respond to the woman caught in adultery?

╾══ *Prayer* ══╼

Thank You, Father, for reminding me that You see me, not as a problem but as a person. I know
You are concerned about my doubts, but You are more concerned
about me. I am deeply grateful. Amen.

Decide to Believe

"... when he asks, he must believe and not doubt ..." (v. 6)

For reading & meditation—James 1:2–12

*A*nother important principle to employ when dealing with honest doubts is this: *Make a conscious decision to doubt your doubts and believe your beliefs.* Living an effective Christian life, as we have been seeing, depends on how willing we are to exercise our wills in favor of God and His Word. To do this requires faith in the fact that God has revealed Himself in His Son and through the Scriptures.

As a teenager, I had many doubts about the Scriptures but, one night, I made a conscious decision to accept them as the eternal and inerrant Word of God. Notice, I said "a *conscious* decision." I *decided* by an action of my will to doubt my doubts and believe my beliefs. I then found an astonishing thing. Both doubt and faith are like muscles—the more you flex them, the stronger they become. I had been using the muscles of doubt to a great degree, but unfortunately, I had failed to exercise the muscles of faith. When I made up my mind to accept the truth of God's Word by faith, muscles I never thought I had began to function.

Now, many years later, those muscles are developed to such a degree that I find, where God is concerned, it is easier to believe Him than to doubt Him. I trace the beginnings of my own spiritual development to that day long ago, when I decided to take what one theologian called "the leap of faith." Perhaps today might become a similar day of decision for you. Decide to doubt your doubts and believe your beliefs. Now!

FURTHER STUDY

Heb. 11;
Matt. 15:21–28; 17:20;
Rom. 10:17; 12:3

1. What different aspects of faith are shown in Hebrews 11?
2. How did the Canaanite woman overcome the obstacles that confronted her?

⟶ Prayer ⟵

O God, perhaps this is the secret: I have used the muscles of doubt more than the muscles of faith. From today, things will be different. I decide to take You and Your Word on trust—now let it work. Amen.

Do Your Emotions Take Over?

"... the steadfast love of the LORD is from everlasting to everlasting upon those who fear him ..." (v. 17, RSV)

For reading & meditation—Psalm 103:1–22

*W*e continue exploring ways in which we can become strong at the broken places caused by deep and disturbing doubts. Another point we should keep in mind in relation to this question of doubt is that *some doubts are rooted more in the emotions than in the intellect.*

Our emotions are an important part of our being, and they can do much to make our lives either miserable or meaningful. When emotions take over, they cause our thinking to waver, so that we can come to faulty conclusions about life. Ask yourself this question now: am I a person who is ruled more by my emotions than by my intellect? If you are, then it is likely that your doubts are rooted more in your feelings than in your mind.

Many years ago, a Christian university student came to me complaining that he had serious doubts about the inspiration and reliability of Scripture. As I counseled him, I heard the Spirit say, "This is not an intellectual doubt, but an emotional one." I explored with him the area of his feelings, and he confessed to me that he could never remember a time in his life when he ever *felt* that he was loved. When the emotional problem was resolved, his doubts vanished of their own accord. His problem was not intellectual, but emotional. Reason and emotion are both important in life, but decisions, especially decisions about the Christian life, must be built not on what we *feel* to be true but on what we *know* to be true.

FURTHER STUDY

Job 1–3

1. What were some of the feelings Job expressed?
2. Did he allow them to give rise to doubt?

Prayer

My Father and my God, help me trace my problem to its roots and meet me at the point of my deepest need. This I ask in Jesus' Name. Amen.

Day 288

Thomas, the Doer

"... you will receive power when the Holy Spirit comes on you; and you will be my witnesses ...
to the ends of the earth." (v. 8)

For reading & meditation—Acts 1:6–14

Recognize that if you could not doubt, you could not believe. So don't be threatened or intimidated by your doubts. Robert Browning put it like this: "You call for faith: I show you doubt, to prove that faith exists. The more of doubt, the stronger faith, I say, if faith o'ercomes doubt." Those who doubt most, and yet strive to overcome their doubts, turn out to be some of Christ's strongest disciples.

One commentator points out that Thomas, being a twin, must have developed an early independence of judgment that made it possible for him to break with his brother and become a follower of Jesus. This is an assumption, of course, but I think it is a valid one. It was that independence, perhaps, that led him to reject the testimony of the other disciples when they said, "We have seen the Lord."

Jesus did not reject Thomas because of his doubts, but said to him: "Reach out your hand and put it into my side. Stop doubting and believe" (John 20:27). Suddenly his doubts vanished, and he was transformed in that moment into one of Christ's most committed disciples. Up until then, no one had called Jesus "God." They had called Him, "Messiah," "Son of God," "Son of the Living God"—but not "God." Here Thomas the doubter leaped beyond the others, and became the strongest believer of them all. And this faith of Thomas's did not stop at faith—it resulted in mighty achievement. The doubter became a doer. And how!

FURTHER STUDY

Matt. 8:1–13;
Rom. 10:17; 14:23;
Heb. 11:1

1. Where does faith come from?
2. What did Jesus say to the centurion?

Prayer

O God, what a prospect—my faith, at first so tentative, can, through Your illumination and my response, become a driving force. It can not only save me, but send me. May there be no limits! Amen.

304

Danger in the Home

"Take my yoke upon you and learn from me . . . and you will find rest . . ." (v. 29)
For reading & meditation—Matthew 11:25-30

nother area of life where many are broken is through *troubles in the home.* "Life," as Hemingway put it, "breaks us all," but perhaps nothing is quite as painful as being broken by difficulties in one's home. Have you been broken by problems within your family circle? Then take heart—out of the brokenness God can bring strength.

What kind of troubles bring us to a breaking point in the home? These are just some of them: incompatibility, disagreements, separation, threats or the action of divorce, insensitivity, bickering, quarrels, misunderstandings and violence, not to mention such things as alcoholism, drug abuse, mental and emotional breakdowns, child and adolescent rebellion, or gross neglect of the aged members of the family. Even in some Christian homes, things can get pretty desperate. A study completed at the University of Rhode Island described the American home as the most dangerous place to be—apart from a war or a riot. It's also getting like this in Britain.

All of us have experienced some hurt through broken relationships in the home. Many, out of loyalty to their families, face the world with a smile, but inwardly they are bleeding. I know a woman who was heartbroken by her husband's adultery and the rebellion of her children, but today she has recovered and is busy staunching the bleeding wounds in other people's hearts. So it can be done. To those of you broken by troubles in the home, our Lord says, "Learn from Me: I will make you so strong at the broken places of your life that you shall minister to others out of that hidden strength."

FURTHER STUDY

Pss. 46:1-11; 147:3;
Luke 4:18;
Matt. 12:20

1. What did God say to the psalmist in the midst of upheaval?
2. What does God promise the brokenhearted?

Prayer

O God, You know how easy it is to blunder in this delicate and difficult business of relationships. I need someone to lead me in the right way. You lead me, Father—I will follow. Amen.

Our Three Primary Needs

"... in Him you have been made complete ..." (v. 10, NASB)
For reading & meditation—Colossians 2:1–10

The first principle we must learn if we are to recover from the brokenness caused by troubles in the home is: *Depend on God, and not on anyone else, to meet the deepest needs of your personality.* Allow this truth to take hold of your innermost being and you will become a transformed person.

The most basic needs of our personality are these: (1) the need to be loved unconditionally (security); (2) the need to be valued (self-worth), and (3) the need to make a meaningful contribution to God's world (significance). Human beings can only function effectively to the degree that these needs are met. If they are unsatisfied, our ability to function as a person is greatly hindered; if they are adequately met, then, other things being equal, we have the potential of functioning effectively.

Notice, however, this important point—our needs for security, significance, and self-worth can be *fully* met only in a close and ongoing relationship with the Lord Jesus Christ. If we do not let Christ meet those needs, then because they have to be met in order for us to function effectively, we will attempt to get them met in and through others. Although many do not realize it, this is what draws many people toward marriage, because they see the possibility of having their needs met through their partner. But no human being, however loving, kind, and considerate they may be, can fully meet these needs. I say again: they can be met fully only in a close and ongoing relationship with the Lord Jesus Christ.

FURTHER STUDY

Eph. 1; 2

1. Where is Christ?
2. Where are we?

Prayer

Father, I sense that I am on the verge of something big and challenging. Help me to grasp this, for I sense that if I do, I shall become a transformed person. In Jesus' Name I ask it. Amen.

Are You a Manipulator?

"My command is this: Love each other as I have loved you." (v. 12)

For reading & meditation—John 15:9–17

Yesterday we touched on what is perhaps the biggest single problem causing marital unhappiness—trying to get one's partner to meet needs that can only be fully met through a relationship with Jesus Christ.

What happens if we do not allow God to meet our basic needs? We will try to get those needs met in some other way. Some people try to find satisfaction in achievement. This, however, fails to bring lasting satisfaction, and whenever their inner discomfort reaches the threshold of awareness, they anesthetize it with more activities, achievement, and work.

Another way is to attempt to get these needs met in marriage. But if we enter marriage as a way of getting our needs met, then we consciously or unconsciously become involved in manipulating our partner to meet our needs. Instead of following the Christian vision of marriage, which is to minister to our partners from a position of security in Christ's love, we begin to manipulate them to meet our needs. Thousands of marriages, perhaps millions, are caught up in this treadmill—each trying to get their partner to meet the needs that only God can fully meet. The best way to get our needs met is to depend on God to meet them. When we lock into Him and focus on how much He loves and values us, and on His purpose for our lives, then and only then are we free to minister in the way He prescribes in His Word. Without that inner security, we become exposed and vulnerable to the likes or dislikes of our partner. We become puppets—not people.

FURTHER STUDY

1 Cor. 13;
Rom. 5:8; 8:35;
1 John 3:16

1. List fifteen qualities of love.
2. Is their emphasis on giving or getting?

Prayer

O my Lord and Master, take me in Your arms today and make me so conscious of Your love that I will no longer manipulate others to love me, but will minister to them with the love I already have. For Jesus' sake I ask it. Amen.

Making God More Meaningful

"No one has ever seen God; but if we love one another, God lives in us and his love is made complete in us." (v. 12)

For reading & meditation—1 John 4:7-21

*W*e have been seeing over the past two days that the first principle to follow in healing the brokenness that comes through troubles in the home is to depend on the Lord to meet our basic needs. You might ask yourself: if the Lord can meet my needs for security, self-worth, and significance, why do I need a human partner at all?

The answer to that question flows out of the next principle: *In the relationship with your partner or your children, focus more on what you can give than what you can get.* This can be exceedingly difficult, of course, if you are not allowing God to meet your needs, but once you are secure in Him, *everything He asks you to do becomes possible.* Assuming our needs for security, significance, and self-worth are being met in God, we are then in a position to fulfil God's true purpose for marriage, which is this: God, who is an invisible, intangible, eternal Being, has designed marriage to be a visible, tangible demonstration of the reality of His love as we minister love and consideration to one another.

Just think of it—in marriage we have the marvelous privilege of demonstrating God's love to our partners in a way that they can feel, touch, and understand. Our love will not add to the *fact* of their security in Christ, but it will add to the degree to which they *feel* it. No wonder Martin Luther said that marriage was the greatest way God had of teaching us the truths about Himself. And the second greatest way? You've got it! The church!

FURTHER STUDY

Matt. 10: 1–8;
Luke 6:38;
Prov. 11:25;
Acts 20:35;
2 Cor. 9:6

1. What did Jesus teach His disciples?
2. How can you demonstrate this today?

Prayer

Father, to realize that I have the privilege of bringing the reality of Your love to others, and thus making You more real to them, is so incredible that it almost blows my mind! But I know it is true. Make me worthy of this privilege. For Jesus' sake. Amen.

Accepting Your Partner

"... whoever accepts anyone I send accepts me ..." (v. 20)

For reading & meditation—John 13:12–20

The third principle for healing the brokenness that arises from troubles in the home only works if the previous two are clearly established: *Accept your partner or your children, and don't just endure them.* Too difficult? Look again at the verse at the top of this page, where we are instructed to accept each other just as God accepts us. And remember that when we supply the willingness, God supplies the power.

There is quite a difference, of course, between accepting your partner and enjoying him or her; the former is a scriptural requirement, the latter is something that is dependent on their response and behavior. Marriage sometimes involves living with an irritating, infuriating, and obnoxious person: how can we accept such a person, let alone enjoy him or her? Acceptance does not mean that we have to enjoy everything our partner does: it means rather that we see our partner as someone to whom God wants us to minister, and we pursue that ministry whether we feel like it or not.

Many Christians stumble over this. A lady who recently came through to victory on this point said to me, "But how can I accept my husband, who is nothing more than a loathsome, alcoholic pig?" I said, "It's impossible as long as you are depending on your husband to meet your need for security. Depend on God to meet that need, and then see what happens." She did so, and found that when she no longer depended on her husband to meet her security needs. she saw him in a completely new light. Then she had no difficulty in accepting him.

FURTHER STUDY

Eph. 5:21–33; 1:6; Rom. 15:7

1. How should the husband show his acceptance of his wife?
2. How should the wife show her acceptance of her husband?

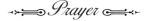

Prayer

O God, this sounds too good to be true. Can life's difficulties be resolved so easily? Give me the courage not to dismiss anything until I've tried it, nor resist any principle that is in harmony with Your Word. Amen.

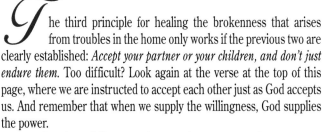

A Check-Up for Husbands

"Husbands, love your wives, just as Christ loved the church . . ." (v. 25)
For reading & meditation—Ephesians 5:22-33

*O*ver the next two days I want to establish two final principles for dealing with troubles in the home: one for the husbands and one for the wives. Today we begin with the men: *Be prepared to give yourself a spiritual check-up on how you are doing as a husband.* Cross out whichever answer does *not* apply.

1. Do you still "court" your wife with an *unexpected* gift of flowers or chocolates? (Anniversaries and birthdays not to be included) (YES/NO)

2. Are you careful never to criticize her in front of others? (YES/NO)

3. Do you make an effort to understand her varying feminine moods and help her through them? (YES/NO)

4. Do you depend on your wife to meet your basic personal needs? (YES/NO)

5. Do you pray together? (YES/NO)

6. Do you share at least half your recreation time with your wife and family? (YES/NO)

7. Are you alert for opportunities to praise and compliment her? (YES/NO)

8. Do you go to church together? (YES/NO)

9. Is she first in your life—after the Lord? (YES/NO)

10. Have you forgiven her for any hurts or problems she may have caused you? (YES/NO)

A score of 7 to 10 yes responses—excellent! Below 7 yes answers—you've got some work ahead of you.

FURTHER STUDY

Eccl. 9:1-9;
Gen. 2:23-24;
Col. 3:18-21;
1 Pet. 3:7

1. What does the word cleave (KJV) mean?
2. Why are our prayers often hindered?

 *Prayer*

Father, You who have set us in families, help me to be the person You intend me to be, both in my marriage and in my home. This I ask in Jesus' Name. Amen.

A Check-Up for Wives

"Wives, in the same way be submissive to your husbands . . ." (v. 1)
For reading & meditation—1 Peter 3:1–12

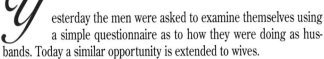

Yesterday the men were asked to examine themselves using a simple questionnaire as to how they were doing as husbands. Today a similar opportunity is extended to wives.

1. Are you depending on the Lord to meet your basic needs for security, significance, and self-worth? (YES/NO)

2. Can you meet financial disasters bravely without condemning your husband for his mistakes, or comparing him unfavorably with others? (YES/NO)

3. Do you dress with an eye for your husband's likes and dislikes in color and style? (YES/NO)

4. Do you keep up your own personal prayer life so that you may meet everything that arises with poise? (YES/NO)

5. Do you avoid daydreaming or fantasizing about other men you might have married? (YES/NO)

6. Are you sensitive to your husband's moods and feelings and know when, and when not, to bring up delicate issues? (YES/NO)

7. Do you respect your husband? (YES/NO)

8. Are you careful never to criticize your husband in front of others? (YES/NO)

9. Do you keep track of the day's news and what is happening in the world so that you can discuss these with your husband? (YES/NO)

10. Are you a "submissive" wife? (YES/NO)

A score of 7 to 10 yes responses—excellent. Below 7 yes answers—it's decision time.

FURTHER STUDY

*Prov. 31:10–31;
1 Tim. 3:11;
Esther 1:20*

1. What are the characteristics of a virtuous woman?
2. What do her children call her?

Prayer

My heavenly Father, I realize the tender relationships of home can be a shrine, or they can be a snarl. Keep my inner shrine from all wrong attitudes and from all worry. Let me approach today's challenge in the knowledge that "I can do all things through Christ who strengthens me" (Phil. 4:13, NKJV). Amen.

When Broken by Stress

"You have let me sink down deep in desperate problems. But you will bring me back to life again, up from the depths of the earth!" (v. 20, TLB)

For reading & meditation—Psalm 71:1–24

*A*nother major cause for brokenness in human life is stress. Often I get letters from people saying something like this: "I feel I am on the verge of a breakdown. No one thing seems to be responsible for it, but I just can't cope. My doctor says I am suffering from stress. Can the Bible meet this need?" I am bold to say that it can. God can take a person overcome by stress and build into their lives insights which will enable them to live above and beyond its paralyzing grip.

What exactly is "stress"? One doctor defines it as "wear and tear on the personality which, if uncorrected, can result in a physical or mental breakdown." Donald Norfolk, a British osteopath who has made a special study of stress, claims that it comes from two main causes: too little change, or too much change. To function at peak efficiency, we all need a certain amount of change. However, when changes come too fast for us to cope with, the personality is put under tremendous stress.

Dr. Thomas H. Holmes measures stress in terms of "units of change." For example, the death of a loved one measures 100 units, divorce 73 units, pregnancy 40 units, moving or altering a home 25 units, and Christmas 12 units. His conclusion is that no one can handle more than 300 units of stress in a twelve-month period without suffering physically or emotionally during the next two years. Holmes, of course, was speaking from a strictly human point of view—with God "all things are possible."

FURTHER STUDY

Luke 10:38–42;
Phil. 4:6;
Ps. 127:2;
Matt. 6:25

1. What was Jesus' response to Martha?
2. How did it differ from His response to Mary?

Prayer

Father, You have taught me much on how to turn my weaknesses into strengths. Teach me now how to handle stress. I cannot change my surroundings—but I can change my attitude. Help me to do this. For Jesus' sake. Amen.

Find the Cause – Find the Cure

"Search me, O God, and know my heart; test me and know my anxious thoughts." (v. 23)

For reading & meditation—Psalm 139:1–24

*W*ere you surprised to discover yesterday that Christmas earned 12 points on Dr. Thomas Holmes's stress scale? In the week leading up to Christmas, there are more suicides and breakdowns than in any other week of the year because the festivity of that season stands out in such marked contrast to the melancholy feelings of the depressed.

What is the first step toward recovery from, or prevention of, stress? *Identify what causes you to feel stress.* One person may revel in frequent change, while another may be thrown into a state of disquiet if a piece of furniture is moved around in a room. Dr. Hans Selye, a world-famous expert on stress, says: "The mere fact of knowing what hurts has a curative value." Get alone in the presence of God with a pen and a sheet of paper, and ask the Lord to help you identify the causes of your stress.

You can help prime the pump of questioning by asking yourself the following: What one thing above all others makes me jumpy and irritable, or gives me the feeling I can't cope? (That could be stress factor No. 1.) How do I react to change? Easily, or with difficulty? How much competition can I take? Keep on questioning yourself until you pin down the things that produce stress in your system. It is only when you establish the origins of stress in your life that you can set about the task of building up biblical principles that will not only modify its impact, but also enable you to turn your weaknesses into strengths.

FURTHER STUDY

Mark 4:35–41;
1 Pet. 5:7;
Matt. 13:22;
Luke 12:29

1. Why were the disciples full of stress when Jesus was not?
2. How did Jesus respond?

Prayer

Father, teach me how to respond to life so that, instead of a breakdown, I may experience a breakthrough—a breakthrough into a new way of living. For Jesus' sake. Amen.

What a Waste!

"Do not be anxious about anything, but in everything, by prayer and petition,
with thanksgiving, present your requests to God." (v. 6)

For reading & meditation—Philippians 4:1–13

We continue meditating on the principles we can use when our lives are threatened by stress: *Recognize the symptoms of stress.* No alarm bells ring in our homes or offices when we are suffering undue stress, but there are adequate warning signs. People under stress generally become irritable and overreact to relatively trivial frustrations. They show a change in their sleep patterns, and become increasingly tired and restless. They derive less pleasure from life, experience no joy while praying or reading the Bible, laugh less, and become plagued with feelings of inadequacy and self-doubt. They sometimes develop psychosomatic complaints such as tension headaches, indigestion and other things.

Some people have what is known as "target organs"—physical organs that are the first to suffer when they are under stress. Harold Wilson confessed that whenever he had to fire a colleague, he suffered acute stomach pains. Henry Ford suffered cramps in his stomach whenever he had to make an important business decision. Trotsky, when under pressure, used to develop bouts of high temperature, and frequently had to spend time in the Crimea recuperating. One businessman I know always has a glass of milk on his desk from which he takes frequent sips in order to calm his nagging peptic ulcer.

Are you able to recognize your own particular patterns of stress? You owe it to God and yourself to find out. The waste that goes on in Christian circles through believers channeling their energies into coping with stress, rather than into extending the kingdom of God, is appalling.

**FURTHER
STUDY**

*Luke 12:15–34;
2 Tim. 1:12;
2 Cor. 11:22–33; 12:7–10*

*1. What was the key to
Paul's trust under stress?
2. List six reasons Jesus
gave for not worrying
about tomorrow.*

 *Prayer*

O God, sharpen my ability to recognize the things I do that contribute to stress in my life, so that all
my energies can be channeled into spiritual activity, not self-activity. For Jesus' sake. Amen.

Stop and Smell the Roses

"... Consider the lilies of the field, how they grow ..." (v. 28, RSV)

For reading & meditation—Matthew 6:25-34

*A*nother principle that helps us cope with stress is this: *Seek to overcome any rigidity in your personality.* You can best understand *rigidity* by comparing it with its opposite—flexibility. A more formal definition of *rigidity* is this: "The inability or refusal to change one's actions or attitudes even though objective conditions indicate that a change is desirable."

The rigid person clings to certain ways of thinking and acting, even when they are injurious to the personality and burn up their emotional energy. Someone described it as similar to driving a car with the brakes on. Take the housewife who worries herself into a migraine attack because she cannot maintain a scrupulously tidy home while her grandchildren are visiting. Or the businessman who triggers off another gastric ulcer because he falls behind with his schedule when his secretary is away sick.

Inflexible goals can be crippling fetters. It's no good saying, "But there are things that have to be done, and if I don't do them, they just won't get done." Perhaps you need to rearrange your priorities, adjust your lifestyle and learn to say "no." As someone put it, "We must not drive so relentlessly forward that we cannot stop and smell the roses by the wayside." You may be caught up in the midst of one of the busiest weeks of your year, but pause for a moment and ask yourself: am I driving, or am I being driven? Am I in control of my personality, or is it in control of me? Today, decide to take a step away from rigidity by pausing to "smell a rose."

FURTHER STUDY

Gen. 1; 2:1-3;
Heb. 4:1-11;
Ps. 37:7;
Matt. 11:29

1. What was man's first day?
2. How can we enter into God's rest?

Prayer

O God, I am now at grips with the raw material of living; out of it must come a person—Your person. Help me to be rigid only in relation to You, and flexible about everything else. For Jesus' sake. Amen.

Don't Push the River!

"There is a time for everything, and a season for every activity under heaven . . ." (v. 1)

For reading & meditation—Ecclesiastes 3:1–4

*R*efuse to be obsessed with time. It is right to be concerned about time, but it is not right to be obsessed with it. Do you live life by the clock? Then you are a candidate for stress.

When filmmakers want to create tension, they show a clock relentlessly ticking away. Such tactics are pointless when applied to the ordinary issues of everyday life. Nervous glances at a watch will generate tension when you are caught in traffic, but they will not make the traffic move any faster. Fretting will do nothing to alter the situation. So learn to relax, and do not become intimidated by time.

Some people live life as if they are on a racing track, and set themselves rigid lap times for the things they want to accomplish during the day. Two motorists were given the task of driving for 1,700 miles. One was asked to drive as fast as he could without breaking any speed limits; the other was told to drive at any comfortable pace. At the end of their journeys, it was found that the faster driver had consumed ten gallons more gas and doubled the wear on his tires; by driving at a speed which, in the end, proved to be only two miles per hour faster than the other driver! A man said to me in a counseling session when I advised him to slow down: "The trouble is that I'm in a hurry—but God isn't!" Learn the wisdom of letting things develop at their own pace, and follow the maxim that says: "Don't push the river—let it flow."

FURTHER STUDY

Eph. 5:1–21;
Col. 4:5;
James 4:14

1. How can we redeem the time?
2. To what does James relate this?

Prayer

O Father, save me from being obsessed by time. Help me to see that I have all the time in the world to do what You want me to do. And when I am overconcerned, I am overwrought! Help me, dear Father. Amen.

Keeping Fit for Jesus!

"... physical training is of some value, but godliness has value for all things ..." (v. 8)
For reading & meditation—1 Timothy 4:1-12

*W*e spend one last day meditating on the ways by which we can overcome stress in our lives. This final principle is: *engage in as much physical exercise as is necessary.*

One laboratory experiment took ten underexercised rats, and subjected them repeatedly to a variety of stresses: shock, pain, shrill noises, and flashing lights. After a month, every one of them had died through the incessant strain. Another group of rats was given a good deal of exercise until they were in peak physical condition. They were then subjected to the same battery of stresses and strains. After a month, not one had died.

More and more Christians are waking up to the fact that God has given us bodies that are designed to move, and the more they are exercised, the more effectively they function. Studies on how exercise helps to reduce stress are quite conclusive. Exercise gets rid of harmful chemicals in our bodies, provides a form of abreaction (letting off steam), builds up stamina, counteracts the biochemical effects of stress, and reduces the risk of psychological illness. The Bible rarely mentions the need for physical exercise, because people living at that time usually walked everywhere and therefore needed little admonition on the subject. In our world of advanced technology, however, common sense tells us that our bodies need to be exercised, and we should not neglect it. It may not be a spectacular idea, but often God comes to us along some very dusty and lowly roads. We must not despise His coming just because He comes to us along a lowly road.

FURTHER STUDY

1 Kings 19;
1 Cor. 3:16–17; 6:19

1. What caused stress in
   Elijah's life?
2. How did God
   help him?

Prayer

Lord, help me not to despise this call of Yours to exercise my body. Forgive me that I am such a poor tenant of Your property. From today I determine to do better. For Your own Name's sake. Amen.

Transformed!

"Blessed is he whose transgressions are forgiven, whose sins are covered." (v. 1)

For reading & meditation—Psalm 32:1-11

We come now to speak of all those who have been broken, or are on the verge of being broken, by *the memory of some deeply grievous sin.*

I am not thinking so much of those who have committed sin and have not come to Christ for forgiveness, but of those who, though they have been forgiven by God, are unable to forgive themselves. A man came to me recently at the end of a meeting at which I had spoken, and told me the details of a particularly horrendous sin in which he had been involved. He said, "I know God has forgiven me, but the memory of what I have done is constantly with me. It is quietly driving me insane."

This brought to mind a story I heard many years ago of a father who taught his son to drive a nail into a board every time he did something wrong, and then to pull out the nail after he had confessed the wrong and had been forgiven. Every time this happened, the boy would say triumphantly, "Hurray! The nails are gone!" "Yes," his father would say, "but always remember that the marks made by the nails are still in the wood." The message I want you to get hold of and build into your life is this: the Carpenter of Nazareth can not only pull out the nails, but can also varnish and beautify the wood so that the marks become, not a contradiction, but a contribution.

FURTHER STUDY

1 John 1;
Ps. 103:3;
Acts 5:31;
Eph. 1:7

1. How can we know full forgiveness?
2. Why not ask for it today?

⇥ *Prayer* ⇤

Lord Jesus Christ, You who once were known as a carpenter's son, take the stains and blemishes of my past and work through them so that they contribute, rather than contradict. For Your own dear Name's sake. Amen.

Grace – Greater Than All Our Sin!

". . . where sin abounded, grace did much more abound . . ." (v. 20, KJV)

For reading & meditation—Romans 5:12–21

*W*e are meditating on how to recover from the brokenness caused by the memory of some deeply grievous sin. By that we mean a sin which God has forgiven but which, for some reason, still burns in our memories.

The first principle is this: *Realize that God can do more with sin than just forgive it.* I heard an elderly minister make that statement many years ago, when I was a young Christian, and at first I resisted it. I said to myself: "How can God *use* sin? Surely it is His one intolerance?" Then, after pondering for a while, I saw what he meant. God uses our sin to motivate our will toward greater spiritual achievement, to quicken our compassion toward sinners and to show God's tender heart for the fallen.

We must be careful, of course, that we do not fall into the error which Paul refers to in Romans 6:1–2: "Shall we continue in sin, that grace may abound? God forbid" (KJV). If we sin in order that God may use it, then our motives are all wrong and we fall foul of the eternal purposes. If, however, we commit sin, but then take it to God in confession—*really* take it to Him—then He will not only forgive it, but make something of it. Is this too difficult for you to conceive? Then I point you to the cross. The cross was the foulest deed mankind ever committed, yet God used it to become the fulcrum of His redemption. It was our lowest point—but it was God's zenith. Hallelujah.

FURTHER STUDY

Heb. 10:1–22;
Isa. 43:25; 44:22; 55:7

1. What will God not remember any more?
2. What is the "full assurance" we can have?

Prayer

O Father, I am so relieved to know that You take even my sins and make them contribute to Your purposes. Grace turns all my bad into good, all my good into better and all my better into the best. Hallelujah!

319

Why Do I Do These Things?

"If we confess our sins, he is faithful and just and will forgive us our sins and purify us from all unrighteousness." (v. 9)

For reading & meditation—1 John 1:1–10

*W*e continue meditating on the principles that enable us to recover from the brokenness caused by the memory of some grievous sin. A second principle is this: *Understand the major reason why you tend to brood on the past.* People who brood on the past, and keep the memory of their sin alive, do so for several reasons.

Let's take them one by one: (1) *They are not sure that God has forgiven them.* If you have this kind of doubt, it is really a *denial.* It is taking a verse, like the one before us today, and flinging it back into God's face, saying "I don't believe it." If you don't accept God's forgiveness, you will try to make your own atonement in feelings of guilt. Once you confess your sin, then, as far as God is concerned, that's the end of it. Believe that—and act upon it. It's the gospel truth!

(2) *They are in the grip of spiritual pride.* You should be asking yourself, at some deep level of your mental and emotional life: How could *I* have ever done a thing like that? What this really amounts to is that you have too high an opinion of yourself. And that's about as bad as too low an opinion of yourself. (3) *They have not forgiven themselves.* It might help to stand in front of a mirror with your Bible open at the verse at the top of this page, reassure yourself that God has forgiven you, and say to yourself, by name: "_____, God has forgiven you—now I forgive you too!"

FURTHER STUDY

Ps. 51:1–19;
Eph. 4:32;
Col. 3:13;
Mark 12:33

1. Why can we forgive ourselves?
2. Forgive yourself today.

Prayer

Gracious Father, although I understand many things, I fail so often to understand myself. Teach me more of what goes on deep inside me, so that, being more self-aware, I may become more God-aware. For Your own dear Name's sake. Amen.

Remembering to Forget

"... forgetting what lies behind and straining forward to what lies ahead, I press on toward the goal ..." (vv. 13-14, RSV)

For reading & meditation—Philippians 3:1-14

O ne more principle in relation to recovering from the brokenness caused by the memory of some dark sin: *Forget it by
reversing the process of remembering.* Puzzled? Let me explain. Memory
works like this: one revives an image of some past event, holds it in the
mind for a certain length of time, and then this process is repeated until
it is locked into the memory for good. Now begin to reverse that
process. The matter has been forgiven by God, so don't let your mind
focus on it. When it rises to the surface by itself, as it will, turn the mind
away from it immediately.

Have in your mind a few interesting themes "on call." Think of
another and more profitable theme. I know a Christian man, involved
in one of the deepest sins imaginable, who has learned to blot out
unwanted memories the moment they rise to the surface by focusing
his thoughts on the cross. It does not matter what the substitute image
is so long as it is wholesome and can thrust the unwanted memory
from your attention.

Another thing you can do when the memory of your sin returns—
even if it is only for a moment—is to turn your mind to prayer. Don't
pray about the sin itself—that will keep it in the memory—but pray that
God will build into you love, forgiveness, peace, and poise. Images that
are consciously rejected will rise less and less in your mind. When they
do occur, they will occur only as *fact*; the emotions will no longer reg-
ister a sense of burning shame.

FURTHER STUDY

2 Sam. 12:1-14;
Mark 2:5;
Col. 2:13;
Heb. 8:12

1. What was Nathan's message to David?
2. What does God do besides forgive?

 *Prayer*

O my Father, how can I cease thanking You for the answers You give—they are so right. Everything within
me says so. Now help me to put the things I am learning into practice. Amen.

321

The End of the Beginning

"... thanks be to God, who always leads us in triumphal procession in Christ ..." (2:14)

For reading & meditation—2 Corinthians 2:12–3:11

Although this is the end of the theme of "Strong at the broken places," I pray that, for many of you, it will be the beginning of a new approach to handling your weaknesses.

How thankful I am that, in the early years of my Christian life, God impressed into my spirit the truth that my weaknesses could be turned into strengths. With just a few years of Christian experience behind me, I stumbled and fell. The temptation was to wallow in self-pity. But by God's grace, I got up, brushed myself off, and said, "Devil, you won that round, but I'll work on that problem until it is no longer a weakness, but a strength." I did work on it, and today I can testify that the weakness which caused me to stumble has indeed become a strength. I say that humbly, recognizing that the strength I have is not my own, but His.

Today is a new day. How will you face it? Are you ready to face your weaknesses in the assurance that, no matter how life breaks you, you can draw out from each experience a lesson that will live on inside you and help you to find victory in a future situation? Just as a broken bone, when it is healed, becomes stronger at that place than it was before it was broken, so you can become stronger by your very weaknesses. Thus when you stumble, you stumble forward; when you fall, you fall on your knees and get up a stronger person. When we are Christians, everything is "grist to our mill."

FURTHER STUDY

Eph. 3;
2 Cor. 12:9;
Isa. 40:31; 41:10

1. What was Paul's testimony?
2. What is your testimony?

Prayer

O Father, I sense today that this is not the end, but the end of the beginning. From now on, I shall face the future knowing that, however life breaks me, in You I can become strong at the broken places. All honor and glory to Your peerless and precious Name. Amen.

Section Six
Going Deeper with God

Going Deeper with God

*P*salm 46:10 says, "Be still and know that I am God." Being still is not something that comes naturally to most of us. Larry Dyke is happiest when he's out hiking in the Rockies or the Tetons looking for new scenes to paint. When he's not doing that, chances are he's involved in a meeting, gallery showing, or book signing. And somewhere in the midst of everything else he has to have time to paint.

Be still? It isn't easy, but as Selwyn Hughes notes, it's one of the most effective ways we have of getting closer to God. We live in a people-centered world; Selwyn reminds us that we have to build a quiet world for ourselves that is God-centered in order to experience full, rich unity with Him. God deserves the best of our time, not a harried minute or two stolen from some other commitment on the calendar. The Bible verses and commentaries in these lessons will help even the busiest person focus on drawing nearer to the Lord.

Hughes rightly observes that too much of the spiritual seeking in devotional books is done by the writers, and not enough by the readers. His thoughts and verse selections here will pull you into the process. Before you know it, you move from passive observer to active participant, working your way closer to God instead of reading about how it's done.

Quiet, still moments are rare and wonderful opportunities to know God better, but there are other ways Selwyn Hughes also identifies for us. Repentance is one, bringing us closer to Him by reaffirming our need for forgiveness. Grace is another, underscoring the truth that ours is an unequal relationship; we can't earn God's companionship, we can only have it bestowed on us as a blessing and a gift. In addition, prayer, public worship, and obedience all have a part in bonding us with God.

We also come closer to God when we work to be like Him. Every time we accept a heartfelt apology, forgiving others as God has forgiven us, we feel His embrace a little tighter.

L.G.G.

No Fixed Rate

"But grow in the grace and knowledge of our Lord and Savior Jesus Christ." (v. 18)

For reading & meditation—2 Peter 3:1–18

We are going to consider the things we need to know and do in order to gain a deeper and more intimate relationship with God. One of the questions put to me most frequently during the years in which I have been a minister and a counselor is this: "Why does one person seem to have a closer relationship with God than another, even though both have been on the Christian way for the same length of time?" Even the most casual observer of the Christian life cannot help but notice that people do not travel along the road leading to deeper knowledge of God at the same rate. We grow old at the same rate. But progress in spiritual things is not made at a fixed rate.

From time to time I meet people who have fewer years of Christian experience than I do, yet they seem to know God more profoundly. They leave me feeling seriously challenged and humbled. You have come across this yourself, haven't you? Surely you have met people who, though younger than you in terms of discipleship, are able to forgive injuries more readily than you, seem to be free of the nasty censoriousness you sometimes struggle with, and are swift to praise others whom they see doing more effectively the things they want to do themselves. Why?

This is the issue which over the coming weeks we must make plain. Lovers of Scripture will have no doubt that God wants to move closer to us. The question we have to decide is: Do we want to move closer to Him?

FURTHER STUDY

1 Cor. 3:1; 14:20;
Eph. 4:1–14

1. How does Paul
describe the Corinthians?
2. What was Paul's desire
for the Ephesians?

Prayer

Father, make this time in my life a time of vision and venture in the things of God. May it become a time of spiritual advancement to a degree I have never before known. I ask all this in Christ's Name. Amen.

A Crucial Element

"... but now [God] commands all people everywhere to repent." (v. 30)

For reading & meditation—Acts 17:16–34

There are, of course, many reasons why some people move along the path of discipleship at a snail's pace, while others appear to cover twice the distance in half the time. It has much to do with the way we enter the Christian life.

Those who have studied the manner in which people become Christians tell us there are two main ways of coming to faith in Christ. One is through a dramatic conversion, whereby a person confronted with the claims of Christ yields to Him in a single moment. The other is when a person moves more slowly into faith, and sometimes cannot even pinpoint the exact moment when he or she made the great surrender. What must be remembered is that both experiences are valid. The best evidence that we are alive is not our birth certificate but the fact we are going about our daily lives as living, breathing people. I myself find no problem when individuals say they do not know the day or hour when they committed themselves to Christ, providing they show evidence that they belong to Him by such proofs as a desire to be alone with Him in prayer, a longing to know Him better through His Word, and an eagerness to meet and have fellowship with other believers.

But no matter how one enters the Christian life—suddenly or slowly—the most essential element is repentance. I have no hesitation in saying that if we do not understand what is involved in living repentant lives, then regardless of how we start the Christian life there will be no successful continuance.

FURTHER STUDY

*Acts 3:11–20;
Luke 13:3;
Acts 17:21–32*

*1. What was Peter's message to the onlookers?
2. How important is repentance?*

Prayer

My Father and my God, if repentance is so important—and I see that it is—then help me understand it more deeply. I am at Your feet. Teach me, dear Lord. In Jesus' Name I ask it. Amen.

A Change of Mind

Day 309

"... your sincere faith, which first lived in your grandmother Lois and in your
mother Eunice ..." (v. 5)

For reading & meditation—2 Timothy 1:1-12

Yesterday we said that there are two types of entry into the Christian life—sudden and gradual. Paul the apostle had one of the most sudden and dramatic conversions in Christian history, yet Paul's disciple Timothy does not seem to have had a similar experience. We cannot tell for sure, but Timothy's coming to faith, a process apparently greatly influenced by his grandmother and mother, seems to have been much more prolonged. We said also (and some may have found this surprising) that without a clear understanding of repentance, and all that it entails, there can be no successful continuance in the Christian life. So what is repentance and why is it vitally important?

The Greek word for repentance, *metanoia*, means "a change of mind." But a change of mind about what? About where life is found. Prior to coming to Christ our minds are shot through with the idea that life depends on such things as self-sufficiency, self-management, and ego-building. The Bible confronts this self-centered approach to living and says that for our lives to work the way God designed them, the ego must be marginal and not central. In other words, Christ must be central, and the ego revolves around Him just as the planets revolve around the sun.

This is quite a radical thought for any mind to grapple with, but be sure of this—if there is no acceptance of it, the soul will not go on to experience a deep and developing relationship with God. No change of mind about where life is to be found—no spiritual progress. It is as simple as that.

FURTHER STUDY

Gal. 2:20;
Rom. 6:6;
Col. 2:1-20

1. In what graphic way
did Paul describe
repentance?
2. What concern did
Paul have for the
Colossians?

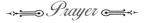 *Prayer*

O Father, help me examine my heart and decide just who is central in my life—You or me. Show me even
more clearly how I can be more Christ-centered and less ego-centered.
In the Name of Your Son I ask it. Amen.

329

How Kind of God

"... not realizing that God's kindness leads you toward repentance?" (v. 4)

For reading & meditation—Romans 2:1–16

One of the places where Christianity parts company with modern-day psychology is over the matter of our ego. The ego is that part of us which contains our sense of individuality—our self-esteem. Secular psychology says the stronger our ego and the more central it is, the better equipped we are to handle life and to live it to the full. Christianity sees the ego as important and does not (as some critics might suggest) seek to demolish it; rather, it puts it in its proper place—at the feet of Christ.

On August 12, 1973, Charles Colson, President Nixon's right-hand man, was feeling deeply disturbed by the events in which he was involved. He went to see a friend who read to him from C. S. Lewis's *Mere Christianity.* Later that evening, he began to sob so deeply that he became quite alarmed. He realized that something spiritual was happening to him and cried out to God: "Take me, take me." That night was the beginning of the period during which this strong, ego-centered man found a new focus for his life—the Lord Jesus Christ.

That is what repentance is all about: it is a change of mind as to where life is to be found—brought about in conjunction with the Holy Spirit. Real life is not to be found in the pursuit of self-centered goals, but in living out God's will and purposes for one's life. Charles Colson is one of Christ's most powerful modern disciples. He appears to have continued the way he began—with a mindset that puts Christ first and himself second.

FURTHER STUDY

*Matt. 19:16–30; 16:24;
Gal. 5:24;
Matt. 8:18–22*

1. What requirement did Jesus lay down for following Him?
2. What was the area of repentance that the young ruler struggled with?

Prayer

O God, may I have this same mindset too—a mindset that puts Your will ahead of my own. Teach me more of what is involved in the act of repentance for I see that without an understanding of it I can make no real spiritual progress. In Christ's Name. Amen.

Jesus Christ Is Lord

"From that time on Jesus began to preach, 'Repent, for the kingdom of heaven is near.'" (v. 17)

For reading & meditation—Matthew 4:12–25

There is a strange lack of emphasis on repentance in many parts of the church today. Our text tells us that our Lord's very first sermons in His preaching ministry was "Repent." We see from other passages in the Gospels that He stresses this message again and again. Peter took up this same theme on the Day of Pentecost, in the first sermon he ever preached (Acts 2:38). Indeed, the word *repentance* appears in one form or another throughout the whole of the New Testament.

Why, then, is repentance such a missing factor (generally speaking) in contemporary Christianity? Is it because in our anxiety to get more converts we avoid the subject of repentance and prefer the quick sales job of getting people to pray the kind of prayer that requires no radical transformation? Once I heard an evangelist tell his converts: "Pray this prayer after me, and you will have a mansion in heaven . . . perhaps even have charge of ten cities when Christ returns to this earth to establish His kingdom." The prayer he then invited them to pray went something like this: "O God, make me a Christian . . . and grant that I might inherit all that is available to me in Christ." What bothered me about the prayer was not that it was invalid but that it was not based on first principles.

The primary thing we have to understand on entering the Christian life is that *Jesus Christ is Lord*. That means we are no longer lord over our lives—He is. Happy are those who enter the Christian life with this clear understanding.

FURTHER STUDY

Isa. 55:7;
Acts 2:38;
1 John 1:9;
Luke 15:11–32

1. What has God promised to the penitent?
2. How did the prodigal son display repentance?

Prayer

O God, help me put first things first. I see that successful Christian living depends on You being first and me being second. Am I really ready and willing for this? Help me search my soul. In Jesus' Name. Amen.

Flightless Butterflies

"... I preached that they should repent and ... prove their repentance by their deeds." (v. 20)

For reading & meditation—Acts 26:1–20

Some evangelists asked me: "Why don't we see more of the kind of converts coming into today's church that we used to get a few decades ago—those who from the very start seem 'out and out' for Jesus?" I replied that I thought it had something to do with the way we present the truths of Christianity to potential converts, and I told them the story I heard John White, a Christian psychiatrist, tell.

A butterfly, struggling to get out of its chrysalis, was given a helping hand by a well-meaning observer. As a result, however, the butterfly was unable to fly because it is in the struggle to emerge that it develops the strength to soar. The observer, intent on making it easy for the butterfly to leave the chrysalis, inadvertently contributed to its early demise.

We do something similar when we help people avoid the struggle that radical repentance invariably brings. The modern-day church (with some exceptions) is like an inexpert midwife bringing damaged children into the world—damaged by lack of attention to basic principles. To return to the metaphor of the butterfly, in the church today there are many butterflies unable to fly because when they emerged from their spiritual chrysalis someone made it easier for them than they should have. We can do that by wrong statements or incomplete statements or even by a misplaced emphasis. Evangelism is making it easy for men and women to be saved, but we must be careful that we do not make it easier than it should be.

FURTHER STUDY

Luke 14:25–35;
Mark 10:28;
Luke 5:27–28

1. What was Jesus' message to the crowd who followed Him?
2. What was Peter able to say?

Prayer

O Father, stir us as Your church to put the emphasis where You put it—on the lordship of Christ and the need for complete and utter surrender to Him in the very first moments of conversion.
In Christ's Name we pray. Amen.

Agreeing with God

"In repentance and rest is your salvation . . ." (v. 15)
For reading & meditation—Isaiah 30:12–21

A definition of repentance I once heard someone use and which I like very much is this: "Repentance is agreeing with God." When we repent, we adopt the attitude that God is right and we are wrong. When you think about it, there is very little point in disagreeing with God over anything because being God, He is always right.

So many problems people have brought to me during the years I have been involved in Christian counseling were rooted in a difficulty they had in their relationship with God. Time and again I have heard people say things such as: "But God can't really expect that of me." "Isn't God being too hard on me in wanting me to yield to Him on this?" "Sometimes God seems to forget that we are human." What underlies all these statements? A difficulty in believing that God is right in everything He says and does. This is why whenever I hear such statements I ask people to tell me something about how they entered the Christian life. Almost always I find that they never underwent a radical repentance when they first became Christians. Because they never knew what it was to agree with God (that is, fully repent) when they first came into the Christian life, subsequently they seemed to want to argue with Him (or at least raise objections) over any issue that appeared to threaten their self-centeredness.

Our wills have to capitulate to God's will if we are to develop a deep relationship with the Almighty. And the best moment to understand this is at the moment of conversion.

FURTHER STUDY

Phil. 3:1–8;
Rom. 6:2–11;
Col. 3:3

1. What attitude did Paul take?
2. How did he describe the result?

 *Prayer*

Father, forgive me if my response to Your challenge is one of resistance and argumentation. If my ego is not at Your feet then help me put it there today. For the sake of Your Son who gave His life for me.
In His Name I pray. Amen.

Failure to "Feel" Saved

"Godly sorrow brings repentance that leads to salvation and leaves no regret . . ." (v. 10)

For reading & meditation—2 Corinthians 7:1–16

*S*ometimes I am asked: "If a person does not undergo a radical repentance at the time they turn to Christ, does that mean they are not converted and will not go to heaven when they die?" My answer is usually along this line: "It is better if a person experiences a radical repentance at the time of their initial commitment to Christ, as this sets the tilt of the soul in the direction of agreeing with God. But God will come in and live in a person's life by invitation, even though the repentance is not as complete as it should be."

The advantage of a radical repentance at the time of one's commitment to Christ is, as I have said, that it bends the ego in God's direction and teaches it right from the start that submission is essential. A major reason for lack of spiritual assurance (people who have committed themselves to Christ not *feeling* saved) is this issue of incomplete repentance. When repentance is incomplete and there is no "godly sorrow" over sin, the effects of sin (guilt and shame) are not eliminated from the soul. Radical conversion siphons off these things and leaves the soul feeling free. It ensures there are no regrets, no hankering for former things.

To change the metaphor, if the soul is not plowed up by radical repentance, the seeds sown by the Holy Spirit and the Word of God will not take deep root. Those who have never fully repented ought to do so now—without delay. Take time this day to evaluate your spiritual condition. Make Christ *Lord*.

FURTHER STUDY

Hos. 10:9–13;
Pss. 34:18; 51:17;
Joel 2:13

1. What had Israel depended on?
2. What was God's word to them?

Prayer

O God, help me not to move beyond this day without clarifying my spiritual commitment. Am I first in my life, or are You? May I know the godly sorrow that leads to deep repentance. In Jesus' Name I pray. Amen.

The First and Last Word

"... for in you the fatherless find compassion." (v. 3)

For reading & meditation—Hosea 14:1–9

*R*epentance is commonly thought of as simply an acknowledgment and confession of sin. But the repentance God desires of us is not only contrition for particular sins; it is a daily attitude, an ongoing perspective. Martin Luther started the Reformation when he nailed his 95 Theses to the door of the Castle church at Wittenburg, and the very first of his statements read thus: "When our Lord Jesus Christ said 'repent' He willed that the entire life of believers be one of repentance."

Note that—"the *entire* life of believers." Repentance is not a one-time act, it is a process—the process by which we see ourselves day by day as we really are: sinful, needy, dependent people. It is the process by which we see God as He is: awesome, majestic and holy. Repentance is the ultimate surrender of self. The call to repentance is one of the most consistent themes of the Bible.

We must be aware that no matter how radical our repentance at conversion, sinful tendencies remain in varying degrees. Constantly we need to recognize that our carnal nature may surface at any time to disagree with God. We will never be able in move into a deep relationship with God unless we maintain an attitude of repentance. "Every bit of growth in the Christian life," said one theologian, "is based on the re-enactment of the original redemptive occurrence." By that he meant that the way we came into the Christian life is the way we continue in it—by repentance. Repentance is the first word of the gospel—and the last.

FURTHER STUDY

*Rom. 12:1–8;
Prov. 23:26;
1 Thess. 5:23*

1. What did Paul urge the Romans to do?
2. What was Paul's prayer for the Thessalonians?

Prayer

Thank You, Father, for spelling out for me the truth that repentance is not merely an act but an attitude. From now on and by Your grace may this forever be the attitude of my soul. In Jesus' Name I pray. Amen.

Amazing!

"... how much more will those who receive God's abundant provision of grace ...
reign in life ..." (v. 17)

For reading & meditation—Romans 5:12–21

*I*f we are to go deeper with God, we need to know *how to avail ourselves of God's grace.* Our text for today talks about "those who receive God's abundant provision of grace." Though God's grace may be abundant, it is only effective in our lives if it is received. But what do we mean by "grace"?

Grace is spoken of in both the Old and New Testaments, and the root meaning of the word is that of kindness and favor. In the New Testament it is used chiefly in connection with God's undeserved mercy in redeeming humankind. *Grace,* as undeserved favor, is a term still used in business—especially the world of insurance. Sometimes a representative of a firm will write to a client and say something like this: "In the circumstances you have no claim, we will give you a certain sum as an act of grace." They acknowledge no indebtedness, but out of their kindness (and in hope of business to come) they give the client something to which he has no legal right.

A definition of grace I like very much is this: "Grace is the strength God gives us to obey His commands." Grace is not just a kindly attitude but an impartation of power too. We can be sure that the people who seem to know God in a much deeper way than we do have received more of that power which God imparts "unmerited and free." It is by grace that they leap over all the impediments on their onward way. Grace truly is amazing!

FURTHER STUDY

*Acts 15:1–11;
Rom. 3:24;
Titus 3:7*

*1. What are some of the fruits of grace?
2. Write out your own definition of grace.*

⟶ *Prayer* ⟵

O Father, how can I thank You enough that just as the atmosphere wraps itself around my body so Your grace wraps itself around my soul. May I respond to Your grace as my physical body responds to the atmosphere—and lives. In Jesus' Name. Amen.

Always More to Follow

"'God opposes the proud but gives grace to the humble.'" (v. 6)
For reading & meditation—James 4:1–17

Why have some Christians received more grace? If, as we said, grace is undeserved favor, does that mean God has favorites? Is there something capricious about the Almighty's allocation of help to His children?

Some secular writers have portrayed God as being like men and women, biased in His affections and having an inexplicable preference for one person and disinterest in another. But surely God does not take "a fancy" to some people and not others. There is favor to be found in God, but no favoritism. His favor moves to all who are willing and eager to receive it.

But to return to our question: Why do some receive more grace than others? I think the main reason must be this—they know that there is grace to be had. Sometimes I come across Christians who think that God's only concern is to get us on to the pilgrim way and that He then leaves us to our own devices. You can tell such people by the way they talk about their conversion—and nothing more. They seem unconcerned about the fact that God's great aim is not simply to bring us into the Christian life but to develop us in it. He is not content with calling us "saints" but making us saints; not simply cancelling sin but breaking its power over us. Those who use God's grace are those who know He has plenty to give. Of this they are confident, and thus they keep it in mind all the time. When they have used what they have, they know there is always more to follow.

FURTHER STUDY

Rom. 5:1–15;
Titus 2:11;
1 Tim. 1:14

1. To whom did grace overflow?
2. What was Paul's testimony to Timothy?

Prayer

O Father, what a comfort it is to know that however much I draw on Your grace there is always more to follow. I cannot draw heavily on many things but I can draw heavily on You. May this be more than an idea; may it be a fact. In Christ's Name. Amen.

A Throne of Grace

"Let us then approach the throne of grace with confidence, so that we may . . .
find grace . . ." (v. 16)
For reading & meditation—Hebrews 4:1-16

W e are seeing that one reason some Christians develop a closer relationship with God is because they know how to avail themselves of His grace. They realize it is there to be had and they open themselves to it most eagerly. People who know God intimately view grace as a treasure above all treasures. It is not that they put no value on the things of earth, but they see grace as the most precious thing of all.

John Wesley, the founder of Methodism, had a friend called Fletcher of Madeley—a deeply spiritual man—whom Wesley designated as his successor. He died before Wesley, however, and at his funeral Wesley took as his text Psalm 37:37: "Mark the perfect man (KJV)." He told of how on one occasion Fletcher had made a public utterance concerning the government of the day which had greatly impressed its leaders. Soon after the Lord Chancellor dispatched a representative to Fletcher's home to offer him a promotion. The official was at some pains to hint delicately at his errand and said: "The government would be very happy to . . . er . . . oblige in any way if . . . er . . . there was anything Mr. Fletcher wanted . . ." "How very kind," was the great man's reply, "but I want nothing . . . except more grace."

That is the difference between those who know God deeply and those who don't. They look at the values of earth in the light of heaven and see that the only really valuable thing is—grace. "Let me have that," they say, "and I am content."

**FURTHER
STUDY**

*2 Cor. 8:9; 12:9;
2 Tim. 2:1-10*

*1. How did Paul describe
grace at work?
2. What was Paul's
admonition to Timothy?*

Prayer

O God, help me look at the values of earth in the light of heaven. Show me the folly of accumulating riches,
the absurdity of heaping together the treasures of earth. May I come to recognize what has
the highest value of all—Your matchless grace. Amen.

Effective Service

"... I worked harder than all of them—yet not I, but the grace of God that was with me." (v. 10)

For reading & meditation—1 Corinthians 15:1–11

We considered yesterday the story of Fletcher of Madeley who said to a government official: "I want nothing . . . except more grace." One wonders what account the official gave when he returned to the Lord Chancellor. "Nothing we can offer seems to attract him. The only thing he wants is more grace!"

Dr. W. E. Sangster, in *The Pure in Heart*, said that all who know God deeply have a high view of grace. They have learned to look at all the values of earth in the light of heaven. They have seen how absurd it is to put their trust in riches, the meaninglessness of angling for applause, credits and titles, and they have come to the conclusion that the only really valuable thing in life is grace.

Few will argue with the fact that the apostle Paul was one of the greatest Christians who has ever lived, and so it is interesting to note from today's passage that he labored for God not in his own strength but in the strength God gave him. The grace of God is essential not only to live a holy life but to live a helpful one also. The best way to serve others is to reach out to them in the strength that God gives to us. This is the point the great apostle is making. "I worked harder . . . *yet not I*, but the grace of God that was with me." The work of Christ must be done by Christ Himself for no one else can do it. He who lives in us must labor through us.

FURTHER STUDY

2 Cor. 1:1–12; 6:1;
1 Pet. 4:10

1. What was Paul's boast?
2. What did he urge the Corinthians to do?

Prayer

O God, how foolish I am to try to labor for You in my own strength. In spurning the grace You provide I do myself and others a disservice. And more—I grieve Your heart. Forgive me dear Father and make me a more reliant person. In Jesus' Name. Amen.

"A Christ Not in Us . . ."

"I have been crucified with Christ and I no longer live, but Christ lives in me." (v. 20)

For reading & meditation—Galatians 2:11-21

We saw yesterday that the apostle Paul claimed his labors were energized by the grace given to him by God. He says something similar in the text before us today: "I no longer live . . . Christ lives in me." The apostle had learned that it was not enough to give all of his strength to the work of Christ, though he certainly did that; he had to receive Christ's strength in order to do His work.

I have seen Christians suffer a breakdown as a result of trying to live the Christian life in their own strength. On one occasion I was present at a dinner given in honor of a certain bishop. During the after-dinner speeches I heard a layman make a terrible blunder when he declared: "Bishop, we are both doing God's work; you in your way, and I in His." Question yourself at this very moment and ask: Am I doing God's work in my own way or in His?

"A Christ not in us, imparting His grace to us," said the great preacher William Law, "is the same as a Christ not ours." I don't know about you but I find those words terribly challenging. Is this why so many of us fail to go as deeply with God as we ought? We have received Christ but we do not allow Him to diffuse Himself through all our faculties, to animate us with His life and Spirit. Let William Law's words strike deep into your soul: "A Christ not in us, imparting His grace . . . is the same as a Christ not ours."

FURTHER STUDY

Eph. 3:1–9;
James 4:4–6;
1 Pet. 5:5

1. What did grace enable Paul to do?
2. What did James declare?

Prayer

Gracious and loving Father, your challenges are my salvation. You wound in order to win me. Help me to take my medicine without complaining and open myself up to all that You are saying to me in the words I have read today. In Jesus' Name. Amen.

Grace upon Grace

"From the fullness of his grace we have all received one blessing after another." (v. 16)
For reading & meditation—John 1:1-17

The Amplified Bible translates today's verse thus: "For out of His fullness (abundance) we all received—all had a share and we were all supplied with—one grace after another and spiritual blessing upon spiritual blessing, and even favor upon favor and gift [heaped] upon gift." I love the phrase "one grace after another." The thought contained in the original text is of grace succeeding grace.

Our capacity to receive grace at any level depends on our use of it at the lowest level. Refuse God's grace at one level of your life and you make it difficult to receive it at another level. We must use the present proffered grace to be granted the grace which succeeds it. One preacher said: "I remember when I sat for my first scholarship. I recall going to my professor and saying: 'What will I do when I have used the paper up?' He laughed. 'You needn't worry about that,' he said. 'When you have used all you have, just ask for more.' Much relieved I added: 'Will he give me all I want?' 'No,' replied the professor, 'but he will give you all you can use.'"

God is eager to give His grace to every one of us, and there is so much of it.

> Grace is flowing like a river
> Millions there have been supplied . . .

But it mustn't be wasted. You can have all you are able to use, but to have more you must use what you have. How good are you at *using* God's grace?

FURTHER STUDY

*Phil. 4:14-19;
Eph. 1:7; 2:7*

1. What was Paul
   confident of?
2. How did he describe
   God's grace?

 Prayer

My Father and my God, show me how to use Your grace—really use it. Help me to throw myself on You, to be less self-reliant and more God-reliant. I need to understand this even more, dear Lord. Please help me. In Jesus' Name. Amen.

Moving off the Sandbank

"You were running a good race. Who cut in on you and kept you from obeying the truth?" (v. 7)

For reading & meditation—Galatians 5:1–15

*A*s you read the words of our text today, do you not sense the disappointment the apostle Paul felt over some of the Galatians? "You were running a good race." You were! Ah, there's the problem. They started well but they had been sidetracked.

Might the Savior say as much to you and me? We were keen once. We were responding to grace. It came in like the waves of the sea—grace succeeding grace—and we allowed ourselves to be carried along by it. Then the time came when God led us to some new task or act of surrender, and we sheered away. When we refused the task we refused also the grace. That's when we ran on to the sandbank. People who started after us have swept past us, not because they are specially favored but because they use all the grace God provides. It's no good putting our lack of keenness down to age or impediments.

Before you go to sleep tonight, get alone and be quiet with God. Review your life in God's light. Ask yourself: Where did I fall out of the race? Invite God to show you the place where you drew back. When He does, repent of your unwillingness to use His grace (there will be grace available for you to face up to this) and tell Him you want to be back in the race again, pacing forward spiritually, along with the most ardent souls you know. It will delight God and make the angels sing. "Look," they will say, "he (or she) is moving again. And with *speed*. Hallelujah!"

FURTHER STUDY

Phil. 3:7–16;
1 Tim. 4:15;
1 Cor. 9:24

1. What was Paul able to say?
2. What were Paul's words to Timothy?

Prayer

O God, may this day be a turning point in my spiritual progress. Help me take this truth to heart that when I refuse Your challenge I refuse the grace that goes along with it.
Today I move off the sandbank. By grace. Amen.

Two Extremes

"Praise be to the Lord, to God our Savior, who daily bears our burdens." (v. 19)
For reading & meditation—Psalm 68:11–20

The next thing we must do if we are to go deeper with God is to *spend time with Him*. This means taking time to regularly read His Word, talk to Him in prayer, and cultivate the spiritual sensitivity to listen for His voice speaking directly to our souls.

One of the great tragedies of our day is that spiritual leaders fail to emphasize the need for all Christians to regularly spend time with God in this way. In my opinion, this de-emphasis is due to two things in particular. First, it is a reaction to the legalism of past days. At one time, most Christians were told that the life of discipleship turned on whether or not you established a daily quiet time and never wavered from it. In my youth I heard one Bible teacher say: "If you don't begin every day by reading a chapter of the Bible and spending at least thirty minutes in prayer then you have no right to go into the day expecting God to bless it." What about those times when circumstances—such as sleeping late, a family emergency, personal sickness, an unexpected turn of events—make it impossible to begin the day with the reading of Scripture or a time of prayer?

In turning from the legalism of past days many, however, have replaced it with a more casual approach to personal devotions. If they don't feel like it they don't have a quiet time. And that, I suggest, is as harmful as the legalism from which they might have turned away.

FURTHER STUDY

Ps. 119:1–15, 72, 97;
Jer. 15:16

1. What did the psalmist say he would not do?
2. What did Jeremiah liken God's Word to?

Prayer

O God, if, as Your Word says, You daily bear my burdens, is not this worth a daily response of prayer and praise? I may not be able to spend much time with You every day, but I can spend some time. Help me never to forget this. In Christ's Name. Amen.

343

Our Lord's Two "Customs"

"... on the Sabbath day he went into the synagogue, as was his custom." (v. 16)

For reading & meditation—Luke 4:14–30

One reason there is a casual approach to personal devotions in the Christian church today is a reaction to the legalism of past days. Another reason is the rise of the charismatic movement.

In the early days of the charismatic renewal, many of its leaders from the historic denominations who had been fed on a diet of legalism began to emphasize (quite rightly) the joy of knowing Christ's presence through the indwelling Spirit every hour of the day. People in charismatic services often said: "Now I don't have to have a daily quiet time in order to feel God's presence. Every waking minute is a quiet time." Dangerous stuff. The danger lies not in emphasizing that we are in Christ's presence every hour of the day but the de-emphasis on closeting oneself alone with Him in personal prayer and study of His Word. Although most leaders of the charismatic renewal did not teach or encourage people to dispense with their personal times of devotion with the Lord, many came to believe they could get through the day simply by speaking in tongues.

Nothing must become a substitute for those private and personal moments we spend in prayer and communion with Christ. Our Lord knew and sensed the presence of God with Him and in Him to a degree we will never fully experience here on this earth, but it is said of Him in Scripture that He had two "customs." One custom was to go regularly to the house of God; the other was to pray regularly. And these must be our customs too.

FURTHER STUDY

Matt. 6:5–15; 14:23;
Luke 5:16

1. What did Jesus teach about prayer?
2. How did He demonstrate it?

 *Prayer*

Lord Jesus, if You needed to spend time closeted with Your Father in personal prayer, then how much more do I need to also. Help me steer a middle course between legalism and casualness. For Your own dear Name's sake. Amen.

The Profit of Passion

"I sought the LORD, and he answered me . . ." (v. 4)

For reading & meditation—Psalm 34:1–22

The more time we spend with our families and friends the better we get to know them. It is the same with God too.

Often I am asked to give a plan on how to conduct a quiet time. Here is one I used to give people many years ago. Decide on the amount of time you can spend, preferably in the morning. The morning is best because it tunes your soul for the day. Having fixed the time, stick to it. Take your Bible and a notebook and read a portion slowly. Let it soak in. Make a note of anything that comes to you. Pray then, mentioning any requests or personal petitions you may have. Then relax and listen to see if God has something to say to you. It is far easier to talk than listen, so don't worry if for some weeks or months nothing comes. Tuning in to God takes time and practice.

Nowadays I am reluctant to give people that plan without pointing out the danger of depending on a structure rather than the direction of the Holy Spirit. We would all prefer to go into a quiet time with a plan rather than to abandon ourselves to the Holy Spirit and wait upon Him. Mature Christians should be able to closet themselves alone with God and on occasions simply enjoy His company and presence without even saying a word. The quiet time becomes more effective when we approach it with passion instead of a plan. Good marriages thrive on spontaneity and passion. So does a relationship with the Lord.

FURTHER STUDY

Ps. 46:1–11;
Isa. 30:15; 32:17

1. When can we know God?
2. Find some time today to be still in His presence.

Prayer

Father, help me come to my quiet time with expectancy—expectancy that my weakness shall become strength, my doubt become faith, and my passion become stronger. In Jesus' Name. Amen.

Day 326

A Father and a Friend

"Ask and it will be given to you; seek and you will find . . ." (v. 9)
For reading & meditation—Luke 11:1-13

he great danger of a quiet time is that we will use it as an opportunity to petition God rather than to know Him and be known by Him. I thought back to a statement I remember reading in C. S. Lewis's book, *Prayer: Letters to Malcolm*, to the effect that the older he got the less involved he became in petitionary prayer. "The strange thing is," said Lewis (and I am paraphrasing now), "the more I pray for things the less my prayers seem to get answered. I think God is leading me on to ask less and less for things and more and more for Himself." Then he expressed this profound thought: "Prayer is taking part in the process of being known."

I glanced up as I wrote those words and looked out at the trees in my garden. God knows everything there is to know about those trees, but they are not persons so they cannot join in the process of being known. God knows all there is to know about me, but that objective knowledge is quite different from the process of drawing close to Him in prayer and letting Him know me through my opening up to Him. One is objective knowledge, the other experiential. And what is breathtakingly marvelous about all this is that in every spiritual tête-à-tête I hold with God, He seeks to draw my soul into such a relationship with Him that I know Him as a Father and a Friend. Such knowledge is almost too good to be true. But also too good not to be true.

FURTHER STUDY

*Job 37:14-24;
Pss. 4:4; 131:2*

*1. What did Elihu
admonish Job?
2. What was the psalmist
able to say?*

Prayer

My Father and my Friend, may my times of communion with You be more than just a petitioner talking to a
Supplier. I know You are willing to open Yourself fully to me; help me open myself fully to You.
In Christ's Name I ask it. Amen.

346

Knowing God

"I want to know Christ and the power of his resurrection . . ." (v. 10)

For reading & meditation—Philippians 3:1–11

*I*t is not my purpose at this moment to explore the philosophy of prayer, but I do feel it will be helpful to some if I point out that God delights also to be known. The Father is known by the other members of the Trinity (and of course they by Him), and that undoubtedly brings Him great pleasure. But He longs to be known by His children also. There is something in the heart of the Deity that enjoys being known.

A lovely, though apocryphal, story told by a Jewish rabbi describes a conversation between Abraham and God. It goes something like this. "God said to Abraham: 'Do you realize, Abraham, that without Me you would be nothing?' 'Ah yes, Lord,' said Abraham, 'I do realize that without You I would be nothing.' Then he thought for a moment, and bowing his head low to the ground said: 'Forgive me if I am being presumptuous, O Lord, but it occurs to me that without me You would not be known.'"

This is only a story, of course, and is not intended to convey that God is dependent on His creatures. It simply illustrates the truth that in some mystical way we enrich the heart of God by knowing Him. I am not saying that by knowing God we add to Him or complete Him. That would be foolish. But we can by our deeper knowledge of Him bring Him pleasure. And if there is no greater reason than that for knowing God, then it ought to suffice.

FURTHER STUDY

John 17:1–5;
Jer. 9:23–24;
Job 19:25

1. What is the essence of eternal life?
2. What should our boast be?

Prayer

O Father, I am grateful for the way in which I have come to know You, but I long to know You still more. You open Yourself fully to me; may I open myself fully to You. In Christ's Name I pray. Amen.

Day 328

Stated Times

"But when you pray, go into your room, close the door and pray to your Father, who is unseen." (v. 6)

For reading & meditation—Matthew 6:1-15

*I*n order to go deeper with God we must sit quietly in His presence, talk with Him, and let Him talk with us. Those who say they can develop their relationship with God without stated times of prayer and the reading of His Word are fooling themselves. Jesus (as we saw) is our best example. He knew God's presence better than anyone, yet He made time to get alone with Him and talk to Him in private prayer.

To say that we can develop a rich relationship with God by recognizing we are always in His presence but without taking time to have a spiritual focus is as senseless as saying that we can live in a state of physical nourishment without having regular meals. As I travel I often ask Christians I meet if they have a daily or regular quiet time, and sometimes the answers I receive astonish me. One man told me: "Yes, I get up early, sit quietly in my garden and watch the birds feeding or the goldfish swimming in the pond . . . and I feel rejuvenated in my spirit and ready to start the day." The modern idea of a quiet time!

The whole purpose of the quiet time is to take in the spiritual resources of God. Nature is wonderful and restorative, but for the intake of spiritual resources we need the blessing that comes from the Word of God and prayer. The quiet time is where the soul grows receptive, where prayer becomes powerful. In turn we gain the quiet heart, that becomes quiet confidence, and that becomes quiet power.

FURTHER STUDY

Acts 10:1-9; 10:30; James 5:17

1. What was the pattern of Peter and Cornelius?
2. How focused was Elijah?

Prayer

O Father, deepen the conviction within me that I cannot develop my relationship with You without taking the time to commune with You. Help me make my meeting times with You one of life's great priorities. In Jesus' Name. Amen.

348

Ah, What Then?

Day 329

"Be still, and know that I am God . . ." (v. 10)
For reading & meditation—Psalm 46:1–11

*I*n the quiet time the soul is stilled so that it concentrates on God, and it is through this concentration that the spiritual life is deepened. The great French Christian Blaise Pascal once declared that "nearly all the ills of life spring from this simple source, that we are unable to sit still for long in a quiet room." In this modern age people seem to find it difficult to sit quietly for long. They must have a radio blaring or something else to drown the silence.

Sitting still can be therapeutic, but what if in the stillness we meet with God? We then receive spiritual therapy. God waits to offer us infinite resources—for the asking and the taking. The quiet time is where the soul grows receptive, where prayer becomes, as a poet put it, "the organ of spiritual touch," where the touch becomes, as effective and as healing as the touch of the woman on the hem of Jesus' garment, where peace flows into our turbulence, where love absorbs our resentments, where joy heals our griefs, and where we enter into the process of being known. The quiet time shuts us in with God, the door closes upon us, and then infinite resources flood into our soul. The door opens and we move out, with an increased awareness of God, ready to face a world that knows so little about Him. There is, as we have said, great benefit in stillness, but when we meet with God in the stillness—ah, what then?

FURTHER STUDY

Pss. 33:17–22; 62:1–2; 130:5–6; 40:1

1. What did the psalmist do?
2. What was the result?

Prayer

My Father and my God, I see that I need to think more seriously about the whole nature of my quiet times. In avoiding legalism, help me not to go in the other direction either—the direction of casualness. In Your Son's precious Name I pray. Amen.

Can God Be Trusted?

"Some trust in chariots and some in horses, but we trust in the name of the LORD our God." (v. 7)

For reading & meditation—Psalm 20:1–9

We consider now another matter that is essential if we are to go deeper with God—*confidence in His character.* Is God good and can He be trusted? The manner in which we answer this question is crucial to our ongoing relationship with Him. If we have doubts about His character—His justice for example—it will most certainly affect the way we view Him and approach Him.

You may have heard the story of the farmer whose one and only tractor failed. So he decided to walk across the fields to a neighboring farmer whom he knew had three. As he strode to the neighbor's farmhouse, he reflected on what he knew about his fellow farmer. He remembered that he never appeared at any of the village's social events, and he had heard somewhere that he had a reputation as a skinflint. More negative thoughts about the farmer entered his head, but by this time he found himself at the door of the farmhouse. The farmer, who had seen him coming across the fields, appeared at the doorway and asked: "What's the problem?" "I've come to tell you," said the man, "that you can keep your jolly old tractor!"

Many do not realize how profoundly the way we think about God and His, character influences the way we worship Him, the way we work for Him, and the way we witness to Him. Any doubts about the goodness of God will result in our souls keeping their distance from Him. If we do not have complete confidence in Him, we will not desire a close relationship with Him.

**FURTHER
STUDY**

*Neh. 9:19–25;
Ps. 23:6*

1. What did the children
of Israel revel in?
2. What was the
psalmist's conviction
about his life?

Prayer

Father, I see how crucial is this issue. Help me deal with any doubts that may be circulating in my mind. I don't want any distance between You and me; I want closeness. I am listening, dear Father. Continue leading me on. Amen.

Doubt and Disobedience

"[The serpent] said to the woman, 'Did God really say, "You must not eat from any tree in the garden"?'" (v. 1)

For reading & meditation—Genesis 3:1–19

We continue discussing the point that unless we have a strong conviction that God is entirely trustworthy, we will not desire a deep and ongoing relationship with Him. Yesterday we spoke of the distance from God our souls experience when we entertain doubts about His goodness. Do you realize that the reason for the distance between God and the first human couple in the Garden of Eden was doubt about God's goodness? Doubt about God soon leads to dislike of God, and dislike of God soon leads to disobedience.

When Eve responded to the Tempter's insinuation that God did not have her best interests at heart (by withholding something from her), the doubt she entertained soon led to dislike of God, and then it was relatively easy to take the next step and disobey Him. The moment her doubt about God's goodness expressed itself in taking the forbidden fruit, the foundation on which her relationship with God was established—trust—crumbled beneath her feet. Adam rapidly followed her in committing the same kind of sin (doubt about God's goodness) and then, inevitably, distance replaced closeness.

Since the Fall, every child born into this world has within its nature a basic distrust of God. Paul puts it like this: "The sinful mind is hostile to God" (Rom. 8:7). The word *hostility* can be translated "enmity." No one trusts someone they regard as an enemy. Distance between humankind and God arose when the first human couple doubted His goodness. Closeness between human beings and God comes when we have confidence in His goodness. As we said yesterday, no confidence—no relationship.

FURTHER STUDY

Pss. 145:1-13; 31:19; 16:2

1. What do the people of God celebrate?
2. What did the psalmist say to the Lord?

Prayer

O God my Father, help me have an unshakable confidence in Your character so that no doubts prompted by the devil will ever penetrate my soul. I want no distance between us, but an ever growing closeness. Grant it, in Jesus' Name. Amen.

Build on the Rock

"'. . . everyone who . . . does not put [Jesus' words] into practice is like a foolish man who built his house on sand.'" (v. 26)

For reading & meditation—Matthew 7:15-29

*T*he biggest problem we face in the Christian life," said Dr. Cynddylan Jones, a famous Welsh preacher, "is distance." He continued: "The only way that distance can be overcome is by having the perspective of Job who said: 'Though He slay me yet will I trust Him.'"

When I talk to counselors in training I tell them that what they should be listening for as a counselee tells his or her story is distance. That's what underlies most problems that bring people into counseling. This does not mean we should ignore or make light of the surface problems with which people may be struggling. But the plain fact is this—when we are close to God and have a deep and intimate relationship with Him, we may feel downcast but not destroyed. Therefore, every Christian counselor's ultimate goal should be to close any distance there may be between the person and God, and to develop spiritual oneness. Counseling is not effective or complete until this is accomplished.

How does distance come between ourselves and God? There are many causes—bitterness and resentment against another, persistent sin, failure to establish a devotional life—but largely it arises through a lack of trust. If you cut your way through the maze of human problems that's what you find—an inability to trust. That's what happened in the Garden of Eden, and that's what happens in our personal Garden of Eden also. To try to develop a close relationship with God and fail to deal with this most basic issue is about as effective as building a skyscraper on an acre of sand.

FURTHER STUDY

*James 4:7–11;
Prov. 3:5–6; 29:25;
Heb. 10:22*

*1. When does God come near to us?
2. How should we draw near to God?*

⟶⟹ *Prayer* ⟸⟵

O God, I see so clearly that although there are many things that bring about distance between You and me, the most basic is lack of trust. Help me settle this issue once and for all over the next few days.
In Christ's Name I pray. Amen.

Where Is God?

"Rise up, O God, and defend your cause; remember how fools mock you all day long." (v. 22)

For reading & meditation—Psalm 74:1-23

How do we develop trust in the goodness of God when so much that is happening in the world seems to contradict it? If God is good, how can He allow disasters?

Dr. M. Scott Peck opens his book *The Road Less Travelled* with these words: "Life is difficult. This is a great truth because once we truly see this truth, we transcend it." I have great difficulty with some of Dr. Scott Peck's statements, but I fully endorse these remarks. Once we accept the fact that life is difficult—that the mystery of why calamities and suffering occur will never be fully solved while we are here on earth—then we will stop demanding that a satisfactory answer be found and begin to get on with life.

Christians go down different routes regarding this matter of calamities and suffering. One is to close their eyes and pretend the tremendous problems are not there. But integrity requires that we face whatever is true. Reality is grim—innocent children are abused, starved, massacred—and countless other forms of atrocity are carried out around the world daily. We must not blind our eyes to these facts and pretend they are untrue because they appear to contradict the concept of God's goodness. Pretense must never be our refuge. We must be willing to look at these things, unpleasant and horrible though they be, and allow ourselves to be jarred by them. When we face life honestly and allow ourselves to be jolted by what we see, then, and only then, are we ready for God to speak.

FURTHER STUDY

Pss. 73:1–17; 25:8; 34:8

1. What was the psalmist's conclusion about God?
2. What did he struggle with?

Prayer

Gracious and loving heavenly Father, give me the courage not to bury my head in the sand and pretend there are no problems. Help me stand even when I cannot understand. For Your own dear Name's sake. Amen.

The God Who Is There

"My ears had heard of you but now my eyes have seen you." (v. 5)
For reading & meditation—Job 42:1–17

The Book of Job records the story of a godly man who underwent some of the most bitter experiences it is possible to meet with in this life. At first Job says very little about his difficulties, but later in the book he begins to face the reality of what has happened to him and declares that if he could have an interview with God he would tell Him exactly what he thought of Him (Job 23:1–17). It was when he faced his hardships, recognized how he really felt and admitted it that God came to him and answered him (Job 38:1–41:34). We must never be afraid of admitting that what we see around us doesn't match up with what we know about the character of God. To blind our eyes to the realities of life for fear that what we observe might turn us against God is utterly foolish. We must face difficult issues, for it is only when we do so that we are ready to hear God speak. If we refuse to face reality, then our souls are not alert to hear His voice. We fear that we might hear something to make us even more uncertain of God, and thus prefer to take refuge in illusion.

When Job faced the reality of his situation and how he really felt, then he was ready for God to speak. But notice God didn't give any answers to Job's questions. He gave Himself. Job had an encounter with God that more than satisfied him. He could live without answers when he knew that God was there.

FURTHER STUDY

Isa. 40:1–31;
Ps. 89:6;
1 Chron. 17:20

1. What question did Isaiah ask?
2. How did he answer it?

Prayer

Loving Father, the more I learn about You the more wonderful I see You are. Help me never to take refuge in illusion but to bring all my doubts and fears directly to You. Do for me what You did for Job—enrich me with Your presence. In Jesus' Name. Amen.

Accepting the Inevitable

"But those who suffer he delivers in their suffering; he speaks to them in their affliction." (v. 15)

For reading & meditation—Job 36:1–15

O swald Chambers said: "Life is more tragic than orderly." Chambers knew that unless Christians are willing to grapple with this truth and accept it, they will be plagued by inner *oughts* and *shoulds* that lead them down the road of illusion. They will find themselves saying, "It *ought* not to be like this" or "Things *should* be different"—and the only thing this kind of demandingness produces is frustration and anger.

The Fall has turned this fair universe of God's into a shambles, and though much about the world is still beautiful, accidents, calamities, and suffering prevail. And these will continue until the time when God brings all things to a conclusion. There is nothing wrong with *wishing* that things were not so, but when we *demand* that they be different, when we say the effects of the Fall must be reversed and reversed *now*, we will end up feeling terribly frustrated.

Life is difficult, as Scott Peck stated, and though prayer does move God to work supernaturally in some situations, life will go on being more "tragic than orderly" until Christ returns and finalizes His plans for this fallen planet. This is reality—and the sooner we face it the better. True faith is not built upon illusion but upon reality. We may not like things the way they are in this world, but to avoid facing them because they don't match up with what we know about God is foolish. As I have been emphasizing, it is only when we face honestly the harsh realities of life that we become ready for God to speak to us.

FURTHER STUDY

*Heb. 11:1–40;
2 Cor. 11:16–29; 4:7–10*

*1. What is faith?
2. List some of the difficult circumstances of life faced in the light of faith.*

Prayer

O God, I see that facing the hard things of life honestly drives me to a place where I become desperate for an answer. Then You step in—and give me not an answer but Yourself. I can live without answers, but I cannot live without You. Stay close to me, my Father. In Jesus' Name. Amen.

Day 336

Messed Up Theology

"Though he slay me, yet will I hope in him . . ." (v. 15)

For reading & meditation—Job 13:1-15

A friend of mine who is an instructor in the field of Christian counseling says that one of the things he likes to do with his students is to mess up their theology. He does so by asking them difficult questions about the realities of the universe in order to see how they attempt to square these issues with their view of God. "God always answers the prayer of faith," said one of his students. "Then why," he asked the student, "did I pray for an hour for my father who was desperately sick to have a good night and then hear that he had the worst night since he had been in the hospital?" "You didn't pray in faith," replied the student.

That's the kind of glib answer many people would give to that question. Such people can't sit quietly in the presence of mystery and say: "I don't understand why this is so but nevertheless I still believe God is good." They must have some kind of answer that they can hold on to because when they have no answers they have no faith. Faith is Job saying: "Though he slay me, yet will I hope in him."

Anyone can believe when there are explanations and answers. The person who goes on to know God in a deep and intimate way is the one who can affirm that God is good even though there may be a thousand appearances to the contrary. Pray for me and I will pray for you that together we might come to the place of trusting God even when we cannot trace Him.

FURTHER STUDY

Dan. 3:13–30;
Hab. 3:16–18;
Ps. 46:2

1. How did the Hebrew youths demonstrate faith in God?
2. What does Habakkuk declare?

Prayer

O God, bring us closer day by day to that place of deep confidence and absolute trust. May we know You so deeply that nothing we see around us will shake or shatter our belief in Your unchanging goodness. In our Lord's Name we pray. Amen.

356

"The Old Rugged Cross"

"But God demonstrates his own love for us in this: While we were still sinners, Christ died for us." (v. 8)

For reading & meditation—Romans 5:1-11

C an we believe that God is good even though things may be happening around us that seemingly give the lie to that fact? The only place we Christians can go when we are assailed by doubts about God's goodness is the cross. At Calvary we were given undeniable evidence that God is good. We must cling to the cross when in doubt and remind ourselves that a God who would give His only Son to die for us simply has to be All-Goodness. A songwriter put it like this:

> God is love, I see it in the earth around me;
> God is love, I feel it in the sky above me;
> God is love, all nature doth agree;
> But the greatest proof of His love to me . . . is Calvary.

Many things about the cross are mysterious, but there is no mystery about divine goodness. There at Calvary it blazes forth for all to see. I often wonder to myself what was happening that was good when my wife was dying with cancer. I couldn't see anything, but because I know God is good I accept that something good was being worked out. A good God was in charge, and I am prepared to wait for the clarification of that until I get home. Then I know He will tell me Himself.

God is good no matter what the appearances to the contrary. The "old rugged cross" makes that crystal clear. Let us cling to it, come what may.

FURTHER STUDY

Gal. 6:1–14;
1 Cor. 1:17;
Eph. 2:16;
Col. 1:20

1. *How did Paul view the cross?*
2. *Spend some time contemplating the cross today.*

Prayer

O Father, I am so thankful for the cross. It is the one place in a dark and mysterious universe where light breaks through. Help me interpret the darkness by the light, not the light by the darkness.
For Jesus' sake. Amen.

"The Stamp of Eternity"

"'Whom shall I send? And who will go for us?' . . . I said, 'Here am I. Send me!'" (v. 8)
For reading & meditation—Isaiah 6:1–13

*A*nother issue we have to consider as we pursue the question of how we can go deeper with God is that of *worship*. The *Shorter Westminster Catechism* asks the question "What is the chief end of man?" and answers it: "The chief end of man is to glorify God and enjoy Him forever."

A. W. Tozer put it like this: "We're here to be worshippers first and workers second. We take a convert and immediately make a worker out of him. God never meant it to be so. God meant that a convert should learn to be a worshipper and after that learn to be a worker. The work done by a worshipper will have eternity in it." Powerful words. Those who wish to go deeper with God will give themselves more to the worship of God than they do to the work of God. Indeed, one evidence that we are not moving on in our relationship with the Lord is when we become more preoccupied about laboring for God than adoring God.

We need have no concern that we give ourselves too much to worship and thus neglect our work for God because no one can worship God without the necessity of service and action being impressed upon him or her. A vision of God such as Isaiah saw in the Temple leads inevitably to the call to serve. "Who will go for us?" is the cry of the Trinity. The worshiper gladly exclaims: "Here am I, send me." And the work done by a worshiper will have, as Tozer says so effectively, the stamp of eternity upon it.

FURTHER STUDY

Ps. 95:6;
John 4:1–26;
1 Chron. 16:29

1. What does the psalmist encourage us to do?
2. How are we to worship?

Prayer

O God, help me I pray to be a worshipper first and a worker second. Let all I do for You flow out of my worship of You so that my service will be sealed with Your stamp of approval and thus have the mark of eternity upon it. In Jesus' Name. Amen.

358

"The One Thing Needed"

"... but only one thing is needed." (v. 42)

For reading & meditation—Luke 10:38–42

We said yesterday that God wants us to be worshipers first and workers second. Martha, bustling about in her kitchen, complains because her sister Mary is sitting at the feet of Jesus, listening rather than helping to get things done. Our Lord with characteristic insight draws a line between the urgent and the important when He says: "There is really only one thing worth being concerned about. Mary has discovered it—and I won't take it away from her" (v. 42, TLB). Martha's concern to be hospitable was not being ignored by Jesus; He was simply making the point that when it comes to priorities worship comes first, work second. Note too that the Great Commission was given to worshiping people. Matthew writes: "When they saw [Jesus], they worshiped him ... Then Jesus ... said, '... go and make disciples of all nations ...'" (Matt. 28:17–19).

How true it is that unless we are involved with Jesus Christ in a loving and adoring relationship, we have nothing of eternal value to offer to a needy world. We must come to a definite conclusion about this before moving any further—our worship of God must take priority over our work for God. When this happens then we will get the right measure of the work we are to do for Him. It is not the Lord who loads us with tasks that bend and break us. These come from our compulsions rather than from Christ. In the atmosphere of worship we see more clearly what we should do, and our work becomes a daily joy instead of a daily grind.

FURTHER STUDY

Exod. 20:1–21;
Pss. 29:2; 99:5

1. What importance does the Lord place on worship?
2. What is the admonition of the psalmist?

Prayer

Gracious and loving heavenly Father, help me perceive that "only one thing is needed" for life's priorities to fall into place—the worship of You. Seeing You clearly means I see everything else clearly. Thank You, my Father. Amen.

Day 340

Worship — Expected of All

"Exalt the LORD our God and worship at his footstool; he is holy." (v. 5)
For reading & meditation—Psalm 99:1–9

When you can stop in the midst of life's most pressing problems and give yourself eagerly to worshiping God, then you are moving along the road to knowing God more intimately. Sometimes when I have had the occasion to talk face to face with people who were going through difficult circumstances I have asked them: "How does all this affect your ability to worship God?" Most have responded something like this: "I find it very difficult to give my heart in worship as I struggle with these problems." And some have said: "I find it utterly impossible."

Are we justified in refusing to worship God because life has dealt us some hard blows? Those who are at a standstill spiritually might react like this: "Yes, how can God expect me to worship Him when He has allowed these troubles to weigh me down?" Those moving slowly along the road of discipleship might say: "I know I should worship Him, but my preoccupation with my problems makes it almost impossible to do so." The spiritually mature will affirm: "Nothing is more important than the worship of the One who holds my life in His hands. Because He is God then I know that no matter how things might look to the contrary, all will be well. Thus my heart delights to worship Him."

Christian counseling ought to be seen (though in some parts of the church it isn't) as restoring people to worship. This may be hard for some to accept, but it is true nevertheless—*nothing* that ever happens to us can justify a Christian's refusal to worship God.

FURTHER STUDY

Pss. 30:1–12; 96:1–13;
Luke 19:37–40

1. Why does the psalmist say we can exalt the Lord in the midst of trouble?
2. Why did Jesus rebuke the Pharisees?

Prayer

O Father, once again Your truth has gone unerringly to my problem—the problem of my self-centeredness. Far too often I am too concerned with what is happening to me to give attention to You. Forgive me and make me whole. In Jesus' Name. Amen.

A Desire to Worship

"... worship the LORD in the splendor of his holiness." (v. 2)

For reading & meditation—Psalm 29:1–11

The thought I ended with yesterday must have cut like a sharp knife into many souls. I said: "... nothing that ever happens to us can justify a Christian's refusal to worship God." You may ask me: "Do you find it possible to turn your heart in worship toward God when things go terribly wrong in your life?" My answer is this: "I find it difficult, but not impossible." It is easier now to turn to God in worship when things in my life are upside down than it was, say, ten years ago. It is something that comes more readily with practice.

When my wife died some years ago, I found it exceedingly difficult to put together words that would constitute any kind of worshipful prayer as I knelt before the Almighty. Yet I found that though words seemed to freeze on my lips, my heart still *wanted* to worship Him. When I sensed *that*, I knew that I had gone deeper with God than I realized. The pain of bereavement had a numbing effect on me (that in itself was not a negative thing), but within my soul I recognized a desire to worship.

The whole matter comes back to what I was saying earlier concerning the character of God. If we have doubts about His character, then we will not want to worship Him. We are made in such a way that we cannot give ourselves to anyone we doubt. Thus if we say to ourselves in the midst of calamity "God is not good in letting this happen to me," then worship will be almost impossible.

FURTHER STUDY

*Pss. 109:1–31;
136:1–26*

1. What were some of the psalmist's difficult experiences?
2. What was his response and conviction?

Prayer

O Father, how I long to reach the place where, no matter what happens to me, my heart responds in praise and adoration of You. I know that my longing is Your longing too. Help me dear Father.
In Jesus' Name. Amen.

Day 342

A Good and Forgiving God

"... let us draw near to God with a sincere heart in full assurance of faith ..." (v. 22)

For reading & meditation—Hebrews 10:19-31

*T*oday we try to understand the concept that lies behind the word *worship*. The essential meaning of the word, both in Old and New Testaments, is that of reverential service. Our present-day English word has evolved from the Anglo-Saxon *weorthscipe*, which means to give worth to something. Worship, as preachers and Bible teachers are at pains to point out, means *worth-ship*—to give worth to something or someone.

This thought is reflected everywhere in the Scriptures. We see it clearly in the passage before us today. True worship of God takes place when a person draws near to God with "a sincere heart in full assurance of faith," believing, indeed *knowing*, that He is there, and that He is a good and forgiving God, and ascribing to Him the honor and worth that is due His Name. Archbishop William Temple, the great Anglican theologian, wrote some words concerning worship which I consider to be among the most beautiful I have ever read: "Worship is the submission of all our nature to God. It is the quickening of conscience by His holiness, the nourishment of mind with His truth, the purifying of imagination by His beauty, the opening of the heart to love, the surrender of will to His purpose—and all this is gathered up in adoration to the most selfless emotion of which our nature is capable, and therefore the chief remedy for that self-centeredness which is the original sin and the source of all actual sin."

In worshiping God we are not demeaned but developed. We were *made* for worship. In glorifying God, we complete ourselves.

FURTHER STUDY

Pss. 73:1-28; 145:1-21

1. What did the psalmist say was good for him?
2. What reasons did the psalmist give for worshiping God?

⟶ Prayer ⟵

O Father, help me draw near to You now in the way that Your Word says I should—"with a sincere heart in full assurance of faith." I am sincere and I have faith, but I long too that they may be deepened and enlarged. Help me, my Father. In Jesus' Name. Amen.

362

Why God Requires Worship

"If I were hungry I would not tell you, for the world is mine, and all that is in it." (v. 12)

For reading & meditation—Psalm 50:1–23

*D*uring the early days of my Christian experience, I queried why God put so many texts in the Bible that command us to worship Him. It seemed to me that many of these commands bordered on egotism and self-centeredness. We all despise those people who clamor for our attention or commendation, and a picture of a God who needed constant ego strokes threatened to impress itself on my mind. It happened most when I read the Psalms. "Praise Me, worship Me," the Almighty seemed to be saying everywhere.

Then I read C. S. Lewis's *Reflections on the Psalms* and the whole matter dropped into the right perspective. This is what he said: "The miserable idea that God should in any sense need or crave for our worship like a vain woman wanting compliments or a vain author presenting his new books to people who had never met or heard of him is implicitly answered by the words: 'If I be hungry I will not tell *thee*' (Ps. 50:12). Even if such an absurd Deity could be conceived He would hardly come to us, the lowest of rational creatures, to gratify His appetite. I don't want my dog to bark at my books."

He went on to point out that in commanding us to worship Him the Almighty is demonstrating far more interest in us than in Himself. Our worship of Him completes us. We perfect our personalities to the degree that we give ourselves to God in worship. In eternity we shall experience full joy because we shall be able to worship Him fully. Meanwhile we are tuning our instruments.

FURTHER STUDY

1 Chron. 16:8–36;
Rev. 4:8–11; 5:11–13

1. What is the anthem of heaven?
2. Why not echo the anthem yourself today?

Prayer

O God, I want to worship You in the way You deserve to be worshipped. Help me give You my worship not because I am completed by it but because You are so worthy of it.
I worship You, Father, with all my heart. Amen.

Day 344

Worship Is Central

"Let us go to his dwelling place; let us worship at his footstool . . ." (v. 7)
For reading & meditation—Psalm 132:1–18

*W*e spend one more day meditating on the suggestion that if we are to go deeper with God, then we must understand both the importance and meaning of worship. Dr. Dick Averby, professor of the Old Testament at Dallas Seminary, claims that the antidote to every human problem is worship. I am sure he is thinking of personality problems, not physical problems, and allowing for this caveat, I would agree with him. Dr. Larry Crabb, professor of counseling in Colorado Christian University, says something similar: "Worship means, in the middle of life as it is experienced, that you find some way to be caught up in God's character and purpose so that His will becomes central."

Mature Christians are people who think of themselves first and foremost as worshipers. They will see their other roles in life—as fathers, mothers, factory workers, business people, farmers, doctors, evangelists, pastors, and so on—as secondary.

Some worship the servants of God more than they worship God Himself. A story is told of an occasion when Christmas Evans, the great Welsh preacher of a past century, was due to preach. Prior to the service the church was packed with people eager to hear the great orator. As the service was about to begin, it was announced that Christmas Evans was unable to keep the engagement and a lesser-known preacher would take his place. People began to show signs of leaving until the moderator said: "All those who have come to worship Christmas Evans may leave. All those who have come to worship God may stay." No one left.

**FURTHER
STUDY**

*1 Cor. 1:1–17;
Acts 3:11–16; 14:11–15*

1. What was a problem in
the early church?
2. How did Peter and
John deal with
this problem?

Prayer

My Father and my God, may this emphasis on worship remain undiminished as I turn to other things. I see it is so central. Help me not only to remember it but to apply it. In Jesus' Name. Amen.

364

Spiritual Passion

Day 345

"O God, you are my God, earnestly I seek you; my soul thirsts for you,
my body longs for you . . ." (v. 1)

For reading & meditation—Psalm 63:1–11

A further issue we must face if we are to go deeper with God is the need to understand the importance of *pursuing Him with passion*. Here I am talking about something much greater than spending time with Him, but allowing the deep thirsts and longings for God which the Almighty has built into our souls to find their freest and fullest expression.

One of the saddest things to come across in the Christian church is the attitude that says: "I have found God so there is no longer any need to pursue Him." To have found God and yet be filled with an immense desire to pursue Him is one of the great paradoxes of the Christian life. Such an idea is scorned by the easily satisfied religionist who seeks for nothing more than a guarantee of heaven. The paradox of which I am now talking is expressed most powerfully by St. Bernard of Clairvaux:

> We taste Thee, O Thou living Bread,
> And long to feast upon Thee still;
> We drink of Thee, the Fountainhead,
> And thirst our souls from Thee to fill.

One of the blights of modern-day Christianity is that so many of Christ's followers are too easily satisfied. They drink from the Fountainhead, and seem to be so satisfied with what they have received that they have no desire to drink more. They do not understand the paradox that to drink the water that Christ gives is to be satisfied, but satisfied with an unsatisfied satisfaction.

FURTHER STUDY

Isa. 55:1–9;
Pss. 42:1–2; 38:9; 73:25

1. *How did Isaiah express his longing for the Lord?*
2. *What conclusion did the psalmist come to?*

Prayer

Father, can it be that in spiritual things I am too easily satisfied? That I am content with what I have and do not seek for more? Help me search my heart as I ponder this issue day by day.
In our Savior's Name I pray. Amen.

365

"The Soul's Paradox"

"But seek first his kingdom and his righteousness . . ." (v. 33)
For reading & meditation—Matthew 6:25-34

I am dealing with issues that can easily be misunderstood. They are so crucial, however, that failure to understand them can hinder us in our quest to go deeper with God. Yesterday we ended with a paradoxical thought. Christ most certainly quenches our soul's great thirst, but in quenching it He arouses within us the thirst for more. Many in today's church do not understand this paradox and as a consequence are spiritually poor. "To have found God and still to pursue Him," said St. Bernard of Clairvaux, "is the soul's paradox of love."

As I was thinking about this I checked my dictionary to remind myself of the meaning of the word *paradox*. This is what I read: "Paradox: a seemingly absurd though perhaps actually well-founded statement." To say that God satisfies but leaves us thirsting for more seems absurd, but I suggest it is nevertheless "a well-founded statement." Although it seems contradictory, the more one ponders it the more one comes to see it is true.

Some types of people don't like to struggle with paradoxes; they prefer what they describe as "simple logic." When I was in Malaysia a man said to me: "I am grateful I've found Christ, but it seems logical now to pursue my career with all the energy I possess and leave the knowledge of God until I get to heaven." I felt a chill descend on my spirit as I heard this. It is not wrong to pursue one's career or other interests, but as the verse before us today makes clear—not at the expense of pursuing God.

FURTHER STUDY

Luke 6:17–21;
Pss. 143:6; 84:1–2

1. What is promised to those who hunger?
2. How did the psalmist describe his thirst?

Prayer

Gracious and loving heavenly Father, I have tasted deeply of You but yet my soul longs for more. Does this mean I am really growing? It must be so. Lead me on, my Father. I ask for more and more and more. Amen.

How Wonderful...

"Then Moses said, 'Now show me your glory.'" (v. 18)

For reading & meditation—Exodus 33:12–23

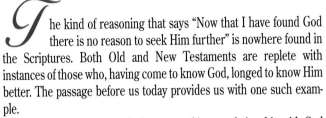

The kind of reasoning that says "Now that I have found God there is no reason to seek Him further" is nowhere found in the Scriptures. Both Old and New Testaments are replete with instances of those who, having come to know God, longed to know Him better. The passage before us today provides us with one such example.

Moses uses the fact that he has entered into a relationship with God as an argument for knowing Him more deeply. The Living Bible puts it: "You say you are my friend, and that I have found favor before you; please, if this is really so, guide me clearly along the way you want me to travel so that I will understand you and walk acceptably before you" (vv. 12–13). That is the kind of daring and powerful praying that only someone who longs after God with great passion will undertake. Later he makes the bold request which forms the words of our text for today: "Now show me your glory." Clearly the Almighty was pleased with Moses' request for He invites him to come up the Mount the very next day where He reveals His glory to him.

How wonderful it would be today if we were gripped by such an overwhelming desire to know God better, to taste more of Him, to feel Him at work more powerfully in our souls, to see Him as Moses did with our inner eyes, that we turn from this moment and find some quiet spot where we too will pray: "O God, show me Your glory."

FURTHER STUDY

Phil. 3:1–11;
Hos. 6:3;
Col. 1:10

1. What was Paul's great desire?
2. To what lengths was he prepared to go?

Prayer

O Father, I have tasted of Your goodness and grace, and although I am satisfied I am thirsty to know more. Show me Your glory, and begin in me this day a deeper work of love than ever before. In Christ's Name. Amen.

Only an Appetizer

"My heart says of you, 'Seek his face!' Your face, LORD, I will seek." (v. 8)
For reading & meditation—Psalm 27:1–14

One of the things that characterizes the saints and seers of Scripture is the heat of their desire for God. King David is another example. Though he was guilty of two of the vilest of sins—murder and adultery—yet it is clear that he yearned after God with intense spiritual passion. His psalms ring with the cry of the seeker and the glad shout of the finder. Even then he is eager to know more.

The same longing can be seen in the life of the apostle Paul—one of the most outstanding Christians in history. Has anyone known God more intimately than did the great apostle? Yet this is his plea in the letter he wrote to the Philippians: "That I may know him, and the power of his resurrection" (Phil. 3:10, KJV). But he did know Him. Ah yes, but his plea is that he might know Him *more*.

"Today we have most of our seeking done for us by devotional writers," said a critic of daily devotional aids in a recent magazine article. "They set out what we should think about in our quiet times." In part I feel he is right. I tell you, if you are satisfied with this devotional aid and do not go beyond it to seek God for yourself then you are spiritually impoverished and too easily satisfied. It is meant to be a spiritual primer, not a satisfier; an appetizer, not the feast. The longings God has put within your soul for Himself can be met only by Himself.

FURTHER STUDY

*John 6:25–58;
Isa. 55:2;
1 Cor. 10:3–4*

1. What did Jesus declare?
2. Why did the Jews stumble over it?

Prayer

O God, my soul is too big to be satisfied with the writings of a mere man. I can be inspired by human words but I can be fed only by Your words. May I continually seek You. Amen.

There's More!

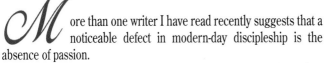

"... my soul thirsts for you like a parched land." (v. 6)

For reading & meditation—Psalm 143:1–12

*M*ore than one writer I have read recently suggests that a noticeable defect in modern-day discipleship is the absence of passion.

The devotional writer A. W. Tozer pointed out that the best thermometer for measuring the health of the church is its current songs and literature. He claimed that comparison of modern songs and writings with those of, say, even fifty years ago reveals a marked difference in the mood of the church. In times past, people's thoughts were preoccupied with knowing God more deeply. Nowadays (generally speaking) the focus is on what we have already found in God. I cast my mind back and think of the songs I sang as a youth, which had lines like these: "His track I see and I'll pursue," or "My soul follows on hard after Thee." Are these same sentiments to be found in contemporary songs? Not to the same degree, it seems. We must, of course, rejoice in what we have found in God, but we must not lose sight of the fact that there's more.

It is the same with contemporary Christian literature. So much of today's writing is experience-oriented, and can lead to our seeking God not for who He is but for what we can get out of Him. To know God and not to yearn to know Him more is a sign of ill health rather than, as some might see it, a sign of spiritual satisfaction. Never be ashamed of your lack of satisfaction. To know God, really know Him, is to be made more thirsty still.

FURTHER STUDY

Eph. 3:14–21;
1 Chron. 28:9;
Ps. 100:3

1. What does Paul pray the Ephesians will come to know more?
2. What was David's admonition to Solomon?

Prayer

Father, help me grasp this paradox that the more I am satisfied the more my soul yearns for greater things. Take me deeper into You, dear Father. In and through the Name of Your precious Son Jesus I ask it. Amen.

Day

350

The Panting Heart

"As the deer pants for streams of water, so my soul pants for you, O God." (v. 1)

For reading & meditation—Psalm 42:1–11

*I*t is time now to ask ourselves: Do we yearn after God? *Pant* after Him? The psalmist paints a picture in the passage before us today of a deer panting for water. Perhaps he had just seen such an animal being chased by a predator and, having escaped, desperately looking for water to quench its thirst. The Hebrew word for *pant* literally means a desire so intense that it becomes audible. Nothing mattered more to the psalmist than the pursuit of God.

Panting, of course, presupposes a thirst. Are we thirsty for God to such a degree that we long after Him in the same way that a thirsty deer pants for water? The thirst for God is there in all of us, but the problem is that we do not sense that thirst. Prior to our conversion we either denied or suppressed it, or attempted to satisfy it in ways apart from God. At conversion we give up (to some degree at least) such things as denial, suppression and attempting to satisfy the ache in our soul through ways other than God, and we find ourselves getting more and more in touch with the desire for God which the Almighty has placed within us. This becomes evident when we realize that we have a longing to read His Word and talk to Him in prayer.

Those who go deeper with God are those who know how to get in touch with the thirst which God has placed in the soul and allow it its full expression.

FURTHER STUDY

Pss. 63:1–11; 105:4; 119:20; 119:131

1. How did David seek God?
2. How does the psalmist describe his inner passion?

⸰⟶⟩══⟩ *Prayer* ⟨══⟨⟵⸰

O Father, if You have placed such a deep thirst in my soul, why do I not feel more thirsty for You? Why do I not pant after You as did the psalmist? Take me through this issue to greater clarity and understanding. In Jesus' Name. Amen.

Renouncing Independence

"My people have . . . forsaken me, the spring of living water, and have dug their
own cisterns . . ." (v. 13)

For reading & meditation—Jeremiah 2:1-14

*W*hat must we do to get in touch with the deep longing for
the Lord which our Creator has put at the core of our
beings?

The major reason is the stubborn commitment to independence
which, due to the Fall, characterizes every one of us. We like to feel we
are in control of the way our soul's thirst can be slaked. In the passage
before us today we see Israel being charged with two evils—forsaking
the spring of living water and digging their own cisterns for holding
water. Why would Israel do such nonsensical things—turning away
from a fresh spring and digging cisterns, *broken* cisterns that could not
hold water? Because they liked the feeling they got from seeking *inde-
pendently* to find water for their souls.

The opposite of independence is dependence. And that is the main
prerequisite for experiencing the great thirst that God has put within
us. But giving up our independence and trusting God to come through
for us is not easy. None of us likes giving up control. The major reason
for ISD (Inhibited Sexual Desire), a common problem among women
in marriage, is a fear of being vulnerable, of appearing to be out of control. Helplessness, vulnerability, dependence, trust are all words the
carnal nature abhors. Take it from me, it is our independence that prevents us from feeling what God has put deep within us. When we can
learn to give up our independence and enter a life of trust, then the passion for God will not just be experienced in our soul, but will explode
in it.

FURTHER STUDY

*Pss. 36:1–9; 46:4;
John 4:10; 7:37–38*

1. Where can we
   drink from?
2. Where can we find
   its source?

Prayer

O Father, I am aware that though You have put a thirst for Yourself within me, sin is also at work in my soul.
Break down this awful commitment to independence that is within me, and make me a more spiritually
dependent person. In Jesus' Name I pray. Amen.

Christian Forgiveness

"But if you do not forgive men their sins, your Father will not forgive your sins." (v. 15)

For reading & meditation—Matthew 6:5–18

*A*nother issue that must be grasped if we are to have a deeper relationship with God is *Christian forgiveness*. In the same way that we have been forgiven, we are told in Scripture, we must forgive others also. Believe me, no one can have a close relationship with God if he or she bears resentment or ill-will toward another.

The verse before us today is among the most challenging to be found anywhere in the Bible. To ignore it is to put ourselves in spiritual peril. I believe with all my heart that if every Christian grasped the truth of this verse and applied it day by day in their lives, it would bring about a worldwide spiritual revival. One of the characteristic effects of every spiritual revival that has ever taken place in the history of the church is that longstanding bitterness and resentment is rooted out.

If we refuse to forgive others, we break down the bridge over which we must pass to God—the bridge of forgiveness. If we refuse to offer forgiveness to others, then we block the forgiveness of God to us. It is not that God does not want to forgive us but that He can't get it across into our hearts because the bridge is broken at our end. Just think of it—unforgiveness ties the hands of the Almighty and makes it impossible for even the omnipotent God to get through to us. Those who keep saying "I can't forgive" should take this verse to heart. What they really mean is "I won't forgive." If you won't forgive, you can't be forgiven.

FURTHER STUDY

Eph. 4:17–32;
Heb. 12:15;
James 3:14

1. What did Paul exhort the Ephesians to do about bitterness?
2. What is the result of bitterness?

Prayer

O great and forgiving God, forgive me for my refusal to forgive others. As I have been forgiven, so I release now all others who have hurt me or injured me from their indebtedness. In Jesus' Name I pray. Amen.

The Highest Morality

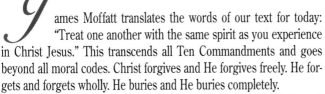

"Your attitude should be the same as that of Christ Jesus." (v. 5)

For reading & meditation—Philippians 2:1-11

*J*ames Moffatt translates the words of our text for today: "Treat one another with the same spirit as you experience in Christ Jesus." This transcends all Ten Commandments and goes beyond all moral codes. Christ forgives and He forgives freely. He forgets and forgets wholly. He buries and He buries completely.

Sometimes I have heard people say: "I can forgive but I can't forget." Usually I respond like this: "You don't really mean that, do you? See how it sounds as you say the Lord's Prayer with that attitude: 'Father, forgive me as I forgive others. I forgive people but I won't forget what they did to me, so when I do something wrong bring up the whole matter again.'" God forgives—and forgets. So must we. Then sometimes, too, I have heard people say: "I'll forgive but I'll have nothing more to do with them." Now put that in the Lord's Prayer and listen to the result: "Father, forgive me as I forgive others. I forgive people but I'll have nothing more to do with them. Now forgive me in the same way; forgive me but have nothing more to do with me. I'll be able to get along without You." You see the absurdity, don't you?

So there is absolutely no justification for a Christian saying "I can't forgive," "I'll forgive but I can't forget," or "I'll forgive but I won't have anything more to do with the person." Bearing in mind what our Lord has taught us about forgiveness, those statements ought never to cross our lips. We are most like God when we forgive.

FURTHER STUDY

Matt. 18:21–35;
Luke 23:26–34;
Col. 3:13

1. What is Jesus teaching in this parable?
2. How did He demonstrate forgiveness?

 *Prayer*

O God, I am so grateful that You don't treat me the way I often treat others. I commit myself to being as forgiving of others as You are of me. I am willing; now grant me Your power. In Christ's Name I ask it. Amen.

"Look to Your Orders"

"... if you ... remember that your brother has something against you ... go
and be reconciled ..." (vv. 23–24)

For reading & meditation—Matthew 5:21–26

For me, forgiveness has never been easy. Though I think I have overcome the difficulty now, I remember going to my pastor as a young man and confessing my strong dislike of someone in the church who had upset me. Somewhat to my surprise he said: "You are a Christian. Look to your orders." "And what are my orders?" I asked. He then read to me from Matthew 5 the passage for our meditation today. Then he said: "Before you next come and worship God, go to the person concerned and put things right." I was very reluctant to follow the "orders" but I did, and the feeling of release and freedom that came into my soul is something I have never forgotten.

But what if we go to someone and attempt to settle an issue and they don't respond? That is their responsibility. You must obey orders and leave the consequences to God. A Christian is under orders not to go halfway, or three quarters of the way to settling disputes, but all the way. Even if the other person does not respond (and that will be a cause for sadness), you have cleared your own soul. Continue to pray for the other person that he or she might be able at some point in the future to see the importance of being reconciled to you.

We must never forget that the Christian faith teaches us that whatever shuts out our brothers and sisters shuts out our Father—automatically. Religious observances are useless if we make no attempt to be reconciled to an estranged brother or sister.

FURTHER STUDY

*Mark 11:20–25;
Luke 11:4; 17:3–5*

*1. Why is forgiving others
so important?
2. How did the disciples
respond to the challenge
of forgiveness?*

Prayer

Father, I know Your grace is available to give me the strength to do anything You command. Help me avail myself of that grace if, as I look to my orders, I find I have to be reconciled to someone.
In Jesus' Name. Amen.

Forgiven . . . So Much

"This is how my heavenly Father will treat each of you unless you forgive your brother from your heart." (v. 35)

For reading & meditation—Matthew 18:15–35

Forgiveness does not come easily or naturally to us. In the film *The Discreet Charm of the Bourgeoise* by Luis Bunuel, one of the characters is a bishop who had been orphaned as a young child when both of his parents were poisoned. The murderer had never been caught. Many years later the bishop was called to the deathbed of a gamekeeper to hear his confession. The bishop listened without showing any emotion as the gamekeeper told him that he was the man who had poisoned his parents. The bishop gave him absolution, then walked over to the corner of the room, picked up the gamekeeper's loaded shotgun, and shot the dying man full in the face with both barrels.

This is an extreme example, but over the years I have met Christians who, when I told them that story, have confessed that if they found themselves in similar circumstances they would probably do the same thing. Some find forgiveness the most difficult issue in the Christian life. We advance some surprising arguments to support our *unwillingness* to forgive. A believer once said to me: "Forgiveness is what God is good at. I'm human. He can't expect me to be as good at it as He is." Like Shylock in *The Merchant of Venice*, we staunchly reserve our right to a pound of flesh and a lifetime of resentment.

The point of today's parable is quite clear: we have been forgiven so much more by God than we will ever be expected to forgive in another. If we refuse to do that, we put our own forgiveness in jeopardy.

FURTHER STUDY

Luke 7:36–50; Ps. 103:3

1. Why did Jesus rebuke Simon?
2. What had he lost sight of?

Prayer

O God, help me never to get over the wonder of Your forgiveness of me. You forgave me not grudgingly but graciously. May I realize how rich I am in forgiveness that I dispense it prodigally to others. In Christ's Name. Amen.

Doing Your Duty

"... you ... should say, 'We are unworthy servants; we have only done our duty.'" (v. 10)

For reading & meditation—Luke 17:1-10

O ur Lord obviously went over and over the point of forgiveness with His disciples during His three-year ministry with them. Here He tells them if someone "sins against you seven times in a day, and seven times comes back to you and says, 'I repent,' forgive him" (v. 4).

Jay Adams, an American Bible teacher, points out the relationship of this to the dialogue that follows. The emphasis of our Lord on forgiving a person seven times in one day demanded what the disciples considered to be an almost impossible level of faith. Imagine trying to forgive someone seven times in one day, possibly for wronging you in the same way each time. A person who apologizes to you seven times in the same day is probably more difficult to forgive than one who does not apologize at all because he appears to be making a mockery of confession, perhaps even goading you with it.

The disciples responded to this aspect of Jesus' teaching with a feeling of absolute helplessness and exclaimed: "Increase our faith!" (v. 5). They thought if they had more faith they could obey, but Jesus goes on to point out (says Jay Adams) that their problem was not lack of faith (because even faith as small as a mustard seed can remove mountains) but lack of obedience. The parable that follows (vv. 7–8) seems harsh but the point is this—the problem is not a shortage of faith but a shortage of obedience. The disciples needed to put into action the faith they already had. Christian forgiveness is our duty. A thankless one sometimes, but a duty nevertheless.

FURTHER STUDY

1 John 1:1–9;
Matt. 7:24;
John 14:23

1. Who is like a
wise man?
2. What does obedience
demonstrate?

Prayer

Father, I see that forgiveness, like the work of the servant in the parable, may be a thankless task, but it is my duty nevertheless. Help me, therefore, to get on with it and forgive others as I have been forgiven. In Christ's Name. Amen.

Choose to Forgive

"He who covers over an offense promotes love . . ." (v. 9)

For reading & meditation—Proverbs 17:1-9

Jesus gives us stern and uncompromising warnings about forgiveness. But if forgiveness is so important and yet so difficult, how do we go about it? We must do several things.

First, we must not try to minimize or dismiss the offense as if it never happened. If it hurts, then we must face it and feel it. A common misconception that keeps people from forgiving is that they think in order to forgive they must come to the place where they look upon the things done to them as being really not that bad. That is excusing, not forgiving. C. S. Lewis says: "Real forgiveness means looking steadily at the sin, the sin that is left over without any excuse after all allowances have been made, and seeing it in all its horror, dirt, meanness and malice, and nevertheless being wholly reconciled to the man who has done it. That, and only that, is forgiveness."

Second, we must see that forgiveness is not an emotional thing (though it can affect the emotions), but a matter of the will. It is making the decision that the wrong done against you will not count or cause a separation. In making that decision, remember you have all the resources of God available to you. This applies not just to minor matters like snubs, but major matters like divorce.

The task of forgiving must be more than a match for the magnitude of the pain involved. Our text today makes clear that a choice is involved. No matter how we are wronged, we can choose out of a desire for love to forgive.

FURTHER STUDY

Mic. 6:1–8; 7:18
Isa. 43:25

1. What does God delight to do?
2. What are we to love?

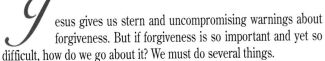

Prayer

Lord Jesus Christ, You looked into the eyes of those who hammered You to a cross and cried: "Father, forgive them." Help me do the same when I am confronted with lesser injury or hurt.
For Your own dear Name's sake. Amen.

Be Like Your Father

"Love your enemies . . . that you may be sons of your Father in heaven." (vv. 44–45)

For reading & meditation—Matthew 5:38–48

We spend one more day on the subject of forgiveness. Forgiveness decides to relinquish any attempts at overt or covert retaliation. No reminders of the offense, no cold shoulder, no angry pouting, no cooled affection, no withheld favors, no elimination of routine kindness, no stubborn uncooperativeness, no superior smiles, no clipped and abrupt conversation, no veiled or open threats to end the relationship, and no humiliation in front of others. The relief and freedom of forgiving can take a great weight off our souls. An unforgiving heart holds resentment, and so carries with it resentment's poisonous effects. Forgiving a friend, a neighbor or one's spouse can produce a gigantic breakthrough in one's relationship with God. And a constant attitude of forgiveness helps maintain our relationship with Him.

A final point we must make about forgiveness is this: forgiveness ends conflict but it is nevertheless only a beginning. It leaves us with a bare foundation on which we must construct a new building. We must not say after forgiving: "Now I am free to end the relationship and forget the person concerned." We should be open to whether or not God wants the relationship to continue. Maintaining some relationships may be impossible or inappropriate, but that is a matter to pray over before coming to a conclusion. In making forgiveness a beginning we imitate God who does not stop at forgiveness but takes us into His family and builds a relationship with us.

And always remember—God provides the Holy Spirit's power which enables us to do whatever He commands. We sin when we do not avail ourselves of that power.

FURTHER STUDY

Matt. 5:1–7;
Luke 6:36;
Titus 3:5;
James 2:13

1. What happens when we show mercy?
2. What did Jesus exhort His listeners?

Prayer

Father, thank You for what You are teaching me about forgiveness. Now for the practice. Help me avail myself of Your Holy Spirit's resources not only to forgive but for every other aspect of my Christian life too. In Christ's Name I ask it. Amen.

Last, but Not Least

"To obey is better than sacrifice, and to heed is better than the fat of rams." (v. 22)

For reading & meditation—1 Samuel 15:10-23

We come now to the last matter we must make a priority if we are to go deeper with God—the necessity of *obedience*. The moment we stop obeying God, that is the moment we stop moving on with Him. We move along the road to a deeper experience of God in relation (as we have seen) to many things, and obedience, though listed last, is certainly not the least in importance. It stands shoulder to shoulder with the other priorities and is equal in significance to every one of them.

In the passage before us today we see Samuel going to the very heart of the issue with which King Saul struggled—desire to go his own way instead of being willing to take God's way. Saul's great sin was that he did not take God seriously. He disobeyed the divine command to destroy all the Amalekites and saved Agag, their king, from the sword. Most probably he said to himself: "As long as I obey most of God's commands, then He will overlook the one I don't obey." Dangerous stuff! When we start such a process of rationalization, we do not know where it will end. For Saul it ended in destruction. No matter how many sacrifices he offered, they could never atone for his willful disobedience. When God tells us to obey, we must heed that word; for no amount of attendance at church services, prayer meetings, or Bible reading can compensate for the sin of willful, continued disobedience.

FURTHER STUDY

Josh. 1:1–8; 11:15; 24:31

1. What did God promise to Joshua as a result of obedience?
2. What epitaph is recorded of Joshua?

Prayer

O God, drive this truth deep into my spirit: that I live dangerously whenever I rationalize any of Your commands. Help me not to think in terms of how I can measure up to exceptions, but in terms of keeping to Your rules. In Jesus' Name. Amen.

Futile Striving

"... he did not know that the LORD had left him." (v. 20)
For reading & meditation—Judges 16:1–22

Which of you reading these lines has not gone through times when you struggled to obey some command that God had given you? Maybe you couldn't see the reason for it. Yet as you thought about the matter, you decided to obey anyhow, simply because God asked it of you. There is, however, a big difference between the struggles that are fairly soon overcome and continued disobedience. Christians who continue to willfully violate the clear commands of God given in Scripture will never, no matter how much they throw themselves into Christian activity, experience the joy of fellowship with God.

A few Christian leaders who became involved in extramarital affairs have claimed: "God doesn't seem to mind as much about this as His people might if they knew, as He appears to bless my preaching more than ever." They were fooling themselves. They were like Samson who, as we see from today's passage, thought to himself: "Everything is fine. I'll go out and shake myself." But he did not know, the Scripture tells us, "that the LORD had left him." The reason why such preachers appear to be blessed is because unconsciously they put more of themselves into their messages in an effort to compensate for the feelings of guilt deep inside them. The tragedy is that so many can be fooled by this.

Sadly, we lack the same sensitivity to the Spirit that was present in the early church, when such things would have been quickly spotted and exposed. Preachers can shake, shout, shriek, and perspire as they preach, but it is all meaningless if there is no obedience.

FURTHER STUDY

Deut. 5:1–29;
1 Kings 3:14;
1 Sam. 12:15;
James 1:25;
Eph. 5:6

1. What was God's desire for His people?
2. What is the result of disobedience?

Prayer

Father, save me from focusing on the disobedience of others and thus overlooking the faults of my own heart. Help me understand what Saul seemed to misunderstand—that without obedience there is no meaning. In Christ's Name I pray. Amen.

Not on Approval

"The law of the LORD is perfect, reviving the soul." (v. 7)
For reading & meditation—Psalm 19:1–14

We live in an age which is increasingly contemptuous of laws and moral prohibitions. Not only the moral teaching of the Sermon on the Mount but the Ten Commandments also are mocked with impunity by millions of people. Sadly, with some exceptions, there seems to be little remorse at what is happening. We Christians must be careful that this attitude does not rub off on us too. We must resist the spirit of the age and refrain from bending the rules, or rationalizing moral or ethical issues, because it suits us to do so.

A curious thing happened in a London court some time ago. A man was summoned before the magistrates for not having a television license. He claimed the TV set was not his and that he had received it from a dealer only "on approval." Until he decided to buy it, he said, he did not feel under an obligation to take out a license. He argued that because of that he was not breaking the law. The magistrate decided to fine him a certain sum and stated: "The law knows nothing about 'approval.' The law is to be obeyed. Pay the fine!"

In some minds today, it would seem, the law is binding upon you only if you approve of it. The reasoning appears to be this: if the law is not to your taste, it ceases to have authority over you. Christians should never hold such a view. God did not give us His commands for our approval. He gave them to us to be obeyed.

FURTHER STUDY

John 14:1–31; 15:10; Rom. 5:19

1. What was Jesus able to say?
2. What did He say was the result?

Prayer

Lord Jesus Christ, my Savior and my Redeemer, like Peter, when I take my eyes off You I am in danger of sinking—into the moral morass of the day. Help me keep my eyes always on You. Then I shall see clearly the ethical issues of the passing hour. Amen.

No Other Way

". . . obedience that comes from faith." (v. 5)
For reading and meditation—Romans 1:1–17

*I*f you are thinking about choosing a new outfit, you can take it or leave it. But when you are thinking about the law of God, as laid down for us in the Scriptures, you can only take it.

G. K. Chesterton said there was once a man who disbelieved in the law of gravity, and to prove his disbelief he walked off the edge of a cliff. He did not prove his disbelief; he proved the law of gravity. It is often said by preachers and Bible teachers that we cannot break the commands of God; we simply break ourselves upon them. When God made us in the beginning, He knew that life could be lived only in one way, and so He gave us His laws and directions for living. When we decide to go against those laws and directions, it is no use standing before God and saying: "I don't profess to be perfect so I should not have to suffer any consequences." What do you suppose would happen in a court of law if someone charged with a serious offense pleaded: "But I don't profess to be perfect"? His effrontery would run the risk of his sentence being stiffened because he had added impertinence to his wrongdoing.

So I say again: God's commands and directions are not a matter for approval. They are binding upon every one of us and none is beyond their sway. If we are to go deeper with God, let's not try to think of exceptions; let's conform to the rules. There is just no other way for a Christian to live.

FURTHER STUDY

*Acts 5:1–29;
2 Kings 18:1–6;
Gen. 6:22*

1. What position did Peter and the apostles take?
2. What did Hezekiah do?

⟿ Prayer ⟽

O God, You have given me many instructions on how to live for You in this world. Help me here and now to dedicate myself to the tasks You have set before me and help me be obedient to them. For nothing counts as much as this. In Christ's Name I pray. Amen.

No Frontiers

**"As obedient children, do not conform to the evil desires you had when you
lived in ignorance." (v. 14)**

For reading & meditation—1 Peter 1:1–16

*I*t seems in many places it is acceptable to practice certain forms of dishonesty, such as bribery, lying, and so on. On an overseas visit recently a pastor told me: "One of my most prominent members boasted to me that he had found a foolproof way of making telephone calls without paying for them and offered to show me how. When I told him I had no desire to know and that he was soiling his soul by practicing this type of deceit, he replied: 'I have no problems with my soul over this—I know many others who do it. And, in fact, as far as my relationship with the Lord is concerned, it is better than ever.'" How sad.

Let us be clear about this—dishonesty is dishonesty no matter how one might try to dismiss it on the basis that others are doing it or that it is the "acceptable" thing to do. It grieves God when Christians allow themselves to be culturally conditioned to such a degree that their consciences fail to work. In the United Kingdom some Christians are not above such things as inflating an insurance claim, avoiding income tax, or telling what they consider "white lies."

The law of the Lord, as we saw a few days ago, is perfect, the statutes of the Lord are trustworthy and right the whole world over. They apply equally in Moscow and Manchester, in Lagos and London. Man-made laws may vary from one nation to another, but God's requirements are the same the world over. "God's laws," it has been said, "know no frontiers."

FURTHER STUDY

*1 Tim. 1:1–19;
Rom. 13:5; 9:1
Acts 24:16;
2 Cor. 1:12*

1. What did Paul admonish Timothy to hold on to?
2. What did Paul strive to do?

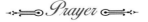

Prayer

O God, awaken Your church throughout the world to the need to put Your Word ahead of culture. Help me
make it a life decision today that where Christ and culture clash, I will choose Christ.
For His dear Name's sake. Amen.

Day 364

God's Laws Never Change

"Blessed . . . are those who hear the word of God and obey it." (v. 28)

For reading & meditation—Luke 11:14–28

Some people today think that because human laws change with the passing of time, God's laws do also. In John Wesley's day, for example, there were no less than 160 different crimes for which men, women, and children in Britain could be hanged. None of those crimes carry the same penalty today. In those days you could be hanged for such offenses as picking a pocket or stealing a sheep. John Wesley records in one place in his journal that he was preaching in prison to two felons who were waiting to be hanged—and one of them was a boy of ten! How the law has altered in two hundred years. Indeed, we seem to inhabit another world.

The consequence of people regarding God's solemn moral laws as being subject to change like man-made laws is that they no longer feel bound by them. In fact, sometimes when one reads a newspaper today one is left with the impression that it is a more heinous sin in certain social circles to break a rule of etiquette than it is to break the moral law of God. What was true of God's laws and commandments in the dim and distant past is true today, and will be true for all the generations that succeed us.

In the midst, therefore, of an age which flouts God's commandments and suggests they can be taken on "approval" or rejected, according to taste, we who want to go deeper with God must stand resolutely in opposition and show by our lives and commitment to Scripture that the law of the Lord is perfect and restores the soul.

FURTHER STUDY

Mark 7:1–9;
Ps. 19:1–7;
Rom. 7:12–14;
1 Tim. 1:7–11

1. What indictment did Jesus level against the Pharisees?
2. What does the law expose?

⤙══ *Prayer* ══⤚

O God, if the world is changing in its attitude to Your moral laws, help us as Your church to show by the way we live that we regard them as unchangeable and inviolable. Purify Your people that the world might see and believe. In Jesus' Name. Amen.

384

Be a Pacemaker!

"If you obey my commands, you will remain in my love . . ." (v. 10)

For reading & meditation—John 15:1–17

Today we conclude our meditations on the issues we need to take on board if we are to go deeper with God. First, we must cultivate an *attitude* of repentance. Our relationship with God *begins* through repentance and it is *improved* in the same way. Second, we must avail ourselves of His grace. God is always eager to give us His grace . . . *and there is so much of it.* Third, we must spend time with Him regularly, and make room in our devotions for Him to talk to us.

Fourth, we must be confident of His character. The great God who runs this universe can be trusted in everything. We cannot see from our perspective the good that underlies everything He does or allows, but we must focus our gaze continually on the cross. There we see most clearly (and starkly) that God is love. Fifth, we must make it a priority to worship Him continually. For worship, as C. S. Lewis put it, "is inner health made audible." Sixth, we must pursue Him with passion. Not just admire Him, but *thirst* after Him. Seventh, we must be forgiving people. God has forgiven us; we must therefore forgive others also and treat them in the same way that we have been treated by Christ Jesus. Eighth, we must obey the Lord's commands. If we love Him, we will be glad to do what He asks.

Commit yourselves to these things. If you do so, then there is no reason why you cannot stride forward with the most ardent souls you know. You too can be a pacemaker!

FURTHER STUDY

Col. 3:1–17;
1 John 2:6, 28; 3:6;
2 John 9

1. Where are we to set
our hearts and minds?
2. What will be
the result?

Prayer

Father, make this time in my life one of vision and venture in the things of God. May it become a time of spiritual advancement to a degree I have never before known.
I ask all this in Christ's Name. Amen.

How to Use the Bible

A question I am often asked especially by young Christians is his: why do I need to read the Bible? We need to read the Bible in order to know not only God's mind for the future but how to develop a daily walk with Him. God uses His Word to change people's lives and bring those lives into a deeper relationship with Himself and a greater conformity to His will. For over four decades now I have spent hours every week reading and studying the Scriptures. God has used this book to transform my life and to give me a sense of security in a shifting and insecure world.

How do we read the Bible? Do we just start at Genesis and make our way through to the Book of Revelation? There are many ways to go about reading the Scriptures; let me mention the three most popular approaches.

One is to follow a reading plan such as is included in the *Every Day with Jesus Devotional Bible* or *Through the Bible in One Year.* The great advantage of following a reading plan is that your reading is arranged for you; in a sense you are being supervised. You are not left to uncertainty: what shall I read today, where shall I begin, at what point shall I end?

A second approach is to thread your way through the Scriptures by following a specific theme. It is quite staggering how many themes can be found in Scripture and what great spiritual rewards can be had by acquainting yourself with them. When I started writing *Every Day with Jesus* in 1965, I decided to follow the thematic approach and I wondered how long I would be able to keep it up. Now, over thirty years later, I am still writing and expounding on different themes of the Bible, and the truth is that I have more biblical themes and subjects than it is possible to deal with in one lifetime!

A third approach is by reading through a book of the Bible. This enables you to get into the mind of the writer and understand his message. Every book of the Bible has something unique and special to convey and, as with any book, this can only be understood when you read it from start to finish.

It is important to remember that all reading of the Bible ought to be preceded by prayer. This puts you in a spiritually receptive frame of mind to receive what God has to say to you through His Word. The Bible can be read by anyone, but it can only be understood by those whose hearts are in tune with God—those who have come into a personal relationship with Him and who maintain that relationship through daily or regular prayer. This is how the Bible puts it: "The man without the Spirit does not accept the things that come from the Spirit of God, for they are foolishness to him, and he cannot understand them, because they are spiritually discerned" (1 Cor. 2:14).

Praying before you open your Bible should not be a mere formality. It is not the act that will make the Bible come alive but the *attitude*. Prayer enables us to approach the Scriptures with a humble mind. The scientist who does not sit down before the facts of the universe with an open mind, will discover little or nothing. He must first be prepared to give up every preconceived idea and be willing to follow whereever nature will lead him. It is the same with the reading of the Scriptures; we must come to it with a humble and receptive mind or we too will get nowhere. Prayer enables us to have the attitude that says, "Speak, for your servant is listening" (1 Sam. 3:10).

If we are to grow in the Christian life, we must do more than just *read* the Bible—we must *study* it. This means that we must give time to poring over it, considering it, thinking about what it is saying to us, and assimilating into our hearts and minds its doctrines and its ideas.

I have already pointed out that one of the ways of reading the Bible is by taking a theme and tracing it through the various books of the Bible. The pleasure this brings can be greatly enhanced by using this as a regular means of Bible study. When we study the Bible with the aid of concordances, lexicons and so on, we feed our minds. But when we study the Bible devotionally, we apply the Word of God to our hearts. Both exercises are necessary if we are to be well-rounded people, but we must see that it is at the place of the devotional that we open up our hearts and expose ourselves to God's resources.

Let me encourage you also to take advantage of a reading plan as a further basis of study. Following this will enable you to cover the whole Bible in a set period. Those who have used this method tell of the most amazing spiritual benefits. One person who had read through the whole Bible in a year said to me, "It demanded more discipline than I thought I was capable of, but the rewards have been enormous." When I asked her what these rewards were, she said, "I used to have a partial view of God's purposes because I dipped into my Bible just here and there as it suited me. Now, however, I feel as if I have been looking over God's shoulder as He laid out the universe, and I feel so secure in the knowledge that He found a place for me in that marvelous plan." There can be no doubt that reading through the entire Bible in a set period enables one to gain a perspective that has tremendously positive spiritual consequences.

The third form of study—reading through a book of the Bible at a time—has the advantage of helping you understand the unity and diversity of the Bible. It is quite incredible how so many writers sharing their thoughts at different times of history combine to say similar things and give a consistent emphasis. Reading and pondering on this gives you such an appreciation of the wisdom of God in putting together this marvelous volume that it fires your soul and quickly brings praise and adoration to your lips.

I have found the best way to study a book of the Bible is to read it through once for a sense of the whole, and then to read it again, making a note of anything that strikes me such as a principle to be applied, an insight to be stored away in my heart, or a thought to be shared with someone who is struggling.

One thing is sure, time spent with the Bible is not wasted. The more one loves God the more one will love the Bible. And the more one loves the Bible the more one will love God. Always remember this unique volume—God's one and only published work—yields its treasures only to those who read it, study it, and obey it.

Selwyn Hughes

Selwyn Hughes – A Brief Biography

Born in Wales to Christian parents who were significantly impacted by the Welsh revivals, Selwyn Hughes trained in theology and counseling in both the UK and USA. During his 18 years pastoring churches around the UK he was asked by a few of his congregation to share his method of daily Bible study. From this inconspicuous start grew *Every Day with Jesus* and for 30 years Selwyn has authored these daily Bible notes which are read by some 500,000 people around the world. In addition to writing, Selwyn travels extensively in many countries presenting a wide range of seminars on different aspects of the Christian life including counseling, marriage, relationships and personal development.

Larry Dyke

Larry Dyke is a native Texan who has traveled, often with his wife and daughter, to some of the world's most beautiful places. Underlying his painting is his deep Christian faith. "When I became a full-time artist, I was impressed to put a scriptural notation on each of my paintings," Dyke states. "It's an expression of what I think the true answer to life is." Dyke's paintings hang in the White House, the Vatican, and the homes of distinguished personalities including Billy and Ruth Graham.

Crusade for World Revival – A Brief History

Founded by Selwyn Hughes in 1965 as a charity, the commission statement of CWR states the purpose of the organization as "Applying God's Word to everyday life and relationships." Today CWR employs 45 people and from its base in the beautiful setting of Waverley Abbey House at Farnham in the south of England provides inspiration, training and support to many Christians throughout the world through an extensive international publishing and training ministry.

For more information about CWR and the training and publishing products available, please apply to your nearest distributor listed elsewhere in this publication or to:

CWR, Waverley Abbey House, Waverley Lane, Farnham, Surrey,
England G U 9 8EP
Tel: 44 1252 784700
E mail: CWRMarketing@compuserve.com
Or visit our Web Site at: www.cwr.org.uk